THE CAPITAL

BUDGETING DECISION

SECOND EDITION

Economic Analysis and
Financing of
Investment Projects

THE CAPITAL

HAROLD BIERMAN, Jr., Ph.D.

PROFESSOR OF ACCOUNTING
AND MANAGERIAL ECONOMICS,
GRADUATE SCHOOL OF BUSINESS
AND PUBLIC ADMINISTRATION,
CORNELL UNIVERSITY

SEYMOUR SMIDT, Ph.D.

PROFESSOR OF MANAGERIAL ECONOMICS,
GRADUATE SCHOOL OF BUSINESS
AND PUBLIC ADMINISTRATION,
CORNELL UNIVERSITY

BUDGETING DECISION

SECOND EDITION

Economic Analysis and Financing of Investment Projects

THE MACMILLAN COMPANY, New York

COLLIER-MACMILLAN LIMITED, London

PREFACE

TO FIRST EDITION

Businessmen and economists have been concerned with the problem of how financial resources available to a firm should be allocated to the many possible investment projects. Should a new plant be built? Equipment replaced? Bonds refunded? A new product introduced? These are all to some extent capital budgeting decisions to which there are theoretically sound solutions. The purpose of this book is to express the solution of the economist in the language of the business manager.

Decades ago, economists such as Böhm-Bawerk, Wicksell, and Irving Fisher laid the theoretical foundation for a sound economic approach to capital budgeting. In recent years the technical literature has contained articles (such as those by Dean, Solomon, Lorie, Savage, and Hirshleifer) that have significantly increased our understanding of what is required for sound capital budgeting decisions. However, these works have not been directed toward business managers and, until recently, the work of these men has had no perceptible influence on the way businessmen actually made capital investment decisions. Businessmen have tended to make capital budgeting decisions using their intuition, rules of thumb, or investment criteria with faulty theoretical foundations and thus are apt to give incorrect answers in a large percentage of the decisions.

The purpose of this book is to present for an audience, which may be completely unfamiliar with the technical literature on economic theory or capital budgeting, a clear conception of how to evaluate investment proposals.

The authors are convinced that the "present-value" method is superior to other methods of evaluating the economic worth of investments that have been discussed in the business literature. They recognize that considerations other than that of economic worth are also important in making investment decisions. The early pages of the book show "cash payback" and "return on investment" may give incorrect results. The "yield" or "investor's method" is shown to be inferior to the present-value method, especially where there are several alternative investments available. The explanation of the reasons for the inferiority of yield to present value is particularly timely, since popular business magazines have carried many articles praising the yield method without mentioning its important drawbacks. In Chapter 4, a positive explanation of the meaning of present value is presented.

The first four chapters present an over-all picture of the method of analysis advocated in this book that would be a suitable introduction for management at any level who need to be informed about the ideas involved in evaluating capital investments, but who are not directly involved in preparing investment evaluations. The remainder of the book is concerned with elaborating on the basic description of the first four chapters and in giving material that will assist a person in actually preparing the analysis of investments.

The authors would like to thank those who aided in the preparation of this book: our wives, who patiently suffered the long working hours and short tempers that accompanied the writing; the Graduate School of Business and Public Administration of Cornell University which provided stenographic assistance; the typists headed by Mrs. Sally Comfort who repeatedly converted the debris of countless conversations between the authors into readable form; and Messrs. Colin Park and James B. Weaver who reviewed early drafts and offered numerous helpful suggestions.

H. B.
S. S.

Ithaca, N. Y.

PREFACE

TO SECOND EDITION

The first edition of *The Capital Budgeting Decision* was written between 1957 and 1959 and was published in 1960. At that time we were convinced that the present-value method was superior to other methods of making investment decisions, and we still believe this. However, in the important area of uncertainty our thinking in recent years has developed along somewhat different lines than presented in the first edition. The most important changes in this edition involve the choice of the rate of discount and general method of incorporating uncertainty in the investment decision process.

In the first edition we suggested that the cost of capital be used as the cutoff rate in making investment decisions. Now, our preference is to consider the present value of the investment, using several discount rates, including a default free discount rate. We are not satisfied that the cost of capital, implicitly including a risk discount in addition to a measure of time value preference, can be used to reject investments with yields less than the cost of capital. There may be situations when we want to accept investments with yields less than the cost of capital.

We have divided the book into three parts. The division enables us to establish the conditions in which the suggested decision rules are relatively effective and those areas and situations where they are less effective. In Part I we have assumed certainty and perfect capital markets. While these assumptions are not descriptive of the world, they do enable us to suggest solutions for some types of problems. As we move into Parts II and III and introduce imperfect capital markets and uncertainty, our suggestions are much less satisfactory. With regard to uncertainty we find that it is difficult to obtain unambiguous decision rules. Instead of clearly defined specific guides for action in the form of one number (such as the net present value), we consider many attributes of the investment. The larger and more unique the investment, the less reliable are the conventional guides for action.

The suggested changes in approach to making investment decisions have important implications to corporation managers and to the economy. Investments previously rejected, using any of the conventional accept or reject criteria, may now become eligible for consideration under our suggested procedures.

We want to thank the many persons in government, academic, and business areas who have raised questions and made suggestions that have advanced our thinking. Also, we greatly appreciate the assistance offered by Robert Blakely in computing tables, and Marge Snedden in all matters secretarial.

H. B.
S. S.

Ithaca, N. Y.

CONTENTS

PART II

Part I

INTRODUCTION

The first seven chapters of this book present a theoretically correct and easily applied approach to decisions involving benefits and outlays through time, that is, capital budgeting decisions. Essentially the procedure consists of a choice of a rate of discount representing the time value of money, and the application of this rate of discount to future cash flows to compute their net present values. The sum of all the present values associated with an investment (including immediate outlays) is the net present value of the investment.

In the first seven chapters it is assumed that the cash flows associated with an investment are known with certainty. In addition, it is assumed that there are markets to borrow or lend funds at the rate of interest used in the time discounting, and there are no constraints preventing the firm from using these markets.

The New York Times on January 17, 1964, reported the following exchange between Alfred P. Sloan, former Chairman of the Board of General Motors, and a reporter:

One questioner asked Mr. Sloan if he had made any mistakes in 40 years as a top executive of General Motors and added: "Think of one."

"I don't want to keep you up all night," Mr. Sloan snapped. "The executive who makes an average of 50–50 is doing pretty good."

1

THE PROBLEM OF

CAPITAL BUDGETING

The controller points to the ancient, gray, six-story structure and says with pride, "This is one reason we can keep our costs down. Our plant is fully depreciated, so we don't have the large depreciation charges our competitors have."

Another company in the same industry sells a relatively new plant because it is not large enough for a three-shift operation. Rather than operate what is considered to be an inefficient production line (the production line had been completely overhauled within the last twelve months), a new plant is being constructed in another state.

The investment philosophies of the two companies making the above decisions were vastly different. One was reluctant to invest money in plant and equipment. The other wanted to operate only the latest in plant and equipment. Which of the two companies was right? Maybe each company was following a policy that was correct for it, or perhaps they were both making faulty decisions. We cannot decide here because the necessary facts are not available to us. But the facts should be available to the responsible executives in both these companies, and these facts should be arranged in a useful manner and then interpreted correctly.

Investment decisions may be tactical or strategic. A tactical investment decision generally involves a relatively small amount of funds and does not constitute a major departure from what the firm has been doing in the past. The consideration of a new machine tool by Ford Motor Company is a tactical decision as is a buy or lease decision made by Socony Mobil Oil Company.

Strategic investment decisions involve large sums of money and may also result in a major departure from what the company has been doing in the past. Acceptance of a strategic investment will involve a significant change in the company's expected profits and in the risks to which these profits will be subject. These changes are likely to lead stockholders and creditors to revise their evaluation of the company. If a private corporation such as Boeing Airplane Company undertook the development of a supersonic commercial transport (costing over a billion dollars), this would be a strategic decision. If the company failed in its attempt to develop the commercial plane, the very existence of the company would be jeopardized.

Future success depends on the investment decisions made today. That businessmen are generally aware of this is indicated by the requirement that important investment decisions must be approved by the chief operating executive or the board of directors. In spite of this fact, the procedures used to help management make investment decisions are often inadequate and misleading. Few manufacturing concerns would sign a long-term contract for supplies of an important raw material without carefully investigating the various sources of supply and considering the relative advantages of each in term of price, service, and quality. Yet, occasionally management groups approve investments without a careful consideration of available alternatives. Even when there is an investigation of alternatives, the information obtained sometimes does not lead to effective decisions, because managements may not organize the information in a way that will help them make better decisions.

Business organizations are continually faced with the problem of deciding whether the commitments of resources—time or money—are worthwhile in terms of the benefits to be expected. If the expected benefits are likely to accrue reasonably promptly after the expenditure is made, and if both the expenditure and the benefits can be measured in dollars, the solution to such a problem is conceptually simple. If the expected benefits are likely to accrue over several years, then the solution is more complex.

We shall use the term *investment* to refer to commitments of resources, made in the hope of realizing benefits that are expected to occur over a reasonably long future period of time. Capital budgeting is a many-sided activity that includes searching for new and more profitable investment proposals, investigating engineering and marketing considerations to predict the consequences of accepting the investment, and making economic analyses to determine the profit-potential of each investment proposal. The primary purpose of this book is to help business management analyze the profit-potential of investments in plant and equipment, marketing programs, research projects, and the like.

INVESTMENTS AS CASH FLOWS

In order to focus our attention on the problems of economic analysis, we begin by assuming that we have investment proposals worthy of preliminary consideration and that for each investment proposal the necessary engineering and marketing research has been completed. We assume that these studies will enable us to measure the dollar value of the resources expended and the benefits received from the investment during each future interval of time. In the early chapters of this book we assume that these dollar values can be estimated in advance with certainty. Later we relax this assumption and consider the additional complications that arise when decision makers are uncertain about the amounts and timing of the cash flows that will result from an investment.

By assuming that the consequences of an investment can be described in terms of the certain (or uncertain) cash flows it will generate in each interval of time, we exclude many investments. Even business organizations, which carry further than most other organizations the attempt to measure all costs and benefits in dollar terms, find that the costs or benefits of many investments cannot be completely described in terms of dollars. Consider an advertising program designed to build up the prestige associated with the name of a corporation. This is an investment, since the expenditures are made in the hope of realizing benefits that will continue long after the advertising expenditures have been made. But it is difficult to estimate in dollar terms the exact value of the benefits that will accrue from the advertising program.

In nonprofit organizations, whether private or public, investments whose costs and benefits cannot be measured reasonably well in dollar terms are made even more frequently than in business. Nevertheless investment proposals for which both the costs and benefits can be measured in dollar terms do arise in all these organizations, and the quantity of resources involved in such investments is considerable. In designing a building, for example, the architect or engineer is frequently faced with alternative means of accomplishing the same objective. The design of the heating or lighting systems are but two examples. Frequently one alternative will have a high initial cost but low maintenance or operating expenses, while another alternative will have low initial costs but high operating or maintenance expenses. A choice between the two alternatives is in essence an investment decision.

Thus, while not all the investment decisions in an organization can be described in terms of the dollar value of the expenditures or benefits, important decisions that can be described in these terms seem to occur in all organizations in modern society. As we increase our ability to forecast the consequences of our decisions, the number of investments that can be described reasonably well in dollar terms will also increase.

In this book we shall be mainly concerned with the economic analysis of investments from the point of view of a profit-seeking enterprise. Nevertheless, many of the methods of analysis described apply to investment decisions arising in private nonprofit organizations or in local or national governments, if the investment can be described in terms of cash flows. In these latter organizations, the appropriate definition of the cash flow may be different. For example, in considering whether an investment was worthwhile, a private business would not try to take into account the additional profits that might be earned by other businesses as a result of its investment. A government would normally try to consider such profits. We shall consider these questions briefly in Chapter 16. Also the costs and methods of finance available to business enterprises are often significantly different from those available to governments or private nonprofit institutions. A government cannot sell common stock; a business firm cannot levy taxes to finance the investments it would like to undertake. In other respects, the methods of analysis that apply in business organizations are usually applicable in governments as well.

Frequently an investment proposal will involve both benefits and expenditures during one or more time periods. When this occurs, it will be convenient to combine the dollar estimates of the benefits and expenditures for each period of time. If, during a specific period of time, the benefits exceed the expenditures, we may speak of the net benefits or cash proceeds; if the expenditures exceed the benefits we may refer to the net expenditures or cash outlays. We shall adopt the convention of referring to cash proceeds or outlays during a given period of time by using positive or negative dollar amounts, respectively. We shall refer to the entire series of net proceeds and net outlays associated with an investment as the cash flow of the investment.

If some of the proceeds are subject to taxation, we shall assume that the proceeds are measured after taxes. A business corporation is subject to taxes on its income, and this income in turn depends on the amount of depreciation charges that can be used to offset revenues in computing taxable income. The amount of cash proceeds resulting from an investment in any future year will depend upon the regulations established by the Internal Revenue Service and laws passed by Congress. These laws or regulations will determine the kinds of expenditures that can be charged immediately to expense and those that must be capitalized and written off in subsequent years by depreciating the asset. Nonprofit organizations and governments are not subject to income taxes, and therefore the proceeds they receive from an investment do not depend upon their depreciation accounting method.

It should be stressed that the definition of net benefits or cash proceeds given above is *not* identical with the income concept used in corporate accounting. The major difference is that in estimating cash proceeds, depreciation charges and other amortization charges of fixed assets are not subtracted from gross revenues because no cash expenditures are required.[1]

We shall define *conventional* investments (or loans) as those having one or more periods of outlays (or proceeds), followed by one or more periods of cash proceeds (or outlays). Borrowing money is a kind of "negative investment" in which one or more periods of cash proceeds are followed by one or more periods in which there are cash outlays. There are also *nonconventional* investments that have

---

[1] The cash outlays associated with the investment are subtracted and these substitute for the depreciation expenses. Corporate accounting computes the income of each year and thus must allocate the cost of the investment over its life. For decision purposes we are interested in the overall effect of the investment on income and do not have to measure its effect on the income of any one year.

one or more periods of outlays (proceeds) interspersed with periods of proceeds (outlays). Loan type investments have positive cash flows followed by periods of cash outlays. Any decisions involving measurable cash flows over one or more periods may be implemented by using the capital budgeting procedures to be developed in this book.

THE ESTIMATE OF CASH PROCEEDS

It is frequently stated that refinements in capital budgeting techniques are a waste of effort because the basic information being used is so unreliable. It is claimed that the estimates of cash proceeds are only guesses and to use anything except the simplest capital budgeting procedures is as futile as using racing forms to pick winners at the track or as using complicated formulas to determine which way the stock market is going to move next.

There is truth in the objection that in many situations reliable estimates of cash proceeds are difficult to make. Fortunately, there are a large number of investment decisions in which cash proceeds can be predicted with a fair degree of certainty.

But even with an accurate, reliable estimate of cash proceeds, the wrong decision is frequently made because crude rules of thumb are used in evaluating this information.

When it is not possible to make a single estimate of cash proceeds that is certain to occur, we do not believe it necessarily follows that crude methods of analysis are justified. If it is difficult to predict the outcome of an investment with certainty, and if the investment is large, the use of a more careful and comprehensive analysis is justified, even if this means that the analysis will be more complicated and costly. With small tactical investments, somewhat less involved methods might be used because a more complex analysis would not be necessary, but again there is no need to use inferior methods.

APPLICATIONS OF CAPITAL BUDGETING TECHNIQUES

It is interesting to note that many decisions may be thought of as investments and hence incorporated into the capital budgeting process. We shall illustrate in this section some of the situations of this nature.

Replacement Decision

A company is currently using three pieces of equipment which cost $10,000 each and are 70 per cent depreciated. They can be replaced with one unit of equipment that would cost $20,000. It is expected that at normal activity the new machine would save $4,000 a year in labor, maintenance, etc., for a period of five years. Should the machine be replaced?

Size of Plant

A company must choose between a small plant which would cost $1,000,000 and a large plant which would cost $1,500,000. The earnings of both plants are computed, and it is found that the small plant would yield a return of 20 per cent and the large plant a return of 17 per cent. Which plant should be chosen?

Lease or Buy

A company can either buy data processing equipment or rent it. The cost of the equipment is $300,000 and the rental fee is $10,000 per month. It is estimated that improvements will make this equipment obsolete within five years. Should the company lease or buy?

Refunding of Debt

A company currently has $10,000,000 debt outstanding, bearing a coupon rate of 5 per cent. The debt was issued at a discount which is still unamortized to the extent of $500,000. The company can currently issue bonds to yield 4 per cent. The costs of issuing the new bonds would be $200,000, and there would be a call premium on the old bonds of $300,000. The old bonds have 20 years remaining until they become due. Should the bonds be refunded?

Although none of the above examples contains all the facts that would be necessary for a decision, they illustrate well the kind of problem that will be considered. The analytical methods that will be suggested in this book are applicable to all these examples.

MEASURES OF INVESTMENT WORTH

In the next chapter we shall introduce some methods of evaluating the worth of investments that are in common use or have been frequently recommended as desirable. We shall find that if we take a group of investment proposals and rank them by each of these methods, each measure will frequently give a different ranking to the same set of investment proposals. In fact it can be said that the different measures will only accidentally give identical rankings to a set of investment proposals. Although we shall not be able to rank individual investments in a useful manner, we shall normally be able to make decisions without such rankings.

Various executives faced with the same set of investment possibilities, but using different measures of investment worth, will tend to make dissimilar investment decisions. Clearly, all the measures that will be described here cannot be equally valid. Our problem will be to determine which of the measures have some legitimate reason for use and to isolate the circumstances under which they will tend to give satisfactory results.

In current business practice, each of the methods selected has its advocates, and frequently one is used in combination with another. Since investment proposals are rarely accepted by top management solely on the basis of such analyses, it may be argued that the choice of method is of little significance because the investment decision is likely to be influenced by many different factors. Insofar as the executives making the final decision are intimately familiar with the proposals, aware of the risks involved, know the possible technical or operating problems that may be encountered, and realize the potential erosion of earnings resulting from competitive action or changing technology, this criticism may very well be correct. However, in large organizations it is impossible for the top management officials, who must finally approve or disapprove investment proposals, to be intimately familiar with the details of each and every proposal presented to them. To the extent that this intimate knowledge is impossible or impractical, these executives must rely upon the evaluation of the recommendations from their subordinates. In order to make reasonable choices in weighing alternative investments, it is increasingly necessary that various proposals be evaluated as nearly as possible on some uniform, comparable basis. In such circumstances, although the measure of economic worth of an investment should never be the sole factor considered in making a final decision, it may play an increasingly important part in the majority of the investments under consideration by the firm.

Accordingly the fact that the various measures in common use today give different rankings to identical sets of investment proposals is a matter of concern. Substantial improvements in efficiency and income may result if a more adequate measure can be discovered and widely adopted. Any such progress requires first a more general agreement about the desirable characteristics to be possessed by a good index of the economic worth of an investment. We therefore turn to consider the various criteria that can be used in evaluating the adequacy of a measure of the economic worth of an investment proposal.

CRITERIA FOR EVALUATING MEASURES OF INVESTMENT WORTH

As anyone who has ever attempted the task will recognize, it is difficult to develop an explicit statement of the goals of an organization. The task becomes even harder if, as in the present instance, the purpose of the statement of goals is not to provide a symbol around which sentiment and loyalty can develop, but rather is a test of the extent to which activities and programs are appropriate for the organization. In the case of business organizations the measures of investment worth that have been proposed and are developed in this book concentrate on the profit-maximization goal but attempt to include equally important conditions such as the risks associated with the investments undertaken and the future structure of assets and liabilities that will be determined in part by the investment decisions currently being made. It is recognized that a complete statement of the organizational goals of a business enterprise would have to embrace a much wider range of considerations, including such things as the prestige, security, freedom, and power of the management group. But directed activity always leads to a hierarchy of goals in which the goals of one activity become the means to achieve further goals. Insofar as the attainment of a reasonable profit position, without unnecessary risks or an unduly awkward financial structure, is a means of accomplishing the other goals mentioned, the assumption that the pecuniary objectives are the proximate goals of a business organization is tenable.

The measure of investment worth that best describes the profit-potential of a proposed investment is the net present value of the cash flows associated with the proposed investment. It is more consistent with furthering the stockholders' interests than straight maximization of income because the accounting measures of income do not take into account alternative uses of the funds that would be tied up in investments. However, the present value method does not necessarily provide a useful measure of the additional risks to which the owners of a business will be exposed as a result of accepting an investment. Methods of incorporating such risks into the analysis are discussed in Parts II and III of this book.

CAPITAL BUDGETING, THE BUDGET PROCESS, AND PLANNING

Frequently we think of the budget of a firm as being part of the cost control apparatus and forget that it is an important tool for planning. The capital budget for the coming period will affect the cash budget and will be affected in turn by sales forecasts; thus the capital budget must be incorporated into the budgetary process.

The timing of cash flows resulting from capital expenditures is extremely important to the corporate officer attempting to plan the cash needs of the firm. Information is needed as to the specific days the bills will have to be paid and when cash will begin to be generated by the investment. Of course it will hardly ever be possible to predict these events with certainty, but it should be possible to make reasonable estimates that will be useful.

Some firms will prepare a five-year capital budget. If an attempt is being made to project other financial data over one or more years, the composition of the capital budget will affect the nature of the other planning budgets. For example, if an automobile company is planning to enter the steel industry, this would be disclosed in the capital budget and would certainly affect all other budgets.

Thus the capital budget should be an integral part of the budget and planning process. The officer in charge of the capital budget must be in effective communication with the budget officer of the firm (if the positions are separate), since the decisions they make will result in a considerable amount of interaction.

BASIC COMPUTATIONS FOR DISCOUNTING CASH FLOWS

Assume there is an investment opportunity with the following cash flows:

	Period		
	0	1	2
Cash flow	−$12,337	$10,000	$5,000

We want first to compute the present value of this investment using .05 as the discount rate. Appendix Table A gives the present value of $1.00 due n periods from now. The present value of

$1.00 due 1 period from now discounted at .05 is .9524.
$1.00 due 2 periods from now discounted at .05 is .9070.

The present value of the investment is

(1) Cash flow	(2) Present-value factor	(3) = (1) × (2) Present value
−$12,337	1.0000	−$12,337
10,000	0.9524	9,524
5,000	0.9070	4,535
	Net present value	$ 1,722

The net present value is positive, indicating the investment is acceptable.

Now we will compute the yield (rate of return) of the investment. We want to find the rate of discount that causes the sum of the present values of the cash flows to be equal to zero. Assume our first choice (an arbitrary guess) is .05. In the preceding we found that the present value using .05 is a positive $1,722. We want to change the discount rate so that the present value is zero. Should we increase or decrease the rate of discount for our second estimate? To decrease the present value of the cash flows we should increase the rate of discount (thus causing the present value of the future cash flows that are positive to be smaller).

Let us try .20 as the rate of discount:

Cash flow	Present-value factor	Present value
−$12,337	1.0000	−$12,337
10,000	0.8333	8,333
5,000	0.6944	3,472
	Net present value	−$ 532

The net present value is negative, indicating that the .20 rate of discount is too large. We shall try a small amount for our next estimate. Assume we try .16:

Cash flow	Present-value factor	Present value
−$12,337	1.0000	−$12,337
10,000	0.8621	8,621
5,000	0.7432	3,716
	Net present value	0

The net present value is zero using .16 as the rate of discount, indicating that .16 is the yield of the investment.

We can describe as an annuity a series of equally spaced payments of equal amounts. Table B in the Appendix gives the present value of a dollar a period for n periods discounted at r rate of interest, the first payment being received (or paid) one period from now and the last payment n periods from now.

EXAMPLE

Assuming an effective interest rate of .05 we want to find the present value of annual interest payments of $100,000 a year. The first payment is one year from now and there will be twenty payments. Using Appendix Table B we find the present value of a dollar period for twenty periods is $12.4622. The present value of the interest payments is

$$\$100,000 \times 12.4622 = \$1,246,220$$

QUESTIONS AND PROBLEMS

1–1. Assume you are given the choice between $100 now and $100 one year from now and that both payments are certain. Which would you choose? Explain. How large would the amount one year from now have to be for you to be indifferent between the two choices? What does the answer to this question imply as to your rate of interest (time value of money) during this time period?

1–2. What types of errors may a budget officer in charge of investment decisions make? How would you evaluate his performance?

1–3. Assume a .05 per year time value of money. Using the tables in the Appendix, compute the value of $100 (a) received one year from now; (b) received immediately; (c) received at the end of five years; (d) received at the beginning of the sixth year; (e) received at the end of fifty years; (f) received at the end of fifty years, but the interest rate is .10.

1–4. Assume a .05 time value of money. Using the tables in the Appendix, compute the value of the following series of payments of $100 a year received for (a) five years, the first payment received one year from now; (b) five years, the first of five payments received immediately; (c) ten years, the first payment received one year from now; (d) ten years, the first of ten payments received immediately.

1–5. Assume a .05 time value of money. The sum of $100 received immediately is equivalent to what quantity received in ten equal annual payments, the first to be received one year from now? What would be the annual amount if the first payment were received immediately?

1–6. Assume a .05 time value of money. We have a debt to pay and are given a choice of paying $1,000 now or some amount X five years from now. What is the maximum amount that X can be for us to be willing to defer payment for five years?

1–7. We can make an immediate payment now of $10,000 or pay equal amounts of R for the next five years (first payment due one year from now). With a time value of money of .05, what is the maximum value of R that we would be willing to accept?

1–8. Assume you are given a choice between incurring an immediate cost (and outlay) of $10,000 and having to pay $2,310 a year for five years (first payment due one year from now); the time value of money is .05. What would be your choice? Explain.

1–9. Each of the following is sometimes listed as a reasonable objective for a firm: (a) maximize profit (accounting income), (b) maximize sales (or share of the market), (c) maximize the value of a share of common stock *t* time periods from now, (d) insure continuity of existence, (e) maximize the rate of growth, (f) maximize future dividends.

Required: Discuss each of the items listed and the extent of its relevance to the making of investment decisions.

1–10. Explain what is meant by conventional and nonconventional investments. Why is it important to know whether you are discussing a conventional or nonconventional investment?

1–11. Classify each of the following types of business decisions as conventional investments, loan-type investments, or nonconventional outlay-benefits-outlay investments. Explain the reason for your classification in each case.

a. To enhance the attractiveness of its cars an automobile manufacturer is considering giving a guarantee to purchasers that certain parts will be replaced if they become defective within a five-year period.

b. A young man who has just earned his bachelor's degree is trying to decide whether to accept an attractive job offer, or to enroll in a two-year graduate program.

c. The patent on a highly successful product will expire in three years. The company is considering an immediate and drastic price reduction to discourage competitors from entering the market after the patent protection has expired.

d. To attract a key executive, a company is planning to offer him a five-year contract guaranteeing a minimum of $80,000 per year. The company is obligated to pay this salary even if the executive is fired before the end of the five-year period.

e. A city is considering using a recreation field for an exposition. The exposition will last three years and then the fields will be converted back to their original use.

1–12. Compute the present value for a bond that promises to pay interest of $50 a year for thirty years and $1,000 at maturity. The first interest payment is one year from now. Use a rate of discount of .05.

1–13. Estimate the present value of a bond that promises to pay interest of $30 a year for thirty years and $1,000 at maturity. The first interest payment is one year from now. Use a .03 rate of discount. After estimating the present value, compute it, using the present value tables.

1–14. A twenty-year $1,000 bond promises to pay .045 interest annually. The current interest rate is .05. How much is the bond worth now? How much is the bond worth if the current interest rate were .04?

1–15. Exactly twenty years from now Mr. Jones will start receiving a pension of $10,000 a year. The payments will continue for thirty years. How much is the pension worth now, assuming money is worth .05 per year?

1–16. Assuming a .05 interest rate, how much is a perpetuity of $1,000 per year worth?

1–17. Comment on the following:

a. Company A, after paying taxes and its customary dividends ($1.00 per share), has $1,000,000 of retained earnings available for reinvestment. If the money is invested it would earn $20,000 per year after taxes for perpetuity. This would raise earnings per share from $3.00 to $3.08. The directors approve the investment.

b. Company A is considering a large expansion program. If it could raise capital of $20,000,000 it could earn $1,000,000 more per year after taxes. However, the stockholders have rejected the projects because the earnings are too low to justify the investment.

How far the majority of our agricultural and industrial plants lag behind the most progressive model establishments in their own fields! And even the latter, in all probability, fall just as far short of the ideal of truly perfected equipment.

—Eugene von Böhm-Bawerk, "Capital and Interest," **Vol. II,** *Positive Theory of Capital* (South Holland, Ill.: Libertarian Press, 1959; first published in 1888), p. 85.

2

ILLUSTRATING THE MEASURES OF INVESTMENT WORTH

In this chapter we shall describe and illustrate the applications of six different measures of investment worth, which were chosen either because they are used in current business practice or because logical arguments in favor of their use have been advanced. These six measures by no means exhaust the possible investment measures. Others, in many cases variations of those discussed, have been suggested or are known to be used by one or more firms. After studying this chapter, the reader should be able to analyze and evaluate for himself the probable performance of other measures of investment worth with which he may be familiar.

Before proceeding to a discussion of the measures of investment worth, we shall describe a series of four hypothetical investments. The four hypothetical investments have been designed so that for two selected pairs it is possible to decide that one investment is clearly preferable to the other. If a measure of investment worth indicates that one investment is better than a second, when it is obvious that the second investment is actually better, then clearly there is a danger in using that measure. We shall find that of the six measures considered, four can easily be eliminated because in certain situations they

give obviously wrong answers while another measure gives the "right" answer.

THE CHARACTERISTICS OF THE INVESTMENTS

In Table 1 a series of four hypothetical investments is described in terms of the initial cost of each and the net cash proceeds expected during each year of earning life. The salvage value or terminal value of each is assumed to be zero. We shall illustrate the ranking that may be given to these investments by each of the measures of investment worth under consideration.

Table 1. Description of Hypothetical Investments

Investment	Initial cost	Net cash proceeds per year	
		Year 1	Year 2
A	$10,000	$10,000	
B	10,000	10,000	$1,100
C	10,000	3,762	7,762
D	10,000	5,762	5,762

Some comments on the interpretation of these hypothetical investments are in order. In the first place, nothing has been said about the risk characteristics of the various investments. An evaluation of the risk or uncertainty associated with an investment is a crucial part of the investment decision process. However, the concepts of risk or uncertainty are complex and need to be clarified before they can be discussed intelligently. It has seemed advisable to take these problems up separately later in the book, and for present purposes the reader may assume either that the hypothetical investments described in Table 1 are completely riskless or that at least they have equal risk; thus there is no basis of choice between them on these grounds. We could also assume the figures presented are mean values, and it is appropriate to use mean values in computing the worth of an investment.

Secondly, the question of income taxes needs clarification. Investment proposals should be evaluated on an after-tax basis. Since this is commonly recognized, the discussion of income tax adjustments is

deferred to Chapter 7. In the present instance, however, the explicit introduction of income taxes would complicate the task of describing the various hypothetical investments and of illustrating the rankings that would result from the use of each of the various measures. Moreover, an explicit consideration of income taxes would not change, in any of their essentials, the conclusions we reach. For this reason we shall assume in the present chapter that corporate income taxes have already been taken into consideration and that the net cash proceeds used in the computations are proceeds after deducting the income tax of the period.

The outlays are made at the beginning of the first year, and proceeds are earned at the end of each year. Each investment is of a conventional nature—i.e., there are one or more periods of outlays followed by one or more periods of positive cash proceeds. If there were nonconventional investments, e.g., more than one period of outlays interspersed with periods of positive cash flows, the yield method would require additional refinements, since in this type of situation a higher yield may indicate a less desirable investment opportunity.

RANKING BY INSPECTION

It is possible in certain limited cases to determine by inspection which of two or more investments is more desirable. The two situations in which this is true are as follows:

1. Two investments have identical cash flows each year through the final year of the short-lived investment, but one continues to earn cash proceeds in subsequent years. The investment with the longer life would be more desirable. Thus investment B is better than investment A, since all things are equal except that B continues to earn proceeds after A has been retired.

2. Two investments have the same initial outlay and the same earning life and earn the same total proceeds. If at the end of every year (during their earning life) the total net proceeds of one investment are at least as great as, and for at least one year are greater than, the total for the other investment, then the first investment will always be more profitable. Thus investment D is more desirable than investment C, since D earns $2,000 more in year 1 which investment B does not earn until year 2. The earning of $2,000 more in the first year leads to the conclusion that investment D is more desirable than investment C.

THE PAYBACK PERIOD

The payback period is one of the simplest and apparently one of the most frequently used methods of measuring the economic value of an investment. The payback period is defined as the length of time required for the stream of cash proceeds produced by an investment to equal the original cash outlay required by the investment. If an investment is expected to produce a stream of cash proceeds that is constant from year to year, then the payback period can be determined by dividing the total original cash outlay by the amount of the annual cash proceeds expected. Thus if an investment required an original outlay of $300 and was expected to produce a stream of cash proceeds of $100 a year for five years, the payback period would be 300 divided by 100, or three years. If the stream of expected proceeds is not constant from year to year, then the payback period must be determined by adding up the proceeds expected in successive years until the total is equal to the original outlay.

Ordinarily the administrator would set some maximum payback period and reject all investment proposals for which the payback period is greater than this maximum. Investigators have reported that maximum payback periods of two, three, four, or five years are frequently used by industrial concerns. The relatively short periods mentioned suggest that different maximum payback periods are required because some kinds of investments (construction, for example) can seldom be expected to have a payback period as short as five years.

The payback period can also be used to rank investment alternatives, those having the shortest payback periods being given the highest ranking. The investments described in Table 1 are ranked by this method in Table 2.

Table 2.   The Payback Period

Investment	Payback period (years)	Ranking
A	1	1
B	1	1
C	1.8	4
D	1.7	3

Let us check the reasonableness of the ranking given the investments by the cash payback approach. Investments A and B are both ranked as 1, since they both have shorter payback periods than any of the other investments, namely one year. But investment A earns total proceeds of $10,000, and this amount merely equals the cost of the investment. Investment B, which has the same rank as A, will not only earn $10,000 in the first year but also $1,000 in the next year. Obviously investment B is superior to A. A ranking procedure, such as the payback period, that fails to disclose this fact is deficient.

Consider investments C and D modified so as to cost $11,524. Both would be given identical rankings because both will return their original outlay by the end of the second year. The two investments are in fact identical, with the single exception that out of identical total returns, more proceeds are received in the first year and less in the second year from investment D than is the case with C. To the extent that earnings can be increased by having $2,000 available for reinvestment one year earlier, D is superior to investment C, but both would be given the same ranking by the payback period measure.

Thus the cash payback period measure has two weaknesses: (1) It fails to give any consideration to cash proceeds earned after the payback date. (2) It fails to take into account the differences in the timing of proceeds earned prior to the payback date. These weaknesses disqualify the cash payback measure as a general method of ranking investments.

PROCEEDS PER DOLLAR OF OUTLAY

The investments are ranked according to the total proceeds divided by the amount of the investment.

This ranking fails to consider the timing of the proceeds. A dollar of proceeds in year 2 receives the same weight as a dollar received in year 1. This is inconsistent with the generally accepted principle that a dollar today is more valuable than a dollar in the future. Since the rankings obtained from this procedure ignore the fact that the early proceeds are more valuable than the later ones because the early proceeds can be reinvested, it is inferior to the procedures which take into consideration the timing of the proceeds.

The failure of this procedure to rank investments correctly is indicated by the rankings given to investments C and D. Investments C and D are given the same ranking, although D is obviously superior

Table 3. Proceeds per Dollar of Outlay

Investment	Total proceeds	Investment outlay	Proceeds per dollar of outlay	Ranking
A	$10,000	$10,000	1.00	4
B	11,100	10,000	1.11	3
C	11,524	10,000	1.15	1
D	11,524	10,000	1.15	1

because the only difference in the two investments is that D receives $2,000 of proceeds a period earlier.

AVERAGE ANNUAL PROCEEDS PER DOLLAR OF OUTLAY

This measure is closely related to the method of proceeds per dollar of outlay. Instead, however, of taking the ratio of the total cash proceeds over the initial outlay, the total proceeds are first divided by the number of years during which they are received, and this figure (the average proceeds per year) is then divided by the original outlay required by the investment.

This procedure is actually an oddity, and its prime weakness is enough to disqualify it from further consideration. By failing to take properly into consideration the duration of the proceeds, it has a bias for short-lived investments with high cash proceeds. The procedure is dangerous, since it *seems* to take all years into consideration. Only in the special situation where the lives of the investments being con-

Table 4. Average Annual Proceeds per Dollar of Outlay

Investment	Total proceeds	Average annual proceeds	Original outlay	Average annual proceeds per dollar of outlay	Ranking
A	$10,000	$10,000	$10,000	1.00	1
B	11,100	5,550	10,000	.555	4
C	11,524	5,762	10,000	.576	2
D	11,524	5,762	10,000	.576	2

sidered are equal does this procedure give reasonable results, and then only if we are willing to ignore the qualification of proper timing of the cash proceeds.

The fact that this method seems to take proper account of the timing of investment is deceptive. Consider investments C and D. As previously pointed out, D is superior, although this method gives them an equal rating. Investments A and B are also incorrectly rated. The method ranks investment A above investment B, although the latter is clearly superior.

By taking the *average* annual proceeds, actually no weight is being given to the duration of the proceeds. For example, investment A has average proceeds of $10,000 per year, since it earns that amount for one year. An investment that earned $10,000 of proceeds each year for ten years would also have average proceeds of $10,000 per year.

AVERAGE INCOME ON THE BOOK VALUE OF THE INVESTMENT

In attempting to get a measure of efficiency, analysts frequently use the ratio of the firm's income to the book value of its assets. Some companies also use this measure as a means of choosing among various proposed internal investments. When this measure is used, the average income is computed after depreciation. If the denominator in the ratio is the book value of the investment, the value of both the numerator and the denominator will depend upon the depreciation method used. An alternative procedure is to divide the average income by the cost of the investment (the accrued depreciation is not subtracted). The use of both the book value (net of depreciation) and the cost of the investment will be reviewed here.

The income on book value is a common and useful measure of performance, but it is less useful as a device for ranking investments. Table 5 shows that the same rankings are given to investments C and D, although D is preferable to C. This procedure fails to rank these investments correctly, since it does not take into consideration the timing of the proceeds.

An alternative procedure is to divide income by the cost of the investment (accumulated depreciation not being subtracted). For purposes of measuring performance and computing return on investment, the use of undepreciated cost has certain advantages over the use of book value. These advantages are not so important in capital budget-

Table 5.   Average Income on Book Value

Investment	Average proceeds	Average depreciation *	Average income (proceeds less depreciation)	Average book † value	Income on book value, %	Ranking
A	$10,000	$10,000	$ 0	$5,000	0	4
B	5,550	5,000	550	5,000	11	3
C	5,762	5,000	762	5,000	15	1
D	5,762	5,000	762	5,000	15	1

* Assuming straight line depreciation.
† Investment divided by two.

ing and are relatively unimportant compared to the failure to take into consideration the timing of the cash proceeds. It is this failing that leads to the same incorrect rankings resulting from the use of book value.[1]

Table 6.   Average Income on Cost

Investment	Cost	Average income	Average income on cost, %	Ranking
A	$10,000	$ 0	0	4
B	10,000	550	5.5	3
C	10,000	762	7.6	1
D	10,000	762	7.6	1

INTRODUCTION TO DISCOUNTED CASH FLOW METHODS

We have considered four proposed methods for measuring the value of an investment. In the case of each proposed measure, we have been able to find at least one pair of investments in which it was obvious that one of the pair was more desirable, and yet the proposed measure of investment worth gave either the same ranking to both

[1] The methods described in this section are commonly referred to as "rate of return analysis" or "return on investment analysis." Terminology is a problem, since both these terms are also used to describe other procedures.

investments or a higher ranking to the less desirable of the pair. On the basis of such evidence we have been able to reject all four of the proposed measures of investment worth because of their undesirable characteristics.

One of the flaws that eliminated from consideration each of the measures reviewed has been the inability of the measure to take proper account of the timing of cash proceeds from the investments. The payback period represents one extreme in this regard, since all the proceeds received before the payback period are counted and treated as equals, and all the proceeds received after the payback period are ignored completely. In the other measures analyzed, the proceeds were related by simple averaging techniques to such things as the original cost of the investment, its book value, and the number of years over which the proceeds were received. None of these methods succeeded in bringing the timing of cash proceeds into the analysis.

We turn in the following sections to two proposed measures of investment worth that employ different methods for evaluating the timing of future cash proceeds. As a group these could be called the *discounted cash flow measures*. Before proceeding to analyze them, it is necessary to introduce and explain the concept of the present value of a future sum, since in one way or another this concept is utilized in both these measures.

The present value of $100 payable in two years can be defined as that quantity of money necessary to invest today at compound interest in order to have $100 in two years. This will depend upon the rate of interest at which the money will grow and the frequency at which it will be compounded. We shall assume that funds are compounded annually. The manner in which a rate of interest will be chosen will be discussed later in the book. For the present let us assume we are given a 3 per cent rate of interest. Let us examine how the present value of a future sum can be computed by using that rate of interest.

Suppose an investment promises to return a total of $100 at the end of two years. Since $1.00 invested today at 3 per cent compounded annually would grow to $1.0609 in two years, we can find the present value at 3 per cent of $100 in two years by dividing $100 by $1.0609. This gives $94.26. Therefore, a sum of $94.26 that earns 3 per cent interest compounded annually will be worth $100 at the end of two years. By repeated applications of this method, we can convert any series of current or future cash payments (or outlays) into an equivalent present value. Since tables are available that give the appropriate conversion factors for various rates of interest, the calculations involved are relatively simple.

We have seen that the measures of investment worth previously considered may give obviously incorrect results because they fail either to consider the entire life of the investment or to give adequate attention to the timing of future cash proceeds. The discounted cash flow concept provides a method of taking into account the timing of cash proceeds and outlays over the entire life of the investment. We now turn to a consideration of two measures of investment worth that incorporate present-value concepts.

THE YIELD OF AN INVESTMENT METHOD

This method utilizes present-value concepts but seeks to avoid the arbitrary choice of a rate of interest in evaluating an investment proposal.[2] The procedure is to find a rate of interest that will make the present value of the cash proceeds expected from an investment equal to the present value of the cash outlays required by the investment. Such a rate of interest can be found by trial and error. For example, if we know the cash proceeds expected and the cash outlays required by an investment in each future year, we can start with any rate of interest and find for that rate the present value of the cash proceeds and the present value of the cash outlays. If the present value of the cash proceeds exceeds the present value of the outlays, then ordinarily some higher rate of interest would make them equal. By a process of trial and error, the approximately correct rate of interest can be determined. This rate of interest is referred to as the *yield* of the investment.

The method is commonly used in security markets in evaluating the yields of bonds and other debt instruments. The yield on a bond having a coupon rate of 5 per cent will be equal to 5 per cent only if the current price of the bond is 100. If the current price is greater than 100, the yield will be something less than the coupon rate; if the current price is less than 100, the yield will be greater than the coupon rate.

The yield of a conventional investment has an interesting inter-

---

[2] Other terms used to define the same concept are interest rate of return, internal rate of return, return on investment, present-value return on investment, discounted cash flow, profitability index, investor's method, and marginal efficiency of capital. In this book yield and rate of return are used interchangeably.

pretation that may be referred to at this point. It represents the highest rate of interest an investor could afford to pay, without losing money, if all the funds to finance the investment were borrowed and the loan (principal and accrued interest) was repaid by application of the cash proceeds from the investment as they were earned.[3]

The use of the yield method to make investment decisions under conditions of certainty will be discussed in the next chapter.

In Table 7 we show the yield for each of the investments listed in Table 1 and the ranking of investments that would result if this method were used.

Table 7. Yield of an Investment (Rate of Return)

Investment	Yield (%)	Ranking
A	0	4
B	10	1
C	9*	3
D	10	1

* Approximate measure.

It will be instructive to examine the rankings given by this method for each of the pairs of investments in this list for which we were earlier able to determine which one of each pair was more desirable.

We previously compared two pairs of investments and decided that investment B was preferred over A, and D over C. In each case if preference had been determined by using the yield of an investment method, the pairs would be given the correct ranking. This is the first method that we have used which gives the correct rankings of both pairs.

> A, 0%   C, 9%
> B, 10%   D, 10%

NET PRESENT VALUE

This measure is a direct application of the present-value concept. Its computation requires the following steps: First, choose an ap-

---

[3] It should be remembered that all investments being considered in this chapter are conventional investments, consisting of periods of outlays followed by periods of proceeds. For other patterns of cash flows, the interpretation of yield given above may not apply (see Chapter 3).

propriate rate of interest. Second, compute the present value of the cash proceeds expected from the investment. Third, compute the present value of the cash outlays required by the investment.[4] The present value of the proceeds minus the present value of the outlays is the net present value of the investment. The recommended accept or reject criterion is to accept all independent investments whose present value is greater than or equal to zero and to reject all investments whose present value is less than zero.

Since the present value of an investment will depend upon the rate of interest used, there is not one present-value measure but a group of measures, depending upon what rate of interest is chosen. This should not be interpreted as meaning that this approach provides purely arbitrary indications of the worth of an investment.

The present value of an investment may be described as the maximum amount a firm could pay for the opportunity of making the investment without being financially worse off. Since usually no such payment must be made, the expected present value is an unrealized capital gain from the investment, over and above the minimum required return on the company's capital. The capital gain will be realized if the expected cash proceeds materialize. If the rate of interest is 10 per cent, a company could make a maximum immediate outlay of $11,000 in the expectation of receiving $12,100 a year later. If it can receive the $12,100 with an actual outlay of only $10,000, the net present value of the investment would be $1,000. The $1,000 represents the difference between the actual outlay of $10,000 and the $11,000, the most the company would have been willing to spend to receive $12,100 a year later.

It will be instructive to note the rankings that will be given to the hypothetical investments of Table 1 by the present-value method, using two sample rates of interest. In Table 8 we present the results of using the present-value method and a 6 per cent rate of interest.

In discussing the measures of investment worth that do not use the discounted cash flow method, we pointed out that the relative ranking of certain pairs of these four investments was obvious. That is, it is obvious from examining the cash flows that investment B is preferable to A, and D is preferable to C. The reader may note that in each

---

[4] If all the cash outlays required by the investments are made in the first period, then, of course, the present value of these outlays is equal to the actual amount expended. This is true of all the hypothetical investments described in Table 1, and which are used as examples in this chapter.

Table 8.   Present Value of the Investment

Rate of Interest: 6 per cent

Investment	Present value of proceeds	Present value of outlay	Net present value	Ranking
A	$ 9,430	$10,000	$−570	4
B	10,413	10,000	+413	3
C	10,457	10,000	+457	2
D	10,564	10,000	+564	1

case the present-value method using a 6 per cent rate of interest ranks these investment pairs in the correct relative order.

In Table 9 the same investments are ranked by the present-value method, using a 30 per cent rate of interest instead of 6 per cent. The relative ranking of investments C and D does not change with the change in the rate of interest. Investment C, which was ranked second when a 6 per cent rate of interest was used, is ranked fourth when the 30 per cent interest rate is used. The ranking of investment D is changed from first to second by the change in the rate of interest. The higher rate of interest results in the proceeds of the later years being worth less relative to the proceeds of the early years, thus B's ranking goes from 3 to 1, but D is still ranked ahead of C.

Even with a 30 per cent rate of interest, the present value method maintains the correct ordering of each of the two pairs of investments for which an obvious preference can be determined. Thus we still find investment B preferred to A, and D preferred to C.

Table 9.   Present Value of the Investment

Rate of Interest: 30 per cent

Investment	Present value of proceeds	Present value of outlay	Net present value	Ranking
A	$7,692	$10,000	$−2,308	3
B	8,343	10,000	−1,657	1
C	7,487	10,000	−2,513	4
D	7,842	10,000	−2,158	2

This result is not an accident resulting from the specific choice of hypothetical investments and interest rates used in our examples. Whenever it is possible to determine obvious preferences between pairs of investments by the methods described earlier, the present-value method will rank these investments in the correct order, no matter what rate of interest is used to compute the present value.[5] Thus we are justified in concluding that, in the sense that it will not make certain kinds of obvious errors, the present-value method even when used with the "wrong" rate of interest will give better results than measures that do not incorporate the discounted cash flow method.

SUMMARY OF RANKINGS

The rankings given by each measure of investment worth for each of the hypothetical investments described in Table 1 are summarized in Table 10.

Table 10. Summary of Rankings

Measure of investment worth	Investments			
	A	B	C	D
Payback period	1*	1*	4	3
Proceeds per dollar of outlay	4	3	1*	1*
Average annual proceeds per dollar of outlay	1	4	2*	2*
Average income on book value or cost	4	3	1*	1*
Yield of an investment	4	1*	3	1*
Present value: at 6 per cent	4	3	2	1
at 30 per cent	3	1	4	2

* Indicates tie between two investments.

The most striking conclusion to be drawn from Table 10 is the tendency for each measure of investment worth to give a different ranking to the identical set of investments. This emphasizes the need to give careful consideration to the choice of measures used to evaluate proposed investments. Obviously all these measures cannot be equally valid. By considering specific pairs of investments, we have

[5] This conclusion is true only if the same rate of interest is used to determine the present value of both the investments.

shown that the measures of investment worth that do not involve the use of the discounted cash flow method can give rankings of investments that are obviously incorrect. For this reason these measures will be excluded from further consideration.

The rankings given the investments by the present-value measures are not identical with that given by the yield of an investment measure. Neither of these rankings can be eliminated as being obviously incorrect; yet, since they are different, they could lead to contradictory conclusions in certain situations. In Chapter 3 we shall continue our investigation in an attempt to determine whether the present value or the yield of an investment measure gives the most satisfactory results.

A NOTE ON THE RELATIONSHIP BETWEEN PAYBACK PERIOD AND LIFE OF AN INVESTMENT

If an investment is expected to earn equal proceeds each year of its life, and if the life of the investment is known, then it is possible to construct a theoretically correct payback period which will lead to the same accept or reject decisions as the present value rule. Because of the limiting assumptions, especially equal annual proceeds, this formula has limited usefulness in making decisions, but it does illustrate the weakness of certain payback conventions. In particular it shows that the longest acceptable payback period depends on the life of the investment and the time value of money.

The payback period is defined as the period of time required to recover the initial investment, or as the cost of the investment divided by the proceeds per period. In equation form:

$$\text{Payback period} = \frac{\text{Cost of investment}}{\text{Proceeds per period}}$$

The present value rule is that an investment should be accepted if the sum of the present values of the proceeds from the investment is greater than the cost of the investment. The symbol $A_{\overline{n}|r}$ stands for the present value of an annuity of a dollar per period for n periods (the life of the investment) discounted at a rate of r per period. We assume that r is known and is the appropriate discount rate for the firm. With equal annual proceeds we would accept the investment, using the present value rule, if the following inequality is satisfied:

$$(\text{Proceeds per period}) \times (A_{\overline{n}|r}) \geqq \text{Cost of investment}$$

As long as proceeds per period are positive, we can divide both sides of the above inequality by the proceeds per period without changing the sense of the inequality sign. If we do this, the right-hand side becomes cost of investment divided by proceeds per period, which is the payback period. This leads to the following formulation of the present value rule:

$$A_{\overline{n}|r} \geqq \text{Payback Period} \quad \text{or} \quad \text{Payback Period} \leqq A_{\overline{n}|r}$$

The payback period for an investment with a life of n years must be equal to or less than $A_{\overline{n}|r}$. As the life of the investment increases, so does the maximum acceptable payback period. As the life tends to infinity, the maximum acceptable payback period approaches an upper limit of $1/r$.

Sometimes we may not be sure what life we can expect for an investment. In this case the above formula can also be used to find the minimum acceptable life for an investment whose payback period is known. To do this we find the smallest value of n for which $A_{\overline{n}|r}$ is greater than the investment's payback period. The values of $A_{\overline{n}|r}$ are listed in Table B in the Appendix to this book.

Example: The ABC Company requires a two-year payback period or less before accepting equipment. A piece of equipment is being considered that costs $5,000 and is expected to earn cash proceeds per year of $1,000 for a life of ten years. The relevant discount rate is 10 per cent per year. Should the equipment be purchased?

The equipment has a payback period of five years; thus it seems to be undesirable in view of the company's two-year payback criterion. However, since it has a life of ten years, it could have a payback period up to six years ($A_{\overline{10}|.10} = 6.1446$) and would still be acceptable.

Now assume that the equipment has a perpetual life. The reciprocal of the payback period of five years is .2. This is also the yield of the investment.

$$\text{Yield} = \frac{\text{Income}}{\text{Investment}} = \frac{1,000}{5,000} = .2$$

If instead of a perpetual life we had assumed a very long life, the reciprocal of the payback period would have approximated the yield of the investment.

QUESTIONS AND PROBLEMS

2-1. For each of the following cash flows, compute the net present value. Assume a cost of money of 10 per cent.

	Period				
0	1	2	3	4	5
A ($1,000)	$100	$100	$100	$100	$1,100
B (1,000)	264	264	264	264	264
C (1,000)	. . .	. . .	. . .	. . .	1,611

2-2. For each of the cash flows in problem 2-1 compute the yield.

2-3. For each of the cash flows in problem 2-1 compute the payback. Assuming a maximum payback period of four years, which (if any) of the cash flows would be accepted as a desirable investment?

2-4. Assuming a cost of money of 5 per cent, compute the net present value of the cash flows of problem 2-1.

2-5. Assuming a cost of money of 15 per cent, compute the net present value of the cash flows of problem 2-1. Compare with the results obtained from problems 2-1 and 2-4.

2-6. The Arrow Company is considering the purchase of equipment that will return cash proceeds as follows:

End of period

1...................	$5,000
2...................	3,000
3...................	2,000
4...................	1,000
5...................	500

Assuming a cost of money of 10 per cent, what is the maximum amount the company could pay for the machine and still be financially no worse off than if it did not buy the machine?

2-7. The Ithaca Machine Company has a maximum two-year payback period for equipment and a nine-year requirement for buildings. The cost of money for the firm is considered to be 10 per cent. Equipment commonly lasts between 10 and 20 years. Buildings are expected to last in excess of 20 years. Do you consider the company's criteria to be useful? Explain.

2–8. For each of the investments compute the net present value (use a cost of money of .15) and the yield (rate of return).

Investment	Period 0	1	2
A	(1,000)		1,322
B	(1,000)	615	615
C	(1,000)	1,150	

2–9. For each of the investments of 2–8 recompute the present values using (a) A cost of money of .20. (b) A cost of money of .05.

2–10. Prepare a schedule showing that with a rate of growth of .15 per year, $1,000 will grow to $1,322 in two years.

2–11. Determine the rate of return of the following investment.

Period	Cash flow
0	(9,120)
1	1,000
2	5,000
3	10,000

2–12. How much could you pay in excess of the indicated cost for the investment of 2–11 if you had a cost of money of .10?

2–13. Consider the three investments of 2–8 to be mutually exclusive investments.

Required: (a) Using the rates of return of the three investments, which is preferred? (b) Using the present value method and a cost of money of .05, which is preferred?

2–14. A company uses a 10 per cent discount rate. Assuming equal annual cash proceeds, what should be the maximum acceptable payback period for equipment whose life is 5 years? What are the maximum acceptable paybacks for lifes of 10, 20, 40 years, and infinite life?

2–15. Answer problem 2–14, assuming the discount rate is 5 per cent.

2–16. Assume $r = .06$. A new machine that costs $7,000 has equal annual cash proceeds, and a payback period of 7.0 years. What is the minimum number of full years of life it must have to be acceptable?

2–17. Compute the yield of the following investments:

		Period		
Investments	0	1	2	3
A	−10,000	4,747	4,747	4,747
B	−10,000			17,280

Compare the two investments. Which do you prefer? Are you making any assumption about the reinvestment of the cash flows?

2–18. Determine the yield of the following investment:

Period	Cash flow
0	−15,094
1	10,000
2	10,000
3	1,000

2–19. *Wellesley Woolen Company*
The Wellesley Woolen Company was an old established Massachusetts textile company. It specialized in woolens used in high-style garments.

The controller stated that the company had not made a major investment decision in recent years. Machines were modernized, but were not frequently replaced. In fact, almost all of the machines had been purchased over 15 years ago.

Another member of top management stated, "The woolen industry is intensely competitive. This is illustrated by the fact that mills must work three shifts in order to make a profit. The Wellesley Woolen Company has been able to exist by limiting capital expenditures to modifications of equipment. A large number of the machines now owned were purchased as secondhand equipment. The advantages of more modern equipment are that they are somewhat faster, have larger cards, and require less maintenance. These savings do not justify the purchase of new equipment. Firms which have brought new equipment have run into difficulties. For example, a new southern mill was recently closed because they couldn't pay for the capital equipment they had purchased."

A salesman of textile machinery justified the policy of the Wellesley Woolen Company. The large number of textile firms going out of business created an extensive market in secondhand textile equipment. This machinery was only slightly less efficient than more recent equipment. In fact much of the used equipment was built after World War II. Prior to 1950 much of the secondhand equipment had been shipped to foreign markets, but in recent years this market had greatly disappeared. For example, the South American textile manufacturers would rather buy new German textile machinery than secondhand American machinery. They considered the German machinery more efficient and less likely to break down.

One problem encountered by textile machinery salesmen was the reluctance of textile manufacturers to accept radical changes in machinery. They preferred small changes because this did not create new problems of maintenance and repair. They also preferred to have all machines of one type to simplify the spare parts problem.

Required: Does Wellesley Woolen have an investment decision?

2–20. Assume a discount rate of 3 per cent, and a machine that generates a constant annual amount of savings. What is the maximum acceptable payback period if the life of the machine is 5 years? What if the life of the machine is 10 years? 15 years? 20 years?

2–21. Answer problem 2–20, assuming interest rates of 6 per cent and 12 per cent.

2–22. Assume a discount rate of 3 per cent and a machine that generates a constant annual amount of savings. If the machine has a payback period of 5 years, what is the minimum acceptable life? What are the minimum acceptable lives for machines with paybacks of 8, 12, and 20 years?

2–23. Answer problem 2–22, assuming a discount rate of 12 per cent.

2–24. Find the net present value at a 5 per cent discount rate for each of the following three investments.

Investment	Period 0	Period 1	Period 2
A	−18,594	10,000	10,000
B	−18,140	0	20,000
C	−19,480	20,000	0

2–25. Find the net present value of each of the three investments in problem 2–24, assuming an interest rate of 5 per cent from time 0 to time 1 and of 7 per cent from time 1 to time 2.

2–26. Find the net present value of each of the three investments in problem 2–24, assuming an interest rate of 5 per cent from time 0 to time 1 and for an interest rate of 3 per cent from time 1 to time 2.

2–27. Can the yield method be used for accept or reject decisions on an investment when the interest rate is not the same in all future time periods?

Long-range investing under rapidly changing conditions, especially under conditions that change or may change at any moment under the impact of new commodities and technologies, is like shooting at a target that is not only indistinct but moving and moving jerkily at that.

—J. A. Schumpeter, *Capitalism, Socialism, and Democracy* (New York: Harper & Brothers, 1947), p. 88.

3

PRESENT VALUE
VERSUS YIELD

In the preceding chapter we saw that neither of the discounted cash flow procedures for evaluating an investment could be eliminated as being obviously incorrect. In many situations the yield procedure will lead to the same decision as the net present-value procedure. However, there are also situations where the yield method may lead to different decisions from those obtained by using the present-value procedure. When the two methods lead to different decisions, the present-value method tends to give better decisions.

It is possible to use the yield method in such a way that it gives the same results as the present-value method.[1] In this sense the two methods are identical, and *if* they are used correctly, either one is acceptable. However, *if* is the biggest two-letter word in the English language. It is easy to use the present-value method correctly. It is much more difficult to use the yield method correctly—more difficult to describe what comparisons are appropriate for a given decision, and more difficult to carry out the required calculations. For both these reasons this book will consistently recommend the use of the present-value method. In the remainder of this chapter we shall ex-

[1] This statement is true as long as the rate of discount at which it is appropriate to discount future cash proceeds is the same for all future years. If the appropriate rate of interest varies from year to year, even if that pattern of variation is known in advance, then the two procedures cannot be used in a way that will give identical answers.

plain why we believe the yield method is inferior, and in the process
we shall show how that method could be used correctly in arriving at
the same answers as the present-value method.

ACCEPT OR REJECT DECISIONS

Frequently the investment decision to be made is whether or not to
accept or reject a project. We speak of this type of investment as
being an independent investment. With the yield procedure the usual
recommendation is to accept an independent investment if its yield
is greater than some minimum acceptable rate of discount. If the cash
flow corresponding to the investment consists of one or more periods
of cash outlays followed only by periods of cash proceeds, then this
method will give the same "accept" or "reject" decisions as the present-
value method, using the same discount rate. Since most independent
investments have cash flow patterns that meet the specifications described above, it is fair to say that in practice the yield and present-
value methods would give the same recommendations for independent
investments.

It is sometimes suggested that one of the advantages of the yield
procedure is that it may be utilized without deciding on a minimum
acceptable discount rate, whereas the present-value method requires
that this rate be incorporated into the computations. The weakness of
this suggestion becomes evident when we consider the accept or reject
type of investment decision. The yield of an investment must be compared with the minimum acceptable discount rate to reach a decision.
The discount rate is no less important to yield than to present value,
although it enters at an earlier stage in the computations of the
present-value method.

In the following pages the terms *cost of money* and *minimum acceptable discount rate* will be used interchangeably.

MUTUALLY EXCLUSIVE INVESTMENTS

If undertaking any one of a set of investments will decrease the
profitability of the other investments, the investments are substitutes.
An extreme case of substitution exists if undertaking one of the investments completely eliminates the expected proceeds of the other investments. Such investments are said to be mutually exclusive.

Frequently a company will have two or more investments, any one of which would be acceptable, but because the investments are mutually exclusive, only one can be accepted. For example, assume that a company is trying to decide where to build a new plant. It may be that either of two locations would be profitable. But the company will have to decide which one is likely to be the more profitable, since only one new plant is needed. An oil company may need additional transport facilities for its products. Should it build a pipeline or acquire additional tankers and ship by water? Either of these alternatives may result in a net profit to the firm, but the company will wish to choose the one that is more profitable. Suppose that it has decided to build the pipeline. Should a 6- or 10-inch-diameter pipeline be installed? Again the problem is to choose the more profitable of these alternatives. In all the above discussion, the choice is between mutually exclusive investments.

Mutually exclusive investment alternatives are common. The situation frequently occurs in connection with the engineering design of a new installation. In the process of designing such an installation, the engineers are typically faced at a great many points with alternatives that are mutually exclusive. Thus a measure of investment worth that does not lead to correct mutually exclusive choices will be seriously deficient. In this light, the fact that the two discounted cash flow measures of investment worth may give different rankings to the same set of mutually exclusive investment proposals becomes of considerable importance.

INCREMENTAL BENEFITS

The yield method gives less correct recommendations for mutually exclusive investments than those that result from the application of the present-value method because it reflects the average rather than the incremental cash flows. Let us assume that we must choose one of the following investments for a company whose cost of money is 10 per cent: investment A requires an outlay of $10,000 this year and has cash proceeds of $12,000 next year; investment B requires an outlay of $15,000 this year and has cash proceeds of $17,700 next year. The yield of A is 20 per cent and that of B is 18 per cent. A quick answer would be that A is more desirable, on the hypothesis that the higher the yield, the better the investment. To see why this answer may be wrong, consider that a yield of 1,000 per cent on an investment of a dime is a poor substitute for a yield of 15 per cent on $1,000 if only one of the investments can be undertaken.

Clearly, when only the yield of the entire investment is considered, something important is left out—and that is the *size* of the investments. The important difference between investment B and investment A is that B requires an additional outlay of $5,000 and provides additional cash proceeds of $5,700. The yield of the incremental investment is 14 per cent, which is clearly worthwhile for a company that can obtain additional funds at 10 per cent.

Two mutually exclusive investments may have different yields, but both may require the same initial outlay. This case seems to be different from the one we have just discussed because there is no incremental investment. Actually the difference is superficial. Consider investments Y and Z described in Table 1. Suppose they are mutually

Table 1

Invest-ment	Year	Cash flows		Yield, %	Net present value at 5%
		Outlays	Proceeds		
Y	0	$100.00	. . . . .	20	$27.89
	1	. . . . .	$ 20.00		
	2	. . . . .	120.00		
Z	0	100.00	. . . . .	25	23.58
	1	. . . . .	100.00		
	2	. . . . .	31.25		

exclusive investments for a company whose cost of money was 5 per cent. The yield of Y is 20 per cent, while that of Z is 25 per cent. However, if we take the present value of each of the investments at 5 per cent, we find that the ranking is in the opposite order. The present value of Z is less than the present value of Y. Neither investment can be said to be obviously superior to the other, and both require the same cash outlays in the first year. Which is preferable for a company with a 5 per cent cost of money?

Suppose we attempt to make an incremental comparison as follows:

Period 0	0	Cash flows identical
1	$80.00	Cash flow of Z exceeds that of Y
2	$88.75	Cash flow of Y exceeds that of Z

We see that the cash flow of Y is $80.00 less in year 1, and $88.75 more than Z in year 2. As before, we can compute the yield on the incremental cash flow. An outlay of $80.00 that returns $88.75 one year later has a yield of 10.9 per cent. An investment such as this would be desirable for a company whose cost of money is only 5 per cent. Again we are really dealing with a problem of the scale of the investment, but in this case the opportunity for the additional investment occurs one year later.

The same result can be reached by a somewhat different route if we ask how much cash the company would have on hand at the end of the second year if it accepted investment Y and if it accepted investment Z. Both investments give some cash proceeds at the end of the first year. The value of the investment at the end of the second year will depend upon what is done with the cash proceeds of the first year. Since the cost of money is 5 per cent, we can assume that the cash proceeds of the first year could be reinvested to yield 5 per cent.[2] Then investment Y would result in a total cash accumulation by the end of the year of $141.00 (105 per cent of $20 plus $120). Investment Z would result in a cash accumulation of only $136.25 (105 per cent of $100 plus $31.25).

One of the disadvantages associated with the use of the yield method is the necessity of computing the yield on the incremental cash proceeds in order to determine which of a pair of mutually exclusive investments is preferable. If there are more than two mutually exclusive investments, we shall have to conduct an elimination tournament among the mutually exclusive investments. Taking any pair, we compute the yield on the incremental cash flow and attempt to decide which of the two investments is preferable. The winner of this round would then be compared in the same manner with one of the remaining investments until the grand champion investment was discovered.

[2] The term *cost of money* as used in the initial chapters of this book refers to a rate of interest which measures both the lending rate (the yield of available investments outside the firm) and the cost of borrowing (obtaining capital from sources outside the firm). The *lending rate* is assumed to be equal to the *borrowing rate;* thus funds have a minimum cost to the firm equal to this cost. (The firm can lend the funds and obtain a return equal to that yield.) It would *not* be appropriate to assume that funds have a cost *higher* than the cost of obtaining new capital, since the firm can always borrow funds to take advantage of such investments. Compare the above discussion with Chapter 10, where we examine the consequences of relaxing the assumption that the lending rate and the borrowing rate are equal.

MULTIPLE YIELDS

When the yield method is used, the ability to choose the best of two investments depends on whether a given series of incremental cash flows is like a conventional investment, in which case the higher the yield, the better; or is like a loan, in which case the lower the yield or interest cost, the better. The following example illustrates a case where the choice is not obvious. The cash flows represented by two mutually exclusive investments, R and S, are given in Table 2. The last line, labeled I, shows the incremental cash flows.

Table 2

| | Cash flows | | |
Investment	Period 0	Period 1	Period 2
R	$−162,727	$+190,909	$+ 60,000
S	− 90,000	+ 20,000	+160,000
I	− 72,727	+170,909	−100,000

The cash flows, R and S, are conventional investments because they have outlays *followed by proceeds.* But for investment I, the outlays of period zero are followed by proceeds in period 1 and then by further outlays in period 2. With this kind of cash flow we cannot say, "The higher the yield, the better," or "The lower the yield, the better."

Suppose the mutually exclusive investments R and S are available to a company whose cost of money is 15 per cent. If the yield of the incremental cash flows I is 10 per cent, should the company accept R or S? If the yield of the incremental cash flows I is 25 per cent, should the company accept R or S? It turns out that the present value of the cash proceeds is equal to the present value of the cash outlays at a 10 per cent rate of discount and at a 25 per cent rate of discount. The yield of I is *both* 10 and 25 per cent.

INTERPRETATION OF MULTIPLE YIELDS

To help illustrate the relationship between the yield of an investment and the present-value measure, and to explain why multiple yields occur and how they should be interpreted, it is helpful to introduce a graph at this point. In Table 3 we describe three series of cash flows, T, U, and I. T can be thought of as a simple 1-year loan at 15 per cent interest, as seen from the point of view of the

Table 3

	Cash flows		
Investment	Period 0	Period 1	Period 2
T	− 100	+ 115	
U	+ 100	− 115	
I	−72,727	+170,909	−100,000

lender. U is the same loan, as seen from the point of view of the borrower, who first receives funds and later repays them with interest. I is the multiple-yield, incremental cash flow described previously. For T, U, and I in Figure 1, the vertical axis represents the net

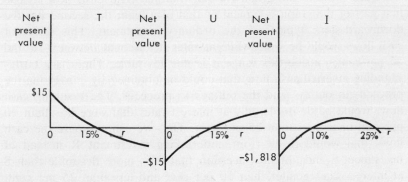

Figure 1.

present value of the corresponding cash flow for various possible rates of interest, which are measured along the horizontal axis. By net present value we mean the algebraic sum of the present value of the proceeds and the present value of the outlays.

Since the yield of a cash flow is defined as the rate of interest that makes the net present value zero, the yield is the point at which the net present-value line crosses the horizontal axis (which measures the rate of interest).

In Figure T the net present-value line drops as the rate of interest increases. At interest rates lower than 15 per cent, the net present value is positive; at interest rates greater than 15 per cent, it is negative. This general configuration typifies those conventional investments in which a series of cash outlays is followed by a series of cash proceeds. For such cash flows, the yield represents the highest rate of discount at which the net present value would be positive and the investment desirable.

Figure U is similar to Figure T but inverted. From the point of view of the borrower, the loan is worthwhile only if the rate of interest at which he finds it appropriate to discount future funds (which represents how much these funds are worth to him) is greater than the rate of interest he pays on the loan. Thus, for the borrower, the net present value of the transaction is negative for rates of discount less than 15 per cent and positive for higher rates of discount. For the loan type of cash flows, the yield represents the lowest rate of discount at which the net present value would be positive and the borrowing desirable.

Figure I shows the graph for the multiple-yield cash flow I. The first part of the graph is typical of that of a loan; the second has the downward slope typical of the ordinary investment. This series of cash flows would be worthwhile at rates of discount between 10 and 25 per cent; outside this range it is not advisable. There is a corresponding inverted cash flow that could be obtained by converting the proceeds to outlays and the outlays to proceeds. The resulting cash flows would be desirable only at interest rates that were less than 10 per cent or greater than 25 per cent. Thus we can compare the cash flows that would result from undertaking investment R instead of investment S and obtain a decision that R is more desirable than S at interest rates greater than 10 per cent and less than 25 per cent. Or we can compare the cash flows that result from undertaking S instead of R and obtain a decision that S is more desirable than R at interest rates less than 10 per cent and greater than 25 per cent. These are equivalent ways of saying the same thing.

In each case, a simple calculation of the net present value of the investment at the correct rate of discount would have provided the correct answer and would have by-passed the problem of multiple yields and the loan type of investments. Figure 2 shows that investment R has a higher present value at rates of interest of 10 to 25 per cent.

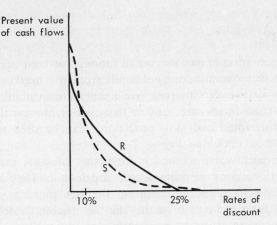

Figure 2.

SIGNIFICANCE OF NONCONVENTIONAL CASH FLOWS

In Chapter 1 we defined conventional investments (or loans) as those in which there were one or more periods of net cash outlays (or net proceeds) followed by one or more periods of net cash proceeds (or net outlays). It is important to determine whether a series of cash flows is conventional because *a conventional investment will have one and only one yield.*

If an investment is not conventional, we consider it to be a nonconventional investment. With a nonconventional investment, any of the following is possible:

1. The investment has *no* yield.
2. The investment has *one* yield.
3. The investment has *more than one* yield.

An example of a nonconventional investment with two yields was given in the preceding section. An example of a nonconventional investment with no yields would be an investment having cash proceeds of $100 and $150 in periods 1 and 3, respectively, and cash outlays of $200 in period 2. This "investment" has no yield, but it has a positive present value for all rates of interest.[3]

---

[3] Mathematically, finding a yield for this series of cash flows is equivalent to finding a real number x that would satisfy the following equation:

$$0 = 100 - 200x + 150x^2$$

But this equation has no solution in the domain of real numbers.

SUMMARY

If a corporation knows its cost of money (at least approximately) and can either obtain additional funds from the market at that cost of money, if desirable internal investments are available, or can invest any excess funds externally at that cost of money, then either of the two discounted cash flow procedures can be used to make correct investment decisions.

If the present-value method is used, the rules for making correct investment decisions are quite simple in principle. They are: (1) For each investment proposal, compute the net present value of the proposal, using the cost of money as the discount rate. (2) If the choice is between accepting or rejecting the investment, accept it if its net present value is greater than zero, and reject it if the net present value is less than zero. (3) If a series of investment proposals is available and the present value of each is greater than zero, but only one can be accepted, then accept the one for which the present value is the greatest, provided its present value is greater than zero.[4]

The yield method can also be used to make correct investment choices, provided the cost of money is the same in all future time periods. If properly used, the yield method will in fact lead to the same choices as the present-value method. But the rules that must be followed if the yield method is to be used properly are quite complex. The complexities arise from the following considerations:

1. A single investment may have more than one yield. The present value of the cash proceeds from an investment may equal the present value of the costs at x and at y per cent. This may mean that the investment is profitable only if the cost of money is between x and y per cent, or it may mean that the investment is profitable only if the cost of money is either less than x per cent or greater than y per cent.

2. If a group of two or more mutually exclusive investments is available, a direct comparison of their yields will not necessarily lead to the correct choice of the best alternative. It is necessary to analyze the investment proposals two at a time, decide which one of each pair is more desirable, and then compare the more desirable investment with one of the others, to decide which of those two is more

---

[4] The problem of time-period comparability complicates this analysis. See Chapter 5 for an explanation of the procedure to be followed when the lives of two mutually exclusive investments are unequal.

desirable, continuing until by a process of elimination the best one can be determined. By contrast the present-value method indicates immediately which one of a group of mutually exclusive proposals is more desirable.

3. In interpreting the yield of a single investment, it is necessary to first determine whether the cash flows correspond to an ordinary investment or to a loan from the point of view of the borrower.

4. It may not be possible to define the yield for a cash flow series. In this case the easiest procedure is to interpret the cash flow series using the present-value method.

5. If the cost of money is not expected to be the same in all future time periods, then the yield method as defined in this book cannot be used to give the same decisions as the present-value method.

For most of us, the present-value method is simpler, safer, easier, and more direct. The remainder of this book will proceed in terms of this approach. However, the yield method may be useful to dramatize the desirability of an investment. For example, an investment may have a net present value of $10,000, using the cost of money of 10 per cent. The relative desirability of the investment (the desirability of undertaking it compared to not undertaking it) may be judged better if we know that the yield is 60 per cent or if we know that the yield is 10.1 per cent. Theoretically and mathematically all independent investments with a positive present value should be undertaken, but the practical businessman may want some measure of how much "elbow room" he has before he is financially worse off because of having made the investment. The present-value method does not accomplish this, since the net present value may result from having made cash outlays of $5,000 or $5,000,000.[5] The yield method does accomplish this to some extent.[6]

[5] Some authors suggest dividing the present value of the cash proceeds by the present value of the investment type of outlays to obtain an index of present value (proceeds per dollar of outlay, both expressed in terms of present value). This procedure is not recommended by the present authors because of the impossibility of distinguishing between investment type of outlays and expense type of outlays. For example, is advertising a subtraction from the cash proceeds or an addition to investment?

[6] For a detailed explanation of why the ranking is only approximate, see Harold Bierman, Jr., and Seymour Smidt, "Capital Budgeting and the Problem of Reinvesting Cash Proceeds," *The Journal of Business,* October 1957, pp. 276–279.

A NOTE ON CONTINUOUS CASH FLOWS AND CONTINUOUS DISCOUNTING

The assumption is made throughout this book that all cash flows occur instantaneously, usually at the end or beginning of a period, and that interest is compounded annually. Either of or both these assumptions may be varied. Interest may be compounded monthly, weekly, daily, or continuously. Instead of assuming that the cash flows occur at the end of a period, they may also be presumed to occur monthly, weekly, daily, or continuously.

If there is a finite number of compoundings and payments, then the following formula may be used to compute the present value of an annuity.

$$A = R \frac{1 - \left(1 + \frac{j}{m}\right)^{-mn}}{p\left[\left(1 + \frac{j}{m}\right)^{\frac{m}{p}} - 1\right]}$$

where R = annual rate of payment
  j = nominal rate of interest
  m = number of compoundings per year
  n = number of years
  p = number of payments per year
  A = the present value of the annuity

If we allow m and p to increase beyond bound, that is, to approach infinity, then we have the situation in which interest is being compounded continuously and cash flows are occurring continuously.

Continuous Interest

To convert a nominal rate of interest j, which is compounded m times annually, to an effective rate of interest r, compounded annually, we make use of the fact that

$$(1 + r)^{-n} = \left(1 + \frac{j}{m}\right)^{-mn}$$

Since the present value of a dollar may be computed by using $(1 + r)^{-n}$, we can substitute the right-hand side of the equation and compute the present value of a dollar by using $[1 + (j/m)]^{-mn}$. If m is allowed to increase beyond bound (approach infinity), we have:

$$\lim_{m \to \infty} \left(1 + \frac{j}{m}\right)^{-mn} = e^{-jn}$$

e is equal to 2.71828 and is the base of natural or Naperian system of logarithms.

Thus the present value of a dollar for n periods with interest compounded continuously may be computed by using the nominal interest rate.

Example. Let

$$j = 0.02$$

$$n = 1$$

To compute the present value of a dollar, assuming that interest is compounded continuously,

$$e^{-jn} = e^{-0.02}$$

$$e^{-0.02} = (2.71828)^{-0.02}$$

We can make use of Table E in the Appendix to this book for finding values of e^{-x}.

$$e^{-0.02} = 0.9802$$

The 0.9802 resulting from continuous compounding should be compared with 0.9804, which is the present value of a dollar, using 2 per cent compounded annually.

Continuous Payments

Instead of $1.00 being received at the end of each year, there may be k payments per year, each payment being of an amount $1/k$ dollars. The total received during each year is one dollar. The present value of a series of such payments extending over n years, with interest compounded continuously at a rate r will be

$$\sum_{t=0}^{n \times k} \frac{1}{k} e^{-rt}$$

Investment	0	1	2	3	Yield (%)
			Period		
A	($1,000)	$ 505	$ 505	$ 505	24
B	(10,000)	2,000	2,000	12,000	20
C	(11,000)	5,304	5,304	5,304	21

(b) Considering only investments B and C in problem 3–2 (a), compute the corresponding incremental cash flow. Compute the yield or yields of this incremental cash flow. Is investment B or C more desirable?

3–3. The Apple Company is attempting to choose between two different machines that accomplish essentially the same task (the machines are mutually exclusive). A comparison of the cash flows of the two machines shows that if the less expensive of the two machines is chosen, there will be a saving of $1,000 at the time of purchase, but there will be additional outlays of $333 per year over the five-year life of the machines. The cost of money of the Apple Company is 10 per cent.

Required: Compute the yield of the incremental cash flows and determine whether or not the cheaper of the two machines should be purchased. Make the same decision, using the present-value procedure.

3–4. There are two mutually exclusive investments. Assume a cost of money of 10 per cent. Choose the better of the two investments.

Investment	0	1	2	Yield (%)
		Period		
A	($16,050)	$10,000	$10,000	16
B	(100,000)	60,000	60,000	13

3–5. There are two mutually exclusive investments. Assume an interest cost of 5 per cent. Choose the better of the two investments.

Investment	0	1	2	Yield (%)
		Period		
A	(10,000)	0	12,100	10
B	(10,000)	5,762	5,762	10

3–6. Assume an interest rate of 15 per cent. Choose the better of the two investments of problem 3–5.

3–7. There are two mutually exclusive investments. Assume an interest rate of 5 per cent. Choose the better of the two investments.

	Period		
Investment	0	1	2
A	−600	500	600
B	−700	800	400

3–8. Continuing problem 3–7, compute the relative cash flows of investment (B-A). Comment on the computation of the yield of this investment.

3–9. There is an investment with the following cash flows:

Period		
0	1	2
−50	150	−100

Assuming an interest rate of .05, is the investment acceptable? What are the rates of return of the investment?

3–10. Using continuous discounting, compute the present value of $1,000 for the following situations:

Annual discount rate r	Number of years until receipt of the cash n
1. .01	100
2. .10	10
3. .20	5
4. .25	4
5. .05	20
6. .05	40
7. .05	100

3–11. Using continuous discounting, compute the yield of the following investment.

Period	Cash flow
0	−15,094
1	10,000
2	10,000
3	1,000

3–12. The ABC Company is considering undertaking an investment that promises to have the following cash flows:

$$\frac{0}{-50} \qquad\qquad \frac{1}{90}$$

If the firm waits a year it can invest in an alternative (i.e., mutually exclusive) investment that promises to pay

$$\frac{1}{-60} \qquad\qquad \frac{2}{100}$$

Assuming a time value of money of .05, which investment should the firm undertake? Use the present-value and the yield methods.

3–13. The IBC Company is considering undertaking an investment that promises to have the following cash flows:

$$\frac{0}{-100} \qquad \frac{1}{150} \qquad \frac{2}{50} \qquad \frac{3}{50}$$

If it waits a year it can invest in an alternative (i.e., mutually exclusive) investment that promises to pay

$$\frac{1}{-150} \qquad \frac{2}{250} \qquad \frac{3}{50}$$

Assuming a time value of money of .05, which investment should the firm undertake? Use the present-value method and the yield approaches. With the yield approach, use the incremental cash flows.

3–14. The Arabian Oil Company is considering an investment that can be undertaken this year or be postponed one year. The investment cash flows if undertaken now would be:

Period

0	1
−100	200

The cash flows if delayed one period would be:

Period

1	2
−100	200

Required: Assuming a time value of money of .05, should the company invest now or delay one year? First use the yield method and then use the present-value method.

3–15. *Norwalk Screw Company*

The Norwalk Screw Company was located in Norwalk, Connecticut. It was a privately held corporation and capital expenditures were financed entirely out of funds generated by operations.

In choosing among different investment possibilities, management relied heavily on its experience. Because management generally had between 15 and 40 years' experience, the capital budgeting computations frequently were not made for specific decisions, though a capital budget was prepared.

An example of an investment decision which was decided affirmatively was the purchase of a zinc plater. The plater was purchased for $20 thousand. It increased capacity, eliminated expensive subcontracting, and reduced direct labor on this particular plating process from two workers to one. Management was very satisfied with the purchase. Equipment used in the manufacture of screws generally had a long life. It rarely became obsolete, though it was modified and improved.

A decision which was encountered was whether or not to operate a truck instead of using common carriers in the states of Connecticut and Rhode Island. The traffic manager prepared an analysis of costs and pounds of product transported during December (see Exhibits 1 and 2). The product transported included raw material, finished goods, and product requiring outside work. The analysis of the traffic manager indicated large savings, but the controller rejected the plan.

The cost of a new two and one-half ton truck was $5,000. The

EXHIBIT 1

NORWALK SCREW COMPANY

INTER-WORKS COMMUNICATION

To   Controller
Subject   Truck Operation in Rhode Island & Connecticut

The New England Motor Rate Bureau is increasing the trucking rates 6% effective March 10th. In an effort to avoid this increase and other future increases we are planning to operate our own truck on a limited scale in the states of Rhode Island and Connecticut.

At the present time we are planning to use our two and one-half ton truck to start this operation. Connecticut has been selected as the major point due to the fact that we have a round trip movement to Shelton, Connecticut. Each day we have considerable tonnage going to and coming back to our plant from Shelton. In addition, we have good accounts at New Haven, New Britain, and Hartford which would enable us to load approximately 5,000 pounds each day. Coming in to our plant we also have freight from Bridgeport, Hartford, Torrington, and Providence. The freight from Providence is ideal in that it consists of set-up boxes, a class one commodity which would ride perfectly over a load of screws or coils of brass.

Figures based on actual shipping and receiving during the month of December show that we paid $1,761.81 for both shipping and receiving charges covering nineteen shipping and receiving days an average of $92.72 per day or $463.60 per week.

Based on an average round trip of 280 miles per day at $.06 a mile for gas, oil, depreciation, etc., it would cost us $16.80 per day or $84.00 a week. The driver's wages would be approximately $100.00 per week based on 40 hours at $1.82 per hour and 10 hours overtime at $2.73 per hour. Our cost weekly would be $184.00 against $463.60 via common carrier or a savings of $279.60 per week and $14,259.60 per year.

The service would be by no means limited to the points mentioned above and would be very flexible operation to satisfy our customers' and our needs. Eventually it could develop into our using our own larger trucks over a greater area. This operation is scheduled to start March 1.

Your comments will be appreciated.

> Very truly yours,
> R. Smith
> Traffic Manager

Exhibit 2. Norwalk Screw Company

Analysis of Shipments in Rhode Island and Connecticut

(Pounds of Freight)

Month of December	Shelton Out	Shelton In	New Britain Out	Hartford Out	Hartford In	Paw-tucket Out	New Haven Out	Bridge-port In	Middle-ton In	Torring-ton In	Water-ville In	Provi-dence In
1	3,000	5,000					1,628					
2	2,662	5,475	2,552									
5	5,000	4,494							306			
6	3,791	4,412	459	783	2,935							600
7	624	940	519				57		1,010			
8	5,673	2,977						2,954	128			2,000
9	1,530	1,075	3,701		831							
12	4,123	5,297					522					
13	704	3,288	430	319	1,360	443			22			
14	2,279	2,206			1,057			2,730				
15	1,928	2,180	2,870	47	374				608			2,000
16	2,773	2,935		1,035	365							1,700
19	5,000	1,090			217				145	3,500		
20	4,052	1,900		1,002	210					3,000		
21	5,000	815			50				247		4,000	
27	4,953	4,825			48							
28	3,400	5,000				1,584						
29	2,112	1,532	2,015								3,500	
30		1,161	4,951		384						3,500	

company already owned one truck of this type and a pick-up truck. Both of these vehicles were used for odd trips and were driven by one man.

The controller stated:

> "We generally reject if payback is more than two years. This is the usual approach to investments where the decision can be based on payback or return. Obviously, many investment decisions are made on other basis."

Required: What action should the controller take, based on Mr. Smith's letter?

the theory is one of *investment opportunity* and *human impatience* as well as *exchange.*

—Irving Fisher, *The Theory of Interest, as Determined by Impatience to Spend Income and Opportunity to Invest it.* (New York: Kelley & Millman, Inc., 1954), p. 149.

4

THE MEANING OF
PRESENT VALUE

In the preceding chapters we have argued that measures of investment worth that do not utilize discounted cash flow concepts can frequently give incorrect rankings of investments. But the fact that a measure of investment worth incorporates discounted cash flow concepts is no guarantee that it will give correct results in all cases.

The thoughtful reader will have noticed that the argument up to this point has been largely a negative one. We have emphasized the shortcomings of the methods in common use. But we have done little more than hint at the reason for preferring the discounted cash flow approach for measuring the value of an investment. In this chapter we shall attempt to present in a systematic and positive way our reasons for recommending the use of the present-value measure. We hope to make clear the advantages as well as the limitations of this method. It is by no means a cure-all for the problem of the businessman harassed by the difficult problems of developing, evaluating, and choosing long-run investments.

We believe that the present-value method can make a definite and important contribution to the solution of the problems of making investment decisions. But it is vitally important that the user understand what it is he is accomplishing by discounting the cash flow of an investment, and what he is not accomplishing. Unfortunately some of those who have advocated use of this procedure have done so for the wrong reasons or have made claims for it that cannot be fulfilled. All of us recognize that the simple screwdriver is a useful tool when properly used. There is no need to revise that opinion because an inexperienced do-it-yourself enthusiast reports disastrous consequences from his attempt to use a screwdriver where a chisel was required.

A BIRD IN HAND VERSUS TWO IN THE BUSH

Most businessmen will agree that a dollar in hand today is more valuable to them than a dollar to be received a year from now. If we pursue the matter, we would very likely find a variety of reasons for this preference. A survey may reveal the following answers to the inquiry, "Why is a dollar in hand today worth more to you than a dollar to be received in one year?"

1. "As a businessman I live in an uncertain world. A dollar in the bank is something I can count on. A promise to pay me a dollar in one year is only a promise until I actually get the money. The promise may be made in perfectly good faith, but any number of things may occur between now and next year to prevent the fulfillment of the promise."

2. "Human nature naturally attaches more weight to present pleasures than to the more distant joys. Offer a young man the choice between a trip to Europe during the coming summer, or a trip five summers from now, and he will nearly always choose the earlier trip. Since future income is meaningful in terms of the pleasant things it makes possible, we would always prefer to receive a given total amount of income as nearly as possible in the immediate future, unless considerations of tax effects dictate another choice."

3. "A dollar received now is more valuable than a dollar to be received five years from now because of the investment possibilities that are available for today's dollar. By investing the dollar received today, I can have considerably more than a dollar in five years. For that reason, future receipts should always be discounted."

Our three hypothetical respondents have suggested three separate reasons for attaching more weight to dollars on hand than to dollars that may be received in the future. Each of the reasons is a correct one in important respects. But only the last one of them is sufficient justification for using discounted cash flow procedures in evaluating investment proposals. The other two reasons, insofar as they are appropriate in any situation, need to be taken into account in other ways. Let us consider each of the three reasons in turn.

UNCERTAINTY

Our first hypothetical respondent stressed the fact that one can never be certain about the receipt of future cash. We would not disagree. In fact, we would generalize and say one can never be certain, even about the future value of present cash held. It can be lost or stolen, the bank in which it is deposited might fail, or our ability to benefit from it may be impaired by death or injury.

It is not the need to allow for uncertainty that is in question, but the suitability of using the present-value approach to make this allowance. The inappropriateness of using high discount rates as a general method of allowing for uncertainty may be illustrated by cases in which there is great uncertainty about the cash flows in the near future, but relatively little uncertainty about the more distant cash flows. Suppose we are considering investing in a building which, once it is built, could be rented on the basis of a long-term lease. The prospective lessor is willing to sign a contract now, and his credit standing is excellent, so that there is minimum uncertainty about his ability to meet the rental payments. However, there may be considerable uncertainty about how much it will cost to construct the building. In a situation such as this, it is difficult to justify using a high rate of discount applied to the relatively certain future cash receipts. There is considerable uncertainty about the magnitude of the cash outlays required to build the building, but varying the discount rate will have little effect on the present value of these outlays, because they will occur in the near future.

Some suggestions for handling data to improve the judgments of the risks involved in investments will be discussed later. However, no completely satisfactory and universally applicable method is known. In particular, the application of present-value discount factors to preliminary estimates of expected cash flows *will not* ordinarily be an acceptable way of adjusting for risk.

SUBJECTIVE TIME PREFERENCE

The second reason suggested above as a justification for discounting future income is the time preference of the individuals involved. Undoubtedly there are individuals who, if given the choice, would prefer an additional $100 of consumption immediately to the opportunity of obtaining an additional $110 of disposable income available a year from now. Such an individual might be acting rationally if he rejected a riskless opportunity to invest $100 today in such a way that it would return $110 in one year. The investment should be rejected if acceptance of the investment requires a corresponding reduction in the investor's immediate consumption.

But acceptance of the investment will not require a reduction in immediate consumption if opportunities to borrow money at less than 10 per cent are also available now. Suppose the individual in question accepts the investment and at the same time borrows $100 at 5 per cent to maintain his immediate consumption. At the end of a year the proceeds from the investment will enable him to pay off the loan, plus its accrued interest, and still retain an additional $5.00.

In general, the subjective time preferences of the owners of a corporation do not need to be consulted in making investment decisions for that corporation, provided the corporation can obtain additional funds in the capital market and invest its excess funds, if any, on the capital market. It is only the rates at which it can obtain or lend funds that are relevant. Accordingly the purpose of a business enterprise in discounting expected future cash proceeds is not to take account of the subjective time preferences of the owners (unless the owners do not for one reason or another have access to the capital market).

The manager of a business owned by a small group of individuals may, and sometimes should, adjust the investment policy of the company to take into consideration the cash requirements of the owners. But the shareholders of a large corporation are usually a diverse group. They may pay marginal tax rates on dividends of anywhere from zero (for certain individuals and nonprofit institutions) to 70 per cent for wealthy individuals. At any given time, some shareholders will be reinvesting a part of their dividend receipts, while others will be reducing their portfolios. The large corporation cannot easily adjust its investment policy to the needs of individual shareholders.

ALTERNATIVE USES OF MONEY

The purpose of discounting the cash flows expected from an investment is to determine whether the investment yields more cash than alternative uses of the same amount of money. In the case of an independent investment proposal in a firm not subject to capital rationing,[1] whose current dividend has been determined, the consequences of accepting the investment are to borrow more funds or to invest less outside the firm. If the costs of borrowing are the same as the rate that could be earned by investing elsewhere, the alternatives are equivalent. It should be mentioned that the term *borrowing* is used here in a very broad sense to include raising additional equity capital as well as the more conventional forms of debt.

MEANING OF THE PRESENT-VALUE CALCULATION WHEN THE ALTERNATIVE IS TO BORROW LESS

To illustrate the meaning of the present-value computation when the investment must be financed by borrowing, we may use an investment that requires an initial outlay of $10,000 and offers proceeds of $5,000 per year for three years. At a 6 per cent rate of interest, compounded annually, the present value of the proceeds is $13,365, so that the net present value of the investment is $3,365. The value of the proceeds expected from the $10,000 investment is sufficient to pay off the principal and accrued interest on a loan of $13,365 at 6 per cent payable in three installments of $5,000 each. One way of interpreting the meaning of the present-value calculation is to realize that a firm could borrow a total of $13,365 at 6 per cent, apply $10,000 of the loan proceeds to the investment, and immediately distribute the remaining $3,365 as income to the owners. The proceeds of $5,000 per year from the $10,000 investment would be sufficient to repay the loan and interest by the end of the third year. The calculations in Table 1 illustrate this arrangement.

Table 1.   Loan Values Outstanding at the End of each Period when a Loan Equal to the Present Value of the Proceeds of an Investment is made and Proceeds are used to Repay Loan

Period	Loan outstanding at beginning	Accrued interest (6%)	Total amount owed before payment	Investment proceeds applied to loan	Loan outstanding at end
1	$13,365	$802	$14,167	$5,000	$9,167
2	9,167	550	9,717	5,000	4,717
3	4,717	283	5,000	5,000	0

[1] For a discussion of capital rationing, see Chapter 10.

We mentioned earlier that making allowances for the subjective time preferences with respect to receipt of income is not the purpose of the discounting process as long as the income recipient has access to the capital market. In the case of the above example we assumed that the owners of the firm chose to receive the profit resulting from the investment in the year it was made. Actually any pattern of income receipts, such that their present value was equal to $3,365, could have been selected. If some of or all the income withdrawals were deferred past the year in which the investment was made, the actual withdrawals that could be made would exceed $3,365. Suppose the owners elected to borrow $10,000, the amount required to undertake the investment, and to withdraw their proceeds only after the initial loan had been repaid. Under these circumstances the owners would be enabled to withdraw $4,008 at the end of the third year, since this amount has a present value of $3,365 with an interest rate of 6 per cent. Table 2 illustrates the loan balances outstanding at various times under this arrangement.

Table 2.   Loan Balances Outstanding at the End of each Period when a Loan Equal to the Initial Investment Outlay is made and Proceeds are used to Repay Loan Before any Withdrawals

Period	Loan outstanding at beginning	Accrued interest (6%)	Total amount owed before payment	Investment proceeds applied to loan	Loan outstanding at end
1	$10,000	$600	$10,600	$5,000	$5,600
2	5,600	336	5,936	5,000	936
3	936	56	992	992	0

Proceeds available for distribution to owners = $4,008

If the owners preferred to withdraw the same amount each year over the life of the investment, then annual payments of $1,259 could be withdrawn. The reader may wish to test his understanding of the meaning of present-value calculations by working out an example to prove to himself that annual payments of this amount could be made to the owners, the remainder of the cash proceeds applied to repayment of the loan, and the loan completely paid off by the end of the third year.

MEANING OF PRESENT-VALUE CALCULATIONS WHEN THE ALTERNATIVE IS TO LEND MONEY OUTSIDE THE FiRM

So far we have considered the case where the investment within the firm was to be financed by obtaining additional capital from outside the firm. This may seem to be an artificial comparison to a company whose past operations are generating enough cash to undertake all the worthwhile investments that seem to be available within the company. This situation is not uncommon. However, it is a mistake to assume that such funds are "free," since there is the possibility of investing funds outside the firm. For example, if a riskless possibility of earning 6 per cent from investments outside the firm is available, then risk-free internal investments ought to be compared with these external profit opportunities; otherwise, the company may undertake internal investments that are not so profitable as those obtainable outside.

Consider the previous example. In the situation in which the funds to finance the investment were obtained from outside the firm, we said that we could interpret the fact that the investment had a present value of $3,365 as meaning that a loan equal to the amount required to finance the investment, plus $3,365, could be negotiated, the excess over immediate needs ($3,365) withdrawn, and the proceeds from the investment then would be sufficient to repay the entire loan.

Assume that the firm has funds available from internal sources. The owner has estimated that by applying $10,000 of those funds to the internal investment, the company could generate cash proceeds of $5,000 per year for three years. We could ask how much money would the firm have to invest outside at 6 per cent per year in order to generate cash proceeds of $5,000 per year for three years. Since the present value of $5,000 per year for three years at 6 per cent is $13,365, it would require an external investment of that amount to generate the same cash proceeds that would be generated internally from an investment of only $10,000. This is illustrated in Table 3. The reader will note that the figures used in Table 3 are precisely the same for each period as those in Table 1. The only difference is that a different set of labels for the column headings is appropriate in this instance.

In the case where funds are available from internal sources, and external investment opportunities to earn 6 per cent per year are available, the fact that an internal investment with a present value of $3,365 is available means that $13,365 would have to be invested externally to generate the same cash proceeds as the internal investment of $10,000.

Table 3. External Investment Earning 6 Per Cent Required to Produce Cash Proceeds Identical to Those Produced by an Internal Investment

Period	Initial external investment	Accrued earnings (6%)	Total external investment before withdrawal	Equivalent proceeds withdrawn	Remaining external investment
1	$13,365	$802	$14,167	$5,000	$9,167
2	9,167	550	9,717	5,000	4,717
3	4,717	283	5,000	5,000	0

As in the previous case, the subjective time preferences of the owners should not affect the choice between the internal or external investment. The reader may verify for himself by working out examples that any pattern of cash generated by investing $13,365 externally could also be generated with a commitment of $10,000 in the investment of the example and an appropriate decision in regard to the application of the proceeds.

One further interpretation of the net present value of $3,365 of the investment is possible. The $3,365 is like an unrealized capital gain. For an expenditure of $10,000 we obtain proceeds whose present value totals $13,365 and whose net present value is $3,365. Before investing, we have $10,000 in cash; after investing, we have prospects of cash proceeds whose present value is $13,365. Thus our asset position can be improved in terms of present values (by $3,365) by making the investment.

CONDITIONS AND LOGIC FOR THE NET PRESENT-VALUE METHOD

In our discussions of the net present-value method we have consciously chosen to present our explanation in terms that we hope have a maximum intuitive appeal. If the desirability of the net present-value method depended only on its intuitive appeal, there would be the possibility that somebody might discover or invent another method that had even stronger intuitive appeal. Our confidence in the net present-value method is derived from the fact that it is at least as good as any other solution to the problem of measuring the economic worth of an investment under certain well-defined circumstances.

First of all we assume a decision maker wants investment choices that give him the greatest satisfaction. The decision maker can be thought of as a single individual, a family unit, a business firm, or some other organizational entity. The satisfaction the decision maker derives from the investment decisions depends upon the amount and timing of the cash flows he is able to withdraw from his business operations. It may be helpful to think of these cash flows as consumption. In a business organization, the analogue to consumption on the part of an individual is dividends paid to stockholders.

The decision maker faces two sets of decisions that together determine the pattern of consumption he will be able to enjoy. One set of decisions concerns his investment choices; the second determines how these investment choices will be financed.

Each possible investment alternative may be described by a series of cash flows representing the amount that would be paid out in each period or the amount that would be received in each period. The size and timing of the cash flows associated with each investment choice are assumed to be known in advance and with certainty. The number of separate investment choices open to the decision maker may be small or may be extremely large.

The cash flow of a period will be positive if the decision maker receives money in a certain period and negative if he is required on balance to pay out money in that period. The cash flow received can be used either for consumption or for lending, in which case it will become available for consumption at some future date. Similarly, if outlays in excess of the current period's cash flows are required in the investment process for a particular period, these outlays may be obtained either by borrowing against future cash flows or by using proceeds from loans made in previous periods.

It is assumed that there is a known market rate of interest at which the individual can lend as much as he wants or borrow as much as he wants. The only restriction on borrowing is that loans must be repayable out of future cash flows.

How should the decision maker select from among the investment options open to him in such a way that it will be possible for him to achieve the maximum attainable level of satisfaction? All the investment opportunities should be arranged into groups of mutually exclusive investments. Some of these groups may contain only one option; others may contain a large number of mutually exclusive options. From each mutually exclusive group, select the investment whose net present value is algebraically the largest when the net present value is computed at the market rates of interest. If this investment has a positive net present value, accept it; otherwise reject all of the investments in that mutually exclusive group.

Now imagine that the decision maker has selected from among all the investment options open to him the ones that have a positive net present value, and do not violate the restriction that no more than one of a set of mutually exclusive investments can be accepted. These investments will determine the amount of money he will receive or must pay out in each time period as a result of his investments.

Assume the decision maker has two independent investment opportunities with the following cash flows projected:

	0	1	2
A	−$ 900	$1,000	
B	−$1,500		$2,000

The rate of interest (this is both the borrowing and lending rate) is assumed to be .05. All we need to know to make the investment decisions is the present value of these two investments ($52.40 for A and $314.00 for B). Because the two present values are positive, the investments should be undertaken, and no further information or computations are required. The investor can borrow the funds at a cost of .05 and repay the debt using the cash flows from the investments. There is no question that the funds should be obtained to finance the investments. The conclusion not only holds for the two investments illustrated, but is valid for any investment with a positive present value using the .05 borrowing rate (remember there is no uncertainty; thus the cash flows of the investments are known).

So far we have not taken consumption preferences into consideration. It is not necessary to make restrictive assumptions about the nature of these preferences. We are assuming that the decision maker knows which one of several alternatives he prefers, or whether he is indifferent. Assume also that other things being equal, he prefers more consumption to less. Specifically, if two patterns of consumption are identical in all time periods except one, and if the first pattern of consumption results in more consumption in a given time period than the second pattern of consumption, the decision maker will prefer the first to the second.

Accepting investments A and B will enable the investor to finance any pattern of consumption he may desire, provided the present value of the amounts consumed do not exceed the sum of the net present values of the investments accepted, in this case $366.40. If the investor is presented with a third independent investment option whose net present value is positive, he should accept it. By doing so he will be able to increase the amount he consumes in one or more periods without having to decrease consumption in any period. On the other hand, if the investor is presented with another investment option whose net present value is negative, he should reject it. Accepting it would require him to reduce, in one or more periods, the amounts he consumed. The details of the investor's consumption preferences do not need to be known in order to advise him about which investments to accept. One would need to know something about these consumption preferences in order to advise him about how to finance the investment—that is, what loans he should make and when they should be repaid.

Assume a decision maker selects his investments using the present-value procedure and then makes the appropriate financial decisions —that is, he does not borrow more than he can eventually repay. The appropriate financial decisions are those that enable him to reach as high a level of satisfaction as is possible given his opportunities. No other method of selecting investments can, in these circumstances, lead to a different selection of investments that will enable the decision maker to reach a higher level of satisfaction than that reached using present value. It is possible that a different method of selecting investments may lead to the same level of satisfaction.

THE QUALIFICATIONS

The problem we have just described is not exactly the problem faced in practice by businessmen. There are two important ways in which businessmen might feel the problems they face are different from the problem just described.

The businessman may feel that the financial alternatives open to him are not considered in the preceding problem. He may feel that he is not able to obtain any additional funds, or he may have to pay a higher price if he borrows more than a given amount, or he may not know for future dates what the cost of borrowing or the return from lending will be. In any of these circumstances the present-value method, as we have described it, is not strictly applicable. Secondly, the businessman may not feel he is able to predict with perfect certainty the cash flow consequences of his investment alternatives. Thus, he cannot describe the outcome of making an investment in terms of a single set of cash flows. Rather, there may be a large number of possible cash flows, any of which could be the outcome of selecting the particular investment, and the businessman does not know in advance which one of the possible outcomes will occur.

Later in this book we will consider what modifications should be made to the net present-value method in order to make it more useful as a method of selecting investments in these more general circumstances.

QUESTIONS AND PROBLEMS

4–1. Assuming a cost of money of 10 per cent, how much could you afford to pay now for $1,000 per year (payable at the end of each year, with the first payment a year from now) for (a) five years; (b) ten years; (c) twenty years; (d) thirty years; (e) perpetuity?

4–2. It costs $20,000 to make a new machine that promises to return cash flows of $10,000 per year for five years. Assume a cost of money of 10 per cent. How much could you pay the owner for the patent rights to this machine and still be no worse off than if the new machine were not made?

4–3. If the patent rights for the machine described in problem 4–2 could be purchased for $10,000, what is the largest extra dividend the company could declare immediately on the basis of the net cash flows expected from these transactions?

4–4. Assuming the transactions described in problem 4–3 were financed by a "loan" costing 10 per cent, how large a loan would be required? Set up a payment schedule for this loan so that the machine is self-financing.

4–5. If the "loan" described in problem 4–4 were to be repaid in a single payment (including "interest") at the end of five years, what financial arrangements would be required?

4-6. There are two investments that have different degrees of risk associated with them. With the first investment it is thought that a dollar to be received one period from now is worth $.9524 today (implying a 5 per cent rate of discount).

With the second investment it is thought that a dollar to be received one period from now is worth $.9091 (implying a 10 per cent rate of discount). Using the implied rates of discount, what is the value today of a $1 to be received fifty years from now for each of the two investments?

4-7. Mr. Jones can borrow $1,000 or more at a cost of 6 per cent. He has an investment opportunity costing $1,000 that will earn 10 per cent. Should his consumption preferences affect the amount he invests or borrows?

4-8. The ABC Company has an investment opportunity that costs $6,000 and has a life of 1 year, and will return $10,000 one period from the time of the investment. Money can be borrowed at a cost of 5 per cent.

Required: (a) What is the net present value of the investment? (b) Assume the company borrows $9,524 from the bank and purchases the investment. How much can it pay as immediate dividend and still repay the loan? (c) If the investment cost $9,524, what would be the yield of the investment?

4-9. The ABC Company has an investment opportunity that requires an immediate outlay of $10,000 and will have a payoff of $12,155 four years from now. It can borrow short-term funds now for the investment at a cost of .04 and then at the end of first year it will be able to issue a long-term debt at a cost of .06.

Required: Should the investment be undertaken?

4-10. *The N Manufacturing Company*

A product is currently being manufactured, and the costs of the product are:

	Unit Costs
Labor, direct	$ 4.00
Labor, variable indirect	2.00
Other variable overhead	1.50
Fixed overhead	2.50
	$10.00

In the past year 10,000 units were produced and sold for $18 per unit. It is expected that with suitable repairs the old machine can be used indefinitely in the future, but it has no salvage or trade-in value. A new machine would cost $60,000 and the projected costs associated with new machine are:

Labor, direct	$2.00
Labor, variable indirect	3.00
Other variable overhead	1.00
Fixed overhead	3.25
	$9.25

The fixed overhead costs are allocations from other departments plus the depreciation of the equipment.

The new machine has an expected life of ten years.

The appropriated time discount rate for this company is .05.

It is expected that future demand of the product will remain at 10,000 units per year for the next ten years. After ten years the product will be obsolete.

Required: (a) Should the new equipment be acquired? (b) If the product can be purchased at a cost of $7.00 per unit from a reliable supplier, should it be purchased or made?

What is usually called a reasonable wage, or a reasonable profit proves on investigation to be not so much "reasonable" as "usual," to be in fact the wage or profit determined by free competition under the prevailing conditions of time and place.

—Knut Wicksell, *Lecture on Political Economy,* **Vol. I** (London: George Routledge and Sons, Ltd., 1946), p. 51.

5

CLASSIFYING INVESTMENTS

In Chapter 1 an investment was defined as a "commitment of resources, made in the hope of realizing benefits that are expected to occur over a reasonably long, future period of time." According to this definition, neither the resources nor the benefits need be in the form of explicit cash flows. A decision to have an accounting executive spend a month studying the capabilities of various types of electronic data processing equipment would be an investment in the sense of this definition. The executive's time is a scarce resource, since he could have spent the month in other activities that are valuable to the firm. In the first instance, at least, the expected benefits will be increased knowledge by management of a relatively new technology. Thus there is no explicit cash outlay or cash inflow, but there is an investment.

Any useful scheme of controlling investments must be based on a classification of types of investments. Different kinds of investments raise different problems, are of different relative importance to the firm, and different persons will be competent to evaluate their significance. By classifying types of investments, each investment proposal will receive attention from persons qualified to analyze it.

Investments may be classified in many ways. Some of these are described as follows:

1. According to the kinds of scarce resources used by the investment. For example, does the investment require important amounts of cash, of floor space, of the time of key personnel (and personnel

may be also classified: sales, production, research, top management, legal staff, etc.)?

2. According to the amount of each of the resources that are required. For example, with respect to the amount of immediate cash outlays required, we could classify investments as requiring less than $500, between $500 and $5,000, and over $5,000.

3. According to the way benefits from the investment are affected by other possible investments. Some investments stand on their own feet. Others will be improved if supplementary investments are made; still others will be useless if competing investments are accepted. For example, the worth of another fork-lift truck may depend on whether or not the plan for adding an automatic conveyor system is accepted.

4. According to the form in which the benefits are received; thus investments may generate greater cash flows, reduce the risks associated with poor business conditions, reduce the accident rate, improve employee morale, or eliminate a community nuisance such as excessive smoke or noise.

5. According to whether the incremental benefits are the result of lower cost or increased sales, or whether they merely prevent a decline in sales or market share.

6. According to the business activity to which they are most closely related. Thus an oil company may classify investments according to which one of the following activities they support: exploration, production, transportation, refining, or marketing.

Many other methods of classification could be suggested.[1] Clearly no single scheme of classification will be equally valid for all uses or for all companies. The essential task is to develop a classification system for investments that is appropriate to the activity of the business and the organizational structure of the particular company.

In this book we are first concerned with investments for which both the resources used and the benefits to be received can be measured to an important degree in terms of cash flows. Secondly, the analytical methods developed in this book will be most useful for investments that are important enough to the firm to warrant a relatively careful study of their potential profitability. In the remainder of this chapter we shall consider a classification of investments that is based on the

---

[1] An interesting discussion of possible methods of classifying investments can be found in Joel Dean, *Capital Budgeting* (New York: Columbia University Press, 1951), pp. 82–88.

way the benefits from a given investment are affected by other possible investments, when the benefits can be predicted with little or no uncertainty. A method of classifying investments that considers uncertainty is discussed in Chapters 15 and 16.

DEPENDENT AND INDEPENDENT INVESTMENTS

In evaluating the investment proposals presented to management, it is important to be aware of the possible interrelationships between pairs of investment proposals. A given investment proposal may be economically independent of, or dependent on, another investment proposal. The first investment proposal will be said to be *economically independent* of the second if the cash flows (or more generally the benefits) expected from accepting the first investment would be the same regardless of whether the second investment is accepted or rejected. If the benefits to be expected from the first investment are affected by the decision to accept or reject the second investment, then the first investment is said to be economically dependent on the second. It should be clear that when one investment is dependent on another, some attention must be given to the question of whether decisions about the first investment can or should be made separately from decisions about the second.

ECONOMICALLY INDEPENDENT INVESTMENTS

In order for investment A to be economically independent of investment B, two conditions must be satisfied. First, it must be technically possible to undertake investment A whether or not investment B is accepted. Thus it is *not* possible to build a school and shopping center on the same site, and therefore the proposal to build the one is not independent of a proposal to build the other. Secondly, the net benefits to be expected from the first investment must not be affected by the acceptance or rejection of the second. If the estimates of the cash outlays and the cash inflows for investment A are not the same when B is either accepted or rejected, then the two investments are not independent. Thus it is technically possible to build a toll bridge and operate a ferry across adjacent points on a river, but the two investments are not independent because the proceeds from one will be affected by the existence of the other. The two investments would not be economically independent in the sense in which we are using the term, even if the traffic across the river at this point were sufficient so that both the bridge and the ferry could be operated profitably.

Sometimes it will happen that two investments cannot both be accepted because the firm does not have enough cash to finance both. This situation could occur if the amount of cash available for investments were strictly limited by management rather than by the capital market, or if increments of funds obtained from the capital market cost more than previous increments. In such a situation the acceptance of one investment may cause the rejection of the other. But we shall not then say that the two investments are dependent. To do so would make all investments for such a firm dependent, and this is not a useful definition for our purposes.

ECONOMICALLY DEPENDENT INVESTMENTS

The dependency relationship can be further classified. If a decision to undertake the second investment will increase the benefits expected from the first (or decrease the costs of undertaking the first without changing the benefits), then the second investment is said to be a *complement* of the first. If the decision to undertake the second investment will decrease the benefits expected from the first (or increase the costs of undertaking the first without changing the benefits), then the second is said to be a *substitute* for the first. In the extreme case where the potential benefits to be derived from the first investment will completely disappear if the second investment is accepted, or where it is technically impossible to undertake the first when the second has been accepted, then the two investments are said to be *mutually exclusive*. It is also possible to define an extreme case for investments that are complements. Suppose that the second investment is impossible (technologically) or would result in no benefits whatsoever if the first investment were not accepted. Then the first investment can be said to be a *prerequisite* of the second.

It may be helpful to think of the possible relationships between investments as being arrayed along a line segment. At the extreme left we have the situation where investment A is a prerequisite to investment B. In the center of the line we have a situation where investment A is independent of investment B. At the extreme right-hand end of the line we have the situation where investment A is mutually exclusive with respect to investment B. As we move to the right from the left-hand side of the line, we have varying degrees of complementariness, decreasing as we proceed to the right. Similarly, on the right-hand side of the line, we represent varying degrees of substitutability, increasing as we proceed outward to the right. A graphic representation is presented below.

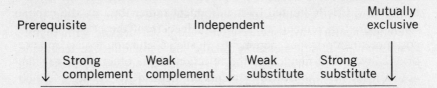

One additional complication in connection with complementary investments should be mentioned here. The complementary relationship need not be symmetrical. Suppose that we consider the building of a new factory as one investment and the purchase of an air-conditioning unit for the factory as the second investment. The two investments are clearly complementary. But the relationship need not be symmetrical, since the new factory may be profitable without air conditioning. With air conditioning, worker efficiency may go up, so that the factory is even more profitable. The additional efficiency resulting from the addition of air conditioning may properly be called the return or benefits resulting from the expenditure on air-conditioning equipment. But the air-conditioning equipment by itself is useless unless there is a factory in which it can be used. The factory is a prerequisite to the investment for the air-conditioning equipment, but the air conditioning is not a prerequisite to the investment in the factory building.

STATISTICAL DEPENDENCE

It is possible for two or more investments to be economically independent but statistically dependent. For example a firm could produce high-priced yachts and expensive cars. The investment decisions affecting these two product lines are economically independent. However, the fortunes of both activities are closely associated with high business activity and a large amount of discretionary income for the "rich" people. This statistical dependence may affect the risk of investments in these product lines, since the swings of profitability of these two product lines will be wider than those of two product lines having less statistical dependence. Statistical dependence is defined and its importance for investment decisions is discussed in Chapters 15 and 16.

ADMINISTRATIVE IMPLICATIONS

The number of possible relationships that may exist between pairs of complementary investments is very large. In dealing with investments that are complementarily related, the most effective technique is to combine sets of investments proposals in such a way that the new proposal is either an independent proposal or one of a set of mutually exclusive proposals. In the preceding example, instead of considering two complementary investment proposals, a factory and the air-conditioning equipment for the factory, we can reformulate the problem as one involving a choice between mutually exclusive investments alternatives, namely a factory with air conditioning or a factory without air conditioning.

In most large organizations, operating procedures require that proposals for capital investment which exceed specified limits must be submitted by the sponsor to higher executive levels for review and approval before actual expenditures can be authorized. Except in unusual circumstances such proposals should consist of independent investment proposals for which an accept or reject decision is appropriate; or they should comprise a set of mutually exclusive proposals, such that either the whole set must be rejected or only one of the mutually exclusive alternatives can be accepted. No system of controlling capital expenditures can operate effectively if management finds that after having approved a seemingly highly profitable investment, additional investments that do not generate any profits on their own account are presented as being absolutely necessary to implement the profit potential of the initial investment proposals.

EXAMPLE

The research and development section of a large chemical manufacturing firm submitted technical data on a new product to one of the firm's operating divisions. After investigation of the product by the engineering, production, and sales staffs, the operating division management decided that the product should be added to their line. Since existing facilities were not adequate for the production of the new product, a capital appropriation request for the new plant and equipment was submitted for review and approval to the firm's executive committee. On review by the executive committee the following deficiencies were uncovered: (1) The appropriation request did not include an estimate of the working capital requirements that would be required to operate the new plant and market the resulting product; (2) one of the raw materials required in the new process would be purchased from another operating division of the company, and the increased output of that division would have required additional plant and equipment expenditures by the supplier division; (3) the new product was partially competitive with one of the company's existing products, and the decline in the profit potential from this existing product had not been taken into consideration; (4) distribution of the new product would require acquisition of additional storage facilities, since demand for the product was seasonal, but efficient production would require a steady rate of production. The proposal was returned to the operating division for further study. After additional investigation it was determined that the company could most effectively utilize the new product by licensing other manufacturers to produce and market it.

In developing an investment proposal to be submitted to higher levels for review and approval, the sponsor and his staff should normally include as a part of the single package whatever complementary investments seem necessary or desirable. Similarly, if the proposed investment will serve as a partial substitute for any investments to which the firm is already committed or which are under consideration, this fact should be noted in submitting the proposal.

If some of the choices involved in planning the investment are considered sufficiently important that the final decision must be made by top management, the investment proposal should be submitted in the form of a set of mutually exclusive alternatives. Examples would be the decision on the location of a new plant or the possibility of including an important piece of auxiliary equipment. This procedure has the advantage of enabling top management to examine in an orderly fashion the major alternatives involved. It also enables management to make decisions at a stage in the planning of the expenditure when the special knowledge, experience, and insight of the senior executives can be effectively brought to bear on the proposal. Too often such choices are not presented to management until previous commitments have largely foreclosed the opportunity to exercise choice, and management is presented in effect with a *fait accompli.*

Ordinarily the cost figures contained in an investment proposal submitted to top management will be based on a careful but necessarily preliminary estimate of the final cost of the proposed project. On major projects, the expensive step of preparing detailed specifications and working drawings should be deferred until the project has actually been approved. Once approval has been obtained, management will proceed with the detailed planning of the project. At this stage a great many decisions will have to be made on such questions as the type of materials to be used in construction, the choice of equipment, and even the location of a plant if no definite decision on this point was made in the preliminary plans. Given the general approval for the project as a whole, these choices are mainly among different ways of accomplishing the same objective—that is, the alternatives are mutually exclusive. Although the most important of these choices, such as plant location, may be submitted to higher management levels, many of the less important decisions will necessarily be made by lower levels of management or by staff personnel.

In order to ensure coordination when decision making is decentralized, it is necessary to set up means of communicating information about policies and objectives of the organization so that decisions made independently in various parts of the organization will contribute to the goals of the organization. When the decentralized decision-making powers grant authority to make investment-type decisions, the procedures recommended in this book can provide an important means of assuring that uniform standards of choice consistent with overall organizational goals are available to the many separate decision-making centers.

As could be expected, these problems occur not only in business organizations but also in nonprofit organizations, both public and private. The following example is based on a situation that occurred in a university.

EXAMPLE

The head of the buildings and grounds department of a large university obtained approval to replace and modernize the lighting system in one of the university gymnasiums. The old lighting system had been installed 30 years earlier when the building was built. It was expensive to maintain, and the quality of the lighting was definitely low by modern standards. The detailed job of designing the new lighting system was turned over to a lighting engineer in the Office of the University Architect. Three types of lighting equipment were initially considered. Of these, one was eliminated on the basis of having excessive glare for this application. The two remaining possibilities were both capable of producing satisfactory light conditions, and therefore an attempt was made to choose between the two on the basis of cost. The cost analysis disclosed that system A would require a high initial outlay but would have low maintenance and operating costs. System B would require lower initial outlays but higher maintenance and operating costs than system A. As a result, the lighting engineer felt that no clear choice could be made on the basis of cost; therefore the final decision was made on the basis of admittedly unimportant differences in the quality of the light produced by the two systems. If the engineer had applied the discounted cash flow approach, taking into account the fact that the university was able to earn a 4.5 per cent return on its funds, it would have been clear that system A had a very decided cost advantage.

COMPARABILITY

The problem of comparability arises if the profitability of future investment proposals will be affected by decisions made currently. A group of investments will be said to be comparable (and mutually exclusive) if the profitability of subsequent investment possibilities will be the same, regardless of which investment is accepted or if all are rejected. Investment alternatives should be combined into groups that are both mutually exclusive and comparable before a final decision is made.

For example, a new plant could be heated by using forced hot air or steam. These are mutually exclusive alternatives. However, they are not comparable if it seems likely that the installation of an air-conditioning system will become necessary at some time in the future. The air-conditioning system would cost less to install in a building already equipped with air vents, and the present value of this difference in expected costs should be taken into account when choosing the heating system.

This simple example brings out two points. First, it is frequently not possible to make a group of mutually exclusive investment alternatives exactly comparable. In designing a new plant, the number of possible changes that may be desirable at some future date (such as remodeling, installation of new machinery, and additions or extensions) is very large, and the cost of each such possible change will depend upon the basic plant design originally adopted. In such circumstances, to make an analysis of truly comparable investments would require consideration of an unduly large number of alternatives.

Secondly, the importance of having mutually exclusive investments comparable is a matter of degree. In choosing a heating system for a new plant, the importance of the fact that future installation of air conditioning would be more expensive with steam will depend on the likelihood that air conditioning will eventually be required, the lapse of time until it may be required, the extent of the extra installation costs, etc. In deciding whether a group of mutually exclusive alternatives is sufficiently comparable for practical purposes, one must apply a reasonable approach.

COMPARABILITY AND THE REPLACEMENT DECISION

When a firm is considering the replacement of equipment with more modern equipment, the problem of comparability of life may arise. The present equipment is likely to have a different expected life than the new equipment being considered. One method of solution is to compute the present values of the costs of the several alternatives for perpetuity (or equivalently for a common life or for a year). The following examples illustrate this procedure.

Assume that a type of pump has an expected physical life of four years and has no expected salvage value at the time of retirement or replacement. All cash flow estimates are on an after-tax basis. The cost of money is 10 per cent. The pump currently in use is one year old. The cash proceeds resulting from running the pump currently in use, the proceeds connected with the pump being considered this year, and the proceeds of the pump that is expected to be developed in the next year are as follows:

Pump	Initial outlay	Expected annual net cash proceeds
Currently in use	. . .	$ 20
Currently being considered	$236	100
Expected at the end of one year	200	100

Let us compare the cash flows resulting from three possible courses of action:

Plan A. Do not replace until three years from now.

Plan B. Replace now, keep the pump for four years, and then replace again.

Plan C. Defer the replacement for one year.

There are other alternatives, such as replacing at the end of the second year or replacing now and again at the end of one year, but these possibilities will be ignored. To include them in the computations would complicate the analysis, and our objective is to illustrate a method of approach.

The table that follows shows the cash flows resulting from each of the three investment plans being considered. The investment that has the largest present value, using a discount rate of 10 per cent, may be accepted as the optimum investment plan. This procedure is essentially experimental in nature. It tests all possibilities and chooses the plan that maximizes the cash flows.

Invest-ment plan	Cash flows at end of year							
	0	1	2	3	4	5	6	7	8
A	. . .	$ 20	$ 20	$ 20 [$200]	$100	$100	$100	$100 [$200]	$100
B	[236]	100	100	100	100 [200]	100	100	100	100 [200]
C	. . .	20 [200]	100	100	100	100 [200]	100	100	100

Note: Outlays to purchase pumps are bracketed.

The above table stops with eight periods, but we should imagine that the table continues past the eight years and extends to perpetuity. Note that for each alternative, there is a pattern of cash flows that repeats itself.

Plan A has an outlay of $200 in period 3 and additional outlay of $200 every fourth year. The cash proceeds are $20 a year for three years and then $100 for perpetuity.

Plan B has cash proceeds of $100 in all periods. It has $236 of investment-type outlay in period 1 and $200 in period 4 and in every fourth year thereafter.

Plan C makes repetitive investment outlays every four years, starting in period 1. It has cash proceeds of $20 in period 1 and $100 in every period thereafter.

By using the present value of cash flows the best of the three investment plans can be chosen. The problem of comparability has been solved by computing the present value of the costs for perpetuity.

The computations indicate that investment plan C is the most desirable. The assumptions made should be noted. We have assumed

Computation

Plan A		Present value of cash flows	Explanations
20 (2.4869)	=	$ 50	$20 a period for three periods
$100 \times 10 \times (1.10)^{-3}$	=	751	A perpetuity of $100 discounted for three periods
$63.09 \times 10 \times (1.10)^{-3}$	=	(474)	The annual equivalent outlay for perpetuity discounted for three periods
		$ 327	Net present value for Plan A

Plan B			
236.00	=	$ (236)	An immediate outlay
100×10	=	1,000	Cash flows of $100 for perpetuity
$63.09 \times 10 \times (1.10)^{-4}$	=	(431)	The annual equivalent outlay for perpetuity discounted for four periods
		$ 333	Net present value for Plan B

Plan C			
$20 (1.10)^{-1}$	=	$ 18	$20 discounted for one period
$100 \times 10 \times (1.10)^{-1}$	=	909	A perpetuity of $100 discounted for one period
$63.09 \times 10 \times (1.10)^{-1}$	=	(574)	The annual equivalent outlay for perpetuity discounted for one period
		$ 353	Net present value for Plan C

Notes for computations:

1. The $63.09 per period is equivalent to $200 every four periods.
2. The factor 10 appearing in each computation is the present value of a dollar per period for an infinite number of periods, assuming a rate of discount of 10 per cent.
3. The present values are being computed as of the end of period 0 or the beginning of period 1. The investment and cash flows of each period are assumed to take place at the end of the indicated period.
4. Instead of converting the $200 outlay every four years to an annual equivalent of $63.09, it is also possible to convert the annual interest of 10 per cent to an equivalent interest of 46.4 per cent over a four-year period, and compute the present value of a perpetuity of $200 per period (each period, four years) using the 46.4 per cent.

knowledge of the investments available now (period 0) and at the end of period 1. We have assumed that the investments available at the end of period 1 will not be improved upon in future periods. If there is reason to suspect that further improvements will be made in a future period (for example, period 2), then this fact may be incorporated into the analysis by considering additional investment plans:

Plan D. Do not replace until period 2.
Plan E. Replace in period 0 and period 2.
Plan F. Replace in period 1 and period 2.
Plan G. Replace in periods 0, 1, and 2.

The computations may become more complex, but solutions are possible if we consider the cash flows from all possible investment alternatives that may be encountered.

If we remove the restriction of the four-year physical life, then the number of alternative investment plans is greatly increased. Obviously, for an investment of small dollar value, it would not be desirable to spend a large amount of time analyzing this type of problem. Where the investment is large (such as a firm renting or owning a large number of automobiles), the decision is important, and a large amount of effort could be expended determining the optimum time to replace equipment.

REPLACING EQUIPMENT WITH INFINITE PHYSICAL LIVES

A piece of equipment may be considered to have an infinite physical life if the replacement of parts as they fail are considered to be maintenance costs. When should equipment of this nature be replaced rather than repaired? An example of this type of equipment is an automobile that may be kept running indefinitely by replacing each individual part as it breaks down.

Assuming that we have the repair cost figures for each year of life, and constant technology, the solution is not difficult. Our goal is to *minimize* the present value of the costs of running automobiles. We can compute the present value of the costs, assuming replacement at the end of one year, two years, etc. It is important that investment streams be made comparable—i.e., that the use of automobiles be considered for an equal number of years for each alternative.

Example: The cost of a new car is $1,000; the cost of money is 10 per cent. Compute the optimum moment of replacement for automobiles, assuming the following fictitious cost information:

Age of car	Repairs for year	Salvage value at end of year
1	$ 500	$800
2	1,000	640
3	1,000	512

Assume that repairs are made at the end of each year if the car is to be retained but that they are not necessary if the car is to be sold for its salvage value.

To illustrate the basic computations, let us first decide whether it would be better to replace at the end of year 1 or year 2. We assume that a one-year-old car is now owned by the company. The cash flows of following the two alternatives are as follows:

Replacement period	Cash flows for year		
	0	1	2
1 year	($1,000)	$800 (1,000)	$800
2 years	(1,000)	(500)	640

An inspection of the cash flows of the two alternatives reveals that the automobiles should be replaced at the end of each year. The outlays required at the end of period 1 are less ($200 compared with $500), and the salvage received at the end of period 2 is greater ($800 compared with $640). At any positive rate of discount the decision to replace annually will be preferable.

It should be noted that the above analysis carried out both alternatives to a common period of two years. If we had included the possibility of a life of three years, it would have been necessary either to carry the analysis to six years (the lowest common multiple of years, which is shown in the following table), compute the equivalent cost per year for each proposal, or find the cost for a perpetuity.

Replacement period	Cash flows for year						
	0	1	2	3	4	5	6
1 year	($1,000)	($200)	($200)	($200)	($200)	($200)	$800
2 years	(1,000)	(500)	640	(500)	640	(500)	640
			(1,000)		(1,000)		
3 years	(1,000)	(500)	(1,000)	(1,000)	(500)	(1,000)	512
				512			

Making use of present-value tables, we find the present value of the costs of the three alternatives to be:

Replacement period	Present value of costs for six years
1 year	$1,307
2 years	2,323
3 years	3,321

Using this analysis, we reach the conclusion that it is desirable to replace the automobile annually. The most undesirable of the three choices is to replace at the end of three years.

It is interesting to note that frequently a decision such as the one being illustrated will result in the old equipment being retained indefinitely. In such cases a replacement verdict may result, not because of cost considerations but because management does not consider the equipment being used to be as attractive in appearance or as safe as more modern equipment.

SERIAL DEPENDENCE

In practice, the question frequently arises, "Must mutually exclusive investment alternatives have the same lives in order to be comparable?" The answer is "no." In some instances, investment alternatives with different lives will be comparable; in other instances equal future time periods are necessary to achieve comparability. Although the principles involved are the same as for other kinds of dependence, serial dependence is sufficiently important to deserve separate comment.

An example of comparable mutually exclusive alternatives not having the same life occurs in connection with deciding how to exploit a new patented product. One alternative is to sell the patent rights to another firm. This results in a single, lump-sum payment. The patent may also be exploited by manufacturing and selling the product.

In this example the two choices are comparable, although the expected cash proceeds from one would extend only one year, and from the second, for a longer period of time.

REPLACEMENT CHAINS

In the preceding example, we considered comparable investments with unequal lives. More commonly we find it is appropriate to compare equal-lived investments. Suppose a real estate company is considering whether to remodel a motel and to continue operating it for an additional ten years, or to raze the old motel and build a new one that would have an economic life of twenty years. On what basis can these two alternatives be compared?

If the alternatives were comparable, we would compare the present value of expected cash outlays and proceeds from the two unequal-lived streams. However, in this instance the two investments are not comparable. If the company chooses to remodel the existing motel now and scrap it after ten years, it will then have the options of selling the land, building a new motel, or using the land in some other way. These possibilities must be taken into account in making the present decision.

One possibility is to convert the two investments into equivalent average annual cash flows. Suppose the company has a cost of money of 10 per cent and that remodeling the old motel would yield a net present value at 10 per cent of $100,000 during the next ten years. To convert this into equivalent annual cash flows, we would find the annual amount for ten years, which has a present value of $100,000. Similarly, if the expected net present value from building a new motel were $125,000, we would find the 20-year annuity which has a present value of $125,000. At 10 per cent the equivalent annual payments are $16,274 and $14,682. With this system the alternative having the largest average annual cash flow is the most favorable. Note that by using net present value, building a new motel is favored; by using equivalent annual returns, remodeling the present motel is better. Using net present value, we ignore the profits that could result from using the land during years 11 through 20, when the present motel will be torn down if it is remodeled now. This creates a bias toward the alternative of building a new motel now. On the other hand, by converting to equivalent annual returns, we assume that an investment as profitable as remodeling the current motel will reappear ten years from now. Another mechanical assumption would be that ten years from now it will be possible to build a new motel that would be as profitable and long-lived as the new motel to be built now. Although it may turn out upon investigation in a particular case that this assumption is reasonable, we cannot assume that this will be the case.

If we considered ourselves sufficiently clairvoyant, we might attempt to estimate the cost of building a new motel ten years from now and also the cash proceeds that would be generated by operating this new motel. Even this would be of little avail if it turned out that this new motel would last for more than an additional ten years, since the two alternatives would not then be comparable.

Sometimes a practical solution is found by putting an upper or lower limit on the value of potential future opportunities. For example, in the motel problem one can safely estimate that if the motel is remodeled now, in ten years there will be a potential cash flow at least equal to the value of the land at that time. It may turn out that even an optimistic estimate of the value of the land will not be sufficient to make the alternative of remodeling the old motel more attractive than the prospect of constructing a new motel.

COST OF EXCESS CAPACITY

It is easy to conclude that excess capacity has no costs—that is, sunk costs are not relevant to incremental decisions. Assume the ABC Chemical Corporation has extra boiler capacity and is considering the addition of a new product which will take one half of the extra capacity. How is the cost of the boiler brought into the analysis? The quick easy answer is to say there is no boiler cost. Unfortunately this conclusion may not be correct. Add the information that undertaking the new product and using one half of the excess capacity moves up the expected date of purchase of a new utility system from five to three years in the future. This acceleration of purchase has costs, and these costs are part of the new product decision.

The means of incorporating the cost of accelerating the acquisition is not obvious. Assume that the expected cost of the boiler acquisition is $2,492,000 and it has an estimated life of 20 years. With a cost of money of .05 the annual equivalent cost per year of use is

$$CA_{\overline{20}|.05} = 2,492,000$$

$$12.4622\,C = 2,492,000$$

$$C = \$200,000 \text{ (a rounded-off approximation)}$$

Without the new product, years 4 and 5 will not have the cost of a new boiler. With the new product there is an equivalent cost of $200,000 for years 4 and 5.

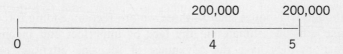

The present value of the additional costs is $321,240.

$$.8227 \times 200,000 = \$164,540$$
$$.7835 \times 200,000 = 156,700$$
$$\overline{\$321,240}$$

An advocate of the new product might argue that the cost should be less because the degree of utilization of the boiler during the first two years will be very low and there will not be much wear and tear. If we assume no wear and tear (also no obsolescence), there would only be the interest cost of $124,622 (.05 of $2,492,000) occurring at the end of years 5 and 6 (beginning of 4 and 5). Just taking interest into account gives a cost of approximately $200,168.

$$.8227 \times 124,622 = \$102,527$$
$$.7835 \times 124,622 = 97,641$$
$$\overline{\$200,168}$$

However, some amortization of cost for tax purposes and some decrease in value (that is, depreciation) should be recognized. Thus the exact present value of the cost of adding the product is not determinable. One estimate is $321,240, but it could be $200,168. Including either of these estimates is better than assuming that there is no cost associated with using the excess capacity.

We may want to include an analysis where we did not include the capacity cost but rather dropped the product when capacity was reached and it was time to add new facilities. This possibility should be checked out, but generally it should be assumed that once the product is added it will be produced in the future. This will tend to occur because of the momentum principle (it is difficult for a firm to change directions) and because after the costs of getting a product under way have been incurred, there is a good chance that an economic analysis would indicate the desirability of continuing the sale of the product and taking advantage of the goodwill that was created.

CONCLUSIONS

Although techniques such as those we are recommending force one to make difficult estimates in the face of imperfect and incomplete information, they have the advantage of focusing attention on the important unknowns. Apparently simpler techniques achieve their simplicity by using general assumptions about the nature of future opportunities rather than conjectures tailor-made to a particular situation. They save time and effort at the expense of a less precise analysis of the decision-making situation.

QUESTIONS AND PROBLEMS

5-1. The Roger Company has the choice between two different types of dies. One type costs less, but also has a shorter life expectancy. The expected cash flows after taxes for the two different dies are as follows:

Die	Period				
	0	1	2	3	4
A	($10,000)	$8,000	$8,000		
B	(12,000)	5,000	5,000	$5,000	$5,000

The cost of money of the firm is 10 per cent.
Required: Choose the more desirable die. Explain.

5-2. Assume that there are two mutually exclusive investments that have the following cash flows:

Investment	Period 0	Period 1	Yield (%)
A	($10,000)	$12,000	20
B	(5,000)	6,100	22

Assume that either investment will require modification to the basic building structure, which will cost $1,000, and that this amount is not included in the above computations. The cost of money is 10 per cent.

Required: (a) Compute the actual yields of the investments. (b) Does the additional $1,000 change the ranking of the two investments? Explain.

5-3. Consider the following two mutually exclusive investments.

Investment	Period 0	Period 1	Yield (Rate of return)
A	(20,000)	30,000	.50
B	(100,000)	130,000	.30

Required: Assuming a cost of money of 0.10, which investment is to be preferred?

5-4. An existing machine must be replaced. Two new models are under consideration. Both cost $15,000. Model X will generate savings of $10,000 per year and has a life of two years. Model Y will generate savings of $18,000 per year; it has a life of one year. The machine will be needed for two years. Which model should be purchased if the cost of money is .05?

5-5. Assume that two pieces of equipment have the following characteristics:

Equipment	Expected life (years)	Initial cost	Operating cost per year
A	9	20,000	10,000
B	5	25,000	8,000

Required: Assuming a cost of money of .10, which equipment is the more desirable?

5-6. The A Corporation's computer currently has excess capacity. The controller would like to prepare and distribute a report that would take approximately one hour a day of the computer's time. The computer could do this task and still have excess capacity. The annual cost of this type of computer is $1,000,000 a year. The discount rate is .05. The long-range planning group estimates that without the report the corporation would be shifting to a more powerful computer five years from now. With the report, they estimate the shift four years from now. The new computer will cost $1,500,000 per year. Assume the computer payments take place at the end of each year.

Required: What is your estimate of the cost of adding the report?

5–7. The New York State Utility Company is considering the construction of a new utility plant. It has accumulated the following cost information:

	Fossil plant (oil and gas)	Nuclear energy plant
Initial outlay	60,000,000	100,000,000
Annual operating cost	15,000,000	20,000,000 *

* This is the projected cost for year one. It is expected that the operating costs will decrease by $2,000,000 per year and level off at $10,000,000. The expected decrease is a result of decreased fuel costs. Both plants have an expected useful life of fifty years.

Assume a time value of money of .05 per year.

Required: (a) Which plant should be built? (b) Assume the only question is the year of construction of the nuclear plant. Should it be built now, assuming that the needed electricity for the first five years can be purchased at a cost of $16,000,000 per year? Should it be built in year 6? (c) If the fossil plant were built, would you replace at the end of 6 years with a nuclear plant? Assume the above cost projections are valid and that the nuclear plant would still cost $100,000,-000.

5–8 (Reference, Problem 5–7 part (b)). Assume that the cost of the needed electricity is $17,000,000: (a) Should the nuclear plant be built now? (b) Compute the present value today of building (that is, completing) the nuclear plant six years from now when the operating costs would be $10,000,000 per year, compared to buying electricity.

5–9. The A Corporation is considering the construction of a new plant to build a component part that it is currently purchasing. It has the following information:

	Cost	Expected life
Plant	20,000,000	40 years
Utilities	10,000,000	20 years
Equipment	15,000,000	10 years

The operating costs are estimated at $5,000,000 per year assuming an output of 1,000,000 units of product per year.

The corporation uses a discount rate of .05. It can purchase the product at a cost of $10.00 per unit.

Should the new plant be built (on a straight economic basis)?

5–10. A company is considering two alternative marketing strategies for a new product. Introducing the product will require an outlay of $15,000. With a low price the product will generate cash proceeds of $10,000 per year and will have a life of two years. With a high price the product will generate cash proceeds of $18,000 but will have a life of only one year. The cost of money for the company is .05. Which marketing strategy should be accepted?

5–11. Compare your answers to problems 5–4 and 5–10. Are the relevant cash flows the same in both problems? If not, why?

5–12. State Electric wants to decide whether to repair or replace electric meters when they break down. A new meter costs $30 and on the average will go 12 years without repair. It costs $18 to repair a meter, and a repaired meter will, on the average, go eight years before it again needs a repair. Repairs can be made repeatedly to meters because they are essentially rebuilt each time they are repaired. It costs $6 to take out and reinstall a meter. The time value of money is .05.

Required: Should the company repair old meters or buy new meters?

5–13. *Fall River Lumber Company*

The Financial Analysis Department of the Fall River Lumber Company in considering the purchase of equipment for debarking logs prepared the following report.

PROPOSED DEBARKING INSTALLATION FOR FLAKEBOARD PLANT

Introduction

The flakeboard plant is using peeled aspen so that our finished board will contain a light-colored appearance. This lighter appearance is felt to be necessary by the Sales Department if we wish to continue to point our product toward a higher quality market.

Moreover, as the plant's operating efficiency is a direct function of the life of its flaker knives, the peeled wood will contribute somewhat to increasing this life by eliminating the abrasive action caused by the sand and dirt that is often found within the bark.

However, the primary consideration in maintaining an adequate knife life is that the moisture content in the aspen be sufficient (above 35% air dry) to act as a cooling agent on the flaker knives.

If the aspen supplied to the plant is too dry, the flaker knives heat up, thereby becoming dull, and the plant's operations are impaired. Past experience has demonstrated to us that the difference in flaker knife life is almost insignificant between using *freshly peeled aspen* and *freshly unpeeled aspen,* but quite significant between using *dry peeled aspen* and *freshly peeled aspen.*

In the initial stages of operations, the plant used fresh "hand peeled" aspen direct from the wood dealers. However, since the hand peeling (commonly known as sap peeling) season lasts only during the trees' annual growth period (a six-week period from spring to early summer), it is only during this time that a sufficient volume (2 cords per man per day) can be maintained. Out of season this type of production drops to ½ cord per man per day, thus becoming uneconomical. While a sufficient year's supply of aspen could possibly be bought during the 6-week sap peeling season, the wood would dry out in storage and the problem of flaker knife life again becomes the critical factor.

Chemical debarking must be ruled out as a possibility since the wood becomes too dry in the one-year period that is required for the tree to die and the bark to fall off.

Thus, the use of some kind of mechanical debarking equipment that would insure a year-round supply of peeled wood with the correct moisture characteristics becomes necessary if we wish to continue producing our lighter colored flakeboard.

Alternative Solutions

The following proposals exist as possible means of supplying peeled aspen to the flakeboard plant:

1. Installing permanent debarking facilities at Fall River employing King or Elmo equipment.
2. Utilizing portable debarkers at Fall River, such as the Leswork.

Recommendations

This study recommends installing a King debarker out in the woodyard. In addition, it recommends the use of mechanical feeding accessories and a bark burner. The estimated savings would be $40,000 per year compared to our present portable Leswork installation. The total estimated investment would be $70,000. The return on this investment would be at the rate of 57% or payback in 1¾ years.

Summary of Findings

The problem as outlined in the introduction of this study of determining the most economical and engineering sound method of debarking aspen for the flakeboard plant is complicated.

Basically, it boils down to balancing our rate of production required to supply the flakeboard operations against a capital investment and estimated debarking cost per cord that we are willing to pay for.

Certain assumptions were made. The main ones, subject to the most variability, are:

1. The estimated useful life of the debarkers,
2. The estimated repair and maintenance costs, and
3. The machine production per hour.

The alternative of *buying peeled wood* is not recommended and such rejection is based mainly on the following considerations:

1. The wide diversity in the location of the aspen stands, creating a difficult peeling set-up in the field.
2. The uncertain supply in the winter season.
3. The higher operating costs for the wood dealer necessitated by his increased handling and depreciation expenses.
4. The possible legal problems arising from buying and renting debarkers to the wood dealers.
5. The reluctance of the wood dealers to debark in the field.
6. The uncertainty of getting clean wood.

Rejection of *portable debarkers at Fall River* is primarily based on a pure cost consideration. In order to maintain our estimated production requirements of 1,000,000 square feet per month in the flakeboard plant, it would necessitate reinvesting in portable debarkers at a rate that would more than offset the initial low investment cost. The low production inherent in these debarkers means running them at their capacity practically around the clock and thereby quickly reaching their estimated life of 5,000 cords.

The choice lies between buying a King debarker, either new or used, or an Elmo. A used King is rejected, since its return on investment is less than that of a new King. Both the Elmo and King are substantially the same machine as far as the efficiency in debarking the wood goes. However, the rugged design of the Elmo has kept its repair and maintenance charges well under that of the King. While there are over 100 King installations in operation, certain companies, such as the United States Paper Company of Flint, Michigan, are replacing their King with Elmos, as the latter seemed to hold up better. Nevertheless, the economic advantage as evidenced by the higher rate of return of the new King as compared to the Elmo, 57% vs. 49% (see Table 4), takes into consideration this more rugged design of the Elmo, yet this report still concludes that the King investment is the more advantageous for our requirements.

It is well to mention that the inherent savings of using an Elmo or a King debarker lie not only with the increased production (both over twice the hourly capacity of a Leswork) which lowers the total unit cost per cord of wood debarked, but also with the longer estimated life of the machines. The savings are not a result of an over-all reduction in manpower.

While the debarkers themselves do not require operating labor, the machine's higher productive capacities require that such men be utilized as spotters on the infeed and outfeed conveying equipment.

The economics of the study are summarized in the following Tables 1–4. Tables 1–3 compare the operating costs and investments

Table 1.   Cost Estimates for Flakeboard Plant Debarkers

	King [a]	King [b]	Elmo	Leswork [c]
Debarker cost (with power)	$23,200	$16,000	$ 44,000	$4,000
Accessories (conveyors & deck, etc.)	37,425	27,700	52,000	—
Installation	9,650	14,600	9,800	300
TOTAL INVESTMENT	$70,275	$58,300	$105,800	$4,300
Fixed costs per cord	$0.82	$1.08	$0.74	$0.95
Variable costs per cord	1.16	1.32	0.72	2.87
TOTAL ESTIMATED COST PER CORD	$1.98	$2.40	$1.46	$3.82

[a] New King
[b] Used King
[c] Present Fall River Operations (estimated 3 Lesworks required to meet production demands)

of a King, an Elmo, and a Leswork debarking installation. Table 4 summarizes the return on investment data of the King and Elmo installations as compared to our present Leswork operations.

Location

The location of a debarker installation is an important factor in determining the efficiency of its operation. The installation could be placed in one of two places, namely:

1. Adjacent to the flakeboard plant, or
2. Out in the woodyard.

Wood handling is a major consideration to this location decision, in particular supplying the infeed side of the debarker. On the outfeed side, stacking the slick debarked logs is also a job. If the sticks are maintained with a minimum end-to-end spacing on the infeed conveyor, full utilization of the debarker is obtained. This requires

Table 2. Analysis of Total Investment Estimate for Flakeboard Plant Debarkers

Type of debarker	King (new)	King (used)	Elmo	Leswork
Debarker (with power)	$23,200	$16,000†	$ 44,000	$4,000
Building	$ (7,000)*	$ (4,500)*	$(No exact break-down given, similar to new King equip.)	
Infeed and outfeed conveyors	9,000	6,000		
Cross Chain Conveyor	10,000	10,000		
Bark Conveyor	5,000	3,500		
Starting Equipment	1,425	1,200		
Cary Lift	(21,400)*			
Bark Burner	10,000	3,000		
Special Roll Conveyor & Flipper		2,000		
Spare Parts	2,000	2,000		
Total Accessories	$37,425	$27,700	$ 52,000	$ —
Dismantling old King equipment and accessories	$ —	$ 5,000	$ —	$ —
Freight—In	250	200	$ 400	$ 50
Power line to woodyard 2,100' wire at $2/foot $4,200 22 poles on 100' intervals at $100/pole 2,200	6,400	6,400	6,400	—
Labor and materials to install equipment (3 men, 3 days)	3,000	3,000	3,000	250
Total Installation	$ 9,650	$14,600	$ 9,800	$ 300
TOTAL INVESTMENT	$70,275	$58,300	$105,800	$4,300

† Estimated.
* Not included in totals for accessories.

Table 3. Analysis of Cost Estimates per Cord for Fall River Flakeboard Plant Debarkers

Type of machine	Elmo	King (new)	King (used)	Leswork (Fall River)
Estimated life *	20,000 hrs. 5 years	14,000 hrs. 3½ years	10,000 hrs. 2½ years	2,000 hrs. ½ year
Rated capacity—rough cords per hour	9	7	6	2½
Fixed costs per cord		Cost Estimate Per Cord		
Depreciation charges: $\dfrac{\text{total equipment cost}}{\text{tot. est. life} \times \text{rated cap.}}$	$0.59	$0.71	$0.96	$0.90
$\dfrac{\$106,000}{20,000 \text{ hrs.} \times 9 \text{ cords/hr.}}$ (sample calculation)				
Interest, taxes, insurance: avg. annual invest. × 10%	0.15	0.11	0.12	0.05
$\dfrac{\$106,000 \times .1}{2 \times 4,000 \text{ hr./yr.} \times 9 \text{ cd./hr.}}$				
Total fixed costs	$0.74	$0.82	$1.08	$0.95

Variable costs per cord

Repairs and upkeep	$0.05†	$0.32†	$0.37†	$0.05
Maintenance (½ hr./8 hr. shift) (routine lubrication & adjust.) $\dfrac{.125¢ \text{ hr.}}{\text{rated capacity}}$	0.01	0.02	0.02	0.05
Operating labor: $\dfrac{2 \text{ men} \times \text{hourly wage} \times 113\% ‡}{\text{rated capacity}}$ $\dfrac{2 \text{ men} \times 2.00/\text{hr.} \times 113\%}{9 \text{ cords/hr.}}$	0.05	0.65	0.75	1.67
Operating supplies and power: 50% hr./rated capacity	0.06	0.07	0.08	0.10
Bark hauling: $\dfrac{\$4/\text{truck/hr.} \times 1 \text{ hr./ld.}}{4 \text{ cords/truck load}}$	—	—	—	1.00
Bark burning	0.10	0.10	0.10	—
Total variable costs	$0.72	$1.16	$1.32	$2.87
Total Estimated Cost Per Rough Cord	$1.46	$1.98	$2.40	$3.82

* Estimated life based on: 16 hrs./day × 5 days/wk. × 50 wks./yr. = 4,000 hrs./yr. × 5 yrs. = 20,000 hrs.
† Estimated from actual operations at Great Falls Paper Company (Elmo), and Paper Products (King installation).
‡ 13% increased for Social Security, Workmen's Compensation, Retirement Benefits.

**Table 4.   Estimated Return on Investment Comparing Proposed
Debarkers with Present Leswork Debarker**

	With bark burner *		
	Elmo	King (new)	King (used)
Estimated savings per rough cord	$ 2.63	$ 1.84	$ 1.42
Estimated required rough cords/ year ** (59 cords/day × 360 days)	22,000	22,000	22,000
Estimated total savings per year	$ 52,000	$40,000	$31,000
Estimated total investment	$106,000	$70,000	$58,000
Estimated return on investment	49%	57%	54%
Payback period	2 years	1¾ years	1⅘ years

	Without bark burner		
	Elmo	King (new)	King (used)
Estimated savings per rough cord	$ 1.55	$ 1.05	$ 0.68
Estimated required rough cords/ year ** (59 cords/day × 360 days)	22,000	22,000	22,000
Estimated total savings per year	$ 34,000	$23,000	$15,000
Estimated total investment	$ 96,000	$60,000	$48,000
Estimated return on investment	35%	38%	31%
Payback period	3 years	2½ years	3¼ years

* Cost of bark burner including installation is $10,000.
** Based on production requirements of 50 finished cords per day, which provides
for 1,000,000 square feet board per month and a 15% bark loss.

production equipment. By having the debarker in the wood yard the
crane could be utilized in unloading the trucks directly onto the infeed line deck conveyors leading into the debarker, thereby producing
at rated capacity. If the volume of trucks is too high at any one
period, the crane could stack the wood in ranks adjacent to the
infeed table and in a slack period feed the debarker from these ranks.
Whereas, if the crane was brought into the plant site, this would cut
down on the yard efficiency for stacking wood when the debarker
is not in use. The only other solution would be to use a Cary Lift
in place of the crane. However, this means an increased investment
of $22,000.

Other advantages to locating the debarker installation in the wood yard are:

1. More space, thereby allowing for flexibility of operations.
2. Possible future infeed application utilizing a "hot" pond. This type of wood handling appears to be the most practical way of solving loading into King-type debarkers. The wood is simply dumped into the pond, which has impellers submerged in the water. If the sticks are not in contact with the water for more than ½ hour, the moisture content of the wood is not affected.
3. Ease of installation, since no interference with the existing supply of wood to the plant would be affected.

The principal advantage to locating near the flakeboard plant site is the reduced material handling on the outfeed end. Instead of stacking the wood or trailers for hauling to the plant or in ranks for inventory, it could be fed directly to the flakers. However, this means that the debarking operation is dependent *directly* on the flakeboard plant's operations, for if the plant shuts down so must the debarker. Otherwise, if the debarker would run when the plant was down, the material handling would increase, since the peeled wood would have to be set off. Out in the wood yard this would not be the case. Wood racks mounted on rails or the present trailers could be placed under the outfeed end conveyor and easily removed sideways away from the flow of materials when each rack has been filled.

Bark Disposal
Another important aspect in a debarking operation is the problem of bark disposal. The bark could possibly be

1. Burned in a regular "bark burner."
2. Utilized as fuel at our boiler house provided the necessary adapting equipment was installed.
3. Possibly pressed into logs and sold as fireplace wood.
4. Hauled away and dumped as refuse.

This study compares returns with and without a bark burner. (See Table 4.)

If the efficiency of burning is high enough to prevent excessive smoke, the investment in such a piece of equipment would pay for itself by the savings ($1/rough cord ×22,000 cords/year = $22,000) resulting from eliminating hauling to the dump.

Discussion of Alternative Solutions
1. *Portable Debarkers at Fall River.* It is possible to utilize *a series* of Leswork portable debarkers for the flakeboard plant's wood requirements. At the present time we are barking approximately 45 rough cords per day (2¼ rough cords/hour × 20 hours/day). This appears to be maximum capacity for these debarkers. Assuming a 15% bark loss and a 2% wood loss this results in a production of 37

finished cords per day (45 × 83%). This is enough capacity for 750,000 square feet of board per month (assuming 1.5 finished cords/1,000 square feet). Basing our wood requirements at a minimum of 1,000,000 square feet/month, we would need a production of about 50 finished cords per day. Thus, it would be necessary to invest in a minimum of two more debarkers (one for reserve) to fulfill our minimum production requirements. This would be an investment of $12,000 (3 × $4,000), excluding the necessary conveying accessories. However, based on an estimated life of 2,000 hours or 5,000 cords, ⅔ of this investment would theoretically be replaced approximately

every 4 months or ⅓ years $\left(\dfrac{5{,}000 \text{ cords}}{45 \text{ cds./day} \times 30 \text{ days/mo.}} = 3.7 \text{ mos.} \right)$.

Thus, a $12,000 initial investment becomes a $28,000 yearly investment.

Expanding this investment to a comparable figure with the King and Elmo debarkers, the following result is seen:

Type	Elmo	King (new)	Portable Leswork
Estimated life	5 years	3½ years	4 years
Total investment	$106,000	$70,000	$112,000

2. *Permanent Debarking Facilities.* In considering permanent debarking facilities for the Fall River flakeboard operations, the first question that must be answered is what type of bark-removable operation is feasible. Some principal methods of bark removal apart from manual labor with a spud or draw knife are:

a. By means of friction by tumbling or rotating action such as the rotating cylindrical drum at Williamsburg
b. By hydraulic pressure
c. By shear principle
d. By the rosser head, or cutter head, principle such as the present Leswork debarker.

An attempt to debark some aspen in the Williamsburg drum was not successful as the wood was not dry enough to experience sufficient friction for effective bark removal. Since the flakeboard operations demand this higher moisture content in the wood, this generally recognized quick, cheap bark removal system cannot be utilized.

A hydraulic pressure debarker is ruled out chiefly on the grounds of the water pollution problem it would create.

The basic feature of a King-type debarker consists of a blunt edge pressure elastically against the log, which then penetrates the bark down into the cell-forming "cambium" layer between the bark and wood. Tangential pressure against the bark produces shear stresses between bark and wood sufficient to overcome the strength of the cambium layer. The principal feature of such a machine is the removal of bark at a substantially low wood loss. The trade names of debarkers of this type are the King and the Elmo. Both of these debarkers could be used for our flakeboard operations.

The rosser, or "cutter head," principle is employed on the Leswork machine we now are using. While these machines remove the bark sufficiently, the wood loss appears to be higher than with the King type. In addition, as these machines are portable, production is not as great as on the King machines. As an example, the Leswork debarks between 2 to 2½ rough cords per hour as compared to 5 to 10 rough cords per hour on the King. Nevertheless, the Leswork is a proven debarker that could be utilized in our operations.

Both the King and the Elmo have been utilized in flakeboard operations. It is generally felt that the King does an excellent job in debarking, but the maintenance requirements are high. Moreover, there seems to be more of a problem debarking wood with varying diameters with the King than with the Elmo. (Our operations use wood ranging from 4″ to 15″ in diameter.)

Since the Elmo has been designed for more rugged operations, its weight is approximately 2½ times the King (22,000# vs. 9,000#). Simultaneously, its cost is $20,000 more ($44,000 vs. $24,000).

The rating of a barker is dependent on the number of sticks per cord, the per cent of bark removal required, and the infeed system to the debarker. In addition, under wintertime conditions it is necessary to slow down the barker in order to maintain the same per cent of bark removal. For this study, the average rated capacity of the King and Elmo barkers was based on automatic conveying accessories. It should be kept in mind that manual feeding to either of these debarkers would tend to reduce their rated capacity.

Required: Assume a zero tax rate and a time value of money of .05. What decision should the firm make?

The chances of success of a given investment (whether of capital or labour) depend on the efficiency with which all those who work in the same firm co-operate with the factor in question.

—J. R. Hicks, "The Theory of Uncertainty and Profit," *Economica* (London, May, 1931), p. 185.

6

THE USE OF
CASH FLOWS IN
EVALUATING INVESTMENTS

We have argued that investments ought to be evaluated in terms of the present value of the cash flows expected from them, in preference to any other measures of investment worth that have been suggested. However, we have not given a complete or careful definition of the term *cash flows*. In the present chapter we shall attempt to do this and also to explain some of the difficulties that arise in applying a cash flow analysis to investment proposals. In Chapter 7, the influence of income taxes on the timing of cash flows will be discussed, and in Chapter 13 a suggested framework for systematically recording estimates of cash flows will be presented.

CASH FLOWS AND PROFITS

Cash flows are not identical with profits or income. Changes in income can occur without any corresponding changes in cash flows. During a period of investment in plant and inventories, a corporation can even experience a decrease in cash at the same time income is increasing.

The popular conception of an investment is typified by a one-period outlay of funds, followed by a series of periods in which incomes are earned. The incomes are then related to the investment, and some type of return on investment is computed. One of the main advantages of the cash flow procedure is that it avoids difficult problems underlying the measurement of corporate income which necessarily accompanies the accrual method of accounting. These problems include the following:

1. In what time period should revenue be recognized?
2. What expenses should be treated as investments and therefore capitalized and depreciated over several time periods?
3. What method of depreciation should be used in measuring income as reported to management and stockholders (as distinct from income measurement for tax purposes)?
4. Should LIFO (last in, first out), FIFO (first in, first out), or some other method be used to measure inventory flow?
5. What costs are inventoriable? Should fixed, variable, direct, indirect, out-of-pocket, unavoidable, administrative, or selling costs be included in evaluating inventory?

There are disagreements as to the answers to each of these questions. Different approaches may lead to different measures of income. If income is used to evaluate investment worth, investments may look good or bad, depending on how income is measured. The cash flow procedure minimizes many of these complications.

WHY CASH FLOWS?

In evaluating an investment we suggest that the cash flows of the investment be used in the analysis. We are not interested in the conventional "cost" of the investment but rather in the cash outlays required and the timing of these cash flows. We are not using the earnings of period 1, but rather the cash flows of period 1. These distinctions can be important. A builder may tell us that a construction project will cost $1,000,000. But this is not sufficient information. We want to know when the outlays will be required. For example, if the outlays are made on completion of the building, then the cost is truly $1,000,000. If the payment is required one year prior to completion, then the true cost is $1,000,000, plus the interest on the $1,000,000 for one year. The use of earnings to measure the benefits would require a much more sophisticated theoretical accounting system than is currently being used by any corporation. The earnings figures resulting from current accounting practices are not usable.

Also, even with improved measures of income, there would remain the question as to whether the use of cash flows or earnings is more appropriate. The advantage of the use of the cash flow is that the receipt of cash is an objective, clearly defined event that leads to a significantly different situation than before the receipt of cash.

A sale on account is an economic event recorded by the accountant and affecting accounting income. However, the firm has not yet received the cash, it cannot spend the cash, and the ultimate collection of the cash is uncertain. For purposes of investment analysis we are more interested in the moment when the cash is received. At that moment the firm reaches a new decision point. The cash may be returned to the stockholders by the payment of a dividend. It may be used to retire debt, increase the working capital, or be reinvested in new long-lived assets.

It might be suggested that to be correct the dollar of cash received in period 1 should be followed to its disposition at the end of the firm's life. However, we find it more convenient to take the receipt of cash associated with a specific asset to be a self-contained event, and we do not normally concern ourselves with the final disposition of the dollar. The assumption that the funds can be borrowed and loaned at a given discount rate allows us to make this simplifying assumption.

Thus for purposes of investment analysis, unlike conventional accounting, we choose the receipt or disbursement of cash to be the crucial event. It should not be thought that a sale on account (or other accruals) are ignored. A sale on account in period 1 will affect the expected cash collection in period 2; hence, it is brought into the analysis in the period in which the firm has the cash in hand and has reached a decision point.

ABSOLUTE AND RELATIVE CASH FLOWS

Every investment analysis involves a comparison of alternatives. If there are not at least two possibilities, then there is no problem of choice. Usually the number of alternatives is large. The question may be whether the company is better off with investment A or without it, or whether investment A is better than investment B, or whether both A and B should be accepted or both should be rejected. In any case, since the investment analysis involves a comparison of two or more alternatives, it is not surprising to find that any estimate of cash flows must also be on a comparative basis.

Suppose the question is whether to start a new business. After a careful analysis we arrive at an estimate of the net cash flows that we expect to occur in each future period after we start the business. Our estimate will tell us how much money we would have to invest during each period as the business got started and how much money would be available after necessary expenses and additional investments in each period after it began to operate successfully. Perhaps we would plan to sell the business after five years if it were successful, and we would include as a cash flow the amount we would expect to receive for the business five years hence. The present value of the net cash flows might then be calculated, using a rate of discount of 10 per cent. What comparisons are we making in analyzing the investment? What comparisons are we making in estimating the net cash flows?

If we say that the cash outlays in the first year is $100,000 (since that amount of money would have to be expended during that period, over and above any cash receipts), then we are implicitly comparing the cash flows from operating the business with a cash flow of zero. When cash flows are being compared with zero cash flows, we shall speak of *absolute* cash flows. In evaluating the present value of these cash flows, using a 10 per cent rate of interest, we are implicitly comparing this investment with an investment that would return 10 per cent per year indefinitely for each net outlay.

Suppose now that the question is whether to start one kind of business or another; for example, a retail store or a wholesale distributorship. One possible analysis would be to estimate the absolute cash flows from each business and compute the present value of the corresponding cash flows. Again, in this case, we are comparing each business separately against a hypothetical investment that could earn 10 per cent. Since the hypothetical standard of comparison is the same for both businesses, the two can be readily compared with each other by noticing which business would probably give a higher present value of cash flows. In practice, the final decision would depend on many other factors as well, such as the degree of risk involved in each business, the degree of confidence we feel in our estimates, and so on. A further discussion of some of these factors is given in Chapter 11.

An alternative analysis would be to compare directly one business with the other. In looking at the cash flow estimates, for example, we can subtract (algebraically) the cash flows of the retail store from the cash flows in corresponding periods of the wholesale distributorship. If the difference is positive in a particular period, it will tell us how much better the cash flows from the wholesale business are than those from the retail business during that period. The cash flows, in this case, can be called *relative* cash flows; the wholesale business is being measured relative to the retail business. Again we can compute the present value of this series of relative cash flows. It can be shown that the present value of this series of relative cash flows will be the same as the present value of the absolute cash flows from the wholesale distributorship minus the present value of the absolute cash flows from the retail business. Thus the present-value method will lead to the same conclusion, whichever approach is used.

There is an important difference between the two series of cash flows, however. With the series of absolute cash flows, if the corresponding investment (the retail or wholesale businesses) were accepted and actually began to operate, we could compare, period by period, the actual cash flows with our previous forecasts. There is not, however, any similarly identifiable series of cash flows that could be compared with the relative cash flow estimates. If we decided to operate the wholesale business on the basis of a comparison of relative cash flows, and wished after a few periods to compare our actual results with those we had forecast earlier, we should need to know what assumptions had been made about the retail business in order to make this comparison.

Frequently, when we are considering investments to be made in a going business, it may be difficult to define the absolute cash flows that would result from the investment. It may be easier to use a relative cash flow concept in computing flows. Suppose, for example, that an automobile manufacturer is trying to decide whether to invest in the tools and dies necessary to make a particular modification in the body style of his product. He might compare what sales would be if he made the investment and what they would be if he did not make the investment. This may still be a very difficult estimate to make since all sorts of other changes are taking place at the same time, both in his product and marketing strategy, and in those of his competitors.

IMPORTANCE OF CONSIDERING ALL ALTERNATIVES

Apart from those difficulties in making estimates of relative cash flows that are a by-product of the difficulties of estimating the incremental effects of various actions of the firm, there is an important conceptual danger that must be avoided in estimating relative cash flows. As previously explained, an estimate of relative cash flows always involves an explicit comparison of two alternatives. The size of the estimated relative cash flows from making a particular investment will depend upon the alternative that is used as a basis of comparison. *This means that almost any investment can be made to seem worthwhile if it is compared with a sufficiently bad alternative.* Consider a problem that was faced by many railroads in the not too distant past. Should the old coal-burning locomotive used on a particular passenger run be replaced with a modern and more efficient diesel? Assuming that the change would not affect passenger revenues, the natural basis of comparison would appear to be to take the present value of the extra outlays required to purchase the new engine (minus the scrap value of the old coal burner) and the cash savings resulting from the difference between the operating costs of the old and the new engines. On this basis it may seem that the investment in a new diesel engine would be quite profitable. But suppose, using the old coal burner, the revenues from the passenger run are insufficient to cover the incremental out-of-pocket costs of operating the train. In such circumstances the purchase of a diesel may serve to decrease the loss, but it may not convert the passenger run into a profitable operation. If there is no possibility of eliminating the passenger run, the decision to purchase the diesel may be wise. But if the passenger train could be eliminated, purchase of the diesel would not be justified. This situation could be handled by examining the absolute cash flows generated by the diesel, i.e., by comparing the cash flows resulting from the passenger train with a diesel locomotive and the cash flows resulting from no train at all. When using relative cash flows, we must remember to consider all alternatives, including the alternative of continuing as we are now or abandoning the operation entirely, if these are possible.

In general an investment should not be accepted unless the relative cash flows generated by it are positive when compared with the next best alternative. Frequently the analyst will be faced with a situation in which there are quite a number of possible alternatives whose relative advantages are not yet known. In such cases any one of the investments can be used as the standard of comparison, and the relative advantage of each estimate can be compared to this standard. If all the other alternatives have a negative present value when compared with the standard, then the standard is the most advantageous insofar as explicit cost and revenue considerations are the determinants. In the railroad locomotive example given above, if continuance of operating the coal-burning locomotive were taken as the standard, it could turn out that discontinuing the passenger train altogether would give a higher present value than buying a diesel, although the latter is better than continuing to operate the coal-burning locomotive. As long as all the feasible alternatives are considered, it makes no difference which one of the alternatives is tentatively accepted as the standard of comparison. The final answer will be the same in any case. The choice of a standard of comparison may lead to mistaken conclusions only if some advantageous alternatives (such as ceasing production entirely) are excluded from the analysis.

OPPORTUNITY COSTS

Usually the cash outlays included in the computation of net cash flows are the outlays incurred because of the investment that would not be incurred otherwise. Outlays that would be incurred by the firm whether or not the investment is accepted should not be charged to a particular investment project. Thus the practice of allocating a share of general overhead to a new project on the basis of some arbitrary measure, such as direct labor hours or a fraction of net sales, is not recommended *unless* it is expected that general overhead will actually increase if the project is accepted.

On the other hand, in some instances an investment project may require the use of some scarce resource available to the firm, although the explicit cash outlays associated with using that resource may be nonexistent or may not adequately reflect the value of the resource to the firm. Examples are projects that require a heavy drain on the time of key executive personnel or that use valuable floor space in a plant or store already owned by the business. The costs of using such resources are called *opportunity costs,* and they are measured by estimating how much the resource (the executives' time or the floor space) would earn for the company if the investments under consideration were rejected.

It may appear that the practice of charging opportunity costs against an investment project when no corresponding cash outlay can be identified is a violation of, or exception to, the procedure of evaluating investments in terms of actual cash flows. Actually, including opportunity costs is not so much an exception to the cash flow procedure as an extension of it. The opportunity cost charged should measure net cash flows that could have been earned if the project under discussion had been rejected. Suppose one floor of a factory building owned by a business could either be rented out at $1,000 per month or used to produce a new product. After an initial outlay for equipment, the new product could produce an absolute net cash inflow of $2,000 per month after taxes but before an allowance has been made for use of the factory space. The figure of $2,000 per month overstates the benefits to be derived from the new product, since the space required could otherwise be used to earn $1,000 per month. By charging a rental opportunity cost of $1,000 per month against the new product, a more meaningful measure of its actual value to the company is obtained. An alternative procedure would be to estimate the relative cash flow from the new product compared with that produced by renting the extra space and not producing the new product.

In some instances it will be extremely difficult to estimate opportunity costs. The temptation then is to use some other more easily identifiable basis of charging for the use of such things as floor space or the time of key executives. This temptation must be viewed with some skepticism. The pro rata share of the costs of owning a building may be much higher or much lower than the true opportunity costs of using that space. When there is really no basis for estimating the opportunity costs associated with the use of a factor, such as the time of certain key executives, it may be preferable to note merely that the proposed project is likely to require considerably more or considerably less than the usual amount of attention from such key executives.

ACQUIRING ASSETS WITHOUT CASH DISBURSEMENTS

The term *cash outlay* is also applied to a transaction where an asset is acquired by incurring a long-term debt or by issuing stock. Even though there may be no explicit borrowing of cash, receipt of cash, and disbursement of cash, these transactions are assumed to occur when an asset is acquired via a promise to pay in some distant time period, and the transaction is treated as if there has been a cash outlay as well as a source of new capital.

Where an asset is acquired by the incurrence of a noninterest-bearing, current liability, the convention is adopted in this book that it is the timing of the actual cash disbursement which is important. Thus if the investment results in an increase in inventories of $100 and the source of capital is an increase in current liabilities of $100, the net cash outlay that is required in the period of inventory acquisition is zero. If the $100 increase in inventories required cash outlays of $20 and current liabilities increased by $80, then the net cash outlay in the period of inventory acquisition is $20.

EXCLUDING INTEREST PAYMENTS

Cash disbursed for interest is normally excluded from the cash flow computation used in analyzing investments. The interest factor is taken into consideration by the use of the present value procedures. To include also the cash disbursement for interest would result in double counting. Assume that the discount factor being used to take into consideration the time value of money is 6 per cent. There is an investment that requires an outlay of $1,000 and promises to return $1,080 at the end of one period. This investment would seem to be desirable. Assume that we can raise money for this investment at a cost of 6 per cent—i.e., obtain $1,000 now and pay $1,060 a year from now. The incorrect analysis would show the $60 interest as a deduction from the cash flows of period one:

	Year	
	0	1
Investment	−1,000	1,080
Interest		− 60
Net Cash Flows	−1,000	1,020

This series of cash flows would lead to a reject decision, using higher than a 2 per cent rate of interest because of a double counting of interest.

SALVAGE AND REMOVAL COSTS

The salvage and removal costs introduce no real problem if we keep in mind that we are interested in the periods when cash outlays are made or when cash flows into the firm. In the following descriptive material, the term *salvage* refers to "net salvage"; removal costs have been subtracted.

reject investments, often it will be necessary to compute the income for tax purposes as a separate computation.

CASH FLOWS AND UNCERTAINTY

It should be recognized that each computation of cash flows makes certain assumptions about the level of business activity, actions of competitors, future availability of improved models of machines, costs of factors of production, future sales, and the like. Since there is a large amount of uncertainty connected with each of these factors, it should be appreciated that computations using the present-value method are indications rather than numbers with 100 per cent certainty and accuracy. A more detailed discussion of the consequences of uncertain estimates and some suggestions for making analyses when basic assumptions are subject to uncertainty are presented in Chapters 11, 15, and 16. It should be stressed that any decision about investments must in the last analysis be based on as complete a consideration of all the relevant factors as it is possible to provide, and that the probable present value of an investment proposal is only one factor, although a very significant one, that must be considered in arriving at a final decision.

QUESTIONS AND PROBLEMS

6-1. The Bright Machine Tool Shop is considering replacement of the equipment in a section of its shop. The equipment performs a function that could be completely eliminated. A comparison of the present equipment being used with the new equipment indicates the following relative cash flows would result if the new machine were purchased instead of continuing with the old:

Period	
0	1
($10,000)	$12,000

The yield of the investment is 20 per cent, and the cost of money is 15 per cent. The net present value of the investment is $435. Based on the positive net present value, the decision was made to replace the present equipment.

In the period of operation, the machine performed exactly as predicted, and all costs were as predicted. The absolute cash flows were as follows:

	Period	
0		**1**
($10,000)		$11,000

Required: Comment on the investment decision made by the Bright Machine Tool Shop.

6–2. The Dotted Airline Company is considering replacement of its fleet of ten two-engine planes with five new model jets. One jet can replace two of the present planes. The airplane company has prepared an analysis showing that each new plane will cost $343,000 and will earn cash proceeds of $100,000 per year for five years. Assume that after five years the salvage value will be zero for both the new and old planes. The analysis was based on the load and operating characteristics of the new plane and the past experience of the airline, as well as number of passengers and the routes traveled, adjusted in a reasonable manner for additional passengers who will be attracted by the new planes.

The planes currently being used are considered to be safe work horses, but are not as glamorous as the new planes. In competition with jets, they are expected to earn net cash proceeds of only $10,000 per year per plane. There is no discernible trend of earnings. The present planes now have a zero salvage value.

The cost of money of the Dotted Airline is 10 per cent. Assume the company has access to the necessary funds.

Required: Should the Dotted Airline purchase the new jets? Explain. What would be your recommendation if the salvage value is, now, $40,000 for the old planes?

6–3. The following facts relate to an investment that costs $10,000 being considered by the ABC Company:

	Period	
	1	**2**
Cash Revenues	12,000	12,000
Depreciation	5,000	5,000
Net Income	7,000	7,000

The Company intends to increase dividends by $12,000 in period 1 and $12,000 in period 2 as a result of the investment. The Company is not subject to income taxes.

Required: What are the cash flows of the two years for purposes of the analysis of the investment?

6–4. For problem 6–3, assume that all the sales were made on account, and collection lagged the sale by one period. The Company will distribute dividends equal to the cash generation.

Required: What are the cash flows of each year?

6–5. An investment will require an increase in the following working capital items:

Cash	$1,000,000
Accounts Receivable	3,000,000
Inventories	6,000,000

It is also expected that current liabilities will increase by $4,000,000.

Required: How will the preceding items affect the cash flows of the investment?

6–6. In computing the cash flows of a period should interest payments be included or excluded? Explain.

6–7. The ABC Company is considering an investment in a new product. The information for the year 1965 is given as follows:

Sales	$200,000
Manufacturing costs of sales	80,000
(includes $20,000 of depreciation)	
Selling and Administrative expenses	40,000
(directly associated with the product)	
Equipment purchases	10,000
Decrease in contribution of other products	5,000
Increase in accounts receivable	15,000
Increase in inventories	20,000
Increase in current liabilities	30,000
Income taxes associated with product income	12,000
Interest on bonds expected to be used in financing	18,000

Required: Compute the cash flow which can be used in the present value computations of this investment.

6-8. A Product is currently being manufactured on a machine that has a book value of $10,000 (it was purchased for $50,000 twenty years ago). The costs of the product are:

	Unit Costs
Labor, direct	$ 4.00
Labor, variable indirect	5.00
Other variable overhead	2.50
Fixed overhead	2.50
	$14.00

In the past year 10,000 units were produced and sold for $20 per unit.

It is expected that the old machine can be used indefinitely in the future.

An equipment manufacturer has offered to accept the old machine as a trade-in for a new version. The new machine would cost $80,000 after allowing $15,000 for the old equipment. The projected costs associated with the new machine are:

Labor, direct*	$ 2.00
Labor, variable indirect	3.50
Other variable overhead	4.00
Fixed overhead	3.50
	$13.00

The fixed overhead costs are allocations from other departments plus the depreciation of the equipment. Repair costs are the same for both machines.

The old machine could be sold on the open market now for $6,000. Ten years from now it is expected to have a salvage value of $1,000. The new machine has an expected life of ten years and an expected salvage of $10,000.

There are no corporate income taxes. The appropriate time discount rate for this company is .05.

It is expected that future demand of the product will remain at 10,000 units per year.

Required: (a) Should the new equipment be acquired? (b) If the product can be purchased at a cost of $8.00 per unit from a reliable supplier, should it be purchased or made?

6–9. The ABC Company is considering an investment in a new product. The information for the year 1965 is given as follows:

Sales (all on account)	$200,000
Manufacturing costs of sales	90,000
(includes $20,000 of depreciation and $6,000 of fixed cost allocations from service departments)	
Selling and Administrative expenses	40,000
(directly associated with the product)	
Equipment purchases	10,000
(purchased on account and not yet paid)	
Decrease in contribution of other products	5,000
Increase in accounts receivable	15,000
Increase in inventories	20,000
(includes $4,000 depreciation)	
Increase in current liabilities	30,000
Income taxes associated with product income	12,000
Interest on bonds expected to be used in financing	18,000
Uncollectible accounts receivable expected to be written off	2,000
Increase in accumulated depreciation	19,000

Required: Compute the cash flow which can be used in the present-value computations of this investment.

People who like this sort of thing will find
this the sort of thing they like.

—Attributed to Abraham Lincoln

7

CORPORATE INCOME TAXES

AND INVESTMENT DECISIONS

Accounting theory suggests three basically different methods of recording a cash outlay for an asset or cost factor; these in turn affect
the measurement of income. The outlay may be considered to be an
expense of the period in which it is incurred, or to represent the acquisition of a wasting asset that will be charged to expense over a
number of future periods, or to represent the acquisition of a nonwasting asset, in which case it is never charged to expense. The first
is typified by outlays for salesmen's salaries, the second by outlays
for plant and equipment, and the third by outlays for land. For some
outlays a reasonable case can be made for one or another accounting
treatment. Thus outlays for research, certain types of advertising, and
some kinds of maintenance may be treated as current expenses or
capitalized and depreciated over a longer period; outlays for land
may be treated as wasting assets if the important characteristics of
the land are its possession of certain minerals or soil fertility, or as
partially nonwasting if its site value is considered.

The accounting treatment accorded a particular outlay will influence the amount and timing of income measurement. But in the
absence of income taxes, the choice of investments should not be
influenced by the method of accounting for a particular outlay. It is
the amount and timing of the cash outlays and the amount and timing
of future cash proceeds that are relevant to the choice of investments.

In the case of corporations subject to income taxes, the accounting
treatment adopted for income tax purposes must be considered in
evaluating a potential investment, since it will affect the amount and
timing of the income tax payments. Since income taxes do not affect
all investments in the same manner, it is necessary to place cash flows
associated with each investment on an after-tax basis before evalu-

122

ating the investments. In this chapter we shall be concerned with the mechanics of computing the after-tax cash flows associated with investments. We shall consider separately the problems associated with depreciable assets, nondepreciable assets, and outlays chargeable to current expense.

MEASURING THE EFFECTS OF DEPRECIATION CHARGES ON CASH FLOWS

Suppose we are considering the purchase of a new piece of equipment that is expected to have no salvage value on retirement. If there were no income taxes, then the cash proceeds resulting from the use of the equipment could be estimated by subtracting the additional cash outlays required to operate the equipment from the additional revenues that result from acquiring it. That is,

$$\text{Before-tax cash proceeds} = \text{revenues} - \text{cash outlays} \qquad (1)$$

The term *cash proceeds* is used here to refer to the proceeds generated by operating the investment. It assumes that all revenues are accompanied by an immediate generation of cash equal to the revenues. It also assumes that all cash outlays, except the initial investment, are charged to expense—i.e., none is charged to inventory—and that inventory is not reduced. Thus cash outlays are equal to the expenses (excluding depreciation) in this simple example.

For a nonprofit hospital or government bureau, this is the only calculation that would be necessary. For a business it is necessary to subtract the additional income tax liability that occurs because of the investment.

$$\text{After-tax proceeds} = \text{revenues} - \text{cash outlays} - \text{income tax} \qquad (2)$$

or

$$\text{After-tax proceeds} = \text{revenues} - \text{expenses other than depreciation} - \text{income tax} \qquad (3)$$

The income tax liability is computed by applying the income tax rate to the additional taxable income. One of the allowable deductions for tax purposes is the depreciation of the investment. It is possible to express the determination of the income tax in the following way:

$$\text{Income tax} = (\text{tax rate}) \times (\text{taxable income}) \qquad (4)$$

and

$$\text{Income tax} = (\text{tax rate}) \times (\text{revenues} - \text{expenses other than depreciation} - \text{depreciation}) \qquad (5)$$

From Equation 5 it can be seen that the higher the depreciation taken for income tax purposes, the lower the income tax will be and the greater the after-tax cash proceeds. Substituting Equation 5 in Equation 3 and simplifying give Equations 6 and 7.

$$\text{After-tax proceeds} = (1 - \text{tax rate}) \times (\text{revenues} - \text{expenses other than depreciation} - \text{depreciation}) + \text{depreciation} \qquad (6)$$

or

$$\text{After-tax proceeds} = (1 - \text{tax rate}) \times (\text{revenues} - \text{expenses other than depreciation}) + (\text{tax rate}) \times (\text{depreciation}) \qquad (7)$$

Equations 6 and 7 are mathematically identical, and therefore give identical answers, although one or the other formula may be easier to use in a particular instance. Equation 7 is particularly useful, since it highlights the fact that the cash proceeds of the period are increased by the allowable depreciation times the tax rate. Thus we can compute the present value of the "tax savings" by multiplying the depreciation by the expected tax rate of each period and discounting that amount back to the present.

Illustration: A piece of new equipment costs $10,000. It can be depreciated for tax purposes in four years, and it has been decided to use the sum-of-the-years'-digits method. It is expected to have no salvage value on retirement. The company uses straight-line depreciation for book purposes. The equipment is expected to result in an increase in annual revenues (sales are all for cash) of $8,000 and additional annual costs requiring cash outlays of $4,000 (not including depreciation of the equipment). The income tax rate is 52 per cent. The cost of money is 10 per cent.

The first step is to compute the taxable income and income tax of each year. This is accomplished in Table 1.

It should be noted that the use of a tax rate of 52 per cent for all years carries an assumption that the tax rate will not be changed. If a change is expected, the tax rates of the future years should be used.

Table 1. Computation of Income Tax

Year	Revenues	Other costs	Depreciation for tax purposes	Taxable income	Tax rate (%)	Income tax
1	$8,000	$4,000	$4,000	$ 0	52	$ 0
2	8,000	4,000	3,000	1,000	52	520
3	8,000	4,000	2,000	2,000	52	1,040
4	8,000	4,000	1,000	3,000	52	1,560

The second step is to compute the cash proceeds of each year. It is important to note that the book depreciation does not enter into this computation at all, but the depreciation for tax purposes influences the income tax and thus does indirectly affect the proceeds.

Table 2. Computation of Cash Proceeds

Year	Revenue	Other costs	Income tax	Cash proceeds
1	$8,000	$4,000	$ 0	$4,000
2	8,000	4,000	520	3,480
3	8,000	4,000	1,040	2,960
4	8,000	4,000	1,560	2,440

The next step is to compute the present value of the cash flows, using 10 per cent as the rate of discount (see Table 3).

The present value of the proceeds, $10,403, is greater than the cash outflows of $10,000; thus the investment is apparently desirable.

In the above example the "other costs" allowed for tax purposes were equal to the "other costs" for which cash outlays were made.

It is possible for these two amounts to differ. For example, costs may be incurred that are not allowable for tax purposes because the cost factors are in inventory. The cash outlays are required, but they do not give rise to decreases in the income tax of the period.

Table 3.   Computation of the Present Value of Proceeds

Year	Cash proceeds	Discount factor (using 10 per cent)	Present value of the proceeds
1	$4,000	0.9091	$ 3,636
2	3,480	0.8264	2,876
3	2,960	0.7513	2,224
4	2,440	0.6830	1,667
			$10,403

A different schedule of depreciation deductions for tax purposes is obtained if the twice straight-line declining balance method is used.

Table 4.   Computation of Twice Straight-line Depreciation

Year	Decreasing balance	Rate (%)	Depreciation of the period	Accumulated depreciation
1	$10,000	50	$5,000	$ 5,000
2	5,000	50	2,500	7,500
3	2,500	50	1,250	8,750
4	1,250	100*	1,250	10,000

* Assuming the asset is to be retired at end of the fourth year.

The company using the twice straight-line declining balance procedure for tax purposes has the option to switch to the straight-line procedure. When the depreciation charge following twice straight line becomes less than it would be following straight line, the company should switch to the latter procedure. This will result in $1,250 of depreciation for year 4. The next step would be to compute the taxable income, income tax, and cash proceeds for each year of the life of the investment so that present value of the cash flows may be computed, just as was done when using the sum-of-the-years'-digits depreciation.

CHOOSING THE MOST ADVANTAGEOUS DEPRECIATION PROCEDURE

Under the Internal Revenue Code of 1954, a company has a choice (among other methods) of depreciating a new asset by using straight-line depreciation, sum-of-the-years' digits, or twice straight line on the declining balance. In the often discussed problem of what depreciation method to use, it has frequently been noted that the choice of depreciation method will affect the profitability of the investment. It has not usually been realized that the best depreciation method for a company may depend upon the discount rate that is appropriate as well as upon the life of the investment and its expected salvage value. The present-value method can be put to use in making this decision. For this purpose Equation 7 for computing the after-tax cash proceeds is most advantageous, since it divides the after-tax cash proceeds into two parts: The first part is independent of the depreciation method, and the second part depends only on the depreciation method. The depreciation method giving the highest present value should be chosen.

Table 5. Present Value of After-tax Cash Proceeds Excluding Depreciation

Year	(1) Revenues less current expenses	(2) After-tax equivalent (Col. 1 × 0.48)	(3) Discount factor	(4) Present value (Col. 2 × Col. 3)
1	$ 4,000	$1,920	0.9091	$1,745
2	4,000	1,920	0.8264	1,587
3	4,000	1,920	0.7513	1,443
4	4,000	1,920	0.6830	1,311
Total	$16,000	$7,680	3.1698	$6,086

As is indicated in Table 5, the present value of the after-tax equivalent of $4,000 a year for four years is $6,086 when the tax rate is 52 per cent and the discount rate is 10 per cent. This part of the calculation is independent of the depreciation method used.

To determine the best depreciation method, we need to compute the present value of the tax saving resulting from the use of each

Table 6. Present Value of Tax Savings from Different Methods of Depreciation, Assuming a 10 Per Cent Rate of Discount

Year	Depreciation method								
	Straight-line			Twice straight-line			Sum-of-the-years' digits		
	Allowable expense	Saving (52%)	Present value	Allowable expense	Saving (52%)	Present value	Allowable expense	Saving (52%)	Present value
1	$ 2,500	$1,300	$1,182	$ 5,000	$2,600	$2,364	$ 4,000	$2,080	$1,891
2	2,500	1,300	1,074	2,500	1,300	1,074	3,000	1,560	1,289
3	2,500	1,300	977	1,250	650	488	2,000	1,040	781
4	2,500	1,300	888	1,250	650	445	1,000	520	356
Total	$10,000	$5,200	$4,121	$10,000	$5,200	$4,371	$10,000	$5,200	$4,317

possible depreciation method. These computations are shown in Table 6, assuming a 52 per cent tax rate and a 10 per cent rate of discount. It is clear from this table that the investment would be most advantageous if it could be used with the twice straight-line method of depreciation, since in that case the present value of the cash proceeds would be $10,457 ($6,086 + $4,371). The present value of the proceeds, when the sum-of-the-years'-digits method of depreciation is used, would be $6,086 plus $4,317, or $10,403, which is less than the $10,457 obtained above.

In this example the present value of the savings from the most advantageous method of depreciation as compared with the next best method amounts to about one-half of 1 per cent of the initial outlay of $10,000, or $54. In the case of a similar investment whose initial cost was $10 million, the present value of the difference between the two depreciation methods would be $54,000.

USE OF TABLES TO CHOOSE OPTIMUM DEPRECIATION METHOD

Tables in the Appendix to this book have been prepared to assist in the choice of method of depreciation and in the computation of the tax saving that will result from making the investment. Two tables have been prepared. One shows the present value, following the sum-of-the-years'-digits method, using different discount rates and assuming assets of different lives. The other table shows comparable data for the declining balance method of depreciation (twice straight line). If an asset has a nonzero salvage value, the tables cannot be used to determine the present value of the depreciation charges for the declining balance method.

To use the tables, it is first necessary to enter the sum-of-the-years'-digits table, using the column that represents the discount rate chosen and going down it until the life of the asset is found. The amount obtained is the present value of the depreciation per dollar of depreciable base. This amount should be multiplied by the depreciable base (cost less salvage of the investment). The next step is to enter the proper table for the declining balance method (assuming zero expected salvage). The column that represents the interest rate should be entered, and the number opposite the proper life of the asset should be determined. This number represents the present value per dollar of cost of the depreciation of the investment and must be multiplied by the cost of the investment to obtain the present value of the depreciation.

The choice of the method of depreciation will be dependent on which of the two present values is the greater. The present value of the tax savings can be found by multiplying the present value of the depreciation times the tax rate.

Where a positive salvage value is expected, the present value of the depreciation deductions using the declining balance method must be computed by following the same detailed procedures which were given earlier in this chapter. If the removal costs are expected to exceed the salvage (the salvage value is negative), the tables may be used. For the purposes of computing income taxes, the salvage is zero.

A change in the tax law in 1962 liberalized the treatment of expected salvage. The taxpayer may reduce the amount of salvage by 10% of the cost of the depreciable property. Thus if $1,000,000 is spent on equipment with an expected salvage of $120,000, only $20,000 would be subtracted from the cost of the asset to compute the depreciable base.

ADDITIONAL COMPLICATIONS AFFECTING CHOICE OF DEPRECIATION METHODS

The examples presented in the preceding section are intended primarily to illustrate the type of analysis that can be undertaken when it is considered worth the effort to determine the most advantageous method of depreciating a wasting asset. The examples chosen were deliberately oversimplified to bring out the point that the present-value approach can be used to determine the most advantageous method of depreciating an asset. A full treatment of the complications arising in determining a proper and acceptable method of depreciation under the Internal Revenue Code would require a book in itself and is beyond the scope of this chapter. However, some of the more important complications that may arise in practice will be mentioned briefly.

In the examples presented, it was assumed that the assets to be depreciated would have no salvage value at the end of their expected useful life. If a salvage value is expected at the end of the asset's useful life, the amount of depreciation expense will be affected. The salvage value will affect the depreciation of each year, using the sum-of-the-years' digits, but by using the twice straight-line, declining balance procedure, it will affect only the change-over point (point at which a shift is made to straight line from twice straight line) and the depreciation after the change-over.

Another complication is that many companies use the group method of depreciation instead of the unit method. Under the group method the rate of depreciation is based on the average life of many units of like items (for example, telegraph poles). This rate of depreciation is then applied to the balance of unretired units. As the units are retired, no loss or gain is recognized at the time of retirement. The depreciation of successive periods is based on the estimate of average life (which is computed by using mortality experience for this type of asset), and the number of units that are retired in each period. Thus the use of the group procedure of depreciation requires a forecast of the number of units in use in each period in order to compute the depreciation of each period as well as a rate of depreciation.

In the examples given in this book, it is assumed that the asset is purchased in year zero and that depreciation expense is not charged until the end of the year. In practice, two other alternatives are also available. Depreciation may be taken on a monthly basis, beginning in the month the asset is acquired. If the cost of the asset is not too large, and especially when straight-line depreciation is not being used, the extra expense involved in computing monthly depreciation charges for each asset may be greater than the possible saving. Another alternative is to adopt what is called the "half-year convention," in which one-half of a year's depreciation is charged in the year the asset is acquired, regardless of when during the year the asset is acquired. When straight-line depreciation is used, the amount to be charged each year under this system is obvious. With the twice straight-line declining balance method, one-half of the usual rate is applied in the first year, and the usual rate is applied to the remaining book value in subsequent years.

A final complication is the timing of tax payments and of tax savings resulting from depreciation. In past years tax payments have lagged the earning of corporate income, but at present they have been advanced to such an extent that assuming the tax payment (or the tax saving) occurs at the end of the period in which income is earned will generally do no great harm.

WORKING CAPITAL AND SALVAGE VALUE

In focusing attention on outlays for plant and equipment, it is possible to lose sight of the fact that the working capital needed to operate the investment project should also be included in computing the investment outlays. Since residual working capital is recoverable at the termination of operations, this leads to the investment having a net terminal value that should be taken into consideration. The term *working capital* is used here in a net sense, and applicable current liabilities are subtracted from the increase in current assets to compute the use of cash. The additional current liabilities are assumed not to change the proportion of current liabilities to other sources of capital.

An investment in plant assets will invariably lead to funds being tied up in working capital. This will include the cash necessary to meet payroll and other bills, funds invested in the raw material, work-in-process and finished goods inventory, and receivables from customers. The size of these items will depend on the exact nature of the capital investment, but all the above-mentioned fund requirements will usually accompany an investment in long-lived assets. The one possible exception would be an investment that would decrease the need for working capital by increasing efficiency. Examples of this nature are accounting machines that expedite the billing to customers, or storage facilities and inventory control devices that reduce the amount of inventory which must be kept on hand.

A working capital increase has the effect of increasing the investment outflow today. Ignoring this factor will lead toward the acceptance of investments which should be rejected. If the investment has a limited life and the working capital is expected to be recovered at the end of the life of the investment, then the recovery of the working capital in the last period should be considered as cash proceeds and treated in the same manner as the other cash flows are treated. It should not be thought that ignoring the working capital investment and the recovery of working capital will balance each other out. The factor that must be considered is the required return on the working capital during the period of use.

SALVAGE VALUE AND TAXES

If taxes are introduced into the analysis of working capital, strange things happen to the conclusions of the investment analysis. The presence of taxes in some situations can actually make salvage value undesirable.

High costs of money, high tax rates, and long-lived assets, combined with accelerated depreciation for tax purposes, can result in the presence of terminal value adversely affecting the desirability of an investment.

Illustration: Assume a discount rate of 5 per cent, a 50 per cent tax rate, a life of 20 years for the asset, and a tax depreciation scheme that allows a company to write off a depreciable asset in five years. In this case $100 of depreciable assets may be worth more than $100 of terminal value.

Solution: The present value of $100 of terminal value, and the present value of a dollar due in 20 years, assuming a rate of interest of 5 per cent, is

$$(1.05)^{-20} = .3769$$

$100 \times .3769 = \$37.69$ (present value of salvage)

The present value of the tax reductions (assuming no salvage value) of the $100 of additional depreciable assets will reduce taxes a total of $50, or $10 per year. The present value of an annuity of $1.00 per period for five periods, with an interest rate of 5 per cent, is $4.3295.

$10 \times 4.3295 = \$43.30$ (present value of the tax deductions)

With the facts as given, tax deduction is worth more than the terminal value. Note that the facts of this situation are reasonable and close to reality: The corporate tax rate in recent years has been close to 50 per cent, depreciable assets do frequently have lives of 20 years, 5 per cent is not excessively high for a discount rate, and assets have frequently been written off for tax purposes over a period of 60 months.

The ideal situation from the point of view of the investor would be to write off the investment for tax purposes as if it had no salvage, and then wait and see if any salvage will develop. The taxpayer is going to be better off with a conservative estimate of salvage. This is even more important if the gain on disposition of the investment were to qualify as a capital gain, thus receiving special tax consideration. There are provisions in the present internal revenue code that tend to result in such gains being taxed as ordinary income, if the asset is held for a short period of time.

The above analysis leads to several interesting conclusions. In the presence of income taxes situations can develop where, all other things being equal, it may be more desirable to accept a depreciable investment that has no terminal value than one which has terminal value. This conclusion must be tested by existing facts; it cannot be assumed. The factors that tend to make it valid are high tax rates, high discount rates, long-lived investments, and the privilege of writing off an investment for tax purposes at a faster rate than its actual service potential warrants. Not all these factors have to be present, but the presence of all leads to the conclusion that a depreciable asset deductible for tax purposes is more desirable than an asset which is not depreciable for tax purposes. Secondly, other things being equal, an expenditure that can be expensed immediately for tax purposes is more desirable than an expenditure that must be written off for tax purposes over a period of years. Thus, under the present tax code, increasing net revenues via research may be more desirable than increasing net revenues by the same amount through increasing plant and equipment.

CHANGES IN INVENTORIES AND INCOME TAXES

The computation of cash flows makes use of the cash expenditures for factors of production in the period of outlay when computing the amount of outlays. Some of these factors of production may be lodged in inventory at the end of the accounting period and thus not charged against the revenues of the period. This would affect the cash flows of the period, since the items would not be expensed for purposes of computing income taxes. The income taxes of this period will be higher than they would be if all cash expenditures were expenses for tax purposes. In some future accounting period, these items will be expensed and will result in taxes for that period being reduced, thus in effect increasing the cash flows (by decreasing taxes) in a period long after the cash expenditure was made. Thus build-ups of inventory required by an investment will adversely affect the desirability of the investment by requiring an immediate cash outlay, while the cash flows, both by reducing income taxes and by generating revenues upon sale of the item, are delayed for one or more periods. The inventories must generate enough cash flows, not only to recover the initial outlay of funds but also to pay the interest costs of the differences in time of outlay and recovery of cash.

THE TIMING OF TAX PAYMENTS

The timing of income tax payments is relevant to the investment analysis if the payment of the tax occurs in a time period significantly later than the earning of the proceeds. There are two possible methods of incorporating the delayed income tax payments into the analysis.

One possibility is to consider the cash outlay to occur when the actual cash disbursement occurs, not when the obligation to pay is created. The second possibility is to consider the incurrence of the obligation to pay income taxes to consist of two simultaneous transactions. The government acts as a source of capital and supplier of assets, the assets are then expended to "pay" for the income tax expense. This second possibility then leads to the inclusion of "Income Taxes Payable" as a noninterest-bearing source of capital in computing the cost of capital. To be consistent with other recommendations made in this book, the first procedure is recommended.

Example: Assume a firm has an opportunity to invest $20,000 today in promoting a sport contest. The promised return to be received one year from today is $24,000. The income tax of $2,080 (assuming a 52 per cent tax rate) is to be paid two years from today. The interest rate is 10 per cent. The schedule of cash flows would be as follows:

Year	Cash flows	Present value factor	Present value of cash flows
0	($20,000)	1.0000	($20,000)
1	24,000	0.9091	21,818
2	(2,080)	0.8264	(1,719)
			$ 99

The net present value is positive and therefore the investment should be undertaken.

If the income taxes are assumed to affect the cash flows of period 1, the cash flows of that period would be $21,920, and the net present value of the cash flows, using a 10 per cent rate of discount, would be a negative $83. This would indicate that the investment should not be undertaken.

INVESTMENT TAX CREDIT

The investment tax credit in effect in 1965 allows most corporations to deduct 7 per cent of the cost of qualified investments from their federal income taxes. Assuming that the company has an income tax liability, this deduction results in a cash flow equal to 7 per cent of the cost of the investment in the initial time period, and effectively reduces the cost of the investment by that amount. A qualified investment of $1,000,000 would have an effective cash outlay of $930,000 in the initial period.

QUESTIONS AND PROBLEMS

7–1. The Internal Revenue Code (in 1965) allows a tax credit of .07 of the cost of eligible investments to be deducted from the amount of federal income taxes payable. It also allows the use of accelerated depreciation.

Assume a marginal income tax rate of .4, and an after tax discount rate of .03. (a) How much is $1 of tax credit worth today? (b) How much is the "right" to deduct $1 of depreciation today worth today? (c) Assume that we are billed and pay $1,000,000 for equipment eligible for the tax credit. The equipment will be depreciated for tax purposes in ten years. What is the cost of the equipment? What is the cash flow of the period associated with the equipment? What do we know about the value of the equipment as of the beginning of the period after the taking of tax credit?

7–2. Assume a rate of discount of 5 per cent. Prepare a set of rules for when to choose the straight-line, double-declining balance and the sum-of-the-years' digits methods of depreciation, if the salvage value is zero. How does your rule change if the rate of discount is 10 per cent?

7–3. Assume a rate of discount of 5 per cent and that a firm is making other income. It is considering an investment eligible for the investment credit that costs $1,000,000. The investment has an expected life of 20 years. Compute the present value of the cash flows that result because of the income tax and the income tax laws (assume a .40 tax rate).

7–4. Assume a tax rate of .4 and a rate of discount of .05. (a) If the firm is basically a profitable operation, what is the present value of $1 of tax deductible expense incurred and paid for at the end of period 1? (b) If the firm is a loss operation what is the present value of $1 of tax deductible expense incurred and paid for at the end of period 1?

7–5. Compute the present value of the right to deduct $1,000,000 in depreciation immediately compared with the right to deduct the $1,000,000 in 20 years from now. The tax rate is .4 and the after tax rate of discount is .05.

7–6. *The XYZ Manufacturing Company*
A product is currently being manufactured on a machine that is fully depreciated for tax purposes and that has a book value of $10,000 (it was purchased for $30,000 twenty years ago). The costs of the product are:

	Unit costs
Labor, direct	$ 4.00
Labor, indirect	2.00
Variable overhead	1.50
Fixed overhead	2.50
	$10.00

In the past year 1,000 units were produced and sold for $18 per unit.

It is expected that the old machine can be used indefinitely in the future.

An equipment manufacturer has offered to accept the old machine as a trade-in for a new version. The new machine would cost $60,000 after allowing $15,000 for the old equipment. The projected costs associated with the new machine are

Labor, direct	$ 2.00
Labor, indirect	3.00
Variable overhead	1.00
Fixed overhead	7.25
	$13.25

The fixed overhead costs are allocations from other departments plus the depreciation of the equipment.

The old machine could be sold on the open market now for $5,000. Ten years from now it is expected to have a salvage value of $1,000. The new machine has an expected life of ten years and an expected salvage of $10,000.

The current corporate income tax rate is .40 and the capital gain tax rate is .25. Any salvage from sale will result in a capital gain at the time of retirement. (For tax purposes the entire cost may be depreciated in 10 years).

The appropriate after-tax time discount rate for this company is .10.

It is expected that future demand of the product will stay steady at 1,000 units per year.

Required: (a) Should the equipment be acquired? (b) If the product can be purchased at a cost of $7.80 per unit from a reliable supplier, should it be purchased or made? Explain.

7–7. Manufacturers of heavy electric generating equipment have been arguing for years the value of buying in advance of need. The following analysis was presented by one manufacturer in order to persuade utilities to order in advance under a "buy and store" plan.

Cost of boiler if purchased a year early and stored:	$1,000,000
(Ninety per cent of the purchase price would be paid immediately and ten per cent one year later when the boiler is completed.)	
Storage costs for one year:	$ 10,000
(This amount would be paid two years from now.)	

It is expected that there will be a 8.5 per cent increase in cost ($85,000) if the purchase is delayed one year (this is based on the experience of the post World War II period).

Assuming a short-term interest rate of .04 the interest cost of buying early is $36,000 and with .52 tax rate, the after-tax interest cost is $17,200. Comparing the $85,000 of cost saving with the storage cost plus the interest indicates that it is desirable to purchase early.

Assume that the boiler is to be placed into use two years from now.

The after-tax cost of money of the company considering the purchase is 7 per cent.

Required: Prepare an estimate of the incremental after-tax cash flows resulting from ordering a boiler immediately. The estimated cash flows should be suitable for determining the value of advance ordering, using a discounted cash flow approach. Assume that the boiler would be depreciated on a straight-line basis over a 20-year period from the date it is installed and ready to use. The 7 per cent tax credit does not apply.

7–8. The dean of a school in a large university while discussing with an executive of a large corporation the pros and con of an automated collator said, "You are lucky, with a tax rate of .40; you only pay $6,000 for a $10,000 machine." Assume there is a labor saving of $2,500 per year associated with the collator being considered. The expected life is 10 years and the before tax time value of money is .05 to both the university and the corporation.

Required: Who has more incentive to purchase the machine, the university or the corporation?

7–9 (continuation of 7–8). Assume that a university and a corporation both are considering spending $5,000,000 for an administrative office building. The expected life is 50 years. Taking the 7 per cent tax credit and depreciation into consideration, what is the net saving to each? The tax rate is .40 and the time value of money is .05 before taxes (.03 after taxes to the corporation). The alternative for both is to rent at a before-tax cost of $300,000 per year with a cancellable lease.

7–10. *The NSV Manufacturing Company*

A product is currently being manufactured on a machine that is fully depreciated for tax purposes and has a book value of $10,000 (it was purchased for $30,000 twenty years ago). The costs of the product are

	Unit costs
Labor, direct	$ 4.00
Labor, variable indirect	2.00
Other variable overhead	1.50
Fixed overhead	2.50
	$10.00

In the past year 10,000 units were produced and sold for $18 per unit.

It is expected that with suitable repairs the old machine can be used indefinitely in the future. The repairs are expected to average $25,000 per year.

An equipment manufacturer has offered to accept the old machine as a trade-in for a new version. The new machine would cost $60,000 after allowing $15,000 for the old equipment. The projected costs associated with the new machine are

Labor, direct	$2.00
Labor, variable indirect	3.00
Other variable overhead	1.00
Fixed overhead	3.25
	$9.25

The fixed overhead costs are allocations from other departments plus the depreciation of the equipment.

The old machine could not be sold on the open market. The new machine has an expected life of ten years and no expected salvage at that time.

The current corporate income tax rate is .40. For tax purposes the cost of the new machine may be depreciated in ten years.

The appropriate time discount rate for this company is .10.

It is expected that future demand of the product will stay steady at 10,000 units per year.

Required: (a) Should the new equipment be acquired? (b) If the product can be purchased at a cost of $7.80 per unit from a reliable supplier, should it be purchased or made? Explain.

Part II

INTRODUCTION

In Chapters 8–14 we introduce the first layer of substantive complications associated with capital budgeting decisions. In previous chapters we used a discount rate in the present value computations, but did not concern ourselves about its origin and nature. The most commonly used rate of discount in business decision making currently is the cost of capital of the firm. Chapters 8 and 9 define the cost of capital and suggest how the computation of the cost of capital may be approached. While the cost of capital is not used in this book as an absolute screening device, it is desirable that the reader understand its nature and how it is computed.

In Chapter 10 the assumption that we can borrow and lend at one rate of interest, with no constraints preventing the firm from using these markets, is discarded.

Implicit in Chapters 8–10 is the assumption that the world is uncertain, and that the use of a model assuming certainty is not valid. Chapter 11 introduces some fundamental notions of uncertainty. This chapter lays the groundwork for questioning the use of the cost of capital as an effective means of incorporating into the analysis attitudes toward the riskiness of the investment.

Chapter 12 studies the buy or lease decision. This chapter is important because it not only suggests a method of analysis for a very important specific decision, but also illustrates the viewpoint that the cost of capital (even without capital rationing)

141

may not be the appropriate rate of discount to use in evaluating investments.

Chapter 13 offers a cookbook approach to the investment decision. It provides us an opportunity to make specific recommendations in instances where there may be a temptation to be vague.

Chapter 14 considers how private investments might be evaluated from the point of view of their effects on the national economy.

The interest rate is not only an expression of the force of nature: it also depends on the wisdom of men.

—Pierre Massé, *Optimal Investment Decisions: Rules for Action and Criteria for Choice* (Englewood Cliffs, N.J.: Prentice-Hall, 1962), p. 15.

8

THE COST OF CAPITAL—I

In our discussion up to this point we have stated the rule that investments should be considered desirable (insofar as quantitative estimates of their profitability are the determining factor) if the present value of the cash flows expected from them is positive. Chapters 2, 3, and 4 demonstrate that this rule has real advantages over alternative methods commonly used in evaluating investment proposals. But we have not explicitly explained the determination of the rate of discount. Unless this concept can be defined in a reasonably useful and correct way, the investment criterion we are suggesting cannot be applied in practice.

In this chapter, and the next, we shall consider the cost of capital, its definition and computation. The "cost of capital" is one possible answer to the question of what discount rate should be used in calculating the present value of future cash flows. Because it is currently the most popular answer to this question, the reader will want to understand what is meant by the term. The main purpose of this chapter and Chapter 9 is to provide this understanding. In later chapters we shall discuss other possible answers to the question of what discount rate should be used and compare these other possibilities with the cost of capital.

Funds to finance an investment proposal may be obtained by a firm in a variety of ways: by borrowing from banks, by allowing short-term liabilities to expand, by selling marketable securities such as government bonds, by selling other assets or parts of its business, by issuing additional securities (either bonds, preferred stock, or common stock), or by committing funds generated by operations. These are only some of the more important sources. For certain types of these sources of cash, such as bank loans, there is a generally accepted, although not necessarily correct, definition of the cost of funds obtained. For other sources, such as funds generated by operations, several definitions of the cost of capital have been proposed, including the notion that funds from this source are free.

If an investment proposal is to be financed by short-term borrowing from a bank, is the interest rate on the specific loan the relevant cost of capital for this investment? If this approach were consistently followed, the cost of capital would be an erratic quantity, fluctuating up or down as the firm obtained additional increments of capital from varying sources. Although there are situations in which a particular investment can be related to a specific source of financing,[1] more commonly there exists on the one hand a group of apparently desirable investment proposals, and on the other, a variety of sources of additional capital funds that, taken together, could supply the financing for the increased investment.

DEFINITION OF COST OF CAPITAL

Before discussing the complexities of the concept of the cost of capital, we shall state the definition of cost of capital that will be developed in this chapter. This procedure is chosen to give the reader a compass that may assist him in following the necessarily complex explanation that will be discussed.

The cost of capital of a firm may be defined as a weighted average of the cost of each type of capital. The weight for each type of capital is the ratio of the market value of the securities representing that source of capital to the market value of all securities issued by the company. *The term* security *includes common and preferred stocks and all interest-bearing liabilities, including notes payable.*

COST OF COMMON STOCK CAPITAL

The cost of common stock capital is equal to the return required by common stockholders. This return can be measured by comparing

[1] For example, in the railroad industry, acquisitions of additional rolling stock may be financed by issuing equipment trust certificates for which the rolling stock acquired is the collateral. In many firms, inventories are assigned as collateral for bank loans. These examples may be misleading, for lenders may actually examine the firm's earning potential and financial structure before deciding to accept securities based on specific collateral.

future dividends to the present market value of the common stock. The rate of discount that equates future dividends for perpetuity to the cost of the stock is the cost of capital for common stock capital.

It is recognized that we cannot be certain as to the amount of future dividends expected by the stockholders. On the other hand it is not unreasonable to assume that the stockholder is in general basing his expectation of the future on the past. It will be shown in Chapter 9 that the cost of capital of common stock equity may be approximated by the formula:

$$r = \frac{D_0}{P_0} + g$$

where r = cost of capital of common stock funds

D_0 = current cash-dividend rate

P_0 = current market price per share

g = expected annual percentage rate of increase in future dividends expressed as a decimal fraction.

Suppose that the current dividend is \$6.00 per share, the current market price is \$150.00 per share, and the dividend per share is expected to increase at about 2 per cent per year. In this case the cost of equity capital could be estimated (as a first approximation) as follows:

$$r = 0.04 + 0.02 = 0.06 \text{ (or 6 per cent)}$$

In estimating the cost of equity capital by using this approach, care must be taken to adjust for expected stock splits and stock dividends, if any. For example, a company may establish a policy of paying a regular dividend of \$6.00 per share outstanding and a regular stock dividend of 2 per cent per year. In this case, although the nominal dividend per share is constant, the actual dividends that can be expected by a stockholder holding 100 shares initially (and assuming that he retained all the additional stock dividends issued) would be \$600.00 in the first year, \$612.00 in the second year, \$624.24 in the third year, etc. In other words the dividend actually received would be growing at a steady rate of 2 per cent per year.

COST OF LONG-TERM DEBT

The cost of long-term debt capital is the current effective interest rate for long-term securities of the specific firm being studied.[2] It must be recognized that the indicated contractual interest rate of an outstanding debt security may not be the effective rate of interest because the security may be selling at a premium or a discount. The effective rate of interest for an outstanding issue can be determined by comparing the current market price for the security with the remaining payment obligations. For example, the effective rate of interest for a bond outstanding can be found by finding the rate of interest which equates the market price and the present value of the amount due at maturity plus the present value of the series of interest payments.

COST OF SHORT-TERM DEBT

The cost of short-term debt is analogous to that of long-term debt in that there may be an explicit interest cost (as with a short-term bank loan).

There are several short-term liabilities that do not have explicit interest costs. Among these are taxes payable and wages payable. There are other short-term debts that may or may not have a cost if they are not paid promptly. For example, a trade creditor may offer terms of 2/10, n/30. There is no cost for not paying the bill in the first 9 days, since the 2 per cent discount may be taken at any time prior to the lapsing of 10 days. If the discount is allowed to lapse, there is a 2 per cent penalty assessed for the use of the funds for a maximum of 20 days. This is equivalent to an annual interest rate of approximately 36 per cent. Some firms may allow the discount to

[2] This effective rate of interest may be a combination of three factors and not a valid indication of the time value of money (the same observation would hold for the cost of common stock capital which we determined above). These three factors are (1) Time value of money. (2) The use of the contractual interest payments, but because of uncertainty of payment the expected interest payments may be less than the contractual. (3) The investors may be risk averters and hence the amount they are willing to pay is less than they would pay for an amount equal to the expected value of the uncertain amounts. The last two factors make it difficult to use the measure of interest cost which is obtained from market prices only to take into account the time value of money.

lapse and then pay the bill some time after the 30-day period. Here a cost is added, arising from the loss of credit standing, supplier ill-will, etc.

In the discussions on cash flows (Chapter 6) and income taxes (Chapter 7) it was suggested that any increase in noninterest-bearing liabilities should be subtracted from the increase in current assets required, and only the net amount (increase in current assets minus the increase in current liabilities) should be considered a cash outlay in computing the cash flows. This method of handling the noninterest-bearing liabilities leads to the conclusion that such liabilities should not be treated as a source of capital when computing the cost of capital, since the implicit receipt (and disbursement) of funds is left out of the analysis.

One can include the noninterest-bearing current liabilities as part of the capital structure when computing the cost of capital. Then the total current assets required by the investment should be considered as an outlay made in the period during which the liabilities increase. Further, the value of a non-interest bearing liability should be recorded at the present value of the amount to be paid. With this procedure any change in the capital structure resulting from an increase in current liabilities would then affect the cost of capital.

The procedure that nets the current liabilities against current assets has been chosen in this book, since it gives reasonable answers and simplifies both the computations and explanations of cash flows.

DEBT AND INCOME TAXES

When dividends are paid to stockholders, the effective cost of the equity funds can be determined by taking into consideration the amount of the dividend, the price of the stock, and the expected rate of change in the dividends. In computing the effective cost of debt, the interest payments must be adjusted to compensate for the fact that interest is deductible for tax purposes.

Example: Compute the average effective rate of interest, assuming that the yield of the debt outstanding is 6 per cent, the tax rate for the corporation is 52 per cent, and the corporation has taxable income.

Since the interest is deductible for corporate income tax purposes, $1.00 of interest will reduce taxes by $0.52, and effective interest cost will therefore be $0.48 per dollar of interest. The effective interest cost is 0.48×6 per cent, or 2.88 per cent, instead of the 6 per cent yield of the debt.[3]

COMPUTING THE AVERAGE COST OF CAPITAL

Suppose the market value of a company's common stock is estimated at $45 million. The market value of its interest-bearing debt is estimated at $30 million, and the average before-tax yield on these liabilities is 6 per cent per year, which is equivalent on an after-tax basis to 2.88 per cent per year (equal to 6 per cent times 0.48, assuming a 52 per cent tax rate).

Assume that the company described in the preceding paragraph is currently paying a dividend of $8.00 per year and that the stock is selling at a price of $100. The rate of growth of the dividend is projected to be 2 per cent per year. Thus the average cost of the common stock equity is

$$r = \frac{\$8}{\$100} + 0.02 = 0.08 + 0.02 = 0.10, \quad \text{or 10 per cent}$$

The average cost of capital for the company as a whole could be estimated as follows:

Estimate of Cost of Capital

Capital Source	Proportion of total capital	Cost	
Equity	0.60	0.10	0.06
Debt, interest-bearing	0.40	0.0288	0.012
Average cost of capital			0.072, or 7.2%

QUESTIONS AND PROBLEMS

8–1. The following facts apply to the ABC Company:

Cost of short term loans	.05
Cost of long term loans	.06
Cost of common stock capital	.10

[3] If a firm does not have taxable income, the effective cost of the interest payments becomes the contractual rate, not adjusted for income taxes. This possibility, if taken into consideration, would tend to make the effective interest cost higher than 2.88 per cent.

	Book Value	Market Value
Current liabilities (noninterest-bearing)	10,000,000	10,000,000
Short term loans (interest-bearing)	5,000,000	5,000,000
Accumulated depreciation	50,000,000	not applicable
Long-term debt	20,000,000	20,000,000
Common stock	25,000,000	75,000,000

Compute the average cost of capital. Assume the income tax rate is .4.

8–2. In problem 8–1 assume that as a result of a decrease in the income tax rate to .3, the market value of the common stock rises to $100,000,000 with no change in the cost of common stock capital. Compute the new average cost of capital for the ABC Company.

8–3. A firm is financed by .2 long-term debt and .8 common stockholder capital. Assume that it has been established that both the common stockholders and the debt holders have a time value of money of .05 (we shall define this as being equal to their cost of capital). The corporate tax rate is .4. Compute the average cost of capital.

8–4. The common stock of a company is selling at $50 per share and is paying a dividend of $2. The expected growth in dividends is .03 per year.

Estimate the cost of common stock capital.

8–5. The ABC Company's stock is selling at $100 and the company is paying a $2 dividend. It has been paying the same amount for five years. The company has many desirable investments available; the cash needs exceed the cash it is generating. On the other hand, the company is earning $5 per share income and feels the stockholders should share in the prosperity of the company.

The President has suggested an increase in the dividend from $2.00 to $2.06. The Executive Vice President has suggested that the corporation conserve its cash and instead of increasing the cash dividend rate it should issue a .03 stock dividend.

There are currently 20,000,000 shares of common stock outstanding.

Required: What do you think the company should do?

8–6. The ABC Company is considering issuing $100,000,000 of 20-year bonds that will pay interest of .05 per year. This is the current long-term interest rate for comparable firms, and it is expected that the bonds will be issued at par. The tax rate is .4.

a. Using the before-tax cash flows and the before-tax interest rate, compute the present value of the debt.

b. Using the after-tax cash flows and the after-tax interest rate, compute the present value of the debt.

c. Assume that the after-tax cost of capital is .10. Compute the present value of the debt.

8-7. The TCG Company has a before-tax operating income of $25,000,000 and no debt. It is subject to an income tax rate of .4. The company allocates half of its after-tax income to dividends and half to retained earnings. It expects to continue dividing its after-tax income in the same proportions in future years. Its common stock is selling at 16.7 times current after-tax earnings. Each dollar of retained earnings generates on the average $0.10 per year of additional before-tax income.

Compute the TCG Company's cost of capital assuming 100 per cent stock equity financing and no change in the earnings-price multiplier.

8-8. The corporate tax rate is cut to .3, but the TCG Company's cost of capital and its operating policies remain the same. How will the tax cut affect the market value of the company's stock?

For respect to future periods we are forced to deal with highly uncertain and merely conjectural data. Under these circumstances it is not only easily understandable but even, from the economic standpoint, commendable that most people do not attempt to repeat, for case after case and for year after year, the tedious and at the same time deceptive calculation of the claims of present and future.

—Eugene von Böhm-Bawerk, "Capital and Interest," **Vol. II,** *Positive Theory of Capital.* (South Holland, Ill.: Libertarian Press, 1959; first published in 1888), p. 376.

9

THE COST OF CAPITAL—II

THE COST OF CAPITAL AND THE GOALS OF ORGANIZATIONS

A satisfactory definition of cost of capital would be helpful in guiding the internal investment policy of corporate management. The choice of investments frequently represents a strategic decision for the management of a firm, since in large part the choices made now will influence the future course of the firm's development. It is not surprising to find that implicit in any definition of a discount rate to guide investment policy is a judgment as to the goals toward which the firm is or should be striving. The goals determine the appropriate definition of capital cost. Certainly we cannot assume without proof that seemingly different goals will lead to identical rates of discount.

The corporate goal that has been conventionally adopted in discussions of this kind is that the corporation seeks to maximize the economic well-being of present stockholders. There are at least two elements in maximizing the economic well-being of stockholders. One is the expected cash proceeds that the stockholder anticipates will result from his stock ownership. These proceeds include dividends and capital gains. In measuring the value of these receipts, adjustment must be made for the timing of their realization. A second element that must be considered is the uncertainty associated with the expected cash flows.

The conventional approach to cost of capital that was briefly presented in the previous chapter and will be discussed in more detail in succeeding pages combines these two elements into one number, that is used as the discount rate. In the concluding pages of this chapter we present another approach to measuring the cost of capital that separates these two elements. One quantity considers the amount and timing of the expected future cash proceeds; a second quantity measures the effect of uncertainty. The advantages of separating these two components of stockholder well-being are discussed in detail in Part III of this book.

It is recognized that corporate managements frequently have other goals that are sometimes in conflict with the goal described above: Management may desire to see the corporate organization expand; to ensure that its own tenure and ability to choose its successors is not threatened; to extend or at least maintain the realm in which it is free to make decisions for the organization without reference to outside groups (be they government officials, minority stockholders, bankers, life insurance companies, or labor union officials); to support what it considers to be desirable nonprofit institutions; to undertake activities in the name of the corporation for patriotic motives; or to achieve a high level of material benefits for itself. In attempting to work out a definition of cost of capital based on the goal of maximizing the economic interests of present stockholders, we do not mean to deny the existence or the importance of other goals. If other goals are in competition with the goal of maximizing present stockholders' economic interests, the development of an adequate definition of cost of capital based on stockholders' interests may help us understand the extent to which the various goals are in conflict.

THE COST OF RETAINED EARNINGS

The costs associated with retaining some part of the current earnings are not always obvious. Frequently corporate officials seem to take the position that these funds are free.[1] If the funds generated

[1] After interviewing the top officials of twenty companies in several different industries, G. Donaldson wrote: "The net conclusion is that the common practice of these 20 companies with respect to quantitative guides to investment decisions suggested a cost-free concept of retained earnings for the so-called mandatory investments in maintaining traditional product lines and a rough internal opportunity cost standard for 'voluntary' investment opportunities."— Gordon Donaldson, *Corporate Debt Capacity* (Boston: Graduate School of Business Administration, Harvard University, 1961), p. 62.

from retained earnings were free, any use of the funds within the corporation that benefited common stockholders would be justified. On the other hand, if there were a cost associated with the use of these funds within the corporation, it would not be sufficient to say that stockholders would benefit. The question must be asked, "Will the benefits be great enough to cover the opportunity cost of the funds?" One suspects that this question is frequently not asked and that the corporate officials too often treat retained earnings as if they were a source of free funds.

If we stipulate the economic interests of present stockholders as overriding, then these funds are not free, and the cost associated with them must be measured by the opportunities foregone in using them in one way instead of in other possible ways. Essentially there are two kinds of opportunities for the use of corporate earnings. They may be retained within the corporation, or they may be distributed to stockholders.

If earnings (or some part of earnings) are retained within the corporation, stockholders are deprived of the current dividends that could have been paid with those earnings. This is a cost to the stockholders. On the other hand there are some benefits, the valuation of which will depend upon what the corporation does with the funds. Suppose they are retained by the corporation. If, as a result, there is an immediate increase in the value of the stock, this increase may more than offset the lower current dividend. If so, stockholders will be better off than if the funds had not been retained and they had received the cash dividends.

Suppose one accepts the propositions that retained earnings are not free but have a cost, and that this cost should be measured by comparing the benefits that stockholders would derive if the funds are retained within the corporation with the benefits that they would derive from having the funds distributed. The difficult problem of deciding how to measure the relative size of the two sets of benefits in a particular instance still remains. If no objective measurement is provided, then the decision must be made on the basis of management's judgment. The theories of cost of capital we describe in this and the preceeding chapter provide possible approaches to measuring the cost of capital.

Management will also need to rely on its judgment to measure the benefits of the uses of capital funds. These funds need not be reinvested in long-lived assets in order to provide net benefits to stockholders. They may be used to reduce bank loans or bonded indebtedness, to start a training program for employees, or to add to the financial liquidity of the corporation by increasing the amount of cash on hand. Whatever the use, if it serves to increase the relative market value of the stock, it will serve to offset partially or completely the loss to the stockholder in not receiving a larger immediate dividend.

The theory we are now describing assumes that if investments are accepted whenever the cash flows associated with them have a positive net present value discounted at the company's cost of capital, stockholders will be better off than if the investments had been rejected.

A simple example will illustrate the theory. Suppose a corporation whose capital structure consisted entirely of equity was considering an investment that would require an immediate cash outlay of $100,000. The officers of the corporation estimated that if the investment proposal were accepted, the corporation would receive additional cash proceeds of $20,000 (after taxes) per year indefinitely. The officials further estimated that if the stock market is informed about the acceptance of this investment, the common stock of the company would immediately increase in value by $200,000. If the investment proposal were not accepted, the company would be able to pay out an additional $100,000 in dividends. It would be to the advantage of stockholders to have the company accept the investment proposal.

The information given could also be used to estimate the cost of retained earnings for this company. This estimate is the rate of discount that makes the present value of the expected cash proceeds equal to the change in the price of the common stock. In this example the present value of a perpetuity of $20,000 per year would equal $200,000 at 10 per cent. Investments having a positive net present value at 10 per cent will be advantageous to present stockholders, since they will result in an increase in the market price of the stock.

Whether a particular stockholder will be better off or worse off as a result of a somewhat smaller dividend and a somewhat larger rise in the price of the stock (or for that matter a smaller decrease in its value than might otherwise have taken place) will depend upon the income tax rates on ordinary income and on capital gains to which the stockholder is subject.[2] Stockholders differ widely in this regard. Some are subjected to high marginal tax rates, and others, such as foundations and universities, are not subject to income taxes. Thus there is no one minimum yield at which stockholders are better off if the corporation reinvests earnings instead of paying greater dividends; rather there are many groups of stockholders whose personal interests are different.

An investor who is not subject to income taxes (e.g., a university or a nonprofit foundation) may be indifferent to the extra dollar in dividends and/or the extra dollar of capital gains. An investor who has to pay a 50 per cent tax on ordinary income and a 25 per cent tax on capital gains may be willing to sacrifice a dollar in dividends in order to gain less than a dollar in capital gains.

If the stock of corporations were distributed between investors in some random manner, the conflicts of interest between investors would be of great practical importance. Actually, however, most large corporations follow reasonably consistent financial and investment policies. The securities of most listed corporations undoubtedly tend to flow into the portfolios of investors whose personal investment goals are consistent with the known policies of the companies whose stock they hold. Thus conflicts of interest between stockholders of widely held corporations are greatly reduced by the ease with which stock may be sold.

A THEORY OF STOCK VALUES

For the purpose of understanding the cost of equity capital, a useful theory of stock values is one which assumes that the price of a share of stock tends to be determined by the present value of the dividends which investors as a group expect to be paid by the company. This theory implies that under present institutional arrangements, the stockholder has an interest in earnings only because they affect future

---

[2] The Internal Revenue Code is only one of many factors that create conflicts of interest among stockholders. At the same time some stockholders are attempting to increase their investment portfolios while others are withdrawing a part of their investments. Even if neither group was subject to taxes, the first would tend to prefer capital gains because it would thereby avoid the brokerage fees required to convert dividends into additional stock holdings. The second group would tend to prefer dividends so as to avoid the expenses and inconvenience of selling a part of its holdings periodically.

dividends or stock prices. As pointed out above, because of personal income tax considerations, some investors prefer situations in which their stock-market gains can be realized in the form of capital gains rather than dividends. But although a stock may for a time show increases in price because some investors come to look upon it as a potential source of capital gains, the stock cannot indefinitely continue to rise in price *only* on the basis of such expectations. If the expectations of capital gains are realized *only* because new groups of investors come to share similar expectations and to act upon them, the situation may be described as a speculative boom, and it will end in a drastic decline in the price of stock as the supply of investors gradually dries up.

If the hopes of capital gains are to be based on a more solid footing, it must be because the stock eventually will become more valuable to some people for a reason other than a desire for capital gains, namely the expectation of dividend payments.

To illustrate this approach to the theory of stock values, we may start with a very simple case in which a company is assumed to have a financial structure consisting solely of common stock. Suppose that by past behavior, announced policy, and an objective evaluation of the investment opportunities open to it, this company has established a firm expectation that its future dividends will continue to be paid at the constant rate of $6.00 per share per year. When the dividend per share is expected to be constant (and no stock dividends are anticipated), the cost of equity capital can be computed simply as the ratio of the expected dividend to the market price of the shares. In symbolic form, we have

$$r = \frac{D}{P_0}$$

where r = cost of capital
  D = (constant) expected future dividend
  P_0 = current market price per share

In the example described, if the market price per share is $150, the cost of capital would be estimated as 4 per cent because this is the rate of discount implied by the market price per share and the expectation of the constant $6.00 per year dividend. It is important to note that we are not suggesting that the cost of equity capital is necessarily equal to the dividend price ratio. It turns out to be equal to this ratio only when the current dividend rate is expected to be continued into the indefinite future and when no stock dividends are expected.

More commonly, the market will expect some changes in future dividend rates. It can be shown that if the current dividend is expected to grow at a steady rate, the rate at which the market is discounting future dividends can be roughly approximated from the following expression: [3]

$$r = \frac{D_0}{P_0} + g$$

where r = cost of common stock capital (rate at which future dividends are being discounted) expressed as a decimal fraction

D_0 = current dividend rate

P_0 = current market price per share

g = expected annual percentage rate of increase in future dividends, expressed as a decimal fraction, and r is greater than g.

The formula in the preceding paragraph assumes that the dividends of each period will increase by a constant percentage of the previous period's dividends. This formula does not explicitly consider expected capital gains or relate dividends to earnings. It is possible to modify

---

[3] To show this, it is convenient mathematically to assume dividends are paid out and discounted continuously. If the initial dividend is D_0, and it is expected to increase at the rate of g per year, then the dividend in year t (i.e., D_t) will be

$$D_t = D_0 e^{gt}$$

By assumption, the current market price will be equal to the present value of this stream of expected dividends. If the (unknown) rate of discount is r, we can write

$$P_0 = \int_0^\infty D_t e^{-rt} dt$$

Substituting and integrating, we have, provided $r > g$:

$$P_0 = \int_0^\infty D_0 e^{t(g-r)} dt = \frac{D_0}{r - g}$$

The expression in the text is found by rearranging terms from the expression

$$P_0 = \frac{D_0}{r - g}$$

See M. J. Gordon and E. Shapiro, "Capital Equipment Analysis: The Required Rate of Profit," *Management Science III*, October 1956, pp. 104–106.

the formula to include these elements if this seems desirable. For example, instead of including all future dividends, we could estimate the cost of capital on the basis of the dividends expected during some limited future period, and the expected price of the stock at the end of the period. If we consider only one future period, the basic equation can be written as follows:

$$P_0 = D_0 + \frac{P_1}{1 + r}$$

where P_1 is the expected price one period from now, and the remaining symbols are defined as before. Rearranging terms, this reduces to the following expression:

$$r = \frac{D_0 + (P_1 - P_0)}{P_0 - D_0}$$

In this form, the role of capital gains becomes explicit; the estimate of the increase in the price of the stock up to some future date becomes a substitute for the estimate of expected dividends beyond that date.[4]

Since the linkage between dividends and earnings is usually quite close, security analysts and others frequently concentrate their attention on estimates of future earnings. It is also possible to develop formulas for estimating the cost of capital that are expressed in terms of earnings instead of dividends. In so doing, it is important to keep in mind that retained earnings are of value to the ordinary investor only insofar as they constitute an economically profitable use of the company's funds.[5]

The formulas presented in the previous paragraphs should not be thought of as ways of estimating a company's cost of capital. Rather they are possible frameworks within which such estimates might be made.

---

[4] We could also define P_0 in terms of the dividend one period from now, assuming the present dividend has just been received.

$$P_0 = \frac{D_1 + P_1}{1 + r}$$

$$r = \frac{D_1 + (P_1 - P_0)}{P_0}$$

[5] On this point, see James E. Walter, "Dividend Policies and Common Stock Prices," *Journal of Finance*, **XI** (March, 1956), pp. 29–41.

CHANGES IN STOCK PRICES AND THE COST OF EQUITY CAPITAL

We all know that stock prices fluctuate quite widely. Does this mean that we are faced with a cost of capital for common stock that changes daily? The answer is a qualified "yes."

Just as bond prices change from day to day as they reflect changes in the interest rate (thus changes in the cost of debt capital), changes in stock prices also will reflect changes in the cost of common stock. There is one prime difference, however, between bonds and stock. The interest payment on bonds is determined by contract and is easily predicted. Common stock dividends are more difficult to predict. They are dependent to some extent on the earnings of the corporation, the cash available, and the decisions of the board of directors. In turn the earnings of the corporation are dependent on numerous factors, such as general business conditions, the actions of competitors, and the desires of consumers. But even if earnings and dividends can be predicted relatively accurately, there are still the whims of the stock market, the waves of optimism and pessimism.

How do the above factors affect the cost of capital? A change in expected dividends and earnings will cause the price of the stock to change, but there may *not* be a change in the cost of common stock capital. For example, if the price of a share of common stock is $10.00 and if future dividends of $1.00 per year are expected, the stock yields 10 per cent. If conditions change and the expected dividends in the future, as seen by the market, are $0.50 per year, the price of the stock may drop to $5.00. The cost of capital remains unchanged at 10 per cent.

It is possible that attitudes toward the company, the industry, or the risks of business in general may change, or there may be a change in the amount of total funds available for investment in industry. In this case the market may still expect the $1.00 dividend to be earned into perpetuity, but the price of the stock may nevertheless change from $10.00 to $8.00. The indicated cost of capital has changed from 10 to 12.5 per cent.

It is, of course, impossible to determine with certainty what factors have caused a change in the price of a stock. Much work remains to be done in the area of isolating the reasons why the price of a share of stock may change.

COST OF CAPITAL AND INFLATION

Inflation, or the expectation of inflation, may affect the computation of the cost of capital of a firm. Let us assume that the market thinks that stock in company X is a good hedge against inflation—i.e., future dividends of company X will increase more as a result of inflation than the dividends of most other firms. In this situation it is possible that if the probability of inflation increases, the price of Company X's stock will rise. Either the cost of capital is unchanged (but higher future dividends are expected) or the desirability of the stock has increased relative to other investments, and its cost of capital has decreased as the risk decreased.

For the decision maker attempting to determine his company's cost of capital, it will be more difficult to forecast the growth in dividends anticipated by the market, since this growth rate is affected by the prospect of inflation.

DEPRECIATION AND THE COST OF CAPITAL

There is some confusion about the relationships of depreciation expense to the generation of cash and of accumulated depreciation to the computation of the cost of capital.

The recognition of depreciation expense for purposes of measuring financial income does not affect the amount of cash available for investments. The two are completely independent. Charging more or less depreciation will not affect the amount of cash held by the firm. The write-off of the cost of a long-lived asset is an accounting expense that does not use cash, and since it does not generate cash, it does not affect the cash balance. However, the amount of depreciation expensed for tax purposes does affect the amount of cash since it affects the amount paid to the government.

In some cases the analyst may add depreciation back to income to compute the cash flow of the period. However, the same result can be obtained by not subtracting depreciation expense in computing the cash flow.

Example: The revenue on a cash basis is $10,000, and the expenses utilizing cash are $6,000. The depreciation for the period is $1,800. One method of computing the cash flow is to exclude depreciation

($10,000 less 6,000 equals cash flow of $4,000). A second procedure adds depreciation back to income.

Cash revenue	$10,000
Less: Total expenses	7,800
Income	$ 2,200
Plus: Depreciation	1,800
Cash flow	$ 4,000

We can say that $1,800 of the fixed assets was converted into cash, and speak of the cash from depreciation. But this is inexact, since the cash came from operations. In any event we should distinguish between the origins of the cash and the sources of capital. Is accumulated depreciation a source of capital? Assume that the balance sheet at the start of the period was

Plant assets	$20,000	Capital stock	$20,000

At the end of the period the balance sheet would be

Cash		$ 4,000	Capital stock	$20,000
Plant assets	$20,000		Retained earnings	2,200
Less: Accumulated depreciation	1,800	18,200		
		$22,200		$22,200

The source of the capital of $22,200 is 100% stockholders' equity funds, and we do not have to concern ourselves with the amount of accumulated depreciation. The total net assets are $22,200, and the sources are fully accounted for by the capital stock and retained earnings.

Now assume that the depreciation expense for the period is $2,500 instead of $1,800. The cash flow would remain $4,000, but the income of the period would be reduced to $1,500 and the retained earnings would be $700 less than with the first computation. The end of the period balance sheet would be

Cash		$ 4,000	Capital stock	$20,000
Plant assets	$20,000		Retained earnings	1,500
Less: Accumulated depreciation	2,500	17,500		
		$21,500		$21,500

The source of the capital (or total assets) is still 100 per cent stockholders' equity funds, and again we do not have to concern ourselves with the amount of accumulated depreciation. Assume we are tempted to include the $2,500 accumulated depreciation in the capital structure, and the $17,500 of plant assets is sold for $17,500 cash. What would the cost of capital now be? There is no accumulated depreciation, and it is apparent that the stockholders are the only source of capital.

If the accumulated depreciation is purposely overstated or understated, then the book value of the stockholders' equity will be incorrectly stated. This should lead to an adjustment of the book value if we were to use the book value. We prefer to use the market value of the stockholders' equity in computing a weighted average cost of capital.

STABLE DIVIDEND POLICY

In a preceding section we discussed the cost of retained earnings as though the alternative to retaining earnings in each year was an increased dividend. Although a discussion in these terms is useful in explaining the ideas underlying the notion of the cost of retained earnings, a too-literal interpretation of the earlier discussion would result in a financial policy that could have disadvantages in practice. Interpreted literally, the preceding section would suggest that in each year the company would estimate its cost of capital, and with the help of this estimate, would determine what investment opportunities available to it would be profitable. If the investment opportunities accepted did not exhaust all the funds available from current operations, the remainder would be distributed to shareholders as dividends. Such a procedure would almost certainly result in a widely fluctuating annual dividend, since both the quantity of funds that could be profitably reinvested and the quantity of funds available from current operations are likely to fluctuate from year to year.

Financial experts generally believe that a highly unstable dividend is not advantageous to a company.[6] The most common reason stated for this belief is that stockholders prefer a steady income from their

---

[6] There is also a school of thought that believes dividend policy does not affect the value of common stock. Much work remains to be done concerning the effect of dividend policy on stock prices, especially under conditions of uncertainty and risk aversion attitudes of investors.

investments. There is at least one other important reason for thinking that a highly variable dividend rate may not be in the best interest of a company. We have suggested earlier that, in the long run, the value of a share of stock tends to be determined by the discounted value of the expected dividends. Insofar as this is the case, a widely fluctuating dividend rate will tend to make it difficult for stockholders to determine the value of the stock to them, and as a result the stock is likely to sell at a somewhat lower price than comparable stocks paying the same average amount as dividends but making payments at a steady rate.

A comprehensive study suggests that many large corporations tend to pay out a constant fraction of their earnings as dividends. A change in earnings that is expected to be fairly permanent is more or less rapidly reflected in dividend payments, but short-term fluctuations in earnings usually are not allowed to influence dividends. The result is that, although the dividend earnings ratio may vary considerably from year to year, the long-term average tends to be quite constant.[7]

If a policy of this type is adopted, the choice of a long-run pay-out ratio becomes quite important. If the pay-out ratio is set rather high (relative to the quantity of profitable investments available to the company), in many years the company will find that the profitable investments available to it require more funds than are available internally after dividend commitments have been met. In such circumstances one of two major alternatives must be chosen if the alternative of changing the dividend policy is not available. The company must either forego some profitable investments or seek additional funds. On the other hand, if the pay-out ratio is set too low relative to the quantity of profitable investments available, the company may either find itself accumulating an unwarranted amount of liquid assets or may be tempted to accept investments that are not truly consistent with the objective of maximizing the economic well-being of the stockholders.

The disadvantages of too low a dividend pay-out relative to the profitable investments available to the company are perhaps the most serious from the point of view of the shareholder. Also, it is not necessary that a firm keep its dividend pay-out ratio low enough so that profitable investments can always be financed out of retained

[7] John Lintner, "Distribution of Incomes of Corporations Among Dividends, Retained Earnings, and Taxes," *American Economic Review*, **XLVI** (May 1956), pp. 97–113.

earnings, provided the firm is in a position to issue new securities when necessary.

Dividend policy must be set in the form of a goal rather than a rigid rule. On the other hand, having a clear policy has the advantage of providing the investor or potential investor a clear basis of choice. The investor, knowing the dividend policy, can choose the type of company that best fits his individual investment goals. This is desirable, since stockholders differ in the extent to which they prefer dividends rather than opportunities for capital appreciation. With the great emphasis on the tax advantages of capital gains, there is sometimes a tendency to forget not only that many investors are primarily interested in income but also that important groups of investors, such as universities, foundations, and private pension funds, accrue no special advantages from capital gains as distinct from ordinary income.

THE COST OF RAISING EQUITY CAPITAL
BY SELLING COMMON STOCK

A corporation can increase its equity capital by retaining earnings or by selling new common stock. The basic principles underlying the costs of capital under either method are the same. If new common stock could be issued at a price equal to the market value of shares already outstanding, the costs would be the same under either method. In practice, the amount that can be realized per share from a new issue will be less than the market value of existing stock because of the need to price the new issue below the market price in order to attract buyers, and because of the various costs associated with floating a new issue. If the amount realized from a new issue is 20 per cent less than the going market price, the cost of raising equity in this form will be 25 per cent greater than the cost of retained earnings.

A second factor affecting the relative costs of retained earnings versus the issuing of new stock arises because of personal income taxes. Assume that a person is in the 60 per cent marginal tax bracket and that capital gains are taxed at a 25 per cent rate. If the corporation pays a $1 dividend, the stockholder will have $.40 remaining after tax. In order for the stockholder to have $1 to return to the corporation, he will have to receive $2.50 in dividends from the corporation. Alternatively, if the firm retains the $1 and invests it in a reasonable manner so that market had reason to expect future increases in dividends, the price of the stock can be expected to increase and the stockholder can realize his earnings by selling a portion of his holdings so that any gains associated with the portion sold are taxed as capital gains. The required return for an investment using the funds retained by the firm may be lower than it would be if the firm must ask its stockholders for additional funds.

THE OPTIMUM CAPITAL STRUCTURE

So far in our discussion in this chapter we have assumed that all capital utilized in the company was obtained as equity capital. Actually this is rarely, if ever, the case. Most corporations will finance at least a part of their operations with funds obtained from creditors. Bank loans are particularly advantageous (apart from considerations of differences in cost) because the funds can be obtained as needed to meet seasonal fluctuations in the demand for funds. Thus the use of bank loans eliminates the necessity of carrying unused funds for a part of the year. It is not uncommon for a business to be regularly in debt to a bank, and to some extent the bank provides a permanent source of funds, although the actual loans may be for a relatively short term. In addition the inclusion of at least some bonded indebtedness is not uncommon, and in some lines of business this source of funds represents a sizeable fraction of the total funds employed in the business.

At the conclusion of the preceding chapter we indicated how a corporation could estimate its average cost of capital for a given capital structure. So far in this book we have assumed that the investments being considered would not result in a change in the capital structure of the firm, i.e., in the relative proportions of each source of capital. If a relatively large investment undertaken is tied to a particular form of financing, a significant change in the capital structure may result. Examples are the purchase of land financed by a mortgage, the acquisition of equipment by a nonrevocable long-term lease, or a corporate merger financed by a stock issue. It may be that such transactions will temporarily result in a significant change in a company's capital structure. If the capital structure is permanently changed, it ought to be as a result of a separate decision that such a change is desirable.

We have also assumed, and it will be normally useful to assume, that the investments contemplated will not significantly change the risks which investors associate with the securities of the company. For example, the purchase of a plant to make glass by General Motors Corporation would not significantly change the public image of that corporation.

There are times when a company will wish to consider a permanent change in its capital structure because management believes that changes in the relative cost of sources of capital, or changes in the business risks faced by the company, would make a different capital structure more desirable. A decision involving a permanent change in capital structure should be considered on its merits independently of any specific decision to acquire assets.

It may be that the optimum capital structure is not a point but rather a broad range—i.e., the average cost of capital is flat bottomed —in fact, practically the entire curve may be horizontal. It has been argued that under certain conditions the entire curve is horizontal, in which case there is not one optimum capital structure but rather that all combinations of debt and common stock are equally desirable.[8]

In discussing the concept of an optimum capital structure, it is convenient to begin by imagining a company financed entirely by equity, and to consider the consequences of substituting increments of debt for the common stock equity.

The suggested procedure is to estimate the effect of a change in the relative proportions of debt and equity on the company's average cost of capital by using the same procedure recommended in Chapter 8. The procedure recommended is to use a weighted average of the average cost of each source of funds. Thus, if it were estimated that the average cost of equity would be 10 per cent after the issue of the debt and the average cost of debt (after taxes) would be 2 per cent, one could estimate that a structure composed of 90 per cent equity and 10 per cent debt would result in an average cost of capital of 9.2 per cent $(0.9 \times 10\% + 0.1 \times 2\%)$. The change of capital structure would not be desirable if the cost of common stock capital with no debt is less than 9.2 per cent.

Let us assume that with no debt, the cost of capital is 9.0 per cent. It may be tempting to estimate the effect of an increase in the proportion of debt by using the cost of 9.0 per cent for equity, and 2 per

<hr>

[8] *See* F. Modigliani and M. H. Miller, "The Cost of Capital, Corporation Finance and the Theory of Investment," *American Economic Review,* **XLVIII** (June 1958), pp. 261–297.

cent for debt. The proposed change in capital structure would then be expected to lead to a new average cost of capital of 8.3 per cent $(0.9 \times 9\% + 0.1 \times 2\%)$.

This expectation would be incorrect because it ignores the increase in the cost of raising common stock funds that results because of the increased risk.

At least two kinds of risks to which common stockholders are subject when debt is included in the capital structure of a company need to be distinguished for our purposes. These may be called the risk of bankruptcy,[9] and the risk of increased leverage. By using average cost of capital of the firm, an attempt is made to take these risks into consideration.

A company financed only with funds obtained from stockholders may eventually have to cease operations because a combination of operating losses and poor investments has exhausted its funds, but shareholders are not exposed to the risk of bankruptcy unless debt in some form is acquired. With debt it is possible equity holders may lose their interest in a company that may again become a profitable operation. With a well-managed and profitable company, the introduction of a small amount of nonequity capital presumably will not increase the risks of bankruptcy appreciably. In practice, the legal possibility of bankruptcy is nearly always present, since a company will always have at least some accounts payable outstanding. However, as the amount of debt rises, the risks of bankruptcy become greater, until the point is reached where the risk is substantial. Just what this point is may be difficult to specify because it varies, depending upon the activities in which a company is engaged. Nevertheless it is well to remember that a very small increase in the chance that a firm may eventually become bankrupt can have a noticeable effect on the price that investors are willing to pay for its common stock, since if bankruptcy occurs, common stockholders are likely to lose their entire investment.

[9] There is a third category of risks or cost associated with the use of debt. This category of costs is the result of limitations on management's freedom of action, which are usually included as a part of the debt agreements. Provisions requiring that sinking funds be accumulated, limiting the conditions under which the corporation can acquire additional debt, and restricting the directors' freedom to declare dividends are examples. These limitations are frequently of great importance, but they will not be discussed here because it is almost always impossible to quantify such costs, and they must be taken into account on a judgment basis. Omitting discussion of this category does not reflect a lack of appreciation of the importance of such costs.

The advantage of debt capital comes from the financial leverage it provides for the remaining equity capital. However, the introduction of debt or increases in the debt ratio generally have two effects on the earnings per share available to common stockholders: It tends to increase the average earnings per share that can be expected; and it tends to increase the year-to-year variability of earnings per share (including negative earnings arising from bankruptcy or near bankruptcy). The first effect is likely to increase the price per share that investors are willing to pay; the second, by itself, is likely to decrease the price per share that investors are willing to pay.

It is impossible to give any simple rules for determining in advance the optimum capital structure for a particular firm.[10] Theoretically, the optimum structure is reached when an additional debt issue, in substitute for stock equity, will result in a decrease in the price per share of the common stock. The capital structure just prior to the issue of that debt is the optimum capital structure. In determining whether a company's capital structure is optimum, management must to some extent rely on the intuitive judgment of well-informed persons.

THE RISK PREMIUM

The previous sections have developed what might be called a risk-discount approach to the subject of cost of capital. The essence of this approach is that the average cost of a particular source of capital is defined as the discount rate that makes the present value of the expected proceeds that will be received by the capital supplier equal to the market value of the securities representing that capital. With a business corporation proceeds to be received by the capital supplier are uncertain. This is clear in the case of equity capital; and so long as there is a probability of default, it is also true of debt. The excess of the cost so defined over the discount rate that applies to default-free cash flows presumably reflects an adjustment for risk.

Raising the discount rate is not an effective or useful way of allowing for risk. In this and the following sections, we will show how the

---

[10] It has been suggested that the average cost of capital of a company is not greatly affected by the company's capital structure because investors can adjust their own portfolios to either increase or decrease the leverage of the equities they own. The validity of this proposition has not yet been effectively tested. See F. Modigliani and M. H. Miller, "The Cost of Capital, Corporation Finance and the Theory of Investment," *American Economic Review,* **XLVIII** (June 1958), pp. 261–297.

essential ideas associated with cost of capital can be expressed in such a way that discount rates are not used to allow for risk.

Consider the example used earlier to illustrate the cost of common stock capital. We assumed that the current dividend was $6.00 per share, that the current market price $150.00 per share, and that the dividend per share was expected to increase at about 2 per cent per year for perpetuity. These assumptions implied an average cost of equity capital of 6 per cent.

Let us now assume that the rate of interest that would apply on default-free loans is .05. At this interest rate the present value of the expected future dividends from this stock is $200.00.

$$PV = \frac{\$6.00}{.05 - .02} = \frac{6.00}{.03} = \$200.00$$

If there were no uncertainty about the amount and timing of the expected future dividends, we would expect to see the stock selling for $200.00 per share. However, the selling price is only $150.00 per share. The difference between the present value of the expected future dividends at the default-free rate and the actual selling price reflects a risk premium of $50.00. The present value of expected future dividends at the default-free rate minus the risk premium gives the market value of the stock. In symbols, using RP for risk premium, PV for the present value of expected future cash flows, and P_0 for the current price we have

$$P_0 = PV - RP$$

In this particular example we have

$$P_0 = \$200.00 - \$50.00 = \$150.00$$

We will refer to this approach to the evaluation of security prices as the risk-premium approach.

Investment Decision Making

Let us compare the risk-discount and risk-premium approaches and see how they affect investment decision making. For this purpose it will be convenient to think of the company in question as having a capital structure consisting entirely of equity. Suppose that the com-

pany has an opportunity to undertake an investment with expected
cash flows as follows:

	Period		Net present value	
	0	1	5%	6%
Cash flow	($90.00)	$106.00	$10.90	$10.00

Using the risk-discount approach one might say that since the net
present value of the cash flows from the investment was positive,
using the company's average cost of capital of .06, the investment
should be accepted. This approach carries with it the implicit assumption that the discount rate of 6 per cent makes a proper allowance for
the risk of the investment. When the risk characteristics of eligible
categories of investments differ drastically, companies may use different discount rates for these investment categories. The risk-discount
approach gives little guidance as to what particular discount rate is
appropriate to a particular investment.

Using the risk-premium approach, the answer to whether or not
the investment should be accepted will depend on the size of the risk
premium that management decides is appropriate for this investment.
If the risk premium is $10.90 or less, the investment should be ac-
cepted. If the risk adjustment is greater than $10.90, the investment
should be rejected. The size of the risk premium would be determined
either on a judgment basis by management or by application of an
explicit utility function for the firm. Utility functions and their use are
discussed in Chapter 15.

If the utility function approach is used a decision is reached based
on the benefits and costs of the investment. If the expected utility of
the investment is greater than the utility of $0, the investment is ac-
ceptable. The acceptance of the investment implies that:

$$P_0 < PV - RP$$

Problems of Estimation

Returning to the situation where we were using expected dividends
and the price of the stock to estimate the cost of capital, we can also
estimate the risk premium of the stock.

The problems of estimation are no more difficult with the risk-
premium approach than with the risk-discount approach. With the

risk-discount approach the basic relation is that the current price is equal to the present value of expected future dividends. There is one equation with three variables—price, discount rate, and expected dividends. The market price for a share of stock can be observed. If we feel justified in making some assumption about what a well-informed investor might reasonably expect future dividends to be, then we can determine the discount rate that is implied by the price.

With the risk-premium approach the basic relation is that current price is equal to the present value of future dividends (at the default-free rate) minus a risk premium. We have one equation and four variables—price, discount rate, expected dividends, and risk premium. However, two of these four, the current market price and the discount rate, are readily observable. (The default-free discount rate can be estimated from the current market yields on government bonds.) If we are again willing to make some assumption about what well-informed investors might expect as to future dividends, the risk premium can be estimated.

Thus we can see that the same information input is required to make an estimate of either the risk discount or the risk premium. Also in both cases the estimates apply to the average of all of the investments that have been undertaken by the firm. There is no reason to believe that the information obtained may be applied to a single investment of the corporation in any reasonable manner.

Debt and Equity

The risk-premium approach can also be used to consider questions about the capital structure of a firm that obtains its capital from more than one source. A typical risk-discount analysis or cost of capital computation is indicated in Table 1. The firm has a capital structure

Table 1.   Capital Structure: Risk-Discount Approach

| Source of Capital | Market values | | Cost of each source (3) | (2) × (3) (4) |
	Dollars (1)	Proportions (2)		
Equity	1,500,000	.75	.12	.09
Debt	500,000	.25	.03	.0075
Total	2,000,000	1.00		.0975

consisting of 25 per cent debt and 75 per cent equity. The proportion of debt represents the ratio of the market value of the debt to the market value of all of the securities issued by the firm. The average cost of capital for the firm is calculated by estimating a cost for each source of capital funds and then weighting these costs by the proportion of capital coming from the corresponding source. In the example illustrated the average cost of capital is .0975.

In Table 2 one way of organizing a risk-premium approach to

Table 2. Capital Structure: Risk-Premium Approach

Source of capital	Market values (1)	Present value of expected cash flow (2)	Risk premium (3)
Equity	$1,500,000	$3,600,000	$2,100,000
Debt	500,000	600,000	100,000
Total	$2,000,000	$4,200,000	$2,200,000

capital structure is illustrated. The first column shows the market values of the equity (first row) and debt (second row). In the row for equity the second column shows the present value at the default-free rates of the expected cash flows that the equity holders in this corporation might expect to realize if they do not sell the shares. For illustrative purposes this total is assumed to be $3,600,000. Since the market value of the equity is only $1,500,000, the difference, $2,-100,000, represents a risk premium. This risk premium for equity is shown in the equity row under column three. A similar set of entries is shown in the debt row. The present value of the debt cash flows is $600,000 at the default-free rates, and there is a relatively modest risk premium of $100,000.

Changes in Capital Structure

We will now illustrate how changes in capital structure can be analyzed using the risk-premium approach. Suppose there is a second firm exactly like the firm just discussed except that the second firm has a different capital structure. It has twice as much debt. The market value of the debt is twice that of the first firm. For simplicity we assume that the market accepts the same risk premium per dollar of debt that it did with the first firm and that the present values at the default-free discount rates of the total expected payments on the new debt are exactly twice what they were with the old debt. The entries in the debt row of Table 3 present a risk-premium approach to this new capital structure in terms of present values.

Table 3.

Source of capital	Market value (1)	Present value of expected cash (2)	Risk premium (3)
Equity	?	$3,000,000	?
Debt	$1,000,000	1,200,000	$200,000
Total		$4,200,000	

Let us consider now how the entries for the equity line of Table 3 could be determined. Tables 2 and 3 represent companies with the same assets and the same investment opportunities open to them (the only difference being the difference in capitalization). One might expect that the present value of the expected cash flows for the company as a whole will not change simply as a result of the different capitalization. This is a reasonable assumption provided that the cash flows referred to in the tables are on an after-tax basis to the corporations and that by issuing additional debt the second company did not agree to restrict its activities in such a way that the present value of the expected cash flows from the company as a whole would be reduced. We shall assume for this illustration that these provisions apply.

The expected present value of cash flows for the company as a whole remains at $4,200,000. Since there is additional debt, $1,200,000 of this cash flow is committed to bondholders, and only the remaining $3,000,000 is available to stockholders.

We have yet to decide what the market value of the equity interest will be under this new capitalization. If we had the market value of the equity, we could compute the risk premium for the stock equity, then complete the total row for columns (1) and (3).

One theory is that the average cost of capital for the company as a whole is not affected by the debt-equity ratio. This is based on an assumption that the total market value of the company is the same, regardless of the debt-equity ratio. Table 4 shows how this statement would translate into a risk-premium approach.

Table 4.

Source of capital	Market value	Present value of expected cash flow	Risk premium
Equity	$1,000,000	$3,000,000	$2,000,000
Debt	1,000,000	1,200,000	200,000
Total	$2,000,000	$4,200,000	$2,200,000

Assuming a constant total value of the firm, the absolute total of the risk premium for the company does not change as a result of the shift in the debt-equity ratio. Increasing the amount of debt transfers an amount of the risk premium from the equity row to the debt row without changing the total. By assumption, the total present value of the expected cash flows does not change due to a change in capital structure.

There are other theories about how the market value of a firm would be affected by a change in its capital structure; these too can be expresesd in terms of the risk-premium approach. To take one additional illustration, let us consider the theory that up to a certain point a firm can increase its debt-equity ratio without increasing the average cost of its equity capital. Specifically we suppose for purposes of illustration that the firm could double the amount of debt outstanding without increasing the average cost of equity capital. The results, in terms of a risk-premium approach, are expressed in Table 5.

Table 5.

Source of capital	Market values	Present value of expected cash flow	Risk premium
Equity	$1,250,000	$3,000,000	$1,750,000
Debt	1,000,000	1,200,000	200,000
Total	$2,250,000	$4,200,000	$1,950,000

The present value of the expected cash flow stays constant at $4,200,000. Table 2 showed the market value of the common stock to be 15/36 of the expected present value. Using the same ratio gives a market value of $1,250,000 based on $3,000,000 of expected present value.

If this theory were correct, the total market value of the firm would increase from $2,000,000 as shown in Table 2 to $2,250,000 as shown in Table 5 as a result of the change in capitalization. Because the present value of the expected cash flows does not change, this increase is due entirely to a reduction in the total risk premium. This theory implies that the market's evaluation of the total risk premium applicable to the firm can be reduced by shifting from equity to debt (or debt to equity). The statement (in terms of the risk-discount approach) that the average cost of equity will not increase as we add additional debt translates into a statement (in terms of the risk-premium approach) that the risk premium on common stock is a constant proportion of the present value of the expected cash flows attributable to the stock.

We have illustrated how the main ideas about cost of capital and financial structure can be discussed either in terms of a risk discount approach or a risk premium approach. The choice between these two approaches will depend mainly on the way in which adjustments for risk are best made in analyzing investment opportunities. We prefer the risk premium approach for reasons that will be given in Part III.

THE MANAGEMENT OF SHORT-TERM FUNDS AND THE COST OF CAPITAL

This book is mainly concerned with the problem of making good choices in selecting *long-lived* investments. The problem of managing *short-term* funds is closely related and should be solved by methods that are consistent in principle and integrated in practice with those used to make long-run investment decisions. But there are also special problems connected with the management of short-term funds. A thorough analysis and discussion of these problems is beyond the scope of this book. Nevertheless, a few brief comments are appropriate.

It is sometimes suggested that a firm not subject to capital rationing (the lending and borrowing rates are equal) should not accept investments that have negative present values at the firm's cost of capital. The objection is sometimes raised that such firms often hold assets, either permanently or temporarily, that yield less than the company's cost of long-term debt. Tax anticipation notes, 90-day government notes, and commercial paper are examples. The holding of such assets is not necessarily inconsistent with the principles of analysis suggested in this book.

In discussing this topic, it is useful to distinguish two situations. In the first situation, some quantity of low-yielding liquid assets have a more or less permanent place in the firm's asset structure. In the second case a temporary accumulation of such assets takes place (above amounts regularly held).

The reason for holding highly liquid, low-yielding assets on a regular basis is that usually the possession of such assets has advantages to the firm over and above their cash yield. In the case of highly liquid securities, the advantages are related to the fact that such assets can be converted to cash quickly, at low cost, and at an easily predictable price. The ready supply of cash enables the firm to avoid the costs that could result from unanticipated needs for cash, and to take advantage of unpredictable opportunities requiring a readily accessible supply of funds.[11] Inventories are frequently held in part for similiar reasons. Inventories of cash can be held at less expense in the form of short-term marketable notes than in the form of demand deposits. When these advantages are considered, such assets become acceptable investments.

The second situation mentioned above (a temporary accumulation of liquid assets) usually occurs when a firm finds that it has an excess of cash over the amounts needed for contingencies, day-to-day operations, or currently available investment opportunities. When this occurs, the firm can either hold the funds in liquid form or make a permanent disposition of them by declaring extra dividends or acquiring "external" investments of a long-term nature. The choice between holding the funds temporarily in liquid form or making a permanent disposition of them will depend in part on when the firm anticipates a profitable application of these funds for internal investments. If a profitable internal use is anticipated in the near future, it is usually less expensive to retain such funds temporarily in the form of short-term liquid investments, even though the nominal yield of these investments is less than the cost of capital.

In summary, it is not fruitful to treat low-yielding, liquid short-term securities held as a buffer against contingencies, or in anticipation

---

[11] Cash balances are also held to satisfy bank requirements for compensating balances.

of a prompt and more profitable use, as though holding such funds is a violation of the rule that investments should be accepted only when they have a positive present value at the cost of capital.

QUESTIONS AND PROBLEMS

9–1. Prepare an example or an explanation that indicates why each of the following is an insufficient description of the goals of a profit-seeking organization: (a) Maximize profits or earnings per share. (b) Maximize the price per share of the common stock now. (c) Maximize the price per share of the common stock in the future. (d) Maximize sales (or percentage of the market).

9–2. The ABC Company has opened 100 new stores. It has incurred a great deal of expenses associated with opening the stores, and the stores have not yet built up enough clientele to be profitable. On the other hand, the stores are operating at profit levels exceeding expectations, and there are indications that they will be very profitable in the future. It is obvious that the stock market has not yet digested this latter fact, and the stock of the company is currently depressed compared to management's appraisal of value. The company has the opportunity to acquire an additional fifty stores this year, but to do so will require new stockholder capital acquired from the market (it has borrowed all it feels it is prudent to borrow and cannot obtain more capital from its current stockholders). Without the new capital the stockholders can expect to earn an equivalent annual yield of .15 on the current market value of their investment (assume there is $100,000,000 or 1,000,000 shares of stock outstanding). The stock is currently selling at $100 per share and paying $6 per share dividend. The earnings are $7.50 per share $(7,500,000 in total).

The new investments would require $10,000,000 to be obtained by issuing 100,000 new shares of common stock. The investment would return $1,200,000 per year available for dividends for perpetuity. The stockholders desire a .08 return per year on their incremental investments.

Required: (a) Should the corporation issue the new shares and undertake the investment? (b) What would be your recommendation if the corporation had the necessary cash already available?

9–3 (reference 9–2). Change the statement of the problem so that the present stockholders can expect to earn dividends of $6 per share or an equivalent annual yield of .06 for perpetuity, unless the new investment is undertaken. Should the new investment be undertaken?

9–4 (reference 9–2). Change the statement of the problem so that the present stockholders can expect to earn $8,000,000, or an equivalent return of .08 per year on the current market value of their investment, if the new investment is not undertaken. Should the new investment be undertaken?

9–5. The common stock of the BAC Company is selling at $100 per share and currently paying a dividend of $2 per year. The expected growth in dividends is .04 per year. (a) Estimate the cost of common stock capital. (b) Assume that you computed the cost of common stock capital and obtained a figure of .03. What evidence would lead you to think that this estimate is too low to use in making investment decisions? (c) Assume that the expected growth in dividends of the BAC Company is .20 per year. Estimate the cost of capital. (d) Assume that the stock is paying a dividend of $2 per year and that this dividend is expected to grow by 10 per cent per year. The cost of common stock capital is 8 per cent. Estimate the current market price of the stock.

9–6. The CAB Company is currently paying a $2 dividend on its common stock. Assume that an investor thinks that the common stock will sell for $105 one year from now. His best alternative use of money (without risk) will earn him .04. The maximum amount he is willing to pay for a share of CAB Company common is $100. Describe some possible reasons why the investor is not willing to pay more than $100 per share.

9–7. Mr. Jones has a time value of money of .06. He is analyzing a common stock that is currently paying $2 per year dividend, but he expects the dividend to grow at a rate of .04 per year for perpetuity. (a) What is a reasonable estimate of price at which Mr. Jones might consider this common stock to be eligible for purchase (ignore risk considerations)? (b) What is a reasonable estimate of price if Mr. Jones considers the $2 to be about to decline at a rate of .04 per year instead of grow?

9–8. Mr. Smith is reviewing a stock currently selling for $100 per share. He expects the price to increase to $102 in one year and the firm to issue a $2 dividend one year from now. Mr. Smith has a time value of money of .06. (a) What price per share might Mr. Smith be willing to pay? Ignore risk considerations. (b) If Mr. Smith purchased the stock, what return would he be expecting for his year's investment?

9–9. The following is taken from an article in the *Wall Street Journal* of July 23, 1965.[12]

> NEW YORK—Transcontinental Investing Corp., New York, said it had decided to stop paying out preferred stock as a dividend on its common shares.
>
> The company added that its directors had agreed to "establish a program of regular cash dividends consistent with earnings just as soon as the company's capital requirements no longer absorb its funds." It said no date had been set, however, for resumption of cash dividends.
>
> Transcontinental had been paying dividends of preferred stock since 1963, when it stopped making cash payouts. The latest quarterly dividend of preferred was at the rate of one share of $25 par value 6½% preferred stock for each 500 common shares held of record May 12.
>
> The company said it had decided that continued issuance of the preferred "would drastically reduce the future potential of the common" and that the preferred payments didn't "appear to have satisfied investor desires for distribution."
>
> Robert K. Lifton, president, said the board also had concluded it would be "desirable" to reduce the number of common shares outstanding and that it would draw up a plan for accomplishing this. In the meantime, he said, the company might purchase some of its common stock in the open market. Transcontinental had 4,195,113 Class A common shares outstanding at the May 14 record date for the annual meeting.
>
> Transcontinental has subsidiaries in such financial fields as banking and insurance, as well as some real estate investments. Directors yesterday declared the regular quarterly dividend of 40⅝ cents a share on the 6½% preferred, payable Aug. 24 to stock of record Aug. 9, but made no dividend declaration on the common.

The company's common stock is listed on the American Exchange where it closed at 2⅞ on the date this article appeared. The price range for the period studied was 5¼ to 2⅞. The preferred is traded over the counter and was quoted at 17 bid, 18 offered. In 1963 and 1964 dividends on preferred stock absorbed were approximately equal to the company's earnings.

Comment on the corporation's financial policies.

[12] Reprinted with permission of the *Wall Street Journal*.

9–10. Mr. Johnson is considering purchasing a stock currently paying a $2 dividend. He expects this dividend to grow at a rate of .10 per year for ten years and then be constant for perpetuity. He expects the market to apply a .05 discount rate to these constant dividends in obtaining a price at that time. He has a .06 time value for money. Determine a reasonable price for Mr. Johnson to pay for this stock ignoring income taxes and risk considerations. (A knowledge of calculus is useful in solving this problem.)

9–11. Assume that in the previous problem Mr. Johnson is subject to a taxe rate of 40 per cent on ordinary income and 20 per cent on long-term capital gains. The discount rate he uses is $(1-.4)(.06) = .036$. What would the present value of the proceeds of the stock be worth to him if he bought it now and sold it at the end of the tenth year? What is the present value of the proceeds if he holds the stock indefinitely? Assume that the market will discount before tax dividends at 5 per cent. What decisions will lead to the highest present value of after-tax proceeds?

9–12. Discuss the merits of a stable dividend policy from the point of view of a business manager and investor. First assume the investor is investing for his own account and then assume he is a trust officer.

9–13. Assume that cost of capital is constant with respect to changes in the capital structure and that stock equity has a higher cost than debt. Draw on a graph the cost of capital, cost of debt, and the cost of stock for capital structures ranging from zero to 100 per cent debt.

> In practice we have tacitly agreed, as a rule, to fall back on what is, in truth, a *convention*. The essence of this convention—though it does not, of course, work out quite so simple—lies in assuming that the existing state of affairs will continue indefinitely, except insofar as we have specific reasons to expect a change.
>
> —J. M. Keynes, *The General Theory of Employment, Interest and Money* (New York: Harcourt, Brace & Company, 1936), p. 152.

10

CAPITAL BUDGETING UNDER CAPITAL RATIONING

In Part I of this book we concluded that under conditions of certainty, if a firm could borrow or lend funds at a given market rate of interest, it should accept independent investments when the investments have positive net present values at this market rate of interest. In this chapter we consider situations in which the assumption that a firm can borrow or lend any quantity of funds that it desires at a given market rate of interest is not valid. There are two distinctly different situations in which this assumption may not hold.

One of these situations arises because of a decision by management to limit arbitrarily the total amount invested or the kind of investments the firm undertakes or to set acceptance criteria that lead it to reject some investments that are advantageous when judged by market criteria. For example, instead of using the market interest rate it might use some higher rate as a cutoff rate.

A second situation that must be considered is when there is a difference between the market rate of interest at which the firm can borrow money and the market rate at which it can lend.

Both situations are frequently labeled *capital rationing*. To distinguish between them, we shall refer to the former situation as *internal capital rationing* and to the latter as *external capital rationing*. External capital rationing is actually the result of market imperfections.

Two observations should be noted. First, capital rationing in both the first and the second form is present throughout the economy, but usually to a relatively minor degree, and thus may frequently not be incorporated into the analysis (although it should not be ignored without trying to estimate its impact). Secondly, where capital rationing is present, there is no simple solution to the internal investment decision. Two possible solutions are offered. The first possibility is to make simplifying assumptions where appropriate and to recognize that the answer obtained is an approximation. The second solution is to use mathematical techniques to develop possible solutions, following different possible investment alternatives (including all possible combinations of investments through the succeeding years). This analytical technique may lead to a sound solution to the capital-budgeting decision under capital rationing, but it is complex and requires detailed knowledge of future investment alternatives that is frequently not available.

EXTERNAL CAPITAL RATIONING

In this chapter the term *borrow* is used when a firm obtains capital from the market by issuing any type of security. The term *lend* is used to mean the use of funds to purchase any type of security. We specifically assume that borrowing takes place in such a way that the borrowing firm's capital structure (the relative proportion of the various kinds of securities it has issued) is not changed. Thus *borrowing* would normally involve issuing both debt and equity securities. Similarly we assume that *lending* means acquiring a portfolio of securities that have approximately the same average risk characteristics as the assets presently owned by the firm.[1]

---

[1] Under conditions of certainty the term *lending* could be interpreted literally, since there is no problem of risk. Under uncertainty we want to define lending so that the operation does not change the risk characteristics of the firm's assets. Such a change would occur if lending were interpreted to mean purchasing government bonds, for example. A firm is lending if it purchases the securities of other firms whose assets have the same risk characteristics as its own assets.

A firm may purchase its own securities in amounts proportional to their market value. Suppose a firm has only equity shares outstanding and it buys some of its own shares. The effect is very nearly the same as if it had used the same amount of cash to pay a cash dividend. It differs from lending in that it is not expected that the funds will be returned to the corporation.

If capital markets were such that a firm could lend or borrow as much money as it desired at the going rate of interest, this rate of interest would be the same for both the borrowing and lending transactions. The goal of expected profit maximization would then require that the firm accept all independent investments whose present values were positive, using this rate of interest. With such capital markets the choice of investments would not be dependent on the amount of funds available to the firm, since by an appropriate combination of borrowing and lending, each firm could finance investments that had positive present values.

This theoretical situation is an ideal never encountered in practice. There will almost always be some divergence between the rates of interest at which the firm can lend surplus funds and the rates at which it can borrow funds. The size of the gap may vary for many reasons, including the effect of the brokerage costs of raising new money and the fact that there may be hidden costs or risks connected with one or the other of the investments. Another reason is that moneylenders may prefer firms having certain characteristics, thus driving up the cost of borrowing by firms that lack these characteristics.

If the borrowing rate and the lending rate are almost equal, then little is lost by neglecting the difference and speaking of a market rate of interest. If the difference is large, it cannot be ignored in determining the investment and financial policies of the firm. This gives rise to the situation we describe as external capital rationing.

An approximate solution to the capital-budgeting process with external capital rationing can be described as follows: Assume that a schedule is prepared, showing the total current outlays required for investments having a positive present value at various rates of discount.[2] Such a schedule will show greater current outlays at lower rates of interest, since some investments whose present values are negative at high discount rates will have positive present values at low discount rates. The schedules are shown by the curves II in Figures $1(a)$, $1(b)$, and $1(c)$. We let the distance OQ_1 represent the quantity of internally generated funds available for investment during the current period. Three situations are possible. In Figure $1(a)$ the vertical line drawn up from point Q_1 intersects the curve II at a rate of interest higher than r_2, the borrowing rate. This indicates that some investments which would be profitable at a cost equal to the borrow-

---

[2] Current outlays are the net outlays required in period zero.

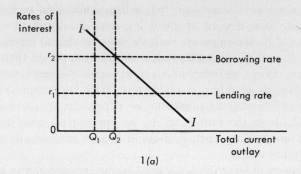

1(a)

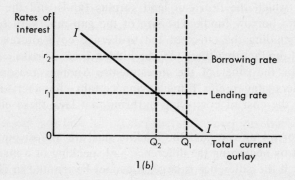

1(b)

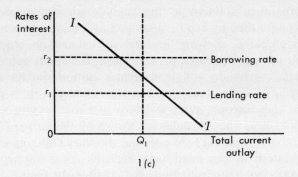

1(c)

Figure 1.

ing rate could not be financed from internally generated funds. It would be profitable for the firm to borrow an amount Q_1Q_2 to enable it to accept all investments that would be profitable at the borrowing rate. It would not be profitable to borrow any more than this amount, since all remaining investments have negative present values at the borrowing rate of discount.

In Figure 1(b) the internally generated funds currently available are more than sufficient to enable the firm to undertake all the investments that would be profitable when evaluated at the lending rate of interest. Only OQ_2 dollars would be invested internally. The remaining funds, Q_1Q_2, would be invested externally by buying the securities of other organizations or by reducing the capitalization of the firm and returning the funds to the original suppliers.

A third possibility is that the firm has sufficient funds to accept all independent investments whose present values are positive when evaluated at the borrowing rate but that the firm does not have enough funds to accept all investments whose present values are positive when evaluated at the lending rate. This is illustrated in Figure 1(c). Under those circumstances the firm would neither borrow any additional funds nor lend any part of its present funds, and the proper rate of discount for investments would be lower than the borrowing rate but higher than the lending rate.

This analysis assumes a capital market with a significant difference between the borrowing and lending rates. The solution suggested is only approximate, since we have not indicated what assumption is being made as to the probable lending and borrowing rates in the future, and the firm's position relative to them. The appropriate interest rates in future time periods are relevant to decisions made in the present because they affect the profitability of funds reinvested at those times. Cash flows expected in each future time period should be discounted at the rate of interest that will apply in that period. But how is this to be predicted? Generally it will not be difficult to predict future lending and borrowing rates. Given these predictions, it will be safe to assume that the appropriate rate of discount for each future period will lie somewhere between these upper and lower limits. Occasionally a firm will have some basis for predicting whether in a given future year it is more likely to be operating somewhere near its borrowing rate or near its lending rate. If a firm, even in a growing industry, is faced with a temporary excess of capacity, it may feel safe in predicting that, for the next few years, it will have more internally generated funds than it needs for the available profitable investment alternatives. This can be reflected by using a rate of discount for these years that is relatively close to the lending rate. In other cases the firm may anticipate product improvements that are presently in the research and development state but which are expected to be perfected within a few years. If the introduction of these innovations will require large-scale capital investments, the firm may feel confident in predicting that it will be likely to be operating relatively close to its borrowing-rate point during the years these investments are being made.[3]

Although such predictions of future cutoff rates under external capital rationing are inevitably rather crude, they serve a useful purpose if the predicted rates are in the right general direction. By using a high rate of discount for a future year in which there is likely to be a shortage of internally generated funds relative to the available investment opportunities in that year, the firm is recognizing that the opportunity cost of funds may be higher in some periods than in others. Investment proposals that release funds for use in periods when the demand is greatest will thus be preferred, all other things being equal, over investments that utilize funds in the periods of high demand. Similarly, if excess funds are likely to be available, the use of a lower discount rate will tend to lead toward the choice of investments that do not generate funds during these periods. The opportunity cost of funds during periods of excess funds is low; thus a low rate of discount is appropriate.

If a company is in a situation of external capital rationing, it may be useful for the top management to predict the appropriate cutoff rate that will apply in future years. By this means the investment planning in various parts of the organization can be coordinated in terms of the best available estimates of future cash needs and requirements for the company as a whole. If fluctuating cutoff rates are expected in the future, the company may wish to prepare and use present-value tables that show the appropriate discount factors to be used for each future period.

EXAMPLE

Suppose a firm expects that the appropriate cutoff rate for it will be 5 per cent for periods 1, 2, and 3, and 10 per cent for periods 4

---

[3] See Figure 1c and assume that curve *II* has shifted upward to the right (meaning there are more profitable investments) until the situation is described by Figure 1a. In this situation the borrowing rate is applicable.

and 5. The firm is considering two mutually exclusive investment alternatives. Both require initial outlays of $100 now. Investment G will return $150 in year 3; investment H will return $200 in year 5. The present value of G's proceeds is $150 $(1.05)^{-3}$ = $150 (.8638) = $130. The present value of H's proceeds is $200 $(1.05)^{-3}$ $(1.10)^{-2}$ = $200 (.8638) (.8264) = $200 (.7138) = $143. Investment H with a net present value of $43 is preferred to G with a net present value of only $30.

INTERNAL CAPITAL RATIONING

There are two types of internal capital rationing. In the first, the firm sets a cutoff rate for investments that is higher than the firm's cost of money. In the second type, the firm decides to limit the total amount of funds committed to internal investments in a given year to some fixed sum, even though investments having positive present values at the firm's cost of money must be rejected as a result of this decision.

Consider the first kind of internal capital rationing. Suppose a firm requires that investments must have a positive present value at 15 per cent, even though the firm's cost of money is only 10 per cent. In this case, if the same cutoff rate is maintained from year to year, the cutoff rate in future years will be known, and the firm can evaluate all investments *as if* the cost of capital were 15 per cent. This will have some advantages compared to many other measures of investment worth. We have shown in Chapter 2 that whatever rate of discount is used, the present-value measures will avoid some errors in making investment decisions that could be committed if the pay-out period or other measures were used.

But although a definite cutoff rate is available, the logic of using that rate to discount cash flows is no longer completely correct. The rate of discount used should measure the alternative uses of funds available to the firm. In the present instance, however, it indicates only that an investment of a dollar now yielding less than 15 per cent will not be undertaken. If next year the company has more internally generated funds than it is willing to invest following the 15 per cent cutoff rule, then an extra dollar of funds that becomes available next year will have an opportunity cost that is less than 15 per cent. How much less will depend on what use the firm makes of the "excess" cash that it will not invest. Usually these excess funds are invested in short-term government securities.

INTERNAL CAPITAL RATIONING AND DIVIDEND POLICY

In the second type of internal capital rationing, the cutoff rate is not specified, but the maximum amount that will be invested is determined by top management because it is unwilling to go to the market to obtain aditional funds, even though there are desirable investments. This reluctance to go to the market may result from a wish to prevent outsiders from gaining control of the business, or from a feeling that there will be a dilution of earnings if additional equity funds are raised under the given market conditions.

In these circumstances, the correct amount and selection of investments will depend on the firm's dividend policy. One possibility is that the firm will maintain (over the life of the investments) the current level of dividends, regardless of any increases in earnings that may come about because of additional investment. Assuming past investments will support the dividend, the net cash flows generated in future periods by the investments of the current period will be available for reinvestment in the period in which they are earned. The amounts of cash available for investment will vary from period to period as will the desirability of investments (the demand schedule for investments may shift). This situation may result in the firm rejecting internal investments with yields greater than the borrowing rate. For this reason it will be very difficult to make predictions of future cutoff rates (the opportunity costs for future cash flows).

A common dividend policy is that whereby the firm pays a dividend equal to a given fraction of its income (the income is measured by ordinary financial accounting techniques). In this case only a fraction of the future cash proceeds generated by current investments will be available for reinvestment. It is theoretically desirable to divide future cash flows generated by investments into that part which will be used as dividends and that part which will be available for the reinvestment. The value of a dollar of reinvestible funds earned in future period t will be greater than the value of a dollar used for dividends in the same future period, if we ignore uncertainty and assume the dollars will be reinvested in projects with positive net present values. But if the firm has an overabundance of cash, it may invest the funds in investments with a negative net present value (the retention of excess cash and marketable securities may have a negative net present value). Such investment will result in the reinvested dollars having less value than the dollars paid as dividends. The firm is accepting investments whose yields are less than the yields of alternative opportunities available to the stockholders.

SUMMARY—CAPITAL RATIONING AND PRESENT VALUE

Capital rationing in one form or another exists to some extent in most corporations. We may distinguish among minor and severe cases of capital rationing. In the minor cases the present-value rules suggested in this book may be used with confidence. In the more severe forms of capital rationing, the present-value method may still be used, but it is no longer correct to use a constant rate of discount for all future years. The rate of discount used for each future year must reflect the cost of obtaining additional funds, the value of external investments available to the firm, or the desires of the owners for present versus future proceeds.

QUESTIONS AND PROBLEMS

10-1. The ABC Company is planning its investment budget. Currently it can raise money at a cost of .06. It assumes that its stockholders are able to invest funds so as to earn .04. There are also opportunities for the company to lend its funds and earn .04. (a) Assuming that the company expected a large amount of investment opportunities, what discount rate should it use in making investment decisions? (b) Assuming that the company expected a large amount of cash compared to internal investment opportunities, what rate of discount should it use in making decisions? (c) Assuming that the company expected a shortage of cash for the coming 24 months, but then expected a surplus amount of cash, what does this imply about the rate of discount to be used?

10-2. The ABC Company has a stable dividend policy (pays $2 a year). It also has a policy of not raising new capital from the market. The policy is to invest the available funds after payment of the dividends (excess cash is invested in marketable securities).

What does this imply about the use of the present value method of making investment decisions?

10-3. The ABC Company has more investment opportunities than it can use (it is unwilling to borrow or issue more common stock).

Management estimated that the investment cutoffs for the next two years will be:

Year	Cutoff
0–1	.20
1–2	.30

It is attempting to choose between two mutually exclusive alternatives both of which will require an initial outlay now and payoff at the end of 2 periods.

What discount rate should be used in evaluating the mutually exclusive investments? What rate would you use if the investments had a life of one year? *Hint:* $(1 + R_n)^n = (1 + r_1)(1 + r_2) \ldots (1 + r_n)$, where r_i is the value of money of period i and R_n is the equivalent interest rate for the n periods.)

10–4. The president of the ABC Company wants a ranking of three investments. The firm considers its cost of money to be .05. The following three independent investments are ranked.

Investment	Cash flow of period			Present net value, using .05	Ranking
	0	1	2		
A	− 1,000	1,120		66.69	3
B	− 1,000		1,210	97.47	1
C	− 1,000	400	775	93.89	2

The firm has $1,000 of uncommitted funds available (without borrowing) for investment. Based on the above ranking the president decides to accept Investment B. It is then brought to his attention that since Investment B has a yield of .10 this could be considered to be the investment cutoff rate (other investments already approved have higher yields).

Evaluate the decision process.

10–5. In September 1964 the Commonwealth Edison Company announced it would discontinue its stock dividend policy. The policy of the company had been to issue stock dividends of 1 to 2.4 per cent for the earnings in excess of the cash dividends. The stated purpose of the stock dividends was to help finance expansion without public offerings of common stock. The dividends were stopped because it was feared that a further increase in the common stock equity ratio would increase the company's overall cost of money.

Required: Discuss the company's use of stock dividends.

10–6. An investor can earn .05 (before taxes) in default-free investments. He is considering purchasing stock in a corporation that will pay a dividend of $10 a year for perpetuity (assume this information is known with certainty). The investor is in a marginal .7 tax bracket. (a) Compute the value of the stock to the investor. (b) Compute the value of the stock assuming an investor has a marginal tax rate of .4. (c) Compute the value of the stock for the investors of parts (a) and (b) assuming there are tax-exempt securities that can be purchased to yield .03.

10–7. Assume a situation where it is known that the dividend of $10 a year will not begin for 11 years and that the price at the end of 10 years will be $200. The capital gains tax rate is .25; the after-tax opportunity cost to high tax investors is .03, and the after-tax opportunity cost to low tax investors is .05. (a) How much would an high tax investor be willing to pay for the stock now? Assume he will sell at the end of 10 years for $200. Why is this selling assumption reasonable? (b) How much would a low tax investor (say zero tax) be willing to pay for the stock now? Would he sell at the end of 10 years?

10–8 (reference 10–7). Recompute parts (a) and (b) assuming the expected price at the end of 10 years is $100.

10–9 (reference 10–7). (a) How much would the high tax investor be willing to pay for the stock at the end of year 9? (b) How much would the low tax investor be willing to pay? (c) How much would the high tax investor realize if he liquidated his investment at a price of $190? Assume he paid $130 for the investment. (d) Compute the present value of the investment at the end of year 9 assuming the high tax investor intends to hold until year 10 and sell at $200.

10–10. Company X's reported net earnings have increased to $3.00 per share after having remained at the $2.00 per share level for a number of years. Dividend payments have been $1.20 per share for quite a few years. Its dividend payout has been somewhat more liberal than that of its industry.

Practically all the increase in earnings has resulted from consolidated earnings of new foreign subsidiaries and affiliated domestic companies. The earnings of these companies are available for Company X dividends only to the extent Company X receives dividends from them. The foreign companies and affiliates are relatively new and their capitalizations are highly leveraged, so that a major portion of their net earnings are currently required to repay debt and provide funds for expansion, leaving only a small portion available for dividend payments to Company X.

The treasurer considers the general financial position of Company X to be quite satisfactory. While cash is kept at the minimum amount necessary to run the business, long-term debt represents only 15 per cent of total capitalization and could be increased readily to finance major capital expenditures. Depreciation is adequate to support replacement of worn-out and obsolete equipment but not a significant expansion of plant and equipment. Long-term debt repayments are equivalent to approximately $0.60 per share of net earnings.

Required: With the increase in reported earnings, management is receiving inquiries as to why the dividend has not been increased. Based on the information presented, the dividend could be increased by about $0.20 per share from parent company earnings plus dividends from foreign subsidiaries and affiliates which may average $0.20 to $0.30 per share over the next several years, but this would reduce or eliminate retained earnings for expansion.

The company's dividend policy is to maintain a dividend rate once established. The problem facing management is whether to increase the dividend or not and, if so, how much and still provide adequately for future expansion.

10–11.

THE UNITED FRUIT COMPANY

During the annual stockholders' meeting held April 21, 1965, the following exchanges took place:

Question: When capital investment is being considered to reduce costs, what minimum rate of return is considered acceptable by the company?

Mr. Fox: To reduce costs, the minimum rate of return that we would be at all interested in would be about 11 per cent after taxes, which is the target we are setting on our return for investments.

There are other considerations than just straight cost reductions. If they improved the quality of the product or improved the safety of our operations, these would also have to be considered. But by and large, anything that didn't enable us to have 11 per cent after taxes would not get serious consideration.

Question: Is there a chance the company again may offer to buy its stock at $26 a share?

Mr. Fox: I think that what you are really asking here is: Are we contemplating acquiring a large amount of our stock and inviting tenders at whatever the price might be at that particular time?

We have better opportunities to broaden and expand this company by using our cash and our credit if need be, to acquire other businesses. And rather than retrenching the company, I would like to see it expand. This, of course, would pretty much preclude a tender in the near future at least.

Question: Would you comment, sir, about our oil leases?

Mr. Fox: There is little to report. We have not made any major strikes and have ceased exploring. We would like to find some way to profitably dispose of these properties to someone who might like to proceed with them. The cost of exploring for oil is too big a gamble for this company to take.

Question: Has there been a tremendous investment of corporate assets in the oil explorations or is it relatively insignificant?

Mr. Fox: No, it has been insignificant.

Required: Discuss the preceding questions and answers.

10–12. The following information was taken from the 1964 annual report of the Inland Steel Company.

The Chairman's letter to the stockholders included the following statement:

We take some satisfaction, and I am sure our stockholders do too, in the fact that our earnings are predicated on accounting principles which are deemed conservative. Specifically, the maximum depreciation allowable for federal income taxes is deducted in full from pre-tax earnings, while the investment credit is prorated over the depreciable life of the facility involved.

As our stockholders know, we are in the midst of a very large and comprehensive expansion and improvement program. Our new mill for the production of thin tin plate is already in operation, and our new quality control center, fully described later in this report, is beginning to serve the Indiana Harbor Works. Other major new facilities—an 80-inch hot strip mill, two 230-ton oxygen steelmaking furnaces, a secondary blooming mill, a billet mill, a unit for producing welded beams and our Caland ore improvement plant—are all scheduled for completion in 1965. Many additional programs—including a coil finishing line for the 80-inch mill, billet conditioning equipment, an addition to our 76-inch mill plate capacity, a new

Inland Steel Company

	1964	1963	1962	Per cent change 1964 from 1963
Net sales	$873,714,553	$808,089,940	$760,141,920	+ 8.1
Net income	$ 71,073,725	$ 56,139,106	$ 52,486,902	+26.6
Per cent of net sales	8.1%	6.9%	6.9%	+17.4
Per share of stock	$3.91	$3.11	$2.94	+25.7
Per cent of stockholders' equity	11.4%	9.7%	9.6%	+17.5
Dividends paid	$ 33,543,987	$ 29,665,532	$ 28,519,906	+13.1
Per share of stock	$1.85	$1.65	$1.60	+12.1
Wages and salaries paid	$231,402,806	$216,760,531	$203,667,559	+ 6.8
Average per employee	$7,782	$7,542	$7,230	+ 3.2
Capital expenditure	$125,586,000	$ 83,726,000	$ 41,978,000	+50.0
Depreciation, amortization, and depletion	$ 62,499,650	$ 60,628,126	$ 60,686,800	+ 3.1
Working capital	$183,876,455	$214,043,622	$225,180,038	−14.1
Long-term debt	$177,400,000	$186,276,200	$193,794,700	− 4.8
Stockholders' equity (book value)	$621,221,903	$578,545,287	$546,486,667	+ 7.4
Per share of stock	$34.19	$32.09	$30.60	+ 6.5
Ingot production (net tons)	6,408,008	5,864,799	5,255,993	+ 9.3
Index (1957–9 = 100)	132.7	121.8	109.2	
Number of employees at year end	31,531	29,487	29,234	+ 6.9
Approximate number of stockholders	40,000	39,300	38,400	+ 1.8
Shares of stock outstanding	18,170,045	18,026,895	17,858,243	+ .8

galvanizing line and expanded cold rolled sheet facilities—have all been approved and will be completed during 1966 and 1967. These new facilities will, of course, be of substantial importance in our competitive efforts and in expanding our sales volume in the years ahead. Our capital expenditures totaled $125.6 million in 1964 and are budgeted at $110 million this year.

Further information may be obtained from the Annual Report or from financial services.

a. What is the optimal capital structure for Inland? b. How should Inland move from its present capital structure to the optimum? c. What is the relationship between the answers to the above questions and capital budgeting decisions?

10–13. The American Telephone and Telegraph Company in 1958, 1961, and 1964 resorted to equity-type financing to raise new capital. In 1959, 1961, and 1964 the company increased the dividend on common stock.

Comment on the financial policies of AT&T implied by the above history of financial events.

Business men play a mixed game of skill and chance, the average results of which to the players are not known by those who take a hand. If human nature felt no temptation to take a chance, no satisfaction (profit apart) in constructing a factory, a railway, a mine or a farm, there might not be much investment merely as result of cold calculation.

—J. M. Keynes, *The General Theory of Employment, Interest and Money.* (New York: Harcourt, Brace & Company, 1936), p. 150.

11

AN INTRODUCTION
TO UNCERTAINTY

Up to this point we have assumed that the basic goal of the business corporation is to maximize the present value of the stockholders' equity, and that this goal had to be consistent with maximizing the economic well-being of the stockholders. A further complication is introduced in this chapter: uncertainty, with the resulting possibility of a loss, though the expectation is that there will be a gain.[1]

UNCERTAIN EVENTS AND FORECASTS OF CASH FLOWS

We can think of the difficulty in specifying unique cash flows as deriving from the fact that there are future events that will affect the cash flows, but we do not know in advance which of these events will occur. It may be that for each possible event, we would make a somewhat different forecast of the cash flows from the investment. The uncertainty arises from the fact that we do not know for certain which of the possible events will occur, and thus cannot be sure which cash forecast will be correct.

[1] The term *uncertainty* is used here to describe all situations in which the decision maker feels that he does not know the relevant consequence of each alternative under consideration. No attempt is made in this book to distinguish between risk and uncertainty.

We shall use the term *event* to describe a future state of the world. For some purposes it may be useful to combine fundamental occurrences to form a master event. For example, rain or snow may result in a cancellation of a game; hence we may use an event "bad weather" rather than one event "rain" and another event "snow."

To take a simple example, suppose you have an opportunity to bet on the outcome of a flip of a coin. If the coin lands heads, you win a dollar; if the coin lands tails you lose a dollar. The cash forecast is a plus $1 with one event and a $1 loss with another event. Before the toss you do not know whether the coin will land heads or tails. Only if you know that the coin is two headed or two tailed will the cash flows be known with certainty.

To take a more immediately relevant case, suppose a firm is contemplating investing in a plant to produce a product whose demand is very sensitive to general business conditions. If general business conditions are good, the demand for the product is likely to be high, and the plant is profitable. If general business conditions are poor, then the demand is low, and the plant is unprofitable. Again, in this case, uncertainty about the cash flows associated with the investment derives from uncertainty about some other event, namely general business conditions. If the future state of general business conditions could be perfectly forecasted, then the outcome of the investment could be predicted.

The example in Table 1 illustrates the effect of business conditions and product design on the potential profits from introducing a new product. In this case, the state of business conditions has some effect

Table 1. **Conditional Forecasts of Net Present Value of a New Product Investment**

	General Business Conditions	
Product Design	Favorable	Unfavorable
Popular design	$1,500,000	$1,400,000
Unpopular design	−$250,000	−$300,000

on the present value of the investment; but product design is more important. If the product design turns out to be unpopular with customers, then producing the new product will result in a loss, and only the exact size of the loss depends on general business conditions. On the other hand, if the product is popular with customers, then it will be profitable, but profits will be somewhat better if business conditions are favorable than if they are unfavorable.

Events could be classified in a great many ways, and no one classification will be useful for all purposes. We might consider as one category those events that affect the level of business activity generally. The international political situation, the monetary and fiscal policies of the government, and the general state of confidence of the business community might be considered to be factors that help determine the actual level of business activity that occurs. Another category might be those events that tend to affect all companies in an industry. For example, all companies in the steel industry would be affected by the outcome of the labor negotiations that determine the wage rates in the industry, by new important discoveries of iron ore, by changes in the cost of rail or water transportation, and by excise taxes affecting steel. A third category would be events directly affecting a particular company such as a change in its management or a natural disaster such as a flood or fire. Similarly, uncertain events affecting primarily one product category or one particular investment project could be isolated.

The classification of events is the first step in focusing attention on those things that are most relevant for a particular decision. The desirability of a decision is likely to be more affected by the occurrence of some events than that of others.

The new product with a popular design would generate positive new profits even under unfavorable business conditions that would eliminate the profits for most of the other lines of activity. A product that could produce high positive profits under those conditions might be extremely attractive to a company. This has very important consequences in considering how this decision will affect the uncertainty about total profits for the company.

PROBABILITY, A MEASURE OF LIKELIHOOD

Probability may be defined as a measure of someone's opinion about the likelihood that an event will occur. If we believe that an event is certain to occur, then we say that it has a probability of one of occurring. On the other hand, if we believe that an event is certain not to occur then we say that its probability of occurring is zero.

Generally we are concerned with events whose probability of occurrence is somewhere between zero and one. Suppose we consider events associated with one flip of a coin. If the coin is a new fairly machined coin that has a head on only one side, most of us would be willing to agree that the probability of landing a head on one fair toss is one-half. If we did not know the coin was fair, for example if the coin were worn unevenly, there would be some question about whether the probability of landing a head would be exactly one-half. One can easily imagine that different people might have different opinions about the probability of a head landing in this case. However, if we were to take such a two-sided coin and flip it in a fair manner a very large number of times, say 100,000 times, the ratio of the actual number of heads to the total number of flips would be a reasonable estimate of the probability of the event "heads" for that particular coin. The probability estimate is based on the objective evidence of 100,000 trials.

If the concept of probability were applicable only to events that could be repeated a large number of times under controlled circumstances, the concept would be of relatively little use in analyzing business investment decisions. Most business decisions are either unique or are made a small number of times. One does not generally make the same decision in essentially the same circumstances a great many times and observe the outcome of each decision. Even where decisions are repetitive, conditions tend to change. If a businessman is considering opening a drugstore in a certain location, there may be a great deal of evidence that helps him form a judgment about whether a drugstore in that particular location could be profitable. But since there is no other location and period of time that is exactly the same in all respects as the location and time he has in mind, the businessman cannot resort to an objective measure of probability to describe the events associated with the drugstore.

Some statisticians have taken the position that it is not very useful to describe a businessman's beliefs in terms of probability (for example to specify a probability that a drugstore opened at that location could be profitable). We believe that a useful measure of probability can be applied to such situations, provided it is kept in mind that the probability measure in this case is a description of the state of belief of the person who makes the probability estimate and that this measure is being used to cause the decision to be consistent with these beliefs. The uses of this concept will be illustrated by examples in the remainder of this chapter and in several of the following chapters. After reading these pages and perhaps attempting to apply some of the ideas to his own decisions, each reader can determine whether subjective probability measures are useful.

Let us consider an election and ask ourselves the meaning of a statement such as the following: Mr. A has a .65 probability of winning this election. The election will not be repeated in exactly the same form, nor has it been held before, although there may be all sorts of evidence relevant to a belief about the outcome. If we say that there is a .65 probability that Mr. A will win the election, this statement implies a comparison of the following sort: Suppose a jar is filled with 100 beads identical in all respects, except that 65 are blue and 35 are red. We mix the jar thoroughly and draw out one bead. The statement that Mr. A has a .65 probability of winning the election means we believe that we are as likely to draw a blue bead as Mr. A is to win the election. Suppose we were willing to bet $10 that the bead drawn will be blue and to pay $10 if it is not blue. If we believe the statement about the election, and are concerned only with how much we win or lose, we should be equally willing to enter a bet in which we would receive $10 if A won the election and lose $10 if A did not win the election. That is, we should be indifferent as to whether the outcome of the bet is determined by the actual outcome of the election or by drawing the bead from a jar of the nature described.

In the case of any unique event (like an election) all observers will not exactly agree on the probability that any particular candidate will win. The adjective *subjective* applied to probabilities suggests that the probabilities described are opinions or statements of belief held by individuals. The purpose of expressing an opinion about the likelihood that an event will occur in terms of a numerical subjective probability is to facilitate the development of decision-making procedures that are explicit and are consistent with the decision maker's beliefs.

By convention, probabilities follow several rules. Among them are: (a) The probability assigned to each possible event must be a positive number between zero and one, where zero represents an impossible event and one represents a certain event. (b) If a set of events is mutually exclusive and exhaustive (covers all possible outcomes), then the total of the probabilities of the events must add to one. For example, if Mr. A is a candidate in an election, then a mutually exclusive and exhaustive set of outcomes describing the election would be that Mr. A wins the election and that he loses. If the probability assigned to the event—Mr. A's winning the election—is .65, then the probability assigned to the event that he does not win the election must equal .35.

UNCERTAINTY AND REPEATED TRIALS

If the investment being considered has uncertainty characteristic similar to those arising from the flipping of a coin, with the amount of possible winnings equal to the possible loss, then definite statements may be made as to the possibility of realizing profits. On any one toss there is a fifty-fifty chance of success in obtaining a selected side of the coin; thus there is .5 probability that we shall be completely correct if we pick heads and an equally large chance that we shall be completely wrong. If, however, there are going to be 100,000 tosses of the coin, we can predict that heads will appear approximately half of the time, and we have a fair degree of confidence that we have chosen correctly. There is obviously a higher degree of uncertainty connected with predicting the percentage of heads with one toss than with 100,000 tosses of the coin. However, the number of heads may differ significantly from the expected number of heads. The presence of different degrees and types of uncertainty may also be true in the area of business.

Let us compare the profit potential of an oil company with the chance of success in tossing coins. If a group of investors organize for the purpose of drilling *one* oil well, they can hire statisticians, geologists, and other experts to compute the odds of finding oil and of finding oil in sufficient quantities to make a profit. In fact it would be possible to make a probability curve of the different possible profits and losses. The actual oil well may result in the maximum possible profits, the maximum possible loss, or something in between. There is a great deal of uncertainty as to the outcome of the operation.

Let us look at a large oil company that intends to drill 50 wells during the coming period. We shall assume that very small and very large oil companies have the same probability of finding a productive well and that this probability is .10. The small oil company drilling one well has a .90 probability of not finding any oil and facing ruin. The large oil company has .9948 probability of finding at least some oil and a probability of .0052 of not finding any oil.[2] The probability of a success for a single well is the same for both companies, but the probability of finding complete failure are greatly different. The likelihood of financial success will depend on the number of wells drilled, on the costs of drilling, and on the profitability of productive wells.

We can arrive at some general conclusions. Even though the outcome of a particular decision may be highly uncertain, if a large number of identical decisions are going to be made, it may turn out that we can predict certain characteristics of the outcomes of the whole collection of decisions with relatively little uncertainty. The proportion of wildcat wells that may be classified as being productive wells over a ten-year period for Standard Oil of New Jersey and the average number of customers per store for A & P may be examples. If we can make reasonably good predictions of the average outcome of the whole collection of decisions, then uncertainty about the outcome of any particular decision may be less important than information about the total investments. In a sense the individual decisions can be treated as components of some master decision whose outcome can be predicted with considerably more certainty.

An accurate statement of the conditions necessary for us to be able to predict these characteristics is too technical for this book. However as a practical matter, we shall obtain reasonable results if the investments are statistically independent; that is the probabilities of all possible outcomes for each single decision are the same regardless of what outcomes occur for the other decisions being averaged, and if for individual decisions the probabilities of extremely good or extremely bad outcomes are not too high. The larger the number of decisions being made, the more accurately the average outcome can be predicted.

Though undertaking several investments tends to reduce the range of possible outcomes, some uncertainty will remain. There is more uncertainty about the amount of oil that will be discovered per dollar of investment if a given amount is invested in drilling one well than if the same amount is invested in shares of fifty separate drilling operations. However, the return on our investment will depend not

---

[2] The probability of not finding any oil is equivalent to the event "no oil" occurring 50 times. The probability of not finding oil on one drilling is .9 and the probability of not finding oil on fifty drillings is $.9^{50}$, or .0052. This example assumes that the probability of finding oil on each drilling is statistically independent of the results of the previous drillings.

just on how much oil is discovered but on how much the oil is worth. A change in the level of world oil prices will have nearly the same effect on the value of a given amount of oil reserves, whether the oil has been obtained by drilling one well or fifty. The element of uncertainty is seldom if ever completely eliminated as a factor affecting business investment decisions.

THE COMPONENTS OF UNCERTAINTY

The consequences of uncertainty can be broken down into at least three components that should be considered in making investment decisions.

1. What is the expected monetary return from the investment? The word *expected* is used in a technical probability sense, and is equal to the sum of possible outcomes weighted by their respective probabilities. Presumably businessmen generally mean expected value when they speak of the estimated cash flows from an uncertain investment. With bonds however, the cash flows usually referred to are not the expected amounts, but the quantities that would be realized if the bond contracts are fulfilled. In the case of an ordinary bond, this amount is also the maximum amount that would be received. The expected amount will be less than the maximum if there is a possibility of default. This possibility of default is the main reason why bonds issued by the federal government carry lower interest rates than bonds of similar maturities issued by private corporations. The higher yield on industrial bonds is a compensation to the holder for the possible loss if the interest payments are missed or if the bond is not paid at maturity.

2. What is the nature of the dispersion of possible outcomes around the expected value? When there is uncertainty, the investor would want to know more than just what the expected return would be from his investment. What is the maximum possible loss that may be incurred if the investment is undertaken? How rapidly, for example, do the proceeds fall with a decrease in business activity? What is the relationship between the return on this investment and the return on other investments that have already been accepted or are currently under consideration? If something happens that causes a low return from the other investments, is it likely to cause a low return on this investment also?

3. Do monetary consequences of the investment accurately meas-

ure their importance to the investor? Consider, for example, an investment requiring an outlay of $100,000 for which there was a .5 probability of a return of zero dollars and a .5 probability of a return of $250,000. The expected return is $125,000. However, most persons whose total wealth was $100,000 would reject this investment.

All the above factors must be considered if a reasonable investment decision is to be made. Just looking at profitability for one given set of assumptions, with no statement as to the uncertainty connected with the assumptions, or the possibility of losses occurring if the assumptions are not realized is not a sound method of decision making.

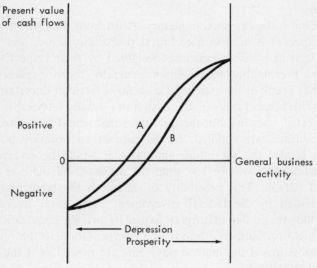

Figure 1.

As one example of the way the range of possible profits could affect the choice of investments, consider investments A and B. The possible net cash flows of the two investments, given different assumptions as to general business activity, are given in Figure 1. Note that both investments have the same maximum possible positive flows and the same maximum possible loss (maximum possible negative cash flows). Yet the diagram indicates that investment A is more desirable. At all points the present value of cash flow of investment A is equal to or greater than that of investment B.[3]

---

[3] We can say that investment A dominates investment B.

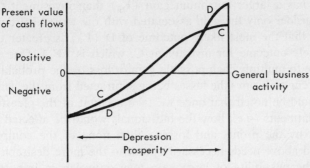

Figure 2.

Consider the mutually exclusive investments C and D as shown in Figure 2. Investment C has a lower maximum cash flow than investment D (the maximum profits are lower). Which of the two would be the better investment? The answer to this question is more complicated. One possible answer is that the investment with the largest area under the curve is the better investment (the negative cash proceeds and the resulting area should be subtracted). The answer might be valid if each possible present value had an equal probability of occurrence. But there is little justification for assuming equal probabilities. Assuming unequal probabilities, another set of curves must be drawn (see Figure 3) showing the likelihoods of the events.

However, in using Figure 3, it is not clear which of the two investments is more desirable. Both investments have the same maximum possible loss (V_1), but the maximum possible gains differ. Invest-

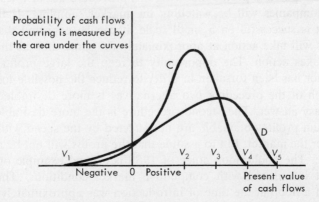

Figure 3.

ment D has a larger maximum gain (V_5) than investment C (V_4). If we consider only the gain associated with the most likely outcome, we note that the most likely outcome of D (V_3) is greater than the most likely outcome for investment C, which is (V_2). One solution would be to multiply each possible gain or loss by the probability that it will occur and sum (the losses being subtracted from the gains).

It should be noted that once we take account of the pleasures and disappointments—i.e., how the individuals would be affected psychologically by the profits and losses—then none of the computations described above needs necessarily point to the more desirable investment. The possibility of large gain may outweigh in importance to the investor the possibility of a very large loss, or just the opposite.

ILLUSTRATION OF UNCERTAINTY— INTRODUCING A NEW PRODUCT

The introduction of a new product is an interesting example of a business decision involving a large degree of uncertainty. The choice is essentially between:

1. Making large initial outlays, thus opening the possibility of large profits if the expectations are realized, or large losses if expectations are not realized; or,

2. Making relatively small outlays and sampling the market. If the product is successful, the scope of operations can be broadened. If the product is unsuccessful, the maximum amount of losses is not large, since the initial outlays were less than under the first alternative. The maximum possible profits following this procedure are also less, since other companies will be watching the market sampling. If the new product is successful on a small scale, it can be expected that competitors will take action at approximately the same time as the originator takes action. The opportunity to reap the large profits of the innovator has been forsaken in order to reduce the possible loss.

Which of the preceding two alternatives is more desirable? There is no easy answer. The second procedure is the more desirable *if* the maximum profits obtainable are not affected by the speed with which we enter the market. But to assume that the profits will not be affected is naïve. The hoola hoop craze of 1958 is a good example of a new product introduced with competitive market conditions. The retail price of a hoop at the time of introduction was approximately $2.00. In a period of three months the price was successively reduced until one could obtain a fine hoop for $0.69. The innovator of the hoop had an investment decision to make before introducing his product. Should he have built up a large inventory and then released a flood of hoops to take advantage of the initial enthusiasm? With the aid of hindsight it may be concluded that this is what the company should have done. As it turned out, other plastic companies were in nearly as good a position to share in the initial profits as the innovating firm.

Actually, instead of two choices, the business manager has a wide spectrum of alternatives, ranging from incurring a small risk (and a small profit possibility) to a large risk (and a large profit possibility). The initial analysis of probable revenues and costs has indicated that this is a desirable product and, in general, a desirable investment. The exact amount of funds to be invested in the product—i.e., the size of plant, amount of advertising, size of the sales organization, and initial finished goods inventory before beginning sales—are managerial decisions requiring judgment. There is no simple formula or procedure that will give the correct answer. The firm must decide whether it desires a relatively safe position and small profits, or whether it is willing to innovate, with the accompanying risks and possible profits that fall to the innovator.

CHANGING THE UNCERTAINTY

It is possible for a company to follow courses of action that will decrease to some extent the degree of uncertainty connected with its operations. Increasing the information obtained prior to making a decision is one method of decreasing uncertainty. For example, a thorough job of market research may make the outcome of an investment in a new product much less uncertain than if the product were launched without the market research.

Another method of reducing uncertainty in some situations is by increasing the size of operations. A large oil company faces less risk of complete bust when it drills 50 oil wells than does a small group banded together to drill one well. On the other hand, a decentralized company may not make use of this fact if a division manager's performance is measured by using the operating data of his relatively small operation. In this case he may be in the same position as the manager of a small firm who fears risky investments because of the threat of insolvency.

Product diversification may also decrease the uncertainty, especially if two products compete with each other. Thus a combined gas and electric company servicing a metropolitan city would have less uncertainty than two separate companies, each specializing in either the electric or gas business. If major industrial users switch from electricity to gas, the fortunes of the specialized companies will be drastically affected, whereas if there were only one company there would be less of a change in the company's profits. Product diversification would also decrease uncertainty if the two products were differently affected by changes in business activity. For example, a combined grocery chain and machine equipment company would have less uncertainty than a specialized machine equipment manufacturer.

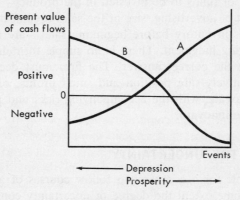

Figure 4.

The interrelationships of two investments on each other to reduce or eliminate risk can be shown graphically. Assume that the horizontal axis of Figure 4 measures different possible states of business activity (for example, the per cent of the work force unemployed or the different possible gross national products for the coming year). The vertical axis measures the mean cash flows of the investment for the year in question. The possible expected cash flows for two investments are plotted in Figure 4.

Taken individually both investments have risk. If a new investment A plus B is considered (adding the results of A and B), Figure 5 shows there is little risk with the joint investment. The objective of diversification is to dampen the swings of the total investment portfolio, hopefully eliminating the possibility of zero or negative results.

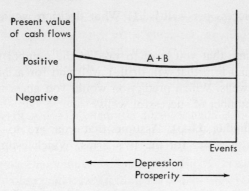

Figure 5.

SUMMARY

Some investments available to a corporation may be more risky than other investments—i.e., there is a higher degree of uncertainty. The introduction of uncertainty opens up the possibility of losses, which in turn forces us to measure the relative importance of the possibility of large profits compared with the possibility of large losses.

It is suggested that management should consciously consider the possibility of not realizing the forecasted results and should incorporate this into the analysis. There remains the question of the psychological impact on business managers and investors of losses and gains. This area of analysis is still in its infancy.

QUESTIONS AND PROBLEMS

11–1. Assume that a small firm has enough funds to drill one oil well and the cost per average well is $1,000,000. A large firm has enough funds to drill 50 wells. (a) What is the maximum loss of the small firm? (b) What is the maximum loss of the large firm? (c) Which of the two firms has more risk?

11–2. Assume that the average oil well returns a present value of benefits of $1,500,000 for every well drilled (a well costs $1,000,000 on the average to drill) resulting in a net present value of $500,000 per well. Assume you are in charge of investing $1,000,000. You have the choice of investing in one well and owning it completely or investing in a series of ten wells and having .1 ownership. The probability of a success per well is .1. What decision would you make? Explain.

11–3. Assume that you have to predict the number of successful wells for a small firm that will drill 1 well and for a large firm that will drill 100 wells. Which prediction would you guess will be closer to the actual number of successful wells?

11–4 (continuing 11–3). Assume that you are to estimate the proportion of successes for the two firms. Which estimate is likely to be closer?

11–5.

INVESTING IN OIL LAND [7]

A lease sale is, from the point of view of the individual oilmen participating, a harrowing, risky poker game for enormous stakes— deuces and one-eyed jacks wild.

First the company must decide which tracts of land it wants to drill on. Once that decision is made, based normally upon the geological evidence available, company personnel enter a strange world of uncertainty and conjecture. How much will they have to bid to get the lease?

The reasoning involved can be infinitely complex. The first and obvious question is: How much has been bid for comparable tracts in the area? In the case of the Hopi sale, the closest tracts were dozens of miles away on Navajo land. The Hopi reservation was a blank page.

Some facts can be learned by watching the competition. It may be known, for example, as the result of painstaking scouting work, that the seismographic crew employed by Company A spent considerable time going over a tract. It may also be known that the company has, in recent lease sales, been willing to spend large sums of money to obtain a tract.

Armed with these facts, Company B may decide it will require a lot of money to outbid Company A for this tract in which so much interest has been shown. Company B makes a very substantial bid, and finds out at the sale that Company A has not even made a bid on the tract. The results of the seismographic tests had been discouraging.

On the other hand, Company B may decide not to compete for this tract but rather to bid a much smaller amount for the mineral rights to a tract immediately beside it. Thus, if Company A does buy the first tract, and if oil is found, Company B may be able to latch on to some oil production next door.

[7] Reprinted from the Winter 1965 issue of *Petroleum Today*.

Sometimes a company will make a bid on a tract primarily to see that a competitor doesn't "get away with anything" by obtaining a tract too cheaply. Or a company will put in a bid just to let the other companies know that it is still around and competing. Or a company that has not been known to be interested in the sale will suddenly appear from nowhere and succeed in picking off a tract that everyone else had, for any one of a hundred reasons, decided to ignore.

No company wants to spend more money than is needed. But as one oilman commented, "The important thing is to get the tract you want, even if you have to leave some money on the table."

How does all this work out in practice? At the Keams Canyon sale, as an example, there was no pattern discernible. In the case of one tract, the top bid was $95,748.76. There were three other bids made on the tract, the highest of which was $2,802.12. Thus the high bidder spent approximately $93,000 more than was necessary to get the tract; he left that amount "on the table." Yet in the case of other tracts, the difference between high and low bids was sometimes only a few hundred dollars.

And the consideration that gives point to the whole unlikely procedure is that until actual drilling takes place, no one knows whether there is oil on the reservation—or, if there is, under which tract it is located.

"You play your cards as you see them," one man commented, "and you don't look back."

Required: Assume the following payoff table applies:

Well Characteristics

Evidence	Probability	Producer	Probability	Dry
Favorable	.10	$4,000,000	.90	$0
Unfavorable	.01	$4,000,000	.99	$0

The following decision matrix is prepared for Company B.

Profits of Company B
(Expected net present value)

Company A's Evidence Is:	Low, Say $2,000	High, Say $100,000
Discouraging	19,000†	− 60,000*
Encouraging	0	150,000†

* Assumes probability of 1 of Company B getting the bid.
† Assumes probability of .5 of Company B getting the bid.

What decision should Company B make?

Now consider Company A's decision. Assume A has two choices, bidding $3,000 or $200,000. It expects that B will bid $2,000 or $100,000. Assume that the results of the evidence were encouraging. The analyst prepares the following payoff matrix for A's president (A's expected profits are shown).

Company A Bids:	Company B Bids:	
	Low, Say $2,000	High, Say $100,000
Low, say $3,000	397,000	0
High, say $200,000	200,000	200,000

What decision should Company A make?

11–6. Assume you are approached about the possibility of investing in a Broadway play. After conducting some research you find that the expected profits are $800,000 per play and that approximately 25% of the plays that open on Broadway show a profit.

Required: Explain whether you would be willing to invest in a play being prepared for Broadway.

11–7. In 1964 a broker argued that while the Dow-Jones industrial average was high there were still many stocks that were far from their own highs.

Assume that common stocks can be divided into 16 groups and that each firm in a group reacts identically to events, but that each group is independent of each other's movements (except for certain major events such as war or depression that we will assume have not occurred). Assume the probability of each group hitting a high during a given period is .6.

What is the probability that all groups will hit a high during that period?

11–8. The ABC Company and the XYZ Company are both currently distributing, through their subsidiaries, automobiles in the country of Afro. The profits per year of the two subsidiaries are currently as follows:

ABC $10,000,000
XYZ $20,000,000

The ABC Company is considering establishing a manufacturing plant in Afro. An analyst has projected a profit of $38,000,000 after the plan begins operations (this assumes that the XYZ Company continues to distribute but not manufacture in the country).

An analyst for the XYZ Company has heard of the plans of the ABC Company. If the plant by ABC is built, he projects XYZ's profits to fall to $4,000,000. If the XYZ Company builds a plant and the ABC Company does not, he anticipates profits of $38,000,000 and a decrease in the profits of ABC to $4,000,000.

If both companies build plants it is expected that they would both earn $5,000,000 per year.

Required: What course of action would you recommend for the ABC Company?

11–9. Answer the following three questions as you would if *you* were faced with the betting situations. Assume the bets are legal and moral.

Situation 1

A fair coin will be tossed fairly. If a head appears you will receive $5. If a tail appears you will receive nothing.

How much would you pay to participate in this game? $_____.

Situation 2

A coin whose characteristics you do not know will be tossed. You can call heads or tails. If you call correctly you receive $5. If you call incorrectly you will receive nothing.

How much would you pay to participate in this game? $_____.

Situation 3

Two evenly matched basketball teams (say Yale and Harvard) are playing this Saturday. You will receive $5 if you pick the winner, $0 otherwise.

How much would you pay for this gamble? $_____.

11–10.

THE ALGONE CASE

Memorandum

TO: Y. P. Student
        Economic Evaluation Manager
        Wedoodit Chemical Corporation

FROM: I. M. Selfmade, President

As you know, the research and development department of our company has developed a new product that we are considering marketing under the brand name of Algone. Algone is an unstable liquid that must be kept under pressure at an extremely low temperature, of approximately −200°F. Above this temperature it decomposes within a few minutes. Algone has only one important known commercial application. When a quarter pound of Algone is sprayed through a specially designed applicator onto the feathers of a freshly killed chicken, the feathers completely disappear within seconds. There are no harmful side effects and the product has been approved for use by the Food and Drug Administration.

Wedoodit Chemical is considering two alternative means of exploiting this new product. One possibility is to sell the exclusive rights to the patent to the Chiselem Corporation which would produce and market Algone. The alternative is for Wedoodit to build a plant to produce the product itself. Chiselem has offered us a straight cash payment of one million dollars for the patent rights.

The attached memoranda from the Market Research Manager and the Engineering Manager provide a basis for evaluating the profit potential of Algone if Wedoodit undertakes to manufacture and market the product itself. As economic evaluation manager, I expect you to specify the type of equipment that would be needed for the most profitable manufacturing facility to produce Algone, to present cash flow estimates for the operation of this facility, and to make a recommendation as to whether or not Wedoodit should sell its patent rights to Algone.

As you know, we have estimated our cost of capital to be 8 per cent, and it is company policy to exploit all available investment opportunities that can earn us at least that much.

We are subject to income taxes of 54 per cent on incremental income consisting of 52 per cent federal and 2 per cent state corporate income tax rates.

Memorandum

TO: I. M. Selfmade
            President
            Wedoodit Chemical Corporation

FROM: V. Gotfigures
            Market Research Manager

SUBJECT: Market Potential for Algone.

Total Market

The only significant potential commercial use for Algone is to remove feathers from chickens (broilers) being processed for market. This requires ¼ lb. of Algone per bird. Approximately 2 billion chickens are consumed in the United States each year. Poultry consumption has been growing rapidly in the last decade as a result of improved technology and lower costs. However, no further growth in this market is expected. The effects of increased population will be offset by growing competition from turkeys and increased consumption of beef as a result of higher consumer incomes.

About half of the poultry are processed in plants in very low-cost labor areas where Algone would be more expensive than other means of removing feathers, or in plants whose layout is not easily converted to this process. Therefore, we expect the total market potential for this process to amount to 1,000,000,000 birds per year for the foreseeable future. This would require 250 million lb. of Algone annually, or about 1 million lb. per working day (based on a five-day week and 50 working weeks in the year).

Market Share

Although Algone is patented, news of our discovery has already leaked out to competitors who are developing similar products not covered by our patents. We are certain to have competitors soon after we begin production. The high capital costs of producing this product and the large potential market will prevent any one firm from dominating the market. We expect to be able to gain and hold 10 per cent of the total U.S. market, equivalent to 25 million lb. annually.

Price

Because alternative means of removing chicken feathers are easily available, a market demand for Algone would be very elastic at prices above 12 cents per pound. It is difficult to know how low the price might go, as this would depend on the costs of our competitors and the danger the industry might overexpand, making the business unprofitable for all concerned. Prices below 8 cents per pound would almost certainly be unprofitable. We estimate the price level will fluctuate around 10 cents, and recommend using that figure for planning purposes. All price quotations are F.O.B. our plant; customers to absorb freight.

Fluctuations in Demand

Fluctuations in demand are particularly important because Algone is an unstable compound. It cannot be stored except at prohibitive costs. The product must be shipped the same day it is produced. The effective market area for our plant will be limited to those customers who can receive product no more than 24 hours after it leaves the plant. The plant will have to operate Sunday through Thursday, because product shipped on Friday would be received on Saturday and would partly decompose by Monday. Poultry processing plants do not operate Saturdays or Sundays.

Poultry consumption does not fluctuate very much seasonally. But poultry processing *plants* normally operate only a half-day on Friday. Our production of Algone would be correspondingly lower on Thursdays.

Thus a plant that expects to have an average daily output of 100,000 lb. should expect a production fluctuation as follows:

Day of week	Daily production
Sunday through Wednesday	111,000 lb.
Thursday	55,000 lb.
Average daily production	100,000 lb.

MEMORANDUM

TO: I. M. Selfmade

FROM: W. E. Triedit
         Manager of Engineering
         Design and Pilot Plant Operations Department
         Wedoodit Chemical Corporation

A plant location has been selected for the Algone project in consultation with Market Research and Traffic Departments. Land and associated development costs (nondepreciable) would be $100,000.00. We hold a 90-day option on the site.

Two methods of producing Algone have been devised and pilot plant tested. Summary cost figures follow:

Method	Equipment and installation per 1,000 lb. of daily capacity	Valuable material and operating expense per 1,000 lb. of Algone produced
A	$80,000	$ 5
B	$34,000	$45

Either type of equipment would last for ten years and the costs of equipment and installation would be entirely depreciable. No salvage is expected. Variable costs do not include any depreciation and are on a before-tax basis.

In addition to the equipment listed, capital costs for office, shipping and miscellaneous utilities would amount to $20,000 per 1,000 lb. of maximum daily output. The variable costs of operating these facilities are included in the variable costs of methods A and B.

It would be possible to design a plant that would include a provision for producing Algone by both methods A and B in whatever proportions seem desirable. For example, a 50,000 lb. daily maximum production could be achieved in a facility having a capacity of 30,000 lb. using method A and 20,000 lb. using method B. There are no significant shutdown or start-up costs for either method of production.

A plant with a daily output capacity up to 125,000 lb. per day could expect fixed costs (for property taxes, insurance, plant guards, etc.) of about $100,000 per year (excluding depreciation). These costs would all require cash outlays and could be charged to expense for income tax purposes. A plant this size would also require working capital (inventories, accounts receivable and cash) of about $50,000.

Practical men, who believe themselves to be quite exempt from any intellectual influences, are usually the slaves of some defunct economist.

—J. M. Keynes, *The General Theory of Employment, Interest and Money.* (New York: Harcourt, Brace & Company, 1936), p. 383.

12

BUY OR LEASE

This chapter will deal with the financial type of lease; i.e., leases where there is a buy or lease option and the firm has a choice. We are not discussing the situation in which the firm has a lease or no lease option but has no opportunity to buy. We shall conclude that many financial leases are very similar to debt, and should be treated in essentially the same manner as debt. A legally oriented person would be able to point out the differences between a lease and debt (especially when there is a failure to pay the required payments), but we shall concentrate on the similarities, and the decision maker can bring the differences into the analysis in a qualitative manner if he so wishes.

ASSUMING ZERO TAXES

We shall first assume a zero tax rate and analyze the financial aspects of the lease versus buy decision. Assume that a company is considering the lease or purchase of a piece of equipment. The equipment will incur operating costs and will generate revenues that are unaffected by whether or not the equipment is leased or purchased. Thus for any lease or buy decision there will be many cash flows that are common to both decisions. There are, however, differences in the cash flows related to the method of financing the equipment. On the one hand, we have the cash flows associated with buying, and on the other, the cash flows associated with leasing. Assume the equipment costs $100,000, and we can borrow the $100,000 at a cost of .05 per year or we can lease the equipment at a cost of $28,201 per year. Should we lease or buy, assuming the equipment has an expected life of four years? The cash flows of the two financing alternatives are as follows:

	Period				
	0	**1**	**2**	**3**	**4**
Buy and borrow:	+ 100,000 − 100,000	− 5,000	− 5,000	− 5,000	− 5,000 − 100,000
Lease:		− 28,201	− 28,201	− 28,201	− 28,201
Difference: (buy minus lease)		23,201	23,201	23,201	23,201 − 100,000

The present value of the cash outlays with leasing is $28,201 times the present value of an annuity for 4 periods or:

$$\$28,201 \times 3.5460 = \$100,000$$

The present value of the cash outlays associated with buying are also $100,000 and in this situation we are indifferent between leasing and buying.

We could compute the yield of this stream. The rate of interest which makes the present value of the cash flows equal to zero is .05.

Cash flow		PV factor		Present value
+ 23,201	×	3.5460	=	82,270
− 100,000	×	.8227	=	− 82,270
				0

Multiplying the differential cash flows by −1, we have outlays of $23,201 for four years and a one-period return of $100,000. In this case we could say that leasing yields a return of .05 compared to buying and borrowing (the higher the yield the better leasing is compared to buying and borrowing). Since we can borrow at a cost of .05, we are indifferent between buying and borrowing and leasing.

There is no reason why we have to choose the method of repayment which is illustrated. For example, we could repay the $100,000 loan, using equal annual payments of $28,201. Since the cash flows of leasing and financing by borrowing would be exactly the same, the computation of a yield rate would not have any meaning in this latter situation. We would again be indifferent between borrowing and leasing.

In general, if the discount rate used in the analysis is the same as the interest rate that the firm would have to pay if it actually attempted to finance the purchase of the asset by a loan, the particular loan repayment schedule chosen will not affect the present value of the loan. Suppose an amount K is borrowed, and interest of r per cent is paid on the principal, plus accrued interest outstanding. Using r as the discount rate, we find that the present value of the payments required to repay the loan will always be K, whatever loan repayment schedule is chosen.

The purpose of this phase of the analysis is to determine whether the proposed lease is financially attractive. Since the lease is presumed to require a contractually predetermined set of payments, it is reasonable to compare the lease with an alternative type of financing available to the company that also requires a contractually predetermined set of payments, i.e., a loan. It follows that the interest rate at which the firm could actually borrow, if it chose to acquire the asset by buying and borrowing, is an appropriate discount rate to use in this analysis.[1] The recommendation holds even if the firm chooses to use some other discount rate for ordinary capital budgeting decisions.

Now assume that the lease payments are $29,000 per year, and the debt is repaid at the end of four years. The cash flows of the two financing alternatives are:

	Period				
	0	1	2	3	4
Buy and borrow:	− 100,000 + 100,000	− 5,000	− 5,000	− 5,000	− 5,000 − 100,000
Lease:		− 29,000	− 29,000	− 29,000	− 29,000
Difference: (lease minus buy)		− 24,000	− 24,000	− 24,000	− 24,000 + 100,000

[1] If a firm is attempting to reduce the amount of leverage in its capital structure, the appropriate discount rate will be the rate that makes the call price of the debt equal to the present value of the reduction in future interest and principal payments.

The yield of this investment stream from leasing is approximately .03, and we would want to borrow and buy rather than lease.

For .03:

$$3.7171 \times 24,000 = -89,210$$
$$.8885 \times 100,000 = +\underline{88,850}$$
$$-360$$

While we can compute and interpret the yield of the financial type of cash flow, the interpretation is somewhat difficult. Is a high yield good or bad for the cash flow difference? Another procedure would be to compute the present values of the two series of cash flows, using the .05 cost of debt as the rate of discount.
Present value of buying and borrowing:

$$5,000 \times 3.5460 = 17,730$$
$$100,000 \times .8227 = \underline{82,270}$$
$$100,000$$

Present value of leasing:

$$29,000 \times 3.5460 = 102,834$$

It is now easily seen that the cost of borrowing is less than the cost of leasing (assuming lease payments of $29,000 per year) and that if we use the asset, it should be purchased not leased.

Using a .05 discount rate, we previously computed the present values of the borrow and lease alternatives, where the lease payments were $28,201 per year, and found that the present values of both alternatives were $100,000 and we would be indifferent between leasing and borrowing.

The conclusions to this point can be summarized as follows: We have a piece of equipment that would cost $100,000 to buy; it has an expected life of four years. The firm could borrow the money to finance the purchase at an interest cost of 5 per cent. The equipment could also be acquired through a lease. If the annual lease payments were $28,201 per year for four years, there would be no financial cost advantage or disadvantage to leasing, because the present value of the lease payments at 5 per cent is equal to the amount that would have to be borrowed to finance the purchase through borrowing. If the lease payments were greater than $28,201 per year (say, $29,000), the lease would leave a financial cost disadvantage. Similarly, if the lease payments required were less than $28,201, it could be shown that the lease would have a financial cost advantage.

An objection to the financial analysis can be considered at this point. Suppose that an analysis along the lines described above led to the conclusion that the lease had a financial cost advantage. One can imagine a company treasurer objecting as follows: "I agree that the lease incorporates very favorable financial terms. However, if we acquire the asset by leasing, we will be adding to the burden of fixed charges (including interest, debt repayment, other leases and noncancellable overhead) which the company must bear. Entering into this lease would add to these fixed charges. For that reason I would prefer that we purchase the equipment outright if we decide to acquire it at all."

One can sympathize with the treasurer's desire not to increase fixed charges, and still disagree with his conclusion about the lease. Assume that the firm does have $100,000 in funds that could be used to purchase the asset. He is correct in saying that if the funds are used to purchase the asset, fixed financing charges will not increase. However, fixed charges could also be kept constant if the company leases the asset rather than buys it by applying the $100,000 to a reduction in other fixed charges, say by prepaying some debt.

Accepting or rejecting a lease does not necessarily imply an increase or decrease in total fixed charges. We have shown above how a company could accept a financially advantageous lease without increasing its fixed charges. If the analysis indicates a financial disadvantage to the lease, then if the equipment is to be acquired at all, it should be bought. Whether the funds for the purchase should be obtained from debt, equity, or some mixture is a separate decision.

The analysis of this section is incomplete, since we cannot tell whether the equipment should be acquired at all until we include all the cash flows (including the revenues and operating costs) in the analysis. Also, it is necessary to take income taxes into account to make the analysis more realistic. Income taxes will tend to influence the choice.

BUY OR LEASE WITH TAXES

Let us now consider the effects of a corporate income tax of 40 per cent. With an income tax we shall want to put all cash flows on an after-tax basis, and since interest expense is deductible for tax purposes, we shall use an after-tax discount rate. If a discount rate of 5 per cent was appropriate on a before-tax basis for borrowed funds, then the corresponding after-tax rate will be assumed to be $(1 - .4).05 = .03$.

Since lease payments are a deductible expense in computing income subject to taxes, annual payments of $28,201 per year will reduce after-tax cash flows to $(1 - .4)28,201$, or $16,921, per year. The present value of the after-tax lease payments, using a 3 per cent discount rate, will be $16,921 \times 3.7171$, or $62,897.

The cost of the equipment is $100,000, and we shall consider borrowing that amount in order to finance purchase of the machine. The exact pattern of after-tax cash flows will depend on the debt repayment schedule. If the lender charges 5 per cent per year, then equal payments of $28,201 per year for four years would be one repayment schedule sufficient to repay the interest and principal on the loan. To put these cash flows on an after-tax basis for the borrower, we need to determine for each year how much of this amount will be considered a payment of interest and how much a repayment of principal. Only the interest expense portion is allowable as an expense for tax purposes. A different repayment schedule would lead to a different pattern of after-tax cash flows, but provided interest was computed on the remaining debt balance, the present value of the after-tax cash flows required to repay the principal and interest of the loan will always be $100,000. For example, suppose the firm pays interest at $5,000 per year for four years and repays the principal in a lump sum at the end of the fourth year. The after-tax interest payments are $3,000 for each year.

$$\$3,000 \times 3.7171 = \$\ 11,151$$
$$\$100,000 \times\ .8885 = \underline{\quad 88,850}$$
$$\$100,001$$

We want to compute the cash flows of buying. If we subtract the present value of the positive cash flows associated with borrowing (plus $100,000), from the present value of the after-tax cash payments (a negative $100,000), we find that borrowing has a zero present value. The present value of the cash flows of buying and borrowing is the $100,000 immediate cost of the asset.

If we compare the purchase price of the asset with the present value of the lease payments, there appears to be an advantage in favor of the lease, when taxes are taken into effect. However, depreciation expenses have not yet been considered. If the equipment is leased, the lessee cannot deduct depreciation. If the equipment is purchased, the right to deduct depreciation expense for tax purposes is also obtained. With a tax rate of 40 per cent, each dollar of depreciation expense will save $0.40 dollars of taxes. The present value of the tax savings due to depreciation will depend on the timing of the depreciation expense. If depreciation is charged on a straight line basis over a four-year period, the present value of the tax savings will be $10,000 \times 3.7171 = $37,171. Subtracting this from the cost of the investment results in a net present value of after-tax cash flows of $62,829 for the borrow and buy decision. This is slightly less than the present value of the lease payments ($62,897).

If a more rapid method of depreciation were used, there would be a more clearly defined advantage in favor of buying. For example if the twice-straight-line declining balance method of depreciation were used, the present value of the tax savings could be computed, using Table D in the Appendix in the back of the book. With an interest rate of 3% and a life of four years, the present value of the tax deduction privilege is as follows: $100,000 \times .4 \times .946539 = $37,862. Subtracting this amount from $100,000 gives a net present value of $62,138 for buying and borrowing, which is $759 less than for leasing.

The tax savings that result from charging depreciation if the asset is owned are not contractual in nature as are the other cash flows we are considering. However frequently there is nearly as little uncertainty associated with the amount and timing of these cash flows as there would be in the case of a contract. Regardless of whether the particular piece of equipment performs as anticipated, the right to charge depreciation expense will generate tax savings as long as the firm as a whole has taxable income. Even if the firm does not have taxable income in any particular year, the tax-loss carryforward provisions of the laws provide a high degree of assurance that tax savings will result, although their timing might change slightly.

The above analysis made the lease and buy alternatives comparable by including financial type cash flows in the purchase decision analysis. This is reasonable since lease payments are a special type of debt, with special tax treatment. The entire amount of payment may be deducted in computing taxable income, unlike the conventional debt where only interest is deductible for tax purposes.

One important difference in buying, compared to leasing, is that the firm that buys an asset owns the asset at the end of the time period of the lease. To the extent that the asset has net value at that time, this is also a net cash flow for the buy analysis. This difference will be illustrated when we discuss the buy-lease analysis for acquisition of land.

RISK CONSIDERATIONS IN LEASE VERSUS BUY AND BORROW ALTERNATIVES

We began this chapter by suggesting that many leases are essentially financing instruments, comparable to debt contracts. Following this line of thought, we compared the advantages of leasing versus buying and borrowing. The question of whether the equipment is worth acquiring has not yet been discussed.

Before we turn to that question, it is desirable to consider the risks associated with the financial decisions we have been considering.

For practical purposes it may be reasonable, in some circumstances, to treat the financial cash flows we have been discussing as being free of any uncertainty. This assumption will not always be valid, as we shall see. If the likelihood of any substantial deviation from our predictions is very small, the time and cost involved in any detailed analysis of the uncertainties may not be worth the effort. The main justification for treating these financial cash flows as essentially certain for practical purposes is that their amounts and timing are largely determined by legal contracts that the firm acquiring the asset will have to fulfill. The lease contract determines the amounts and timing of the lease payments; the debt contract determines the amounts and timing of the debt repayments by the firm acquiring the asset. The depreciation expense charges allowed for tax purposes are not contractual, but they are fixed by law and in the presence of a large amount of other income and stable tax rates are reasonably certain.

Given a specific set of contracts, it might be possible to analyze the cash flows under various foreseeable alternatives. What would happen if the firm cannot meet the legal requirements? Will it be declared bankrupt? Can the lease be terminated earlier? Can the loan be extended, renewed, or is it callable?

Possible changes in the corporate income tax rates are worth considering. If a decrease in the corporate income tax rates is anticipated, it will tend to raise the after-tax cash flows for any of the alternatives considered. However, the effect of this increase on the net present value of any alternative will be somewhat offset by the fact that a decrease in tax rates will also tend to increase the appropriate after-tax discount rate and to decrease the value of the depreciation deductions, thus changing the relative desirability of buying and leasing.

The effects of these sources of uncertainty could be analyzed in detail if such an analysis were considered worthwhile.

IS THE EQUIPMENT WORTH ACQUIRING?

In the previous sections we have shown that the present value of the cost (using twice straight-line depreciation) of acquiring the equipment is $62,138 if it is bought, and $62,897 if leased. To decide whether it is worth buying the equipment, we need to compare the present value of the benefits with these costs.

Suppose the equipment has a life of four years and would lead to before tax-cash savings of $30,000 per year. The after-tax cash savings are $(1 - .4) \times \$30,000$, or $18,000 per year. The present value of the tax savings that would result from the right to charge depreciation expense on the equipment has already been calculated and subtracted from the purchase price of the equipment, so that these tax savings should not be considered again.

Using the after-tax interest rate of 3 per cent, we find that the present value of the savings from operating the machine are:

$$\$18,000 \times 3.7171 = \$66,908$$

Subtracting the present value of the costs of equipment from the present value of the savings, we have a net present value of $4,770 (i.e., $66,908 − $62,138), indicating that we can accept the machine on a borrow-and-buy basis.

In situations such as this, the cost of acquiring the asset can be generally estimated with a high degree of confidence, while the savings that would result from having the use of the asset are subject to some considerable uncertainty. If the firm has not had experience with similar equipment, there may be some question as to whether the savings in cost per unit of product (or other measure of the rate of usage) will be as high as anticipated. In addition there may be some uncertainty about the number of units of product that will be needed, and about the equipment's anticipated life. For these and other reasons a decision about whether or not the machine should be acquired will to a great extent depend upon management's judgments.

How should we present the data to management so as to facilitate management's ability to exercise its judgment? One possibility we have illustrated above is to calculate the present value of the anticipated savings at the debt interest rate and to compare these with the present value of the cost of acquiring the asset. Another possibility would be to indicate various possible savings that might result so as to give management an idea of the range of possible outcomes. For each outcome there might be some indication of its probability or of the circumstances necessary for the outcome to be likely.

LEASING OF LAND

In making investment decisions we generally separate the cash outlay (the investment) from the financing (the source of the cash). The two are tied together by the use of a given rate of discount that measures the time value of money for the firm.

In leasing decisions involving land it may not always be possible to separate an investment from its financing, as they frequently become interwoven. In fact in some situations it is not clear whether the land is being purchased or leased. Assume a situation where land is being leased but the company leasing the land can acquire the land for a nominal price at the end of twenty years. Are the lease payments for the use of the land, or are they for the use of money during the twenty-year period plus payments for the land?

We shall assume the following situation: Company A owns land and has offered to lease it to Company B at a cost of $80,242.65 per year for twenty years. After the twenty years A retains the land, assuming B leases.

B is a very large stable company, and A considers a lease with B to be the equivalent of a certain cash flow. Using the current long-term debt rate of .05, B finds the before-tax present value of the $80,242.65 to be $1,000,000.

A has offered to sell the land to B for $1,000,000 (A would not be taxed on this transaction). Should B buy? B can obtain long-term funds at a cost of .05. These funds would have to be repaid at the end of twenty years. B's tax rate is .40, and B has taxable income.

B's analysis is as follows:

Cost of Leasing

The after-tax cost of leasing is obtained by multiplying the lease by the tax and present-value factors.[2]

$$\text{After-tax cost of leasing} = (80,242.65) \times .60 \times 14.8775 = \$716,000$$

Cost of Buying

If we ignore the method of financing, the cost of buying is the immediate outlay of $1,000,000.

Alternatively we can compute the cost for the twenty years as being equal to the present value of the interest of $50,000 a year plus the $1,000,000 at maturity. Discounted at .05 this has a present value equal to $1,000,000, and the cost of buying is again $1,000,000.

B must compare the after-tax cost of borrowing with the after-tax cost of leasing, which is $716,000. The after-tax cost of borrowing is $1,000,000.

$$\$50,000 \times 14.8775 \times .60 = 446,300$$
$$\underline{\$1,000,000 \times .5537 = 553,700}$$
$$1,000,000$$

The after-tax cost of leasing is less than the after-tax cost of borrowing. This is not surprising, as the entire payment of the lease is tax deductible (thus with a lease only .6 of the amount paid is included as an outlay), but only the interest payments are deductible for tax purposes if we borrow.

There is a tax advantage in repaying the $1,000,000 via a lease compared to repaying the $1,000,000 outlay via a debt if we buy. However, in considering the buy decision we ignored the value of land at the end of the twenty years. Adding this to the cash flow of the twentieth year may affect the decision.

We will compare the $716,000 after-tax cost of leasing with the $1,000,000 after-tax cost of buying and borrowing and compute the break-even value of land (at the end of twenty years). Let X be the value of the land after twenty years.

---

[2] $A_{20/.03} = 14.8775$.

$$716,000 = 1,000,000 - X(1 + .03)^{-20}$$
$$284,000 = .5537\ X$$
$$X = \$513,000$$

Based on the after-tax computation, if the land is expected to have a value of less than $513,000 we should lease; otherwise we should buy.

Lease and Buy

There is an additional complication. Suppose Company B can lease and then buy the land for $300,000 at the end of twenty years. A lease decision is preferable based on the after-tax economic analysis. Unfortunately, the Internal Revenue Service will probably object to the deduction of the lease payment for tax computations purposes and will consider part of the cash outlay as being a payment for the land (which it is). If the lease payments are not completely allowed for tax purposes, this might shift the optimum decision to a buy decision even where the value of the land is less than the break-even value of $513,000. This break-even value assumed that the entire lease payment would be deductible for tax purposes.

We can compare the two alternatives year by year. Assume the land will be worth its present purchase price at the end of twenty years. The lease plan does not have a buy option.

The after-tax cash flows (in dollars) are:

	Year				
	1	2	3	...	20
Lease	− 48,146	− 48,146	− 48,146	−	48,146
Buy	− 30,000	− 30,000	− 30,000	−	30,000 interest
					− 1,000,000 repayment of debt
					+ 1,000,000 value of land
Difference (lease-buy)	− 18,146	− 18,146	− 18,146	−	18,146

The $18,146 is the extra cost (per year) of leasing compared to buying. Assuming the land does not depreciate in value through time, the advantage is clearly with buying.

Changing the timing of the debt repayment would not change the basic conclusion as long as the interest rate of the loan and the discount rate were equal.

It is interesting to note that the after-tax present value of the lease to A is $716,000 (i.e., $80,242.65 × .60 × 14.8775, assuming A has a .4 tax rate).

Conclusions

Leasing of land is a possible method of financing the use of land. If we remove the mystery from the decision process, we find that leasing may be more desirable than purchasing if there exists a difference of opinion relative to the value of the land upon termination of the lease. If Company A thinks the value of land will be increasing, it may lease to B at a price that seems low to B, if B thinks the value of the land will decrease. To the extent that the Internal Revenue Service allows lease payments for land to be deductible where there is an option to buy at a reduced price (i.e., a price less than the expected market price) at the termination of the lease, there may be a tax advantage to leasing land. But this tax advantage cannot be automatically assumed, as it is likely that the lease payments will be interpreted to be a purchase payment, thus not deductible for tax purposes.

QUESTIONS AND PROBLEMS

Problems 12–1 to 12–6 are tied together and should be done consecutively. Assume a zero tax rate.

12–1. The ABC Company has contracted to make three lease payments of $10,000 each for the use of a piece of equipment. The first payment is to be made immediately and the other payments are to be made in successive years. Assume that the cost of debt is .05.

Required: Determine the debt equivalent of the lease payments.

12–2. Referring to problem 12–1, if we could borrow $28,000 and buy the equipment being leased, should we purchase it or lease it?

12–3. Assume that a piece of equipment costs $28,000 and has indicated cash flows of $10,200 a year for three years. Assume the cash flows are received at the *beginning* of each year. With a time value of money of .10, is the investment desirable?

12–4. Assume that $18,000 could be borrowed with the funds being paid back as follows:

Period	
0	
1	10,000
2	10,000

Referring to problem 12–3, is the investment now desirable?

12–5. Referring to problem 12–3, if we could lease the equipment for $10,000 a year, first payment due immediately, would the equipment be desirable?

12–6. Referring to problems 12–3 and 12–4, if we could lease the equipment for $10,000 a year, would it be more desirable to buy and borrow or lease the equipment?

12–7. The RSV Company can finance the purchase of a new building costing $1,000,000 with a .05 bond that would pay $50,000 interest per year and repay the face amount at maturity. Instead of buying the building, the company can lease it for $95,000 per year, first payment being due one period from now. The building has an expected life of twenty years, The company has a zero tax rate.

Required: Should the company borrow and buy or lease?

12–8. The CDE Company is considering leasing a piece of equipment. There are three lease payments of $10,000 due at the end of each of the next three years. The equipment is expected to generate cash flows of $10,500 per year. Assume the cost of debt is .05 and the income tax rate is .40.

Required: Combining the investment and its financing, prepare an analysis showing the net present value of leasing.

12–9. Assume that the equipment of problem 12–8 can be purchased at a cost of $27,232.

Required: Should the equipment be purchased? Use sum of the years digits method of depreciation for tax purposes. Use a discount rate of .03, but exclude the financing from the cash flows.

12–10. Assume that the life of a piece of equipment is uncertain, but that management believes that the probabilities of it having different lives and the present values of cash flows for buying and leasing for different assumed lives are as follows:

Assumed Life	Probability	Present value (buying)	Present value (leasing)
1	.2	(20,000)	(2,000)
2	.3	0	4,000
3	.4	20,000	10,000
4	.1	40,000	16,000
	1.0		

Required: Is it more desirable to buy or lease?

12–11. *The Rocky Boat Company*

The Rocky Boat Company is considering the purchase of a business machine. The alternative is to rent it. The purchase price of the machine is $100,000. The rental per year of the same machine is $30,000. The $30,000 includes all repairs and service. If the machine is purchased, a comparable service contract can be obtained for $1,000 a year.

The salesman of the Business Machine Corporation has cited evidence indicating that the expected useful service life of this machine is five years.

The appropriate rate of discount of the firm is 5 per cent per year. If rented, the company may cancel the lease arrangement with one month's notice.

Required: Prepare a comprehensive analysis for the controller of the Rocky Boat Company, indicating whether purchase or rent is more desirable. Assume a tax rate of zero.

12–12. The Rocky Boat Company (see problem 12–11) has purchased the machine on January 1, 1963. How should the machine be depreciated for tax purposes? Assume a life of five years is acceptable to the Internal Revenue Service and that the tax rate is 52 per cent. The net salvage value of the machinery is zero since the removal costs are expected to be equal to the salvage proceeds. Use a .05 discount rate. (a) Prepare an analysis backing up your answer. (b) Recompute the investment decision of problem 12–11, taking income taxes into consideration and assuming that a five-year life is valid.

12–13. The Able Company was approached by a salesman from the Rochester Machine Tool Corporation. Rochester had developed a machine that could mechanize an Able Company operation now performed by hand. The machine cost $30,000, had a life expectancy of three years, and could save Able Company $14,000 per year in labor costs. Able Company estimated that its cost of capital was 10%. Its analysis of the cash flows that would result from using the machine is given in Table 1. Able Company was subject to a 50% corporate profit tax, and the machine would be depreciated on a straight-line basis for three years.

Table 1. Cash Savings from Buying New Machine

Annual reduction in labor expense	$14,000
Increased income tax liability before allowing for depreciation	(7,000)
Tax saving from depreciation charge of $10,000 per year	5,000
Annual increase in cash flow from using machine	$12,000

Subjecting the purchase price and cash savings from using the machine to a present value analysis, illustrated in Table 2, the Able Company decided it was not profitable to buy the machine.

Table 2. Cash Flow Analysis from Buying Machine

Year	Cash flow	Present value factor (10% cost of capital)	Present value
0	($30,000)	1.0000	($30,000)
1	12,000	.9091	10,909
2	12,000	.8264	9,917
3	12,000	.7513	9,016
Total	$ 6,000	—	($ 158)

When the Rochester Machine Tool salesman heard of the decision, he offered the machine to Able on the basis of a three-year lease. The lease payments required were $11,223 per year. The salesman pointed out that the extra $3,669 the company would pay if it leased the machine just covered the interest costs on the purchase price over a three-year period at 6%. Able figured that the lease payments of $11,223 were $2,777 less than the saving in labor cost. Half the difference would go to the government in extra taxes, but the company would be ahead by $1,388 per year (½ of $2,777) and no capital outlay was involved. They decided to lease the machine.

Only one Able executive disagreed. He felt that the company could borrow the money to pay for the machine from its regular banking connections, and save even more money. His calculations are presented in Table 3. He was overruled because the other executives felt it was not wise for the company to incur any more debt.

Table 3

A. Cash Flows from Buying Machine and Borrowing Purchase Price from Bank at 6%

Item	Year 1	Year 2	Year 3
Reduction in labor expense	$14,000	$14,000	$14,000
Increase interest expense	(1,800)	(1,235)	(635)
Increase income tax before allowing for depreciation	(6,100)	(6,383)	(6,683)
Tax savings from depreciation	5,000	5,000	5,000
Cash flows from operations	11,100	11,382	11,682
Repayment of loan principal	(9,423)	(9,988)	(10,589)
Net cash flows	$ 1,677	$ 1,394	$ 1,093

B. Comparison of Present Values from Leasing vs. Buying and Borrowing

Year	Lease Cash flows *	Lease Present values	Buy and borrow Cash flows †	Buy and borrow Present values	Present value factors (10%)
1	$1,388	$1,262	$1,677	$1,525	.9091
2	$1,388	$1,147	$1,394	$1,152	.8264
3	$1,388	$1,043	$1,093	$ 821	.7513
Total	$4,164	$3,452	$4,164	$3,498	

* (14,000 − 11,223) × .5 = 1,388.
† See Table 3A.

Should Able buy or lease?

12–14. The ABC Company can purchase a new data processing machine for $35,460 or rent it for four years at a cost of $10,000 per year. The estimated life is four years. The machine will result in a saving in clerical help of $11,000 compared to the present manual procedure. The corporation has a cost of capital of .10 and a cost of available debt of .05. The incremental tax rate is .52. Assume the .07 tax credit does not apply. The following analysis was prepared for the two alternatives:

			Year			
Buy:	0	1	2	3	4	Total
1. Outlay	−35,460					
2. Savings before tax		11,000	11,000	11,000	11,000	
3. Depreciation*		17,730	8,865	4,432	4,432	
4. Taxable income (2–3)		(6,730)	2,135	6,568	6,568	
5. Tax on savings (.52 of Income)		(3,500)	1,110	3,415	3,415	
6. Net cash flow (2–5)		14,500	9,890	7,585	7,585	
7. Present value factors (using .10)		.9091	.8264	.7513	.6830	
8. Present values (6 × 7)	−35,460	13,182	8,173	5,699	5,181	−3,225

* Assume the depreciation of each year for tax purposes is computed, using the twice straight-line method of depreciation.

		Year		
Lease:	0	1	2	3	4
Gross savings		11,000	11,000	11,000	11,000
Lease payments		−10,000	−10,000	−10,000	−10,000
Savings before taxes		1,000	1,000	1,000	1,000
Income tax		520	520	520	520
Net savings		480	480	480	480

"Buy" was rejected since the net present value was minus $3,225. The lease alternative was accepted since the present value of the savings is positive for any positive rate of discount.

Required: Comment on the decision to lease. Prepare a report for the president of your firm on the relative merits of leasing and buying of depreciable assets and land.

But no one has ever won contemporary acclaim as a hero for wise economy and rationality, nor is his name celebrated in history books or attached to magnificent dams—our modern equivalent of pyramids.

—J. Hirshleifer, J. C. DeHaven, J. W. Milliman, *Water Supply, Economics, Technology, and Policy.* (The Rand Corporation, The University of Chicago Press, 1960), pp. V–VI.

13

A MANUAL

FOR ANALYZING

INVESTMENT DECISIONS

This chapter is written in the form of a manual. Its objective is to explain in detail some of the computations necessary to analyze investment proposals when the present-value method is used. No attempt is made to explain the theory behind the computations at this point. An attempt is made to give flexible procedures applicable to a wide range of situations.

The manual is aimed at developing skill in the preparation of forms to be prepared or used by three different groups within the organization. In the first group are the sponsors of the project, the persons who are most familiar with what makes the project desirable and how it will operate. In the second group are the staff men who must summarize the information obtained from the sponsors. The third group is top management, who must appraise and make the final investment decisions, using the information prepared for them as well as their experience and intuitive judgment.

This manual focuses attention on the quantitative aspects of the investment decision, but it also allows for the presentation of descriptive material which tells in detail the pros and cons of different investment opportunities. It should be recognized that each computation requires certain assumptions about such things as the future level of general business activity, actions of competitors, costs of factors of

236

production, and sales forecasts. Since there is a large amount of uncertainty connected with each of these factors, it should be appreciated that the resulting computations are, at best, only indications of future operating results.

The authors recognize that it is not possible to devise one set of forms that will be fully satisfactory to every company. The forms presented here are designed to illustrate the main calculations that would be desirable for an analysis of the cash flows that may result from an investment proposal. It is hoped that they will be useful in clarifying the application of the material discussed in earlier chapters and that they will provide a starting point from which a firm unfamiliar with the cash flow method of analyzing investments may proceed in devising administrative practices suitable for its special needs and its particular organizational structure.

The reader will remember that in Chapter 6 we introduced the distinction between absolute and relative cash flows. Absolute cash flows result when cash flows from a given alternative are compared with zero cash flows. Relative cash flows result when we record the difference between the (absolute) cash flows resulting from one alternative and the (absolute) cash flows resulting from a second alternative. The forms presented here can be used directly to compute absolute cash flows or to summarize the results of a relative cash flow comparison. When the figures recorded are relative cash flows, it will ordinarily be necessary to use supplementary work sheets to perform the calculations. Some companies may prefer to have forms that allow space for at least two alternatives and also the difference in cash flows between the two alternatives. The forms suggested here can easily be revised to permit this procedure if it seems desirable.

THE CAPITAL APPROPRIATIONS REQUEST (FORM A)

Suggestions from operating personnel on such problems as how to improve processes, replacement of equipment, and possible new products are, of course, desirable. The procedure described here attempts to ensure that all desirable suggestions are properly reviewed by higher levels of management and are given appropriate consideration.

The sponsor of an investment project (outlays of over $5,000 for plant, equipment, or other out-of-the-ordinary items may be classified as investment projects) should prepare form A and the necessary

Form A

Capital Appropriations Request Form

Plant or division: Date:

Proposal: Code No.: _____

A. DESCRIPTION AND JUSTIFICATION SUMMARY:

B. RISK ANALYSIS SUMMARY:

C. CASH FLOW SUMMARY:
   Outlays are bracketed.   Estimated
                                              life: _____   Yield: _____

Period	Dollars	Most probable outcome	
		Present values	
		Borrowing rate _____%	Cost of capital _____%
Total life			
Year 1			
Year 2			
Year 3			
Year 4			
Year 5			
Years 1–5			
Years 1–10			
Years 1–15			
Years 1–			

D. SUMMARY OF ECONOMIC MEASURES:
   1. Most probable present values using
      a. the after-tax borrowing rate (say 4%).
      b. the average cost of capital (say 10%).
   2. Rate of return (yield) _____.
   3. Cash payback period _____.

4. The effect on accounting income in years:
   1
   2
   3
5. Probability of the net present value being less than $0:
   a. Using a rate of discount of _____ the probability is _____.

Sponsor: _____ Prepared by _____
      (Name)   (Title)   (Name)   (Title)

Routing	Initials	Date	Routing	Initials	Date
Engineering			R & D		
Production			Accounting		
Sales			Div. manager		
Market research					

supporting material. Since these forms are the basis of the quantitative analysis, they must be carefully prepared. It is recognized that many of the items on the forms are estimates, but they should be reasonable estimates. If the project is accepted, the estimates made on the forms will be reappraised after several periods of operations to determine whether they set forth objectives possible of attainment.

Technical assistance for filling out the forms should be available for the sponsor of the project. Since a staff man will have to process the data, it is desirable that contact be made with the Capital Budget Department early in the planning. A staff man should be assigned to assist in the preparation of the forms, to ensure that the data are ready for processing and that all alternatives have been considered. At the time the staff man is assigned to the project, a code number should be selected for the investment project so that references and files of information for the numerous investment projects can be easily identified and coordinated.

EXPLANATIONS

A. *Description and Justification Summary.* This should give a brief statement of the nature of the project and of the type of benefits expected. For example: The purpose of this project is to replace a milling machine with a newer version in order to reduce labor costs per unit processed and to reduce the percentage of defective pieces. An incidental benefit is that there will be a 10% increase in capacity for this operation, but this benefit has not been quantified in the cash flow analysis.

B. *Risk Analysis Summary.*   The purpose of this section is to provide a basis for making a qualitative judgment of the risks to which the project is exposed. This may be done by describing under three main headings uncertain events which, if they occurred, would affect the value of the project to the company. The following classification of uncertain events might be used: (1) uncertain events whose occurrence would affect the cash flows of the project, but not the cash flows of other parts of the business; (2) uncertain events whose occurrence would affect the cash flows of the project and of other parts of the business in the same way; (3) uncertain events whose occurrence would have a favorable effect on the project but an unfavorable effect on the rest of the business (or an unfavorable effect on the project, but a favorable effect on the rest of the business).

C. *Cash Flow Summary.*   The table heading for this section assumes that the cash flow forecast will be based on the most probable outcome. If the forecast is actually made on this basis, the main assumptions about various uncertain contingencies should be explicitly described.

Frequently it will be desirable to prepare more than one cash flow estimate, or to prepare the estimate on a different basis than the most probable outcome. In some respects the expected cash flow would be preferable. The expected cash flow is calculated by taking the sum of each possible outcome weighted by its probability. The calculation is likely to be worth while when the most probable outcome is also the best (or the worst) outcome. When net present values of better and worse outcomes are approximately symetrically distributed around the most probable outcome, the latter can serve as a reasonable approximation to the expected outcome.

D. *Summary of Economic Measures.*

1. *Most probable present values.*   The lowest interest rate used represents the after-tax borrowing rate of the firm. The highest rate represents an estimate of the average cost of capital.

2. *Yield.*   The computation of the yield using the estimated cash flows gives the rate of interest for which the present value of the cash flows is equal to zero. The differences between the minimum accept-

able return and the yield gives one measure of the margin for error, i.e., the amount of risk.

3. *Cash payback period.* Used properly the payback of an investment is an indication of the amount of risk, and is useful information. As a supplemental tool it is constructive. Used as the primary means of making accept or reject decisions, it is misleading. The computation of the payback period requires that we compute the period of time that is required for the investor to recover his original investment.

4. *The effect on accounting income.* This is a measure that is computed by many companies. Management frequently wants to know the effect on income in the short run as well as the effect in the long run. The measure requires the preparation of pro-forma income statements.

Depreciation accounting becomes a crucial computation and component of the income computation. Unfortunately conventional methods of depreciation accounting (straight-line or accelerated depreciation) can make a slow-starting, long-lived investment seem less desirable than it actually is by loading the early years with excessive depreciation and start-up expenses. It should be remembered that these methods are merely accounting conventions and may not be correct accounting. However, the fact remains that the income statement will be affected by the accounting procedures, and management is interested in these effects.

5. *Probability of a loss.* The probability of the net present value being less than $0 (i.e., of there being an economic loss) is of interest, since this is the probability that the decision to accept will turn out to be incorrect.

There are sophisticated methods of computing this probability if we are given the probability distributions of the cash flows of each time period. This is too complex a procedure for this book; hence we shall resort to a subjective evaluation made by the expert most familiar with the task being proposed. This expert should supply the requested probability and explain why he believes it to be valid.

Space is provided in Form A to indicate the routing of the investment proposal from the original sponsor. The particular routing will, of course, vary from one organization to another. However, one of the main advantages of a systematic capital-budgeting procedure is that, with proper procedures, it provides a framework for the coordination of planning in this area. For example, consider a proposal sponsored by the production manager for acquiring a new machine that he thinks will result in cost saving and also in product improvements. An orderly routing of this proposal to the sales manager concerned will provide a routine mechanism for informing him of the proposed product improvement. To take full advantage of the possibilities provided by systematic capital budgeting, the sales manager should be encouraged to do more than merely note, initial, and forward the appropriation request. He should attach his own memorandum, indicating whether or not he agrees with the estimate of increased sales presented by the sponsor, and include any other pertinent comments. The opportunities for consultation provided by this mechanism will frequently result in further improvements in the character of the investments actually submitted to the final authority. In any case it will provide valuable information for top management in weighing the important intangible factors almost invariably associated with an investment proposal. Later on, it can be used in comparing actual experience and costs with those predicted. This discipline will induce the sponsors to be more honest and precise in their estimates, and there will be less likelihood of bargaining or overoptimism.

ESTIMATING CASH FLOWS FROM OPERATIONS (FORM A-1)

Section A

The sales figure should be the dollar value of sales expected to be recognized during the period under consideration. An adjustment for the timing of the actual collection of the cash receipts resulting from such sales is included by incorporating the change in Accounts Receivable under section C. If the product or products are partly substitutes for other products already produced by the company, an adjustment for the decline in cash proceeds resulting from the new product should be included under section D. The physical volume and price per unit underlying these calculations should also be included in a schedule.

Section B

In section B, the production cost estimates for each period should be those incurred for the *actual* rate of production expected during that period and *not* an estimated rate for the sales of the period. The actual rate of production during a period may be greater or less than the rate of sales, depending upon whether inventories are increasing or decreasing. An adjustment for the cash flows resulting from the tax effect of inventory change is included in section E of Form A-1.

Section B should include all costs incurred because of the investment that would have been avoided if the investment had not been undertaken. Any cost that will be incurred, whether or not the investment is undertaken, should be excluded from this section. The value of the alternative uses of any resource for which the cost is unavoidable is discussed in section D.

Section C

In section C, adjustments are made for changes in cash tied up in working capital (other than partly or completely processed inventories). The procedures used in estimating these items are the same as procedures used in preparing cash budgets.

The increase in working cash balances should be the amount estimated as necessary to support the operations resulting from the investment. Excess cash reserves should not be included.

Ordinarily, the items in this section will total to a positive amount (indicating a use of cash) during periods in which the rate of operations is increasing. They will also show negative amounts (indicating a release of cash) during periods when the rate of operations is declining. Similarly, in a period of steady operations, this total will approach zero.

Section D

Most investment proposals will have some effect on the sales, costs, and use of resources in other parts of the organization. Section D is an attempt to allow for such influences. All estimates of cash flows should be on an after-tax basis. Frequently it will be extremely difficult to arrive at a satisfactory basis for estimating the items in this section because they are often difficult to measure, and wide differences of opinion may exist as to the importance of individual items. An example would be a new product that could partly substitute for an existing product of the firm. If no agreement can be reached as to the degree of substitution, the item may be listed as an intangible. However, there may be general agreement that sales of the old prod-

Form A-1

Proposal: _____

Code No.: _____

Summary of Cash Flows from Operations

	Year 1	Year 2	Year 3	Year 4	Year 5	Year 6	Year 7	Year 8
	19___	19___	19___	19___	19___	19___	19___	19___

A. Sales: _____

B. Production expense (except depreciation) and other expenses:

    Direct labor
    Materials
    Indirect labor
    Other manufacturing overhead
    Sales and promotion
    Administrative
    Other (include any investment-type outlays that are expended for tax purposes in the period of outlay)

C. Increases (decreases) in current liabilities and nondepreciable assets (except finished inventory or work in process):

244

Increase in accounts receivable

Increase in inventory (supplies and raw material)

Increase in working cash balances

Increase in current payable (subtract an increase)

D. Adjustments for cash flows in other parts of the business resulting from project

Decrease in cash proceeds of other products

Cost of space utilized (cost of foregoing other uses)

Use of executive time

Other

E. Tax adjustments:

Increase in income taxes before allowing for depreciation (see Schedule E)

Tax savings from depreciation (subtract):

Outlays of cash (B + C + D + E)

F. After-tax cash flows from operations:

[A − (B + C + D + E)]

Form A-1

Schedule E:

Computation of Income Tax (without allowing for depreciation):

	Year 1 19__	Year 2 19__	Year 3 19__	Year 4 19__	Year 5 19__	Year 6 19__	Year 7 19__	Year 8 19__
Sales								
Deductions:								
Beginning inventory *								
Plus: Costs of production incurred †								
Total manufacturing costs								
Less: Ending inventory *								
Cost of goods sold								
Selling and promotion expenses								
Administrative expenses (directly associated with the project)								
Other								
Total deductions								
Amount subject to tax (sales less the total deductions)								
Increase in income taxes before allowing for depreciation (amount subject to tax times tax rate)								

---

* Includes work in process and finished goods.
† Excludes depreciation of the investment.

uct will decrease, although the amount of the decrease may be in doubt. When some agreement can be reached as to the direction of the effect, if not its size, it is usually wise to include an estimate of the minimal effect and to indicate in the intangible section of Form A that only a minimal estimate has been made and that there is disagreement as to the actual amount. In this case the estimate of the minimal decline in after-tax cash proceeds resulting from sales of the old product would be included under "Sales of other products."

Section E

Under section E, the item "increase in income taxes before allowing for depreciation" is computed and obtained from schedule E. The tax rate used in that schedule should be the tax rate expected to apply in that year. The tax rate is applied to the taxable income (excluding the depreciation deduction) expected to result as a result of the revenues and revenue deductions (associated with the investment) allowable for tax purposes. The tax section of the controller's department should be consulted in computing the taxable income to ensure that the assumptions made in preparing schedule E are consistent with the method which will actually be used in preparing the tax returns.

The method of computing the tax saving from depreciation is explained below. The amount is obtained from Form A-2 (*see* Page 251).

Section F

Section F gives the after-tax cash flows from operations that result because of the investment. It should be inserted in column 1 of Form A-3 (*see* Page 254) for further processing.

CHOOSING THE MOST PROFITABLE DEPRECIATION METHOD

There are actually two problems in connection with depreciation. First, there is the question of choosing the most desirable method of depreciation. Second, if an estimate of the cash flow from the investment in each year of its life is desired for Form A, the tax saving resulting from depreciation in each year must be estimated. Once the depreciation method has been chosen, the preparation of such estimates is a routine task.

The method of depreciation accounting that is most desirable for income tax purposes will depend on the firm's rate of discount, the life of the investment, and the salvage expected at the time the investment is scrapped.

If less salvage value than 10 per cent of cost is expected at the end of the asset's useful life, then the most advantageous depreciation method can be determined quickly by consulting the tables in the Appendix to this book. Table C shows the present value of the depreciation charge resulting from a $1.00 asset depreciated over *n* years when the rate of discount is *r* per cent per year, using the sum-of-the-years'-digits method of depreciation. Table D shows a corresponding set of values when the twice straight-line declining balance method of depreciation is used. It automatically allows for switching over to the straight-line method as soon as this becomes advantageous. To determine the most advantageous depreciation method for an asset, look up the values in each table under the column corresponding to the rate of discount being used and in the row corresponding to the life of the asset in years. The highest present value indicates the most advantageous method of depreciation. To determine the present value of the total tax savings, multiply the tabular value by the income tax rate (assuming no change in the rate is expected), and then multiply this product by the original book value of the asset in dollars.

If, in Form A, only the total present value of the investment is to be shown, then the steps described above will suffice. If it is desirable to show separately in Form A the cash flow in each year, then Form A-2 can be used. For this purpose only columns one, two, and three need to be filled in. The entry in column three can then be transferred to section E of Form A-1, on which the after-tax cash flows of each year are computed.

If the asset is expected to have positive net salvage value in its final year of life, Form A-2 is needed to determine the present value of the tax savings that will result from using the twice straight-line declining balance method of depreciation. All five columns must be filled in for this purpose. The present-value factor necessary for each year should be entered in column four from Table A. The sum of the values in column five give the present value of the tax savings for this method. This value must then be compared with the present value of the tax savings that would result from using the sum-of-the-years'-digits method. The latter can be obtained from Table C just as in the case when the expected salvage value is zero, except that the tabular value is multiplied by the tax rate and by the difference between the original cost and the expected salvage value. Again, the most advantageous depreciation method will be the one giving the, highest present value of tax savings.

In discussing the choice of depreciation methods, we have ignored the straight-line method because either one of the alternative methods will *always* be preferable to the straight-line method in the sense that either will always give a higher present value of tax savings for all rates of discount. If the straight-line method is used to reduce the clerical costs involved, the present value of the tax savings from this method can be easily estimated by multiplying the annual depreciation charge by the tax rate and by the present value of an annuity of $1.00 per year for *n* years, choosing *n* equal to the expected life of the asset in years.

In case the basic investment proposal is a complex one with more than one type of depreciable asset involved and with possible replacement of one or more assets required during the life of the operation, it is necessary to summarize the basic information relating to the depreciation of each separate asset.

COMPUTING THE ANNUAL DEPRECIATION CHARGES (FORM A-2)

Sum-of-the-Years'-Digits Method

The same general procedure is used whether or not the asset is expected to have a positive salvage value. Under the sum-of-the-years'-digits method, the depreciation charge will decrease each year by a constant absolute amount during the asset's life. The depreciation charge in the first year can be determined from the following formula, in which *n* represents the expected life of the asset, and *D* is the depreciable base (the original book value minus expected net salvage value).

$$\text{First year's depreciation charge} = \frac{2D}{n+1}$$

To determine the depreciation charge in any later year, subtract from the preceding year's depreciation charge the following amount:

$$\left(\begin{array}{c}\text{Amount to be subtracted to determine}\\ \text{next year's depreciation}\end{array}\right) = \frac{2D}{n(n+1)}$$

EXAMPLE

Compute the depreciation schedule for an investment with a life of five years and which costs $15,000, using the sum-of-the-years'-digits method.

The sum-of-the-years' digits is

$$1 + 2 + 3 + 4 + 5 = 15$$

The depreciation schedule is

Year 1	5/15 × 15,000 =	$ 5,000
2	4/15 × 15,000 =	4,000
3	3/15 × 15,000 =	3,000
4	2/15 × 15,000 =	2,000
5	1/15 × 15,000 =	1,000
		$15,000

Using the formula, the first year's depreciation charge is found to be

$$\frac{2D}{n+1} = \frac{2 \times 15,000}{5+1} = \frac{30,000}{6} = \$5,000$$

The amount to be substracted to determine the next year's depreciation is

$$\frac{2D}{n(n+1)} = \frac{2 \times 15,000}{5 \times 6} = \frac{30,000}{30} = \$1,000$$

The depreciation for the second year is $5,000 − 1,000, or $4,000; for the third year, $3,000; etc.

Twice Straight-line Declining Balance Method: No Salvage

When the twice straight-line declining balance method is used, the Internal Revenue Code allows the taxpayer to switch from this method to the straight-line method applied to the remaining book value and the remaining depreciable life. The switch should be made when the latter method is advantageous. The first step in computing the annual

Form A-2

Computation of Annual Tax Savings from Depreciation

Proposal:

Code No.: _____

Original cost of assets *_____ Expected salvage value _____

Expected life of assets _____ Depreciation method _____

Year	(1) Depreciation expense	(2) Tax rate	(3) Tax saving (1) × (2)	(4) Present value factor	(5) Present value of saving (3) × (4)

* If the outlays are to be made over several periods, attach a schedule showing the timing of the outlays.

depreciation charges by this method is to determine in what year it will be advantageous to switch over. This can be done by dividing the expected life in years of the asset by two, and adding one to the quotient. If the resulting number is an integer (whole number), it represents the year in which the switch takes place. If the resulting number is not an integer, the next largest integer is the year in which the switch takes place. For example, if the expected life is 20 years, the switch will take place in year 11, i.e., $(20/2) + 1 = 11$. If the expected life is 25 years, the switch will take place in the year 14, i.e., $(25/2) + 1 = 13.5$.

If the expected life is n years, the first year's depreciation charge will be $2/n$ times the cost of the investment. The next year's depreciation charge is the preceding year's charge times $[1 - (2/n)]$, up until the year of the switch. The depreciation charge in the switch year and all subsequent years is simply the book value at the beginning of the switch year divided by the number of years of life remaining.[1]

Twice Straight-line Declining Balance Method: With Salvage

Even though an asset has a positive expected salvage value, the first year's depreciation charge under this method is found by applying twice the straight-line rate to the book value of the asset (not the book value minus the expected salvage as in the straight-line or sum-of-the-year's digits methods). Therefore, for the first few years of life the depreciation charge under this method will be the same whether or not the asset is expected to have any salvage value. The computations proceed either until the book value of the asset is equal to the expected salvage value or until it is advantageous to switch over to the straight-line method. However, if a switch takes place, the annual depreciation charge must then be figured by dividing the number of years of life remaining into the difference between the book value at the time of switch and the expected salvage.

If an asset is expected to have a positive salvage value in excess of 10 per cent of cost, there is no simple formula that can be used to determine the year in which it will be advantageous to switch over from twice straight-line on the declining balance to straight-line. How-

[1] The book value at the beginning of any year, up to and including the year in which the switch takes place, can be determined easily from the depreciation charge in the preceding year by multiplying that charge by $[(n/2) - 1]$, where n is the original life of the asset in years.

ever, a switch, if it is ever advantageous, will occur no sooner with positive salvage of the asset than with a zero expected salvage. To determine whether a switch is advantageous, it is necessary to compute the depreciation charge both ways. But there is no need to try this comparison until the year $[(n/2) + 1]$ at least. If the book value of the asset has been reduced to salvage value, no further depreciation will be allowable.

SUMMARIZING THE CASH FLOW INFORMATION AND COMPUTING PRESENT VALUES (FORM A-3)

Form A-3 is provided for the purpose of summarizing all the information on cash flows, and also to allow space for computing the present value of these cash flows by years.

If the sum of the present values of the net cash flows (total of column 5 of Form A-3) is positive, this means that the investment has passed the test of the present value of cash flows. It promises to return a yield greater than the company's rate of discount, thus warranting further consideration, and therefore would ordinarily be recommended to top management. Important exceptions to this rule may arise in the case of mutually exclusive investments (Is there another way of accomplishing the same objective that will be even more profitable?) or in cases where the investment has important intangible disadvantages. Similarly, investments with negative present values would not ordinarily be recommended to top management, but exceptions may occur in cases where the investment had important intangible advantages.

Instructions for Using Form A-3

General: Indicate outflows of cash (cash outlays) by bracketing the corresponding figures.

Column (1): This column is filled in from line F of Form A-1.

Column (2): Information for this column is obtained from Form A-2. Check to be sure that outlays charged to expense have been included in the appropriate line of Form A-1. Also include outlays for assets which are non-depreciable.

Column (3): This is the algebraic sum of columns (1) and (2). Enter this column in the appropriate column of Form A.

Column (4): Copy present-value factors from the appropriate col-

Form A-3

Summary of Cash Flows and Computation of Present Values

Proposal:

Code No.: _____

Year	(1) Cash flows from operations	(2) Outlays for assets	(3) Net cash flows (1) + (2)	(4) Present-value factor	(5) Present-value of cash flows (3) × (4)

umn of Table A. The present value factor for immediate outlays is always 1.000.

Column (5): This column is computed as the product of columns (3) and (4). If the entry in column (3) is bracketed, the entry on the same row in column (5) should also be bracketed to indicate net cash outlays. This column should also be entered into the appropriate column of Form A.

AVOIDING ERRORS DUE TO IMPROPER COMPARISONS

Frequently the gains from making investments will be so large that no formal analysis is required to justify them. For example, a railroad must either replace a broken rail or abandon the line in which the broken rail occurs. The main danger to be avoided in analyzing such investments is the too-ready assumption that if only the present *necessary* investment is made, future cash flows will proceed indefinitely. If the investment is at all a borderline case, then what is required is a projection, not only of the present investment but also of the necessary additional investments that will be required in the future, thus making it possible to decide whether the whole series of these investments will be profitable. Otherwise, one may find oneself rebuilding an unprofitable road, rail by rail and tie by tie, with each small expenditure defended as absolutely necessary.

The sales and expenses estimates must always be on a comparative basis. That is, the estimates should attempt to measure the difference between what would occur if the investment under question were undertaken and if it were not undertaken. If the investment will reduce operating costs but not increase sales, then the appropriate entry for sales is zero. Similarly, if the investment will increase both sales and expenses, the amounts of increase of each should be estimated.

Since every estimate of cash flows involves an implied comparison, it is extremely important that a realistic situation be projected as the one likely to occur if the investment is not undertaken. The weakest professional football team would look good in a contest with an Ivy League college team, but no one would use the score of such a contest to judge the professional team's chances of winning the title in its own league. In the same way, an investment may look good if the cash flow analysis is made by comparing its performance against an absurd and unprofitable alternative. Thus, in deciding whether to replace a five-year-old truck now with a new truck, we should not make the comparison as though a decision against replacement meant that the old truck would be operated for another ten years. Similarly, if operating the old truck is unprofitable from the viewpoint that using a common carrier would be less expensive, a decision to replace the old truck with a new model should probably be supplemented by comparing the costs of the new model with the costs of using a common carrier as well as with the costs of continuing to operate the old truck.

Since it is frequently difficult to decide in advance what alternative to the present investment is "realistic," it is important in such situations to try to analyze simultaneously all the significant available alternatives. If all available alternatives are considered, the choice of an unrealistic alternative as the common standard will not bias the results. Thus, if both replacing the old truck with a new model and using a common carrier are compared with the alternative of continuing to operate the old truck, it may become clear that although buying a new truck may be preferable to continuing to operate the old one (that is, the present value of the cash outlays of the new truck will be less than those of the old truck), using a common carrier is better than buying the new truck (the present value of the cash outlays from using a common carrier is less than from buying a new truck).

Mutually exclusive investments are investments directly and adversely affecting the earning possibilities of each other (e.g., ten different models of furnaces being considered when only one furnace is needed). With investments of this type the appropriate forms should be prepared for each investment. The net cash flow for each investment should be obtained and listed. Form A-3 can be used for this purpose. The investment with the highest present value is the most desirable investment from the point of view of this one criterion. The best investment should be listed on Form A, but the fact that it is one of a set of mutually exclusive investments should be indicated. If top management wants to review the other possibilities, then the entire file of schedules should be presented with this form as a cover sheet.

QUESTIONS AND PROBLEMS

13–1. "To determine whether a contract is acceptable, discount the cash flows using the cost of capital." Is this reasonable if the contract is a debt contract? A lease contract?

13–2. Distinguish between determining the optimum sized plant and the optimum sized firm.

13–3. Is it better to build a small plant and work it intensively (with overtime and double time) or build a large plant and sometimes have idle capacity?

13–4. Is the plant which offers the highest rate of return the most desirable plant (in a set of mutually exclusive alternatives)?

13–5. Assume that a firm has two alternatives: (a) Plant A promises to earn a net present value of $10,000,000 with certainty (assume this is a cost-plus government contract). Instead of plant A we could build a larger plant. (b) Plant B may earn a net present value of $50,000,000 (this has a .5 probability) or it may have a negative net present value of $20,000,000 (this event also has a .5 probability).

Which of the two plants do *you* prefer? Assume your firm's yearly earnings have averaged $5,000,000 a year.

13–6. To make a new product, inventories must be increased by $5,000,000. Should this be considered a cash outlay?

13–7. Would you expect the relevant costs for decision making (such as the make or buy decision) to be higher or lower than the accounting costs computed on an absorption costing basis?

13–8. In making the bond refunding decision: (a) Should the present value of interest savings be computed using the cost of debt or the cost of capital? (b) How does the presence of discount on the bonds which are presently outstanding affect the bond refunding decision? (c) If the new debt will extend the maturity of the debt, how does this affect the bond refunding decision? (d) What are the uncertainties connected with the bond refunding decision?

13–9. The ABC Company has $10,000,000 of debt outstanding which pays .05 (i.e., $500,000) interest annually. The maturity date of the securities is 20 years from the present.

Assume that a new 20-year security could be issued which would yield .04 per year. The issue costs would be $800,000, and the call premium on redemption of the old bonds is $100,000.

Assume a zero tax rate for this company. The cost of capital of the firm is .10.

Required: Should the present bonds be refunded?

13–10. (see problem 13–9). How would your answer be modified if the maturity date of the new issue were 30 years instead of 20 years?

13–11. The BCD Company has $10,000,000 of debt outstanding which pays .06 annually. The maturity date of the securities is 20 years from the present.

Assume that new securities could be issued which would have the same maturity date. The issue costs of the new securities would be $2,700,000; there is no call premium on the present debt. Assume a zero tax rate.

Required: Determine the rate of interest or yield rate of new securities at which the firm would just break even if they refunded. Determine to the nearest per cent.

13–12. The National Money Company, in deciding on to make or to buy decisions, considers only direct labor and direct material as being relevant costs. The sum of these two cost factors is compared with the cost of purchasing the items, and a decision is made on this basis.

Required: Appraise the make or buy procedure of the National Money Company.

13–13. The Ithaca Manufacturing Company currently has excess capacity and is considering manufacturing a component part that is currently being purchased. The estimate of the cost of producing one unit of product is:

Direct labor	$2.00
Material	3.00
Variable overhead	1.00
Fixed overhead (based on accounting procedures of a generally accepted nature)	2.50
	$8.50

The average increase in net working capital which will be required if the item is produced internally is $50,000.

The firm uses 100,000 of the parts per year. The unit cost of purchasing the parts is $6.05. Assume a zero tax rate.

Required: Should the company make or buy?

13–14. The York State Electric Corporation has $100,000,000 of debentures outstanding which are currently paying interest of 5.5 per cent ($5,500,000) per year. The bonds mature in 24 years.

It would be possible to currently issue 30-year debentures of like characteristics which would yield 5.0 per cent. The firm considers its cost of capital to be 8.0 per cent. The marginal tax rate is .4.

The following analysis has been prepared:

Refunding Calculations

	Before taxes	After taxes
Cash Outlays		
Premium @ $50 per $1,000	$5,000,000	$3,000,000
Duplicate interest for 30-day Call period less interest received on principal @ 1.4% due to temporary investment	300,000	180,000
Refunding expense (80% of $250,000, total expense of new issue based on remaining life of old issue of 24 years)	200,000	120,000
Call expense:	50,000	30,000
Less: Tax saving due to immediate write-off of unamortized debt discount and expense		(20,000)
Total cash outlay of refunding		$3,310,000
Interest Calculations		
Annual interest—old issue @ 5.5%	$5,500,000	$3,300,000
Annual interest—new issue @ 5.0%	5,000,000	3,000,000
		300,000
Total after-tax interest—old issue—discounted @ 8.0% for 24 years * (PV = 10.5288)		34,700,000
Total after-tax interest—new issue—discounted @ 8.0% for 24 years (PV = 10.5288)		31,600,000
Total after-tax discounted interest savings resulting from refunding		$3,100,000
Total after-tax cash outlay of refunding		3,310,000
Net savings due to refunding at effective interest rate of 5%		$ (210,000)

* The remaining life of the old issue.

259

Required: Should the firm refund? Explain briefly.

13–15. The Bi-State Electric and Gas Corporation has $25,000,000 of debentures outstanding which are currently paying interest of 4.5 per cent ($1,125,000) per year. The bonds mature in 24 years.

It would be possible to currently issue 30-year debentures of like characteristics which would yield 4.0 per cent. The firm considers its cost of capital to be 8.0 per cent. The marginal tax rate is .50.

The following analysis has been prepared:

Cash Outlays

	Before taxes	After taxes
Premium @ $52 per $1,000	$1,300,000	$650,000
Duplicate interest for 30-day call period less interest received on principal @ 2% due to temporary investment	54,000	27,000
Refunding expense (80% of $220,000 total expense of new issue based on remaining life of old issue of 24 years)	176,000	88,000
Call expense:	25,000	12,500
Less: Tax saving due to immediate write-off of unamortized debt discount and expense		−18,000
		$759,500

Required: Should the firm refund? Explain.

13–16. The XYZ Company wants to know the cost of a new building it has constructed. It paid the builder an advance of $2,000,000 and paid the remainder when the building was completed two years later (total amount paid to the builder was $3,000,000). (a) Determine the cost assuming the building was financed with .05 debentures. (b) Determine the cost assuming the building was financed entirely by stock.

13–17. The company has an investment opportunity that offers $1,000,000 of cash flows a year for perpetuity. It requires a cash outlay of $19,600,000 for plant and equipment and the necessary inventory. It is estimated that an additional $500,000 of cash will have to be carried as a compensating balance during the period of the investment. The company has a time value of money of .05.

Required: Is the investment acceptable?

13–18. The Allen Company is faced with the decision whether to buy or rent data processing equipment. The initial outlay for the equipment is $380,000 if purchased. The rentals are $100,000 per year and are cancellable on one month's notice by the Allen Company. Similar service contracts may be obtained if the equipment is purchased or rented.

The time value of money is 10 per cent. The income tax rate is zero.

The best estimate of service life is five years, but an analysis of the life of equipment of a similar nature indicates that the life may be as follows:

Year	Probability (%)
1	0
2	1
3	2
4	25
5	40
6	30
7	2
8	0

Required: Should the equipment be purchased or rented?

13–19. High Voltage Electric Company has $10,000,000 of debt outstanding which pays 7 per cent interest annually. The maturity date of the securities is 15 years from the present. There are $100,000 of bond issue costs and $200,000 of bond discount currently on the books.

Assume a 15-year debt security could be issued which would yield 6 per cent annually. The issue costs on the new issue would be $300,000, and the call premium on the old issue would be $500,000. (a) The company has a 10 per cent cost of captial. Assuming a zero tax rate, should the old bonds be replaced with new securities? (b) Assuming a discount rate of 7 per cent, what would be your answer?

13–20. Referring to problem 13–19, how would your answer be affected by the possibility of interest rates decreasing in the future and the new bonds being issued for a 30-year period?

13–21. The Giant Motor Car Company is considering the size of plant which would be most desirable for its next assembly plant. We shall assume that there are the following two alternatives:

	Large plant	Small plant
Initial costs	$20,000,000	$4,000,000
Out-of-pocket cost savings per year, assuming the assembly of different numbers of cars per year:		
100,000 cars		1,000,000
200,000 cars	...	...
300,000 cars	2,000,000	
400,000 cars	4,000,000	

A forecast of car sales indicates the following demand for automobiles assembled in this plant:

First year after completion of the plant............100,000 cars
Second year after completion of the plant.........200,000
Third year after completion of the plant...........200,000
Fourth year after completion of the plant..........300,000
Fifth year and thereafter for the expected life
of the plant of 20 years.....................400,000

The company has a cost of money of 10 per cent. For purposes of this problem assume an income tax rate of zero.

Required: Which one of the two plants is the more desirable?

13–22. An investment costs $14,059 and has expected cash flows of

0	1	2
−14,059	10,000	5,000

The time value of money of the firm is .05. Management wants a system for reappraising capital budgeting decisions. (a) Assuming that the accounting measures of expense (except for depreciation)

and revenues would be the same as the preceding, prepare statements of income and return on investment that would be reasonable tools for reappraisal of the decisions. (b) Assume that the cash flows just indicated apply, but the accounting measure of net revenue in period 1 is $14,762. What is the depreciation of periods 1 and 2?

Without development there is no profit, without profit no development.

—Joseph A. Schumpeter, *Theory of Economic Development.* (Harvard University Press, Cambridge, Mass., 1934), p. 154.

14

EVALUATING PRIVATE INVESTMENT PROPOSALS: A NATIONAL ECONOMIC POINT OF VIEW

In the other chapters in this book we have been concerned with methods of evaluating the economic worth of proposed investment projects from the point of view of the managers or owners of a business. An investment proposal that appears desirable to the business that proposes it may be considered to be unattractive from the point of view of a government that tries to measure the investment's impact on the country. Similarly, a proposal that is unattractive to a business may be considered to be attractive to the government. The purpose of the present chapter is to introduce the reader to some of the differences between evaluating investment projects from a business point of view and from a national economic point of view.

Many executives in private business corporations will encounter situations in which to do their jobs effectively they must understand how investments are evaluated from a national economic point of view. In many countries it is necessary to obtain government approval before an important business investment can be undertaken. This is particularly likely in some of the less developed countries of the world, but it is by no means limited to such countries. A businessman contemplating an investment in such a country must be prepared to justify his investment not only to his board of directors but to officials from a finance ministry or a government planning office. These officials will be more interested in the cost and benefits from a national point of view than in the profitability to the corporation. However, many principles of economic analysis relevant to evaluating investments from the point of view of the owners are also relevant to evaluating investments from a national economic viewpoint.

Most businessmen would want to give some attention to the effects an investment might have on groups other than the owners of the business proposing it. In recent years, for example, American businessmen have been called upon to cooperate in helping to solve the balance of payments problems of the United States. It is not difficult to cite examples in which business investments that were economic from the point of view of the business organization proposing them were opposed by others because of water pollution, air pollution, or detrimental effects on scenic values.

The primary considerations to be incorporated in an evaluation of investments from a national economic point of view are

a. How large are the net benefits that would be derived from the proposed investment?
b. Who would receive the benefits?
c. By what means would the benefits become available to the recipients?

The first question refers to matters of economic efficiency. The second refers to matters of income distribution. The relevance of these two questions should be fairly clear. The relevance of the third question may be less apparent. The means by which benefits are distributed to a group may influence the satisfaction they derive from the benefits. It seems likely, for example, that both American farmers, and countries that derive foreign exchange from exports of basic commodities, would prefer an increase in income resulting from a higher price for the commodities they sell, to an equal increase in income in the form of a grant that has the characteristics of an unearned gift.

Although in principle the answers to all three questions are relevant to deciding on the value of a proposed investment, we will concentrate in this chapter on the computations that must be made in order to measure the size of the net benefits.

In the following discussion we will assume that we begin with an investment proposal that has already been analyzed from the point of view of its profitability to the owners of the business using the procedures suggested earlier in this book. The process of adjusting this analysis to a national economic point of view can be thought of as consisting of three basic steps.

In evaluating investments a businessman uses market prices to estimate the relevant cash flows. However, for a variety of reasons, market prices may not reflect opportunity costs of resources used, or the opportunity value of the production. Whenever there is a systematic and material difference between the market price and these opportunity prices, the latter should be substituted for corresponding market prices. This substitution would be applicable to most investments, and its materiality would be particularly important in developing countries where the importance of investment decisions is magnified because of the crucial need for investments.

A second type of adjustment is necessary when an investment is so large relative to the markets in which its factors of production will be purchased, or in which its products will be sold, that acceptance of the investment will appreciably change the relevant market price or opportunity price of one or more of the resources used or produced. When this is the case, neither the market nor opportunity prices that would have prevailed without the project, nor the prices with the project, will exactly measure the benefits or costs of accepting the project. In these circumstances some price in between the price that would have prevailed without the project and the price that will prevail with it should be used.

Some investment projects will lead to changes in the efficiency of other economic activities in the society. Such changes in efficiency may be beneficial or detrimental. In either case, it is desirable to take them into account when evaluating the economic worth of investments from a national point of view.

The following sections discuss each of the preceding adjustments in some detail.

DISCREPANCIES BETWEEN MARKET PRICES AND OPPORTUNITY PRICES

The opportunity price or cost of a resource is the value of the resource used in its most valuable manner. In a competitive market there is a strong tendency for market prices to represent opportunity prices. Customers will tend to purchase additional units of a product whenever the value of the product to them is more than the price.

Similarly, producers will tend to produce an additional unit whenever the price of an additional unit is greater than the extra cost of producing it (where cost is the opportunity cost of the factors of production). In equilibrium, under these conditions, the price of a commodity will measure both the value of an additional unit to customers and the incremental cost of producing it.

Monopoly Pricing

When a commodity is being produced under monopolistic (or oligopolistic) conditions market prices are likely to differ from opportunity prices. A firm in a monopolistic position will find that it can increase its profits by pricing its products at something more than the extra cost of producing an additional unit. The market price will represent the marginal value of the commodity to the user but not generally the cost of producing an additional unit.

If an investment proposal involves using factors of production purchased from a monopolistic firm, a better measure of the cost of the project, from a national economic point of view, can be obtained by substituting an estimate of the marginal cost of the products for the actual market prices.

Unemployed Resources

If in the absence of the project a resource would be unemployed, and if the resource cannot be stored, then the appropriate opportunity price for using that resource in the project may be zero. In underdeveloped countries frequently there are considerable unemployment and underemployment of resources, particularly unskilled labor. If a person who would otherwise be unemployed is put to work as a result of a new investment project, the wages he will be paid may considerably overstate the true opportunity cost of using him in this particular project. In fact, the opportunity to work may have a positive value taking into consideration the morale of the unemployed workers. With some particularly unpleasant or dangerous work the opportunity price may be greater than zero. More importantly, if labor must be induced to move from one location to another or be retrained, there may be some significant opportunity costs in employing the labor even if the alternative would be to leave it unemployed. In addition to the direct cost of moving the workers there may be

costs associated with providing housing, schools, and various government facilities for the additional population at the new location. These
are costs that might be avoided if the workers remained in their old
location. Even allowing for such costs the market wage rates are likely
to overestimate the opportunity cost of unskilled labor in countries
where there is chronic unemployment.

Foreign Exchange Shortages

So far we have considered cases where the market price for using
a resource was higher than its opportunity price. There are also important cases where the market price is liable to be less than the
opportunity cost of employing a resource. An important example
involves the use of imported goods or services. The official exchange
rate may not properly measure the opportunity price of foreign exchange. If a businessman imports a commodity, the price he pays is
likely to be the world market price converted to domestic prices at
the official exchange rate. The opportunity cost for foreign exchange
is a better estimate of the cost to the country of using foreign exchange in this way. Some projects may produce goods for export. The
value of a foreign exchange earned by the exports may be under-
estimated when the official exchange rate is used. The investment
project may produce goods that are not exported but are substitutes
for imported goods. Such goods may save foreign exchange by reducing the amount that would have otherwise been imported. Again
the value of the foreign exchange saving should be estimated by using
an opportunity price for an exchange rate to compute the value of
the imports rather than the official exchange rate.

Savings vs. Consumption

Ordinarily in attempting to evaluate an investment project we
measure the extra income (the benefits less the costs) that would
be generated by the project, but we do not concern ourselves with
how this income would be used. A justification for stopping with a
measure of income is that if the recipients are free to allocate income
in any manner they desire, the opportunity value of an additional
dollar used for savings will have the same value as an additional dollar
used for consumption. In some less developed countries this assumption may not be valid at the national level. If the country's economic

development is inhibited by low levels of savings and investment, an increment of income saved and invested may be of greater value in promoting the economic interests of the country than an increment of income used for current consumption. In these circumstances it might be desirable to go beyond simply measuring the income generated by a project and to attempt to estimate how that income is likely to be used. The proportion of income that goes into savings may be given more weight than the proportion going into current consumption. The additional value attached to income that is saved and is reinvested can be thought of as an opportunity price for savings.

Taxes

A major difference between the way investments would be evaluated from the point of view of the businessman and from the point of view of a national economy is related to the treatment of taxes. The businessman will be concerned only with the after-tax cash flows associated with the investment. This is correct from the national point of view if the taxes are really prices charged for services rendered to the business by government bodies. Examples are tax assessments covering services such as water, sewage, police, and fire protection. Such taxes need to be deducted, but they may require adjustment, as it is unlikely that they reflect the additional cost of providing the additional services used as a result of the investment. Expenditures reflecting the costs of providing such services are a proper deduction from the benefits of an investment from the national economic point of view.

Most tax payments, however, cannot usefully be thought of as payments for identifiable quantities of services rendered a particular business. A large fraction of taxes collected in any country is likely to be used for such things as health, education, and national defense (or paying for past wars). A business may benefit from such services in a general way, but there is not likely to be an identifiable relationship between the amount of taxes paid by the business and the amount of benefit received. Because this is the case, from the national economic point of view, the costs and benefits of an investment should be analyzed on a before-tax basis.

We have previously mentioned that if a country's ability to achieve its economic goals is inhibited because savings are too low to finance the desired level of investment, it may be reasonable to attach a high opportunity price to that portion of the project's income that is channeled into savings. Government savings might be used to finance either its own investment projects or those of the private sector. If a government devoted a proportion of its tax revenues to savings, and if political or administrative complications did not prevent the effective use of these savings, the extra tax revenues generated by a new investment project might have more value in contributing to the country's economic goals than the same amount of funds retained in the hands of consumers. This analysis suggests that an opportunity price may in some situations be assigned to government tax revenues. This will increase the measure of benefits associated with investments that generate tax revenues.

INDIVISIBILITIES

If a project is large relative to the markets of the country so that the operation of the project would change the market prices of one or more of the inputs purchased or of the products being produced, the net benefits of the project to a nation may not be properly measured using market prices. This may be true even where these market prices represent the opportunity costs of using the resources consumed in the project and the opportunity values of the resources produced. This special evaluation problem arises if for some technological reason the investment must be undertaken on at least a certain minimum scale, large enough so that some of the relevant prices would change as a result of building the project. There are many situations where a series of small incremental investments is not feasible technologically. A jet airport runway must be of a certain minimum size; a dam cannot stop halfway across a river; and a railroad must have at least one set of tracks preferably with reasonable starting and ending locations.

Suppose that a hydroelectric project results in a 25 per cent increase in electric output and that a 50 per cent reduction in the price of electricity would result in a sufficient expansion of the use of electricity to absorb this extra power. Even if the new price of electricity appropriately measures both the marginal cost of producing an extra unit of electricity and the marginal value of the extra unit in its various uses, the benefits of the investment cannot be measured in terms of revenues collected. Under the assumptions given, accepting the project would lead to a 37.5 per cent reduction in total revenues collected by the electric power generating system. If revenues were used as a measure of the benefits, one might conclude that the 25 per cent increase in output led to a reduction in total benefits.

One difficulty in this case arises because the price at which all the electricity is sold tells how much one more increment of electricity would be worth when added to the existing supply. In fact, the project added not one small increment to the supply but a very large increment. Consumers as a group would have been willing to pay

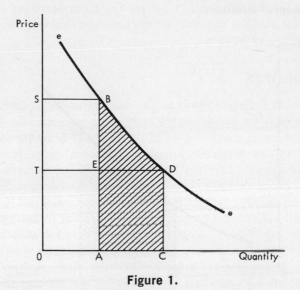

Figure 1.

more for the output of the project. The value of this additional increment, expressed as a price per unit, will be an amount somewhere between the market price that would have prevailed without the project and the market price that will prevail with it.

The appropriate measure of benefits in such cases is illustrated in Figure 1. The vertical axis measures the price per unit, and the horizontal axis measures the rate of consumption in kilowatts per year. The curve *ee* is a market demand curve for electricity. Each point on the curve shows the quantity people would purchase at the corresponding price. Suppose that without the project a quantity OA would be produced (the marginal cost is AB) and sold at a price of AB. The total revenue collected under these circumstances is measured by the rectangle OABS. With the project an additional quantity AC would be produced (with a marginal cost of CD). The market price will now be CD per unit. If all units are sold at that price, the total revenue collected with the new project would be measured by the rectangle OCDT. The additional amount that consumers are willing to pay for an increment of AC units of additional electricity, if the alternative were to do without this increment, is measured by the shaded area ACDB. It is this shaded area rather than the change in total revenues that properly measures the extra benefits from having this increment of electricity.

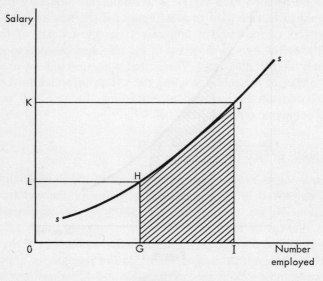

Figure 2.

It is still necessary to subtract from these benefits an appropriate measure of the extra costs of providing this electricity. A problem similar to the revenue calculation occurs if a new investment project would materially change the prices of some of the resource inputs used in the project. Figure 2 presents an example of this sort. Suppose that in a country with only one steel mill it is proposed to build a second steel mill. Both the old and the new steel mills will require metallurgists. With just one steel mill OG metallurgists would be employed in the old mill at a salary of GH. The curve *ss* represents the potential supply of metallurgists at various salary levels. With the new mill let us suppose that the total number who will be required in both the old and new mill increases by an amount GI (the exact amount of the increase will depend on the demand curve of the product). In order to increase the supply by this amount it will be necessary to pay a wage equal to IJ. The total wage bill for metallurgists with one steel mill is given by the area OGHL. The total wage bill for metallurgists with two steel mills is given by the area OIJK. However, the excess of the large area over the small area does not properly measure the extra costs to the country of obtaining the metallurgists required for the new mill. These extra costs are measured by the shaded area GIJH. The additional monetary payments that would in fact be paid to metallurgists if the new mill were built are transfers of income (in this case from the owners of the steel mill to the metallurgists) in excess of the minimum needed to increase the supply of metallurgists.[1] The actual wages would be used by a private owner of the mill, including the excess incentive to the workers; it should not be included in evaluating the new mill from the national economic point of view.

EXTERNAL EFFECTS

An investment project may adversely affect the productivity of resources employed in other economic activities or the welfare of the population. To the extent that such changes are compensated for through market or legal institutional arrangement, their effect will tend to be included in the private benefit-cost evaluation of the investment. If the institutional arrangements do not provide for appropriate monetary compensation, these effects should be taken into account by incorporating implicit costs or benefits in evaluating the investment.

Suppose a factory will produce a large amount of dirt and smoke. Consumers living where the dirt settles will spend more time dusting their furniture and more time and money cleaning clothes. In the absence of an appropriate tax on the factory that reduces its profit and compensates consumers for the additional expense and trouble, the smoke would be an uncompensated external diseconomy that should be taken into account in evaluating a project from the national point of view.

[1] For the minimum amount to take place a discriminatory wage system would have to be used.

In other cases an investment may directly affect the productivity of resources employed in other enterprises. If a farmer installs drainage tiles on his field, the productivity of some of his neighbors' fields receiving the runoff may also be increased. An oil company drilling a wildcat well on its own land may provide valuable information about the possibility of oil on adjacent land it does not control. Sometimes a drilling company is able to obtain compensation from its neighbors for the value of this information in the form of a payment toward the cost of the well, but generally there is no compensation for this type of information. A private utility may build a dam to generate electricity. An uncompensated effect of the dam might be to reduce the danger of flooding on downstream land. Unless it owned the land, the utility would not count this as a benefit derived from its investment. From the national point of view, decreased flood damage is a benefit attributable to the dam.

CONCLUSIONS

It is apparent that different analyses of the desirability of investments may be appropriate for managerial decision making and for decision making where the objective is to take the national economic point of view into consideration. We have suggested several adjustments that might be made to the analysis prepared by the business manager. These adjustments generally require subjective judgments by the analyst.

The business manager might wish for a laissez-faire attitude on the part of government and for the government planners to allow any investment deemed desirable by a person willing to bet his fame or fortune, but the institutional fact remains that in many countries the considerations described in this chapter are relevant.

It is obvious that the businessman should be aware of factors taken into consideration by the government planning organization when it attempts to decide whether or not a private investment project should be approved. In like manner the planning organization that is not aware of the factors considered by the business manager (or owner) in making his investment decision is at a severe disadvantage.

The discussion in this chapter of adjustments that could be made to investment project proposals to make them reflect the projects' effects on the national economy should not be interpreted as a recommendation by the authors that governments should institute controls over private investment activity. A full discussion of this issue is beyond the scope of this book, though some points might be mentioned. Market prices may imperfectly measure the national economic benefits of a project; but it does not follow that a system of investment controls would be preferable. Market prices have the advantage of being relatively objective; their use facilitates decentralized decision making and prompt adjustment to changed circumstances. At best, direct government controls have the disadvantage of adding to the time and expense needed to implement investment decisions. There is no guarantee that an attempt to estimate the national economic benefits of a project, requiring as it does a high level of analytical ability and a detailed knowledge of many sectors of the national economy, possibly influenced by political considerations, will in practice produce an estimate that is consistently closer to the true measure than the unadjusted private estimate.

QUESTIONS AND PROBLEMS

14–1. There are three purchasers of a product each willing to pay the following amounts for one unit per period:

Purchaser	Price they are willing to pay
A	$10 (for first unit)
A	8 (for second unit)
B	7
C	5

There are four suppliers each willing to supply one unit per period at the following prices or higher:

Supply	Price
W	$12
X	10
Y	9
Z	8 (for second unit)
Z	7 (for first unit)

Assume the preceding prices for the suppliers also represent their marginal costs.

Required: (a) At what price would you expect the product to sell, and how many units would you expect to be sold per period? (b) What maximum revenue would the purchasers of the product be willing to pay? At what total cost would the suppliers be willing to sell? (c) Assuming A sold for $18 two units it had purchased, what profit would it report? (d) From the point of view of the economy, what would be the change in position as a result of A buying and selling two units? (e) How much could a planner invest to make it possible for A to buy the two units?

14–2. A major investment project will employ 100,000 workers. Presently 40,000 of these workers are employed but the remainder are unemployed. Those that are employed are currently earning $20,000,000 per year; it is expected that they will earn $60,000,000 per year when the new project begins operation. The other workers will earn $30,000,000.

It will cost $2,000,000 to retrain the workers for their new jobs and $1,000,000 to move them to new living locations. The cost of new governmental and service facilities at their new location will be $10,000,000.

Required: Describe how the above information would be incorporated into the investment analysis from the point of view of the economy.

14–3. The exchange rate for a country is 2 yen for $1. A piece of equipment for an investment project will cost $100,000 or 200,000 yen. The country is short of dollars and wants to conserve its present supply. The planning board wants to choose between two alternative plans: (a) One suggestion is to use an effective exchange rate of 4 yen to $1. (b) Another suggestion is to use a higher discount rate for investments requiring the use of dollars than for investment just using domestic resources. For example, .08 could be used for the former and .04 for the latter. It is felt that there are current uses for dollars that will return, on a present value basis, $2 for every $1 invested.

Required: How would you evaluate the desirability of the equipment?

14–4. The country of Rajah has hired a firm of American consultants to decide on the desirability of a private corporation building a steel mill. The net annual benefits are computed to be $200,000,000 and $90,000,000 on an after-tax basis (the taxes are excise and income taxes). The consultants computed the present value using the $90,000,000 a year benefits.

Required: Comment on the computation of the annual benefits.

14–5. Assume that the appropriate time discount for money is 5 per cent on a before-tax basis and that the income tax rate is 40 per cent. An investment opportunity is available requiring an outlay of $10,000 in year 0 and producing proceeds of $10,500 in year 1.

Required: Compute the present value on a before-tax and after-tax basis.

14–6. The before-tax cash flows are the same as in 14–5, but the outlay of $10,000 in period 0 is chargeable to expense for tax purposes in period zero.

Required: Compute the before-tax and after-tax cash flows.

14–7. The Eastern University has been offered a foundation grant of $2,000,000 to establish a program in the administration of the arts. While the program has been judged to be acceptable from an academic point of view, the president of the university does not want to accept the grant if it will drain resources from ongoing programs.

The following analysis of the program costs has been prepared:

	Annual costs
Three professors of specialized interests	$ 60,000
Support of research personnel	40,000
Fringe benefits	9,000
Office space and other overhead	10,000
Student support	30,000
Administration	11,000
Overhead	20,000
Total	$180,000

Required: Should the president accept the grant?

14–8. The Airplane Company has a cost plus fixed fee contract with the Air Force to build super jet transports. The government will buy any additional equipment that is needed and that is justified on a cost-saving basis.

The incremental tax rate for the company is .4.

The company has computed the following labor saving for a new piece of equipment that costs $18,334:

Time period		
1	2	
$10,000	$10,000	before tax
6,000	6,000	after tax

The company has an after-tax time value of money of .05, and the federal government has a time value of money of .04.

Required: Should the equipment be purchased?

14–9. In 1963 the United States Steel Corporation completed for the United States government "A Techno-Economic Survey of a Proposed Integrated Steel Plant at Bokaro, Bihar State, India."

The following quotations are taken from the study:

> *Profitability*—Operations of the plant at Step I levels alone would be unprofitable even though operations are projected at full capacity following completion of start-up. . . . Each year of the projected period produces a cash deficit which reaches $270 million in 10 years or an average annual deficit of $27 million.

Presumably government of India loans will cover these deficits.

> Upon examination of the profitability of Bokaro it is evident that the heavy burden of excise duties and large interest payments on loans are the greatest influences on the results. Production costs on the other hand indicate that Bokaro could be a relatively low cost steel producer based upon the facilities proposed and the assumptions made with respect to raw materials, manpower and managerial control.

The projected Bokaro expansion in Step II to 2.5 million ingot tons, with operations beginning four years after start of Step I production, will result in profitable operations when close to 100 per cent of capacity is reached and will remain profitable thereafter.

> Since the government of India is assumed to own the mill, it is relevant to mention that during the 20-year period an estimated $1.0 billion of revenue would accrue to the government of India from the Bokaro operation, through excise duties on ingots, finished steel

products and coal chemical by-products. Income taxes paid by Bokaro would give the government an estimated $0.5 billion. In addition, the "surcharge," or difference between the retention price and selling price, would amount to about $1.2 billion during the same period and would accrue to the government.

The selling price is the price paid by a plant's customers, the retention price the amount it is permitted to keep. Both are set by the government.

Required: Discuss how the items described should affect the analysis of the Bokaro steel plant.

All hope abandon, ye who enter here.

—Dante Alighieri (1265–1321), *Divine Comedy, Inferno,* Canto III, Line 9. Translation from *Oxford Dictionary of Quotations,* 2nd ed., 1959. (Oxford University Press, Inc., New York).

Part III

INTRODUCTION

There are two chapters in Part III of this book, both dealing with the problems of investment decision making under conditions of uncertainty (introduced in Chapter 11 of Part II).

We have divided the book into three parts in order to highlight the different functions of the sections. Part I describes easily applied decision rules using the present value procedure. With conditions of certainty and no capital rationing, we are able to make, accept, or reject decisions involving independent investments or to choose the best of a set of mutually exclusive investments. In Part II we introduced a series of complications to which there are few completely satisfactory solutions, but we were able to suggest some reasonable approaches. A business decision maker could possibly read Part III and then despair of ever finding an easily applied rational approach to making investment decisions. We hope that the opposite will occur, namely that a knowledge of the complexities will lead to more reasonable procedures.

We think it is important that the decision maker understands all aspects of the investment decision, and realizes the limitations of the present value procedure as well as the advantages of this very useful tool for business decision making. The purpose of Part III is to insure that the reader is aware of situations in which it may be appropriate to supplement the simple decision rules of the present-value procedure.

"One would hope . . . that some day satisfactory solutions will be found to the pervasive and fundamental problem. At present, however, the problem of uncertainty is clouded by uncertainty."

—Robert Dorfman, *Design of Water Resource Systems,* A. Maass, *et al.* (Cambridge, Mass.: Harvard University Press, 1962), p. 158.

15

UNCERTAINTY AND INVESTMENT DECISION MAKING

If we could always assign to an investment a unique set of cash flows, in the absence of capital rationing it would be possible to use relatively simple, straightforward rules for making investment decisions that maximize the well-being of the stockholders in a firm. We shall use the terms *risk* or *uncertainty* to describe situations in which we cannot assign a unique set of cash flows to a particular investment project, that is, situations in which there are several conceivable outcomes of the investment. In practice, businessmen are seldom, if ever, certain of the cash flows likely to result from a particular investment. The existence of uncertainty complicates the job of the investment decision maker, and makes it difficult for us to offer the decision maker simple decision rules.

The present chapter has two limited goals. First, to discuss some basic concepts that are useful in thinking about the question of uncertainty; and second, to describe different ways in which the existence of uncertainty complicates the making of investment decisions. In Chapter 16 we shall turn to the question of how investment decision making can be adjusted to take uncertainty into consideration more adequately.

ATTITUDES TOWARD RISK

An important factor that must be taken into account when considering investment opportunities that are subject to uncertainty is attitudes toward risk. We shall discuss later the question of whose attitudes toward risk are relevant (for example, those of the decision makers, or those of the persons financing the investment). For the purpose of introducing some basic ideas about risk-preferences we shall make the somewhat oversimplified assumption that the decision maker will also be required to finance the investment himself.

To illustrate the problem let us suppose a potential investor has assets worth $5,000, all held in the form of a savings account earning 4 per cent. The investor considers that the probability is one that if he holds his assets in a savings account for one year, he will have an asset worth $5,200 one year from now. That is, he considers the savings account to be a riskless asset. Now suppose that he is faced with an investment opportunity that would require an immediate outlay of $5,000 and would return either $3,000 (with probability .2) or $10,000 (with probability .8) one year from now. If he accepts this opportunity, the expected cash flow one year from now will be $8,600 (that is, .2 × $3,000 + .8 × $10,000). The yield on this one-year investment will be 72 per cent, if we calculate the yield, using the expected cash flow of one year from now. This is an attractive yield by ordinary standards. However, we cannot use the yield to decide the acceptability of this investment for this potential investor. It is necessary to establish his attitudes toward risk before we can decide whether he should accept or reject the investment, if he must finance it with his own funds.

The reader may be tempted to say that a reasonable way to make the decision is to compare the certain cash flow of $5,200 that would be realized if the investor kept his money in a savings account with the average or expected cash flow of $8,600 if he accepts the investment. The difficulty with this approach is that it buries the fact that at the end of the year the investor will have $3,000 or $10,000 if he accepts the risky investment compared to his initial assets of $5,000. The question which our potential investor cannot avoid is whether the dissatisfactions associated with the possibility of having only $3,000 next year when he could have been sure of having $5,200, outweigh the satisfactions associated with the possibility that he may have $10,000.

The ability to make a decision under uncertainty depends on such comparisons, and requires knowledge of risk preferences or attitudes toward risk. Different investors might answer such questions differently, in which case we shall say that they have different risk preferences. And clearly the same investor may have different risk preferences at different times in his life or under different circumstances. Other investments already undertaken, his state of health, the number of persons dependent on him, and his chances of being unemployed next year are clearly factors that he will take into account in his decision.

It may be possible for an investor to describe objectively his risk preferences. Such a description is called a utility function. Just as subjective probabilities can be used to describe a person's attitude about the likelihood that some outcome will occur, so a utility function may describe his risk preferences.

A utility function assigns a number to each possible outcome of an uncertain event. The number assigned by a utility function can be interpreted as an index of the relative satisfaction the individual would derive if that outcome actually occurred. In Table 1 we illustrate a possible utility function for the potential investor in the above example. Column 1 in the table lists the possible outcomes that are involved in his choice measured in terms of net present value, and Column 2 lists the utilities he assigns to each possible outcome.

If the utility function accurately describes the investor's risk preferences, he will make the choice that provides the highest expected utility. This calculation for the risky investment is presented in Table 1. In Column 3 we list the probability of each outcome if the investor accepts either the bank account or the risky investment. In Column 4 we list the product of the probability of each outcome by its utility. The expected utilities or the sums of these products for the two alternatives are also given in Column 4. For the example given in this table a third party acting for the investor would choose the risky investment in preference to the certain outcome, because the former has a higher expected utility than the latter.

Suppose that we multiplied each of the utility numbers in Column 2 by some positive number. Would this change the decision? The answer is that it would not. If we multiply each utility number in

Column 2 by 3, the expected utility for the risky investment would become 540 and the expected utility for the riskless investment would become 450. But the ranking of the two alternatives, and therefore the decision, would not change. Similarly, if we add or subtract the same number to or from every utility value in Column 2, we will not change the decision. This means that two apparently different utility functions may actually describe the same risk preferences, just as the Fahrenheit and Centigrade scales both measure the same quantity,

Table 1. Computation of Expected Utility

Col. 1 Outcome: net present values *	Col. 2 Utility	Col. 3 Probability	Col. 4 Utility × Probability
Bank account:			
0	150	1.0	150
		Expected utility of bank account	150
Investment:			
(2,115)	100	.2	20
4,615	200	.8	160
		Expected utility of investment	180

* The analysis is made in terms of the net present values using a discount rate of 4 per cent. The present value of the bank account (treating the initial balance as an outlay) is $-\$5,000 + \$5,200$ (.9615) $= \$0$. With the risky investment the possible net present values are either $-\$5,000 + \$3,000$ (.9615) $= -\$2,115$, or $-\$5,000 + \$10,000$ (.9615) $= \$4,615$. The analysis could also have been carried out in terms of the possible terminal values, \$5,200, \$3,000, or \$10,000. The desirability of each outcome is the same whether we choose to measure it as a net present value or as a terminal value.

temperature. By a combination of adding and multiplying by appropriate constants, one can convert temperature readings from one of these scales to the other. In exactly the same way if one utility function can be derived from another by adding and multiplying by appropriate constants, then the two utility functions actually measure the same risk preferences.

It is reasonable to ask at this point whether a utility function can always be derived that describes a person's attitudes toward risk. Certain kinds of attitudes toward risk can in principle be described by a utility function of the sort we have been describing. Several authors have described axioms or sets of postulates that are sufficient conditions for the existence of a utility function. That is, if a person's attitudes toward alternatives satisfy certain conditions, then we know that his risk preferences can be described by a utility function.[1]

We have assumed that the outcomes may be described in terms of monetary consequences that are then translated into utility. It is possible other factors, such as the nature of the lottery, may be important to the decision maker. If a person enjoys being exposed to a certain kind of risk (say, because it makes him feel brave or clever), then his risk preferences are not described by the utility function. For example, a poker player might get more satisfaction from winning ten dollars in a poker game than from another activity, say a lottery, that gave him equal chances of gains or losses. Intangibles such as this may have to be brought into the analysis, possibly in a qualitative manner.

Presumably, in most business situations it is the possible monetary outcomes and their likelihood that are taken into account in analyzing risky decisions, and not the fun or excitement that may arise from being exposed to a risk of a specific nature, although such considerations may sometimes be relevant.

It is a convenience in terms of exposition to assume that risk preferences can be appropriately described by some utility function. We shall make this assumption throughout the remainder of our discussion. Whether or not this particular assumption is valid in the context of business decision making is not as important as the recognition that attitudes toward risk play a critical role in the process of making investment decisions under conditions of uncertainty.

UTILITY FUNCTIONS AND BUSINESS DECISION MAKING

There are several questions that can be raised about the use of an utility function as an aid in business decision making:

a. Can an individual's utility function be obtained?
b. Even if an individual's utility function can be obtained, can we obtain the utility function of a group?

[1] For a relatively simple explanation of these postulates and a proof that they are sufficient conditions for the existence of a utility function, the interested reader can consult William J. Baumol, *Economic Theory and Operations Analysis*, 2nd ed. (Englewood Cliffs, N.J.: Prentice-Hall, 1965), Chapter 22.

c. If we can obtain the utility function of a group, which group should be chosen for making the decisions of a corporation?

d. Is the use of a utility function inconsistent with wealth-maximizing objectives? What conditions are favorable for the use of a utility function, and when can wealth maximization be used without implicit or explicit consideration of utility?

Assuming that the preceding questions can be answered satisfactorily, there remains a question. Is the utility analysis an academic plaything, or is it a tool for the practical business decision maker? We argue that it is a practical tool either as an explicit procedure leading to a definite decision (accept if the utility of the investment is greater than the utility of $0), or as an implicit explanation of why the decision maker has to consider all possible events and not just the expected monetary value of an investment.

Utility and the Individual

There is relatively little difficulty in obtaining a utility function for an individual.[2] It is possible for the individual to misunderstand the questions being posed, or to be somewhat inconsistent if a large number of points are obtained for the utility function. However, the derived utility function should in a reasonable manner reflect the attitudes toward risk of the individual.

This utility function may in turn be used by a third party to make decisions involving risk for the individual whose function has been obtained. If the individual is making his own decisions, it is not necessary for him to determine his utility function. He knows better than us whether or not a particular investment is desirable, though we may be able to help him analyze the investment—for example, help him take time value into consideration. However, if we are required to make the decision without additional consultation with the individual, we are more likely to make the decision consistent with the individual's wishes if we have his utility function than if we did not know his utility function. For example, assume the individual has the opportunity to invest $4,000 and there are two possible outcomes with equal probability. He will receive $10,000 or $0 (that is, he will have $6,000 with probability .5 or lose $4,000 with probability .5). Each of us can make this type of decision for himself. However,

[2] See the last section of this chapter.

you cannot effectively make this decision for another person without knowing his attitudes toward risk—that is, knowing his utility function or at least his utility for an additional $6,000 and the utility of a decrease in wealth of $4,000. The expected monetary value of the gamble is a positive $1,000, but this may be a poor guide for action if the loss of $4,000 will cause the individual to lose his home.

Utility and Groups

The construction of a utility function for an individual is well grounded in economic theory. There is less agreement about the construction of a group utility function. It is agreed that we cannot just add the utility functions of each individual to obtain the group's utility function. One possibility would be to have the entire group answer the standard gambling questions posed to determine the utility function of an individual. The answers would depend on both the risk attitudes of the individuals making up the group and their bargaining and political power. Some of the group (in fact all) may be unhappy at the resulting utility function.

But it is not fair to blame utility theory for the fact that group decision making has some difficulties not associated with decision making by individuals. If the group is making its own decisions, rather than arguing about artificial standard gambles, then the group could argue about the actual business decisions. The decisions they reach will indicate the nature of the utility function of the group. Investigating a series of business decisions reached by the group would be one effective means of arriving at a utility function for the group.[3]

If the group is actively making decisions, we do not have to determine its utility function. The appropriate attitudes toward the risk are being applied directly in the decision process. As with individuals, the use of a utility function and formal analysis become important when the decision making (a selection of investments) is delegated to another person or group.

It may be that we can substitute an alternative procedure for the utility analysis. The group may describe the type of investments that are acceptable to it. For example, it may specify the requirement of

[3] One difficulty would be the fact that if the investments were relatively large, the undertaking of the investments in the past could influence the attitudes of the group toward undertaking additional investments of the same amount of risk. The utility function of income is a conditional function and will change as decisions are made and as results of decisions are made known.

a positive present value and no more than a .10 probability of losing $1,000,000 or more. Other conditions would have to be specified, including the interaction with other investments, but the point is that a surrogate can be obtained for a utility function. There are alternative ways that we can attain much that the utility approach can accomplish, but this is not sufficient reason to reject the use of utility analysis.

WHOSE ATTITUDES?

The point has been made that under conditions of uncertainty, subjective attitudes toward risk-bearing should play an important role in investment policy. However, the issue of whose risk attitudes are relevant for a corporation remains. Any ongoing business affects the interests of a variety of groups, among them the owners, the managers, the workers, the customers, and the suppliers. These groups may consist of separate individuals or there may be considerable overlap. In a small family store or farm, the owners, the managers, and the workers may all be members of the same family. In such a case it is clearly the family's attitude toward risk that will be considered. In a large corporation, there is typically less overlap.

The traditional point of view is that where the owners are a distinct group, a business is run primarily in the interests of the owners, except insofar as their freedom to make decisions in their own interest has been limited by laws, custom, or by contractual arrangements with other interested parties.

In many business situations it is not sufficient to refer simply to the owners. For example, we might distinguish three subgroups. First, there may be those of the owners who exercise a controlling interest in the business. The controlling owners may own a majority of the shares, or they may have a minority interest but a larger block than any other organized group of shareholders. In addition to those who have a controlling interest, there may be a much larger group of persons who have an ownership interest in the business, but do not attempt or cannot effectively control. This latter group has an interest in the financial results insofar as they affect stockholders. Finally, the concept of owners might usefully be expanded, for some purposes, to include not only the present stockholders but also potential stockholders—in effect, the entire financial community. For example, some investment or financial policies that a firm considers might reduce the appeal of the stock to at least some of its present owners but at the same time increase the stock market value by making it more attractive to persons who are not currently owners.

If attitudes toward risk are to be considered in deciding what investments should be accepted, decision makers need a clear idea of whose attitudes toward risk are relevant and to what extent they should be considered. Suppose the group whose attitudes toward risk are relevant in selecting investments has been defined. There still remain important questions of how to implement the investment decision. One difficulty with the current procedures for making decisions under uncertainty is that where there are operating divisions it is likely that different criteria for evaluating (or incorporating) risk are being used. It may be that operating management is rejecting investments as being too risky that from the corporate standpoint would be very reasonable. One can imagine a credit officer of a bank rejecting a loan application, because of the risk, that from the point of view of the firm as a whole is a good investment. On the other hand, a second loan officer might be accepting loans that had too much risk from the point of view of the corporation. The element of personal judgment as to the likelihood of various events cannot be eliminated, but interpretation of the monetary consequences can at least be applied in a somewhat more consistent manner than is currently done.

It is suggested that a utility function be obtained from individuals to be used by other individuals managing the corporation. The fact that persons rather than the corporate entity are used to obtain the function should not be surprising (the corporation entity is a fictional being existing only to satisfy the wants and needs of people). The utility function is by necessity subjective, because we are dealing with reactions to gains and losses. Rather than destroying the usefulness of the concept, the subjectivity of the measure enhances its usefulness. We can take the monetary measures of the outcomes and transform them into utility measures that incorporate our attitudes toward the possible events. Another dimension is added to the available information to be used for making the decision.

If the group whose risk attitudes the decision makers wish to take into account is a relatively small cohesive group with whom the decision makers can communicate directly (for example, if it were decided that investments should be selected in terms of the risk preferences of a small group of controlling stockholders or of an owner-manager or of the professional managers), the persons whose risk attitudes are relevant can be involved directly in the investment decision-making process. An attempt can be made to communicate the nature of the risk alternatives available and to obtain the reactions of the investors.

A second set of circumstances would obtain if it were decided that the relevant risk preferences were those of the present stockholders, but the stockholders are a large and diverse group with whom direct communication is not easily possible. Given present techniques we know of no one who has effectively implemented such an attempt.

A third possibility is that the relevant risk preferences would include those of all present or potential future owners. This is in some respects less difficult to implement than the second situation described. Assume that each stockholder has had ample opportunity to purchase the stock of other corporations (thus diversifying his portfolio, if he so wishes). In this situation, except for a very large investment that jeopardizes the existence of the firm or changes drastically its basic nature, it may be appropriate for the corporation to use the expected monetary value of the investment as the basis of the decision. The expected present value would be computed without taking risk into account. If the investment is a "fair" gamble (i.e., it has a positive monetary expectation), then the firm could follow a policy of accepting this investment. If the stockholder wanted less risk, he could change the risk characteristics of his investment by buying stocks of other companies. The use of such an investment policy implies that the stockholder is reasonably well informed as to the nature of the risks of the firms he is investing in.

If the controlling group whose risk preferences are to be taken into account is also in a position to provide the financing necessary to implement their preferences, then the risk preferences of the financial community as a whole need not be considered. The only question in this case is to determine what the controlling group's preferences are with respect to investment and financial policy (the market opportunities will influence these preferences). The situation is not much different when a relatively small amount of debt financing is required, since it will usually be possible to arrange small amounts of debt financing without severe restrictions on the controlling group's freedom of action.

Even when a firm is effectively controlled by some group that wishes to establish policies that reflect its own risk preferences, the response of the financial community will be relevant whenever a significant proportion of outside financing will be required, either immediately, or in the foreseeable future.

If there is no cohesive group of stockholders that seek to exercise a controlling interest, and if the managers of the firm attempt to operate it in the best interests of the stockholders, then the tastes and preferences of the financial community as a whole will be controlling. Among any large group of stockholders, there will be individuals whose interests and preferences conflict with those of other stockholders. Management cannot hope to satisfy every individual stockholder. Those who are dissatisfied will tend to exercise their privilege of selling their stockholdings. Management can best discharge its interests to a diverse group of stockholders by undertaking policies that tend to lead to the highest sustainable market value for the company's common stock.

UTILITY ANALYSIS AND WEALTH MAXIMIZING

The term *wealth maximizing* is an approximate description of a decision process that accepts investments that have a positive expected present value. The classic example used to disprove the use of the expected monetary value decision rule is the St. Petersburg paradox. A coin is tossed until the first head, the winnings being equal to 2^n where n is the number of tosses required. The expected value of this gamble is infinite, but most of us would pay very little, say $8, for the right to gamble.

Whether you consider the use of expected utility to be inconsistent with the objective of wealth maximizing depends on your interpretation of wealth maximization under condition of uncertainty. Say you could buy a lottery as described (the St. Petersburg paradox) for $100. The expected monetary value is positive, but the probability of winning more than the $100 is very low and the probability of losing is high. Are we serving the wealth-maximizing objective by accepting this type of gamble?

A difficulty with a wealth-maximizing objective is that it is not clearly defined under conditions of uncertainty, unless it is defined in terms of expected value. But we know that expected value may be a poor guide to action.

In certain situations the use of expected monetary value may be reasonable. Assume that a person of known repute approached you and proposed an investment that costs $1 and offers a payoff of $4 with .5 probability and a payoff of $0 with .5 probability (the expected monetary value of the investment is $1). Most of us would accept the investment. However, if the size of the investment were increased a millionfold, most of us would reject the investment. In the first situation the amounts are small, and we can easily absorb the possible loss. In the second case the amounts are large, and the possible loss could result in a mortgaging of our future for this and the next lifetime. With relatively small investments, essentially independent of other assets (both economically and statistically), and with a small variance of outcomes, the use of expected monetary value is a reasonable procedure. Some of the investments may turn out to be bad, but if the investments have positive net present values, and if they are small investments, without too large a probability of loss, then the use of expected monetary values may be a reasonable guide to action.

Now, let us consider a large investment. This may be a machine tool company of $200,000,000 asset size considering going into the automobile industry. In such a situation the use of expected monetary value may be misleading. If the investment does not turn out to be desirable, the entire future of the firm may be jeopardized. The distribution of possible events may be too spread out for the firm, despite a favorable expected value.

Essentially the same type of risk situation may develop with small investments if the investments are not statistically independent of each other. Consider a whole series of investments where each investment is $1, and we can undertake 1,000,000 of these investments. The payoffs are $4 and $0 with .5 probability. If the investments are independent, this is a very fine investment opportunity. If the investments are statistically dependent and we either win or lose on all 1,000,000 investments, the risk of a large loss is much larger, and we might steer clear of this investment.

No matter how large the firm, there is some investment opportunity that it would not want to consider on a straight expected monetary value basis. The analysis of risk (that is, incorporating the consequences of the outcomes) could be performed by a utility analysis or by some other means, but it must be recognized that we cannot inspect one number (say, the yield of the investment or the expected monetary value) to make an investment decision. It is necessary to consider all possible outcomes and the probabilities of these outcomes. One method of systematically accomplishing this is a utility analysis.

For giant corporations it is sometimes difficult to imagine an investment that we could not judge on a straight expected monetary value basis. But even for such corporations there are investments (or classes of investments) of such magnitude that they give rise to the likelihood of events that could be disastrous to the firm. Incorporating this information into the analysis, rather than just using the maximization of wealth (or the expected monetary value criteria), can be done by the use of a utility analysis. Assume that an investment has the characteristic of resulting in a doubling of income or reducing income to approximately zero. Should this type of investment decision be made on an expected value basis?

The expected value decision criterion may at times be consistent with the wealth-maximization objective, but several things should be noted. The consistency holds true only in the long run and assuming we can repeat the trial many times. We are dealing with averages, and there is very little chance that the average event will actually occur on any trial (there may be no chance). In some cases, following the expected monetary value criterion will lead to bankruptcy (that is, ruin) and end of the "game." The possibility of this unhappy event is always present, and it is reasonable that this should affect our decision process. The objective "maximize the wealth of the owners" ignores the fact that this is a maximization of an average amount. This is not a sufficient description of the objectives of the investor. The maximization goal is reasonable, but the things being maximized should not be expected monetary values, but rather expected utility.

THE INVESTMENT MARKET

Easy access to markets for securities greatly facilitates the risk analysis for investment decision makers of corporations that are owned by a large number of stockholders, none of whom have large percentages of their wealth in the securities of the firm. These stockholders can diversify their investments in order to obtain the amount of risk and expected return that they desire. If an investor with a total wealth of $500,000 has $1,000 invested in an oil company, the investment strategy of that corporation can do very little to jeopardize the wealth of the investor. Even a complete disaster would only reduce his wealth by .002. Assuming the investor has knowledge of the types of investments (and their risk) being undertaken by the firm, he could balance off his holdings in a risky firm by buying stock in a less risky firm or by buying government securities or by increasing the size of his savings account.

The ability of investors to diversify and pool risk is extremely important to the decision makers of a corporation. It means the corporation can undertake investments with positive expected net present values, even though they may have significant probabilities of unfavorable results. In general, we can conclude that, in the interests of stockholders, large corporations can accept fair investments—that is, investments with a positive expected net present value. An exception would be investments with a positive expected present value that we might reject because of an extremely large variance of outcomes and a large probability of loss (as with the St. Petersburg paradox).

EXAMPLE

The Airplane Company is considering investing $1,000,000,000 in a new supersonic transport. The plane is expected to either earn a net profit of $2,000,000,000 or be a complete loss (with each event having .5 probability). From the point of view of the corporation this may be thought to be too risky. Consider the individual investor who owns 10^{-7} (one ten-millionth) of the corporation. From his point of view the investment might stand to increase his wealth by approximately $200 or decrease it by $100. Looked at from this standpoint, the large size of the investment is reduced to manageable proportions.

The preceding analysis has indicated that investor diversification helps reduce the importance of the risk analysis, however, there are three important qualifications:

a. Not all investors in the corporation may have diversified portfolios; a risky decision may have a significant impact on the well-being of some of the stockholders.

b. Even with the stock widely held, the corporation may encounter investments that the individual investor would reject if given the opportunity to invest in a proportion of the investment equal to the proportion of his investment in the firm. This can occur when the variance of the outcomes is large and there is a large probability of undesirable outcomes.

c. The management, workers, and the communities where the major units of the firm are located, all have an interest in the well-being of the corporation, and they may not be able to diversify to the same extent as the stockholders.

These important qualifications all point in the direction of utility analysis, or some other formal incorporation of risk attitudes.

AN ILLUSTRATION

Implementing investment decisions with uncertain outcomes can be very complicated. We shall illustrate a procedure, using an artificial situation to make clear the basic steps. Assume that the time value of money is .05 and that we have been given the utility function of an individual. The following measures of utility for the different amounts of dollars apply:

Present value of dollar outcomes	Utility
−$ 500	−1,200
−100	−60
0	0
500	500
1,500	1,000
2,500	1,200

The investment is a two-period investment, with an immediate $500 outlay. At the end of the first period there is .5 probability of $0 and .5 probability of $1,050. At the end of the second period there is .8 probability of $0 and .2 probability of $2,205. The Tree Diagram (Figure 1, on page 298) shows the possible outcomes.

The expected present value is $400.

Event (in dollars)		Probability		Monetary expectation
$2,500	×	.10	=	250
500	×	.40	=	200
1,500	×	.10	=	150
−500	×	.40	=	−200
		Expected net present value		$400

We shall now substitute the utility measures for the dollar outcomes and compute the expected utility.

Event (in utility)	Probability of event	Expectation of utility
1,200	.10	120
500	.40	200
1,000	.10	100
−1,200	.40	−480
	Expected utility	−60

The expected utility is less than the utility of $0 and we would choose the action "do nothing" with zero utility compared to the choice "invest." The negative utility of a loss of $500 outweighs the expected consequences of the other events.

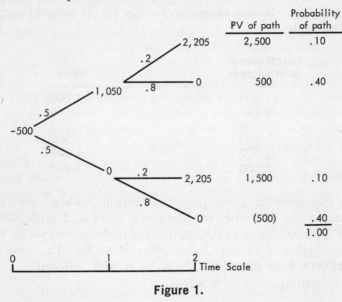

	PV of path	Probability of path
2,205	2,500	.10
0	500	.40
2,205	1,500	.10
0	(500)	.40
		1.00

Figure 1.

In Chapter 9 we introduced the concept of a risk premium. The utility function provides a means of calculating the amount of risk premium a decision maker would attach to a particular investment. In the preceding example the investment has an expected utility of −60. A certain loss of $100 also has a utility of −60. A dollar loss of −$100 is the certainty equivalent of the investment. The expected net present value of the investment is $400. The risk premium for any investment is the expected monetary value of the investment less the certainty equivalent of the investment. In this case the risk premium is $500 (400 − [−100]).

Using this approach to decision making, we go beyond the application of intuition as a means of weeding the list of eligible investments. Attitudes toward risk are systematically incorporated into the analysis, and the procedure leads to a decision that is consistent with the feelings of the decision maker about the likelihood of the possible outcomes and the effect of the outcomes on the investor's financial position. The analysis as presented does leave out the value of immediate information about the outcomes compared with having to wait two periods for the final outcome. In the example which was illustrated, the investment would be rejected even if we assumed that we knew the results immediately. Thus it does not make a difference that we did not incorporate the information factor. If the investment had been marginally acceptable based on the expected utility computation, then we would have had to incorporate a qualitative factor to take into account that we would have to wait two time periods before the final results are known.

In the above example we analyzed a situation in which there were four possible outcomes. Now assume there are a large number of possible outcomes (possibly an infinite number of outcomes). This change would only modify the mechanics.

In the following sections of this chapter we discuss three additional complications that arise and need to be considered when there is uncertainty about the cash flows that will be generated by an investment: (1) the portfolio problem; (2) the problem of information; (3) pooling of risk.

THE PORTFOLIO PROBLEM

The first complication has come to be called "the portfolio problem" because it is analogous to the problem faced by an individual whose investments take the form of purchasing securities in the stock and bond markets. Normally, an individual does not put all his money into the one best stock or bond. The disadvantage of concentrating investments is that if some unfavorable event occurs that affects the one stock he owns, it may have a drastic effect on the value of his investment.

The stock market investor typically attempts to divide his assets into stocks of a number of different companies. When this strategy is followed, an unfavorable event affecting the value of any one company will have relatively less effect on the value of his entire portfolio, since much of his investment will be unaffected by the occurrence of such an event.

The portfolio problem might be defined as the problem of choosing a collection of investments that, taken together, have relatively desirable characteristics. An analytical problem arises because the risk characteristics of a single stock taken by itself may be very different from the change in risk that occurs in a portfolio by acquiring some shares in that stock. The term "diversification" is often used to describe one strategy that is followed to solve this problem in the context of corporate investment opportunities.

As a means of describing the portfolio problem we present in Table 2 data on two investments, A and B. We assume that each of these investments would require an outlay of $1,000 and each could return one year later, either zero dollars, $1,200, or $2,400. In each

Table 2. **Subjective Probability Distributions of Returns from Two Investments**

Triggering events for A	Triggering events for B	Cash flow of period 1	Probability
e_1	e_4	$ 0	.10
e_2	e_5	$1,200	.80
e_3	e_6	$2,400	.10

case the probability of the smallest return is .1, the probability of the largest return is .1, and the probability of a return of $1,200 is .8. The investor is assumed to have a choice of either accepting investment A or investment B or both or rejecting both.

It might appear that the two investments are identical. However, this may not be the case. Assume that with investment A the cash flow of zero dollars would occur if event e_1 occurred. The return of $1,200 would occur if event e_2 occurred, and the return of $2,400 would occur if event e_3 occurred. We assume that e_1, e_2, and e_3 are mutually exclusive and exhaustive events. With investment B the returns depend on three different events, e_4, e_5, and e_6.

To evaluate the consequences of accepting both investments A and B we need additional information that has not yet been presented: the relationship between the events on which investment A depends and the events upon which investment B depends. We will examine possible extreme cases of the relationship between the series of events.

Case 1, the relationship illustrated in Table 3, is that in which the events that investment A depends on are statistically independent of the events upon which investment B depends. In this context the term "statistical independence" means that the probability of any particular outcome for investment A is the same regardless of what

Table 3. Joint Probability of Two Investments: Case 1

Investment B outcomes	Investment A outcomes			
	$0 e_1	$1,200 e_2	$2,400 e_3	
$ 0 e_4	.01	.08	.01	.10
$1,200 e_5	.08	.64	.08	.80
$2,400 e_6	.01	.08	.01	.10
	.10	.80	.10	1.00

the outcome is for investment B. The probabilities listed in the table show the probability that both the event described by the column head and the event described by the row stub will occur. For example, if the outcome of investment B is zero (that is, if e_4 has occurred), any of the three outcomes for investment A is possible and each is relatively as likely as if some other outcome for B had occurred.

To help understand the implications of statistical independence more clearly, divide each of the three probabilities in row one (.01, .08, .01) by the row total of (.10). For example, for row one, column one .01 ÷ .1 = .1. This is the conditional probability of event e_1, given that event e_4 has occurred. In symbolic terms, this conditional probability is expressed by $P(e_1|e_4)$. We can also compute the conditional probabilities given that e_5 and e_6 have occurred: [4]

[4] The general mathematical relationship being used is

$$P(X|Y) = \frac{P(X,Y)}{P(Y)}, \text{ where}$$

$P(Y)$ is the probability of event Y.

$P(X|Y)$ is the conditional probability of event X, given that event Y has occurred.

$P(X,Y)$ is the joint probability of X and Y, that is, the probability of events X and Y both occurring.

$$P(e_1|e_4) = \frac{.01}{.10} = .10$$

$$P(e_1|e_5) = \frac{.08}{.80} = .10$$

$$P(e_1|e_6) = \frac{.01}{.10} = .10$$

It should be noted that the probability of e_1 does not depend on the outcome of investment B. In like manner we could show that the outcomes of investment B are independent of the outcome of investment A.

The following decision tree (Figure 2) illustrates Case 1. Note that all the paths of investment B are independent of the path followed for investment A.

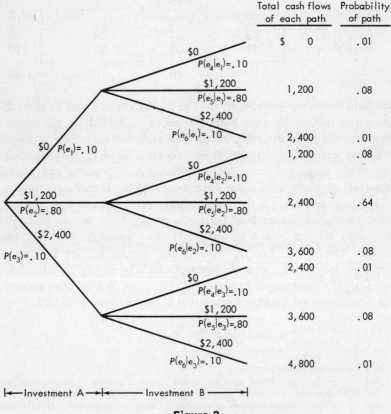

Figure 2.

Let X be any event that determines the outcome of one investment, and let Y be any event that determines the outcome of a second investment. If the events X and Y are statistically independent, then $P(X|Y) = P(X)$, i.e., the probability of the event X given that Y has occurred is equal to the probability of X. The probability of X is the same whether or not Y has occurred. If this relationship holds for every possible pair of events that determines the outcomes of the two investments, the two investments are statistically independent.

We can summarize the results of undertaking both investments by combining the events that have equal monetary outcomes. The expected monetary value is obtained by weighting each cash outcome by its probability and summing.

Col. 1 Cash flow	Col. 2 Probability of cash flow	Col. 3 Col. 1 × Col. 2
$ 0	.01	0
1,200	.16	192
2,400	.66	1,584
3,600	.16	576
4,800	.01	48
	Expected monetary value	2,400

In the second case, illustrated in Table 4 and Figure 3, it is assumed that there is a type of dependence between the returns of investment A and investment B. It is assumed that if event e_4 occurs (investment B has a return of zero dollars), we can be certain that

Table 4.   Joint Probability of Two Investments: Case 2

Investment B outcomes	Investment A outcomes			
	$0 e_1	$1,200 e_2	$2,400 e_3	
$ 0 e_4	.00	.00	.10	.10
$1,200 e_5	.00	.80	.00	.80
$2,400 e_6	.10	.00	.00	.10
	.10	.80	.10	1.00

event e_3 will have occurred (the return from investment A will be
$2,400). If event e_6 occurs (investment B's return is $2,400), then
we can be certain that e_1 will have occurred (investment A's return
is zero dollars). If event e_5 occurs, then we know event e_2 also has
occurred. In this second case, there is uncertainty about which events
may occur and about the returns from either investment taken by
itself. But if both investments are accepted, we can be certain that
the total return will be $2,400.

The decision tree for Case 2 (Figure 3) may be simplified by
leaving off those branches with zero probability. It is apparent that
the expected value of the investments in Case 2 is $2,400.

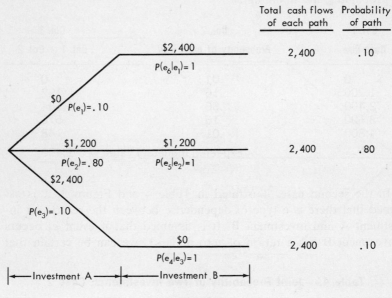

	Total cash flows of each path	Probability of path
$2,400 $P(e_6|e_1)=1$	2,400	.10
$1,200 $P(e_5|e_2)=1$	2,400	.80
$0 $P(e_4|e_3)=1$	2,400	.10

|←——Investment A——→|←——Investment B——→|

Figure 3.

The third case, illustrated in Table 5, is that in which the returns
from the two investments have a type of risk intensifying dependency.
Under these circumstances the occurrence of event e_1 ($0) guaran-
tees that e_4 ($0) will occur. If the return from one of the investments
is $1,200, the return from the other investment will also be $1,200.
Similarly, if the return from one of the investments is $2,400, the
return from the other will also be $2,400.

The decision tree for Case 3 is shown in Figure 4.

Table 5.   Joint Probability of Two Investments: Case 3

Investment B outcomes	Investment A outcomes			
	$0 e_1	$1,200 e_2	$2,400 e_3	
$ 0 e_4	.10	.00	.00	.10
$1,200 e_5	.00	.80	.00	.80
$2,400 e_6	.00	.00	.10	.10
	.10	.80	.10	1.00

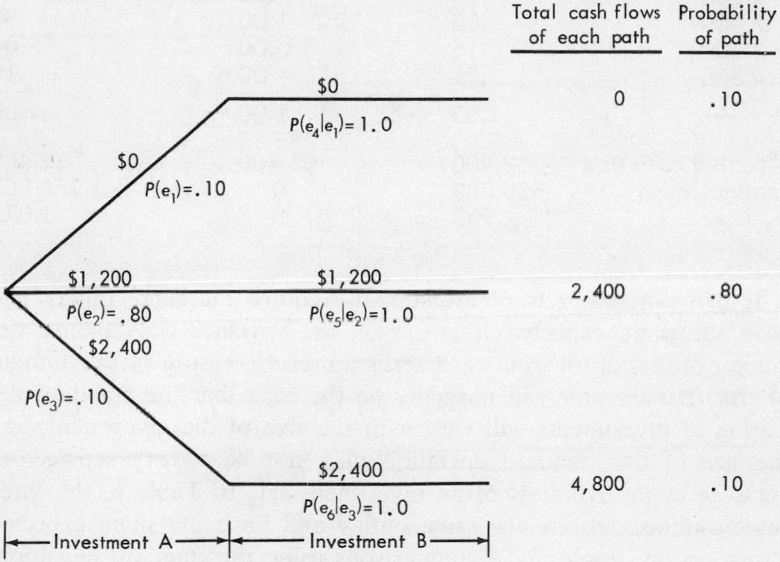

Figure 4.

In Table 6 all combinations of events that yield the same total cash flows are grouped together and the corresponding probabilities for each of the three cases described above are presented in a single table. At the bottom of Table 6 several summary measures are presented. The expected cash flow is computed by multiplying each flow by its corresponding probability and summing the products. The variance of the return is a measure of how much the flow varies around its expected or average value. Specifically, the variance is computed by squaring the difference between each possible flow and the expected cash flow, multiplying that amount by the corresponding probability, then summing the products. The standard deviation of the return is the square root of the variance.

Table 6. Summary of the Results of the Three Cases

Total cash flows	Probabilities		
	Case 1	Case 2	Case 3
$ 0	.01	.00	.10
1,200	.16	.00	.00
2,400	.66	1.00	.80
3,600	.16	.00	.00
4,800	.01	.00	.10
	1.00	1.00	1.00
Expected cash flow	$2,400	$2,400	$2,400
Variance (σ_R^2)	576,000	0	1,152,000
σ_R	759	0	1,073

If two different sets of investments require the same outlay and have the same expected return, then the variance or standard deviation of the return from each set is a useful measure of the amount of risk. However, it will normally be the case that the standard deviation of investments will vary with the size of the investment, and the size of the standard deviation may not be a very satisfactory measure of the riskiness of an investment set. In Table 6, the three cases outlined require the same outlay and have the same expected return, so one could make comparisons using the standard deviation. Case 2 has the least amount of risk associated with it; Case 3 has the greatest amount of risk (using σ_R as the measure of risk).

In practice, most events that tend to stimulate general business conditions will tend to increase the returns from most investments. Similarly, events that affect an entire industry, or all of the operations of a particular company, are likely to increase or decrease the returns of most projects in a particular company. These factors will tend to introduce a situation analogous to Case 3 between the returns of individual investment projects within a company.

THE TIME VALUE OF INFORMATION

We have devoted a considerable portion of this book to discussing the problem of how to compare investments that have different patterns of cash flows over time. Our conclusion is that if the cash flows are certain, the investments can be put on a comparable basis by taking the present value of the cash flows, using an appropriate interest rate. When the amounts and timing of the cash flows are uncertain, a similar but distinct problem arises for which there is no such simple solution. The problem is to determine how to allow for differences in the value of investments when the investments differ because uncertainties about the future cash flows are eliminated at different points in time. A simple example may help clarify the problem of the time value of information.

In Table 7, two lotteries are described. With lottery A there is a .50 probability of winning $100 and a .50 probability of winning

Table 7.

Lottery	Event	Probability	Period 0	Period 1	Present value of receipts
A	A_1	.5	$100	0	$100
	A_2	.5	0	0	0
B	B_1	.5	0	105	$100
	B_2	.5	0	0	0

nothing. If event A_1 occurs, then we win the lottery and the $100 winnings are received in period 0. If event A_2 occurs, then we win nothing in the lottery. Also assume that the appropriate default free rate of interest is 5% per period. With lottery B there is a .50 probability that event B_1 will occur, and if it does occur we will win $105, which will be received one period from now. If B_2 occurs, there are no winnings from this lottery. In terms of the present value of the receipts the lotteries are identical. In each case there is a .50 probability that the present value of the receipts will be $100 or zero. One might ask whether it is possible that a ticket in lottery A will be worth more than a ticket in lottery B?

To get further insight into an appropriate answer to this question we present in Table 8 two alternative joint probability distributions of these lottery incomes. Case 1 assumes that there is a perfect correlation between winning lottery B and winning lottery A. That is, even if we choose to buy a ticket in lottery B, we will know during period 1 from the outcome of lottery A whether or not we have won lottery B. However, even if we win lottery B, we will not actually receive payment until the next period.

Table 8. Alternative Joint Probability Distribution of Lottery Outcomes

Case 1: Outcomes perfectly correlated

	A_1	A_2	
B_1	.50	.00	.50
B_2	.00	.50	.50
	.50	.50	

Case 2: Outcomes independent

	.5	.5	
	A_1	A_2	
B_1	.25	.25	.50
B_2	.25	.25	.50
	.50	.50	

In Case 2 the outcomes of the two lotteries are statistically independent. Knowing the outcome of lottery A gives us no additional information about the probability of winning lottery B, and we will not know whether we have won lottery B until the second period arrives. At that point we will find out whether we have won and, if we have won, receive the winnings immediately.

Let us first consider Case 1 in which we become aware of whether we win the lottery during period 0 regardless of which lottery ticket is chosen. It seems reasonable that under these circumstances there would be no reason for anyone to be willing to pay more for one ticket in lottery A than for one ticket in lottery B, provided that he could lend or borrow money at the risk-free .05 rate of interest. Suppose a person wished to spend any lottery winnings he made during period 0. He might buy a ticket for lottery A. Alternatively, if the price were the same, he could do just as well by buying a ticket in lottery B. If he discovered that he was a winner, he could then borrow $100 to spend in period 0, using the winning lottery ticket as a collateral for the loan. When the winnings became available, they would be sufficient to repay the loan plus accrued interest. If he loses he is no worse off with B than with A.

If the ticket buyer were interested in spending all his winnings during period 1, he could buy lottery ticket A and if he won, invest the money and thus have $105 available for expenditure during period 1. Alternatively, he could simply buy a ticket in lottery B, in which case he would receive the $105 at the time that he wished to spend it.

Now let us consider the second case in which the outcomes are statistically independent. If a person did not wish to spend the potential lottery winnings until period 1, then he might be willing to pay the same price for either lottery ticket, or if they were priced differently to buy the least expensive lottery.

However, suppose that the potential ticket buyer were interested in spending any lottery winnings during period 0. Such a person would be willing to consider purchasing a ticket in lottery A only. It might not be possible for him to achieve his goal by buying a ticket in lottery B because he would not know what his lottery winnings were until after period 0 had been terminated. If there were many people in these circumstances, it is possible to imagine that the market price for tickets in lottery A would be higher than the market price for tickets in lottery B, even though the present value of the expected winnings of the two lotteries were identical. On the other hand, provided lending and borrowing opportunities were available to everyone at the risk-free rate of interest, there is little reason for tickets in lottery A to be less expensive than tickets in lottery B. Anyone who prefers the timing of cash flows generated by lottery B can duplicate the results by buying tickets in lottery A and reinvesting the cash proceeds.

It is possible to imagine a person who would prefer a ticket in lottery B to one in lottery A, even if the tickets in lottery B were as expensive or more expensive than those in lottery A. Such a person would have to enjoy risk for its own sake. He would derive great satisfaction from contemplating the fun he could have spending his winnings; the satisfaction he will receive from actually spending them may be relatively less important to him. Lottery B gives him more time for contemplation than does lottery A, so he prefers it. There is no question that attitudes such as this do play a role in decisions about some types of risky actions. If a mountaineer were interested only in getting to the top of a peak, he might do better to rent a helicopter than to climb. But the enjoyment of risk for its own sake is probably a relatively unimportant component of most business decisions. On this basis, if the lotteries we have been discussing are business investments, one can argue that the "tickets" for investments like lottery B would not, in fact, be more expensive than those for investments like lottery A.

If there is a market for these types of lotteries, there is reason to expect that many persons would not be disturbed by the delay in the information. As soon as lottery A increased in price relative to lottery B, they would start buying B and selling A, tending to narrow the gap between A and B. In this example the dollars involved are in the magnitude of $100. How much would you pay for the opportunity of finding out the result of the gamble one period earlier? For many persons the amount would be very small relative to the total amount of money involved in the lottery.

While this discussion is very simplified, it seems realistic to make the following generalization on the basis of it. If two sets of uncertain outcomes are similar in terms of the present value of their proceeds, and differ only in the timing of the information about the outcomes, it is reasonable to conclude that the investment that provides earlier information about its outcome will either be more valuable or else have the same value as the other.

POOLING OF RISK

In addition to diversification (by acquiring investments with different risk characteristics) we can change the risk characteristics of an investment, if there are other independent investments with equivalent characteristics, by pooling of risk. We accomplish the risk pooling by spreading our investment fund over several investments (the investments are exactly alike, and the results are independent).

It should be noted that we do not change the expected monetary value of the investment by the suggested procedure, but we do change the probabilities of several possible gains or losses.

SPREADING RISK OVER INDEPENDENT BUT OTHERWISE SIMILAR INVESTMENTS

Example: First consider the following two alternatives:
Alternative 1: We can invest $400 and play the following lottery:

$$\$0 \qquad .5$$
$$\$950 \qquad .5$$

The expected monetary value is $(475 - 400)$, or $75.
Alternative 2: We can invest $400 and play the following lottery:

$$\$0 \qquad .95$$
$$\$10,000 \qquad .05$$

The expected monetary value is now $100. Most of us would say that the second investment has more risk despite the higher expected monetary value because there is a .95 probability of losing versus the .5 probability of losing with Alternative 1. Given the choice, we would prefer Alternative 1. However, by changing the amount we gamble on any one outcome we may be able to influence the risk characteristics of our investing in Alternative 2 type of investments. Alternative 3: Now assume that we can purchase .5 of the second investment (that is, pay $200), but can purchase one half of two such investments with our $400, where the results of the two investments are independent. The expected value of the investment is again $100, but the risk characteristics of this alternative are different than those of Alternative 2. We can now win $5,000 or $10,000. This is shown in Table 9.

Table 9. Alternative 3

Total: x	Probability: p(x)	xp(x)
$10,000	.0025	25.00
5,000	.0475	237.50
5,000	.0475	237.50
0	.9025	0
	1.0000	$\bar{x} = 500.00$

It is interesting to compare Alternatives 2 and 3. Alternative 3 gives up some probability of the large gain of $10,000 and at the same time reduces the probability of the outcome $0. While the expected value of Alternatives 2 and 3 are the same, we can change the variance of the results. The nature of the risk changes as we change the amount we bet on each gamble.

If we purchased .25 of Alternative 2 and bought into four of the gambles with the same outcome characteristic, the expected value of the investment would remain at $100 (we are investing $100 on each gamble). The possible results and their probabilities are:

x	p(x)	xp (x)
$0	.814500	0
2,500	.171475	428.69
5,000	.013538	67.69
7,500	.000475	3.56
10,000	.000006	.06
		$\bar{x} = 500.00$

Note that we were again able to reduce the probabilities of winning $10,000 or $0.

These examples have important implications in the art of decision making. If we start with a desirable but risky investment represented by Alternative 2, we can change the risk characteristics by investing in not one, but several of these investments (each with independent outcomes). Assume that Alternative 2 is an oil well. We can drill with 100% ownership and have .95 probability of not striking oil. If instead of drilling one well, we only purchase .25 of the well, but purchase 4 wells, there is now .8145 probability of complete failure. If we carry this further and drill 100 wells (owning .01 of each), the probability of complete failure (i.e., no successes) is .0059. We can change the drilling of the oil well from an investment with characteristics similar to those of Alternative 2 to one which is somewhat safer, the probabilities of the extreme outcomes being reduced.[5]

By now the reader may have observed that the adage "don't put all your eggs in one basket" has justification if we want to minimize

[5] We are assuming that the outcomes of drilling are statistically independent.

the risk of losing all. But there is a price to be paid, since we also reduce the likelihood of the best possible outcome occurring.

ILLUSTRATION OF A DERIVATION OF A UTILITY FUNCTION

We shall illustrate one approach to deriving the utility function of an individual.

The first step is to assign two arbitrary amounts of utility to two arbitrary amounts of money income. For example, we shall arbitrarily choose $0 and $1,000,000 and assign utilities of 0 and 1,000 to these two money amounts. The choice of these two points determines the scale of the utility function as well as its location.

The second step is to set up a sample lottery consisting of one lottery offering $X for certain and a second lottery offering the two amounts arbitrarily picked, each with .5 probability of occurring.

Lottery A	Lottery B
$X for certain	$0 with .5 probability
	$1,000,000 with .5 probability

What amount X for certain causes you to be indifferent between lotteries A and B? If we set X equal to $50, most of us would prefer lottery B. If we set X at $5,000,000, all of us would prefer lottery A. After some introspection we might establish an amount for X equal to $10,000. We then have:

$$U(A) = U(B)$$
$$U(\$10,000) = .5\ U(\$0) + .5\ U(\$1,000,000)$$
$$U(\$10,000) = .5 \times 0 + .5 \times 1,000 = 500$$

Thus the utility of $10,000 is determined to be 500, and we have three points of the utility function. We can continue the process by substituting the $10,000 for the $1,000,000 of lottery B. After obtaining several points, we may decide to find the utility of larger amounts by setting up the following two lotteries:

Lottery C	Lottery D
$1,000,000 for certain	$0 with .5 probability
	$X with .5 probability

Assume that for you to be indifferent to the two lotteries, X in lottery D must be equal to $800,000,000.

$$U (\$1,000,000) = .5\ U\ (\$0) + .5\ U\ (\$800,000,000)$$
$$1,000 = .5 \times 0 + .5\ U\ (\$800,000,000)$$
$$U\ (\$800,000,000) = 2,000$$

The utility measure of $800,000,000 is 2,000. We can continue the process to obtain the utility measures of still larger amounts.

We must still determine utility measures for negative amounts of money. Lotteries of the type E and F accomplish this.

Lottery E	Lottery F
$0 for certain	$10,000 with .5 probability
	$X with .5 probability

If X were equal to or greater than $0, we prefer lottery F; therefore, for us to be indifferent to E and F, X must be negative. Say X is equal to $ - 200. We then have

$$U (\$0) = .5\ U\ (\$10,000) + .5\ U\ (\$ - 200)$$
$$0 = .5 \times 500 + .5\ U\ (\$ - 200)$$
$$U\ (\$ - 200) = - 500$$

We can continue this process and obtain the utility equivalents of other dollar outcomes.

QUESTIONS AND PROBLEMS

15–1. A person may estimate the expected cash flows of year 5 to be $10,000. If this figure is used in the investment analysis, what assumption (or assumptions) is being made?

15–2. What is the maximum amount you would pay for the lottery: (a) .5 probability of $1,000? (b) .5 probability of $0? What does this imply about your utility function?

15–3. For you to be indifferent between the following two lotteries, what value of X must be inserted?

Lottery A	Lottery B
.5 probability of $1,000	1.0 probability of $X
.5 probability of $0	

What does this imply about your utility function? Compare your value of X to the answer you gave to problem 15–2.

15–4. Would the utility function of a firm change after making an investment?

15–5. When is it reasonable to base decisions on the use of money (in the computations) and to ignore utility considerations?

15–6. In making a utility function for a corporation, how would you handle the situation where different corporate executives and owners had different utility functions?

15–7. If we did not try to incorporate utility considerations into the investment analysis, would the investment decisions of the firm still be affected by the utility functions of the individual corporate executives, assuming some degree of decentralization?

15–8. If the firm is small enough for the president to make all the decisions, is it necessary to make a formal analysis using utility functions? Explain.

15–9. If we do not know the exact probabilities of the events which may occur, is it still reasonable to use the utility analysis? Is it reasonable to compute the expected monetary value?

15–10. The following utility function of Mr. Jay will be used for problems 15–10 and 15–11.

Dollars	Utility measure
−3,000	−3,000
−1,000	−1,000
− 600	− 500
− 500	− 350
0	0
100	100
500	150
1,000	200
2,000	350
4,000	500
10,000	1,000

Assume there is a gamble which has .5 probability of $10,000 and .5 probability of $0.

Required: (a) What is the utility measure of the gamble? (b) What is the amount which Mr. Jay would be willing to accept for certain to cause him to be indifferent to the two choices? (c) What is the expected monetary value of the gamble?

15–11. Assume there is a gamble which has a .5 probability of $4,000 and .5 probability of $1,000.

Required: (a) What is the utility measure of the gamble? (b) What is the amount which Mr. Jay would be willing to accept for certain to cause him to be indifferent to the two choices? (c) What is the expected monetary value of the gamble?

15–12. The following problem attempts to illustrate the simulation of the mean utility of a cash flow which has a normal probability density function.

The earnings of a period are normally distributed with a mean of $100,000 and a standard deviation of $20,000. Four random deviations from the mean were obtained (in an actual simulation the number of observations would be much larger).

$$d$$
$$.40$$
$$1.35$$
$$-\ .83$$
$$2.50$$

The following values were obtained from the utility function:

Dollars	Utility measures
0	0
83,400	10,000
108,000	15,000
110,000	16,000
127,000	19,000
150,000	20,000

Required: (a) Compute the four earnings observations. (b) Using the utility function, determine the utility observation for each earnings observation. (c) Determine the mean utility of the observations. (d) Determine the certainty equivalent.

15–13. Assume the following utility function for the ABC Corporation.

Dollars	Utility measures
−20,000	−400
−10,000	−100
0	0
7,200	80
8,600	90
10,000	100
18,600	140
20,000	150
30,000	190
35,800	200
40,000	220
60,000	240

a. Should the corporation accept an investment that requires an outlay of $10,000 and will either be a complete bust or will generate cash flows of $30,000 within a week (each possibility has a .5 probability)?

b. What would be your recommendation if the probabilities were .65 of failure and .35 of success?

15–14. Assume the same utility function as in problem 15–13.

a. Should the ABC Corporation undertake the following invest-- ment? Assume that a .05 discount rate is appropriate.

Period	Cash flow
0	−10,000
1	0 with .5 probability
	30,000 with .5 probability

b. What would be your recommendation if the probabilities were .6 of failure and .4 of success?

15–15. Assume the same utility function as in problem 15–13. The ABC Corporation has been offered an investment that costs $20,000. The investment has .5 probability of not generating any cash the first day and .5 probability of generating $30,000. It also can generate $0 or $30,000 with the same probabilities the second day. The amount received on the second day is statistically independent of the amount received on the first day. Should the firm accept the investment?

15–16. Assume the same situation as in problem 15–15, except that the transactions take place in successive years instead of days. The discount rate is .05. Should the firm accept the investment?

15–17. Assume the same investment as in problem 15–15, except the cash flows of the second day will be the same as for the first day. Should the firm accept the investment?

15–18. Assume the cash flows of an investment are as follows:

Period	Mean value	Standard deviation
0	−8,000	500
1	10,000	1,000
2	10,000	2,000

Compute the mean, variance, and standard deviation of the net present value distribution assuming the cash flows of each period are independent. Use a .05 rate of discount.

15–19. Determine whether the following investment is acceptable. Explain briefly your computations and assumptions.

Period	Cash flows
0	($1,000)
1	.5 probability of $2,100 cash flow
	.3 probability of $1,050
	.2 probability of 0.

The firm has a cost of money of .05. The utility function of the corporation has the following values (interpolate if you need other values).

Money	Utility
−1,000	−300
0	0
500	50
1,000	70
1,050	75
1,300	85
1,500	90
2,000	100
2,100	101
3,000	125

15–20. The cash flows of an investment are independent and have the following distributions:

Period	Mean	Variance
0	−1,600	2,500
1	1,000	4,000
2	1,000	10,000

(a) Assuming that the appropriate rate of discount is .05, compute the mean and variance of the distribution of the net present values of cash flows. (b) Change the assumptions of part (a) to be that the cash flow of the second period will be the same as those of period 1 (there is dependency). Compute the mean and variance of the distribution of the net present values of cash flows. Ignore the preceding description of period 2 specifying a variance of 10,000.

15–21. The ABC Company can invest $1,000,000. The two possible payoffs occurring immediately are

Probability	Payoff
.5	$0
.5	$2,600,000

(a) If you were in charge of making this decision, would you accept? Explain. (b) Assume that you can make two investments similar to that described above and own .5 of each investment. Would you accept this alternative? Do you prefer it to the possibility of investing the entire $1,000,000 in one investment?

15–22. It has sometimes been argued that net present value is "more sensitive" than the yield of an investment to variations in the cash flow estimates. For example, suppose that an immediate outlay of $3,859,000 produces proceeds of $1,000,000 per year for 15 years and an additional end of life salvage value that might range from $0 to $240,000. With a discount rate of 9 per cent the net present values would range from $4,200,000 to $5,400,000 (a variation of about 25 per cent). The yield would range from 25 per cent, if there is no salvage, to 26 per cent if there is the maximum recovery of salvage (a variation of only 4 per cent).

If sensitivity is measured by the percentage variation in the measure of investment worth for a given range of variation in the cash flow estimates, would you agree that in general net present value is a more sensitive measure of investment worth than yield?

15-23. The IBC Company has the choice between two mutually exclusive investments. One requires an outlay of $10,000,000 and has a net present value of $10,000. The second has an outlay of $500,000 and a net present value of $6,000. Both investments have a life of one year. The time value of money is .05.

Assuming certainty, which investment should the firm undertake? With uncertainty, does your answer change?

15-24. The Tin Can Company must choose between two plants. One is large and has sufficient capacity for working efficiently at the higher ranges of possible sales estimates. The other plant is smaller and is more efficient at lower ranges of sales, but is less efficient if sales are high. The net present values of the two plants are shown with different assumed level of budgeted sales. The probability of reaching that level of sales is also shown.

Level of expected sales (as % of budgeted sales)	Probability	Present value Large plant	Small plant
150%	.10	50,000,000	40,000,000
100%	.70	35,000,000	30,000,000
50%	.20	(10,000,000)	20,000,000

Required: Which of the two plants should the company build based on the information presented?

15-25. Assume you have the choice between the following two investments:

Investment A

Probability	Immediate Outcome
.5	$0
.5	$1,000

Investment B

The outcome will be known now, but the payoff is one year from now and consists of the following outcomes:

Probability	Outcome
.5	$0
.5	$1,100

Required: Which investment do you prefer? What amount does B have to offer with .5 probability for you to be indifferent between the two investments?

15–26. (continuation of 15–25). Assume investment B pays off in ten years an amount of $2,594 (with .5 probability and .5 probability of $0). Do you prefer A or B?

> "The fundamental difficulty of uncertainty cannot really be dodged; and since it cannot be faced, it must simply be ignored."
>
> —Robert M. Solow, *Capital Theory and the Rate of Return.* (Amsterdam: North-Holland Publishing Company, 1963), p. 15.

16

UNCERTAINTY AND FINANCIAL POLICY

In the previous chapter we have defined some of the complications that arise when uncertainty is considered explicitly in connection with investment decisions. In the present chapter we offer suggestions as to how uncertainty might be taken into account in making investment decisions. Given the present state of knowledge, these suggestions constitute our evaluation of what management can hope practically to accomplish in dealing with the uncertainty associated with investment decisions. We are confident that as improvements are made in the underlying theoretical knowledge and in the computational techniques available to management, more efficient precedures will be developed.

RISK AND THE DISCOUNT RATE

The weighted average cost of capital is widely used as a discount rate for making investment decisions. However, there are several drawbacks to its use. In order to compute the cost of capital, it is necessary to know the cost of stock equity funds, and this cost is very difficult (and sometimes impossible) to measure. A second and more important drawback is that by including the cost of common stock funds in the computation, there is automatically included a measure of the attitudes toward risk of the investors in common stock. Thus, we speak of an .08 return required for a relatively safe stock and a .15 return required for a stock of high risk. The cost of common stock funds measures both the attitudes of the stockholders relative to the time value of money and their attitudes toward risk. Unfortunately, by combining the two into one measure we end up with neither being measured very well.

It is less obvious than with common stock, but the cost of corporate debt also includes an adjustment for risk, since there is generally the possibility of default. A bond yield of .05 is partially a result of time preference (say, .04) and partially a result of the risk of default and other adverse events that might occur.

As normally defined and computed, the cost of common stock equity funds and the yields of most debt instruments include an allowance for risk, but it does not necessarily follow that the use of a higher discount rate applied to future cash flows is a desirable way of determining the present value of an asset that is subject to risk.

The results of any evaluation of debt can be expressed in terms of yield. For example, suppose a bond contract involves a promise to pay $50 per year for ten years and $1,000 at the end of the ten-year period. If a potential investor decides that he would pay no more than $371 for this bond, we may choose to describe the investor as being willing to buy the bond if it is priced to yield 20 per cent. This statement tells us nothing about how the investor actually decided what the bond was worth. Does the investor have a time value of money of 20 per cent per year, or is it that he has an aversion to risk and fears a possible inability to collect interest and principal?

The use of high discount rates to allow for uncertainty makes a very special assumption about the nature of uncertainty. For example, suppose we consider an investment to build and equip a plant for producing a new product. In some instances the major uncertainty may be related to the cost of constructing the plant, while the demand for the resulting output may be easily predictable in advance with very little uncertainty. This could be the case if the product to be made were to be sold in advance through a long-term sales contract, whereas the design, construction, and operation of the plant may involve new or unusual engineering problems creating an unpredictable cost. The use of atomic energy to generate electric power is a tangible example of this situation. In such a situation the discounting of future revenues, themselves fairly certain, seems a poor way of allowing for the uncertainty about how much the fixed plant will cost. In another instance the main element of uncertainty may revolve around consumer acceptance of the product. The alternatives may be either a very high or a very low level of consumer acceptance, with a corresponding probability of either a series of years of very high cash proceeds or a series of years of little or no cash proceeds. Again there seems to be no reason to suppose that the use of present-value discount factors will lead to a correct or appropriate allowance for uncertainty in this instance.

We shall use two examples to illustrate the difficulty of predicting the effect of using different discount rates in an attempt to take risk into consideration.

Example 1: Assume we have two investments, one more risky than the second. Do not be bothered by the vagueness of the description of the amount of risk. With the first investment we shall use a discount rate of .10, and with the second a discount rate of .20. The two investments have mean cash flows of $10,000 in years 1 and 50.

Year	Cash flows	PV factor using .10	PV using .10	PV factor using .20	PV using .20
1	10,000	.9091	$9,091	.8333	$8,333
50	10,000	.0085	85	.0001	1

Note that the present value of the cash flows of year 1 of the less risky investment is 1.09 times as large as the cash flow of the more risky investment. However, the present value of the cash flows of year 50 is approximately 85 times as large. The use of a larger rate of discount for a more risky investment may move the decision in the correct direction, (i.e., the riskier the investment, the lower the value of the future cash flows). However, it does this in an approximate and somewhat unpredictable manner. We cannot be sure of the impact of the risk discount added to the time value of money without considerable computation, and the effect of the risk discount will not be equal each year.

The use of a risk discount assumes that the risk difference between the two investments is increasing as we move further into the future. As we have already mentioned, this assumption may not be correct. Even if the assumption is correct, we still need to inquire whether the discount factor appropriately measures the disadvantage of this risk.

This difficulty with the use of a risk discount (i.e., a larger interest rate) to take risk into consideration is not limited to situations involving long-time periods.

Example 2: Assume that we are given the opportunity to bet on a horse race being run today, and the information we receive is so good we consider the probability of our obtaining $3 for each dollar invested to be .5. There remains a .5 probability of losing our entire investment, so we want to apply a large interest rate to take the risk into consideration. However, the benefits are zero time periods in the future. When the discount factor $(1 + r)^{-t}$ is computed for t equal to zero, we find the present value factor is 1 and is independent of the choice of the discount rate, r.[1]

We can generalize our experience and conclude that with very short time periods the choice of a large rate of discount fails to incorporate effectively our attitudes toward risk into the investment decision. For practical business decision making, varying the rate of discount is not a good way of accomplishing the objective of taking risk into consideration. It is true that most persons would require a higher return for risky investment than for less risky investments; however, determining the exact amount the rate of discount should be increased for different types of risk in different time periods is a difficult task.

If one attempts to allow for attitudes toward risk by using a risk discount rate added to the time value of money, there is no direct means of deciding how large the risk discount rate should be. By contrast, if the discount rate used reflects solely the time value of money, one could use a utility function to determine how large a risk premium should be subtracted from the expected net present value of the investment and thus calculate the investment's net monetary value to the investor.

With uncertain cash flows, except in very special cases, adding a risk discount to the time value discount rate does not (a) incorporate any consideration of the value of information arising from differences in time at which uncertainty about the magnitude of the cash flows will be eliminated; (b) reflect any information that may be available about the correlation between the returns of a patricular investment and the returns of the other business operations in a particular firm; (c) incorporate attitudes toward risk into the evaluation of an investment proposal in an effective manner.

The theories of time discounting require that we have information about the preferences of the investor for receiving money today compared with receiving money in the future. They also require that we know the production opportunities and the borrowing opportunities

---

[1] Suppose that we receive the information about the race (a tip) an hour before the race results will be determined. Then of course there will be finite discount rates that make the present value of the proceeds equal to the outlay.

that are available. It is implicitly assumed that all this information is known with certainty. The basic logic of time discounting does not justify the use of a discount rate that is adjusted upward for increasing amounts of risk.

We shall summarize where we stand in our analysis. The objective is to take the time value of money into account by discounting, and as a separate operation we want to incorporate the other complications introduced by the existence of uncertainty. The use of the cost of capital as a discount rate implicitly includes a risk factor. At best it may tend to move the investment decision in the correct direction by making it more difficult to accept risky investments. Nevertheless, the use of cost of capital has several drawbacks which makes it difficult (if not impossible) to use it consistently and correctly.

We shall discuss another possible candidate for the choice of rate of discount.

A DEFAULT-FREE RATE OF DISCOUNT

We shall retain the assumption that a reasonable person would prefer to have a dollar now rather than a dollar in the future. This means that there is a positive rate of discount.[2] There are many choices of discount rates that may be suggested for use in making investment decisions. The following are the two possibilities we shall consider in this section: (a) interest rate of government securities, and (b) interest rate of long-term industrial bonds.

Before proceeding further, however, it is desirable to establish more clearly the characteristics we seek in selecting an interest rate. The term *risk free* might be used to describe the interest rate. This is suggestive, but not strictly accurate. There are certain risks that cannot in practice be eliminated and that affect all interest-bearing securities to a greater or lesser extent. The interest rates we have in mind are those at which the investor could lend money with no significant danger of default or at which he could borrow if his collateral were so good that his creditor would feel that there was negligible chance of default.

---

[2] It is possible to have a situation where the discount rate is negative and we are satisfied to invest $1 now and get back less than $1 in the future just to be sure of getting something. Imagine a family with four children approaching college age. They might invest even with a negative discount rate, if holding cash was impractical.

Even if the risk of default is practically negligible, there are other risks inherent in fixed money debt instruments as long as there is uncertainty about the future changes that might take place in the economy. We shall describe these risks from the point of view of the lender. The counterparts of these risks also exist for a borrower.

One source of risk arises because of uncertainty about the future price level. Expectations about possible future price levels influence the market determination of interest rates. Lenders will tend to be hurt if the price level rises; hence they require a higher interest return with an expected price level increase than with an expected price level decrease, or with constant prices.

Another source of risk arises because of the possibility of changes in the term structure of interest rates. Normally the interest rate on bonds will vary with the number of years to maturity even when there is no risk of default. Bonds that mature in a few years may have higher (or lower) yields than bonds that mature in the more distant future. If there is no risk of default, the lender can always be sure of earning the going yield by buying a bond of a certain maturity and holding it until it matures. However the possibility exists that some other strategy would result in earning a higher yield. If an investor wants to lend money for a five-year period and expects a decline in interest rates, he may be able to earn a higher yield by buying a fifteen- or twenty-year bond and selling it after five years than by buying a five-year bond and holding it to maturity. However, when this strategy is followed, there is no longer any guarantee that a certain minimum rate of interest will actually be earned.

Even if a lender wishes to avoid the uncertainty that results from the possibility of changes in the term structure of interest rates, he may be unable to do so. This will happen if he is uncertain about the amounts of cash he will require on various future dates. If he invests in short-term debt instruments, such as treasury bills, he will face uncertainty about the rates he will be able to earn when the time for reinvesting these funds arises. If he invests in longer-term securities, he will face uncertainty about the actual return that will be realized if he must liquidate the securities before they mature.

In spite of these limitations the interest rates on government debt constitute a reasonable choice of discount rates representing default-free lending opportunities. These rates represent actual market opportunities at which firms or individuals could lend money with essentially no risk of default.

Unfortunately, neither private corporations nor individuals can actually borrow money at these rates, even with the best available collateral. For various reasons the rates at which one could actually borrow for a given term would be higher than the rates at which the government can borrow for loans of the same maturity.

THE BORROWING RATE

We have argued that the rate of discount used in computing the present value of cash flows should not attempt to take into consideration risk preferences or aversions. It is appropriate that the time value factor result in a compounding effect; we do not consider it appropriate also to assume that risk results in the same type of compounding phenomenon.

Any individual or private business corporation that attempts to borrow money will find that the interest rate it must promise to pay will be greater than the default-free rate that we recommend be used to discount future cash flows. An analysis of the discounting of debt-type cash flows is an interesting special problem that helps us to understand the discounting process, and it is worthwhile considering this problem even when the difference between the interest rate promised on a debt and the default-free rate is not large enough to be material in relation to investment decision making.

We will ignore income tax considerations. Suppose the interest rate on default-free one-year debts is 6 per cent, and a private corporation offers to sell a bond that promises to repay $1,060 one year from now. If such a bond were offered by the federal government it could be sold for $1,000, because the obligations of the government are default-free. With a private corporation there is some possibility of default, although the possibility may be remote. Suppose the potential buyers judge the probability distribution of future cash payments that would result from purchasing this bond to be as follows:

(1) Possible cash proceeds	(2) Probability	(3) (1) × (2)
$1,060	.9990	$1,058.94
1,000	.0005	0.50
500	.0003	0.15
0	.0002	0.00
	1.0000	Expected value $1,059.59

The bondholders treat the bond contract as nearly default-free because they consider that there are only 2 chances out of 10,000 that they will receive nothing from the bond, and only 1 chance in a 1,000 that they will fail to receive the total amount promised. The bondholders, discounting the expected cash flows of $1,059.59 at the default-free rate of interest, would find the present value of the bond to be $999.62 ($1,059.59/1.06). If the potential purchasers were willing to buy the bond on the basis of the present value of its expected cash flows they would offer $999.62 for it. It is customary to quote bond yields on the basis of the payments promised, not the expected payments. On this basis it would be said that the bond were sold to yield 6.04 per cent (1,060/1.0604 = $999.62).

One might question whether in fact potential buyers would pay $999.62 for the bond. Their expected return on a default-free government obligation would be just as high, although the most probable return on the corporation's bond is higher than on the government's. Suppose the buyers offered to pay $998.00 for the bond, and the corporation sold it at that price. The present value of the expected cash flows is $999.62. The difference of $1.62 is a risk premium that serves to induce the bond buyers to buy this slightly risky asset instead of a default-free government bond.

It is interesting and relevant to note that the analysis made by a potential bond-buyer is essentially the same as the analysis that the corporation would make in analyzing a risky investment. From the point of view of the buyer, a bond is a risky investment. The future cash flows can be adjusted for timing by discounting at the default-free interest rate, but the expected present value is not the amount that would be paid for the asset. The value depends on the risks involved and the risk attitudes of the purchaser.

Now let us look at the debt transaction from the point of view of the issuing corporation. Say the corporation receives $998. It is legally obligated to pay an amount whose most likely present value is $1,000. The corporation may agree with the bondholder's assessment of the possible cash proceeds of the bond and their probability. That is, it may recognize that there is a small probability that it may be unable to meet its legal obligations under the contract. Even so it has received only $998 for entering into an obligation having a present value of expected cash payments of $999.62, for which the most likely consequence (probability .999) is that it will make payments whose present value is $1,000.

In analyzing the consequences of issuing the bond, the corporation should consider the reactions of the stockholders in the corporation. The issuance of bonds may affect the risk premium stockholders use, and thus the market value of the common stock. Despite the incurrence of a liability that exceeds the cash received, the contract is not necessarily disadvantageous to the borrowing corporation. To balance the debt contract it has received cash plus an intangible asset that we may call "increased liquidity." Why does the firm want increased liquidity? There may be several reasons, but we will concentrate on one.

Assume that there is an advantageous investment with a positive expected net present value using the default-free rate. By expending the cash and the intangible asset called "increased liquidity," the firm can acquire this investment. If the expected present value of the proceeds of the investment exceeds its cash cost plus its liquidity cost, the investment might be worthwhile. The financial accountant will record only the cash obtained from liability and the cash cost of the investment. The investment analyst should recognize that the asset is worth acquiring if the cash outlay plus intangible liquidity cost given up is less than the expected net present value plus a risk adjustment. Typically the reason the firm is willing to incur a liability greater than the cash obtained is that it expects to use the cash to acquire an asset whose value is greater than the value of the liability.

If the firm has other assets the decision about whether an investment is acceptable or not may have to be made on the basis of an analysis of its risk characteristics combined with the risk characteristics of the assets already owned by the firm. With uncertainty there are examples of undesirable investments whose expected net present value is positive, and of desirable investments whose expected net present value is negative. Life insurance is an example of the latter type.

If there is uncertainty, the discounting of future cash flows serves to place cash flows to be received at different points in time on a comparable basis relative to time. This process facilitates the making of investment decisions. But expected net present values cannot be used as a sole decision-making criterion when there is uncertainty. Unfortunately we cannot offer a comparably simple and effective decision rule to take the place of net present value when we drop the assumption of certainty.

DISCOUNT RATE—SUMMARY

To summarize, we have argued that when cash flows are discounted at a default-free interest rate, the resulting net present values adjust the cash flows for differences in timing, but not for risk. If any higher discount rate is used, there is an implicit risk allowance, and the decision maker must ask himself whether the appropriate risk allowance has been made. Some firms may prefer to use the rate at which they can borrow long-term funds as a discount rate. If their credit rating is good, this rate will not be far above the default-free rate, and it may be easier to explain and justify to management. Our preference is to use a default-free interest rate and make risk adjustments separately.

Even more important than the choice of a specific discount rate is the recognition that when cash flows are uncertain, some investments may be undesirable, even though their expected cash flows have a positive net present value; whereas other investments may be desirable even with expected cash flows having a negative net present value. Because the risk characteristics of the investment will greatly influence the investment decision and the present value calculation is viewed as only one information input, it is most important that good investments are not rejected by the use of a high rate of discount, so that they drop from consideration. The use of a too low interest rate at worse will merely allow some investments to receive further consideration than they would receive if higher discount rates were used.

CLASSIFICATION OF RISKY INVESTMENTS

Under conditions of uncertainty, using a discounting process does not lead to a simple and exact rule for making investments. The objective of the discounting process is to place the cash flows that may occur at various future dates on a comparable basis with respect to time. With uncertainty there is not likely to be a simple relationship between the net present value of an investment and its desirability; in fact, there will not be a unique net present value. Rather there will be a number of possible net present values that might occur, some of which will be positive and others, negative.

If for some investment, every possible net present value were negative, the investment could clearly be rejected. Similarly, if every possible net present value were positive, the investment could be accepted. In the latter circumstances, there is no uncertainty about the investment's desirability. There is uncertainty only about how desirable it would be.

For practical purposes one may not want to interpret the term "every possible outcome" in a literal sense. Some possible outcomes are so improbable that we may wish to ignore them. Not many buyers of U.S. Savings Bonds consider the possibility of not being able to collect on maturity as being a possible event. Other outcomes might be so disastrous for nearly all investments that they would not affect a choice between alternative investments. The outbreak of a major atomic war is the frighteningly realistic example in this category.

The difficult problems of choice are for those investments for which some of the possible outcomes would produce positive net present values, and other possible outcomes would produce negative net present values. When this is the case we need to be concerned with the dispersion of possible outcomes for the investment under consideration, and with the effect of accepting the investment on the dispersion of possible outcomes (net present values) for the firm as a whole.

One method of making investment decisions would involve computing for each possible combination of acceptable investments the resulting probability distribution of net present values for the firm as a whole. The investment set would be selected which led to the most desirable probability distribution given the attitudes toward risk of the managers and stockholders.

While this method is very attractive in terms of the kind of information that it makes available to management, it is not practical, given the computational techniques available today. The number of alternative combinations of acceptable investment projects that would need to be considered by an average business corporation would be extremely large, much greater than the number of separate investment projects being proposed.[3] Equally important, the task of determining the probability distribution of net present values for the firm that

---

[3] If we let $\binom{n}{r}$ be the symbol for the combination of n things taken r at a time, then $\sum_{r=0}^{n} \binom{n}{r} = \sum_{r=0}^{n} \dfrac{n!}{r!(n-r)!}$ is the number of alternatives, where n is the number of different investment opportunities and r is the number of investments undertaken. This sum can be an extremely large number.

would result from accepting any one set of investment projects would be exceedingly complex. Each possible event that might affect the existing operations of the company or the cash flow of any of the proposed investments would have to be listed, and the joint probability distribution for all such events determined. Finally, the consequences of each possible outcome on the net present value of the company (including the proposed new investments) would have to be estimated.

Sometime in the future we may be able to approximate this process with the help of electronic computers. At present, an analysis of the sort described above, even if it could be carried out, is likely to cost much more than it is worth.

An alternative approach is to recognize that the task the managers of a business firm face in deciding what new investments to accept is in many respects analogous to the portfolio analysis task that is faced by the manager of a mutual fund. In fact, with some modifications, the analysis previously described also fits the case of such a mutual fund manager. Similarly, some of the techniques applicable to portfolio selection problems are applicable to business investment problems as well. For example, the portfolio analyst does not ordinarily explicitly consider all the possible uncertain events and attempt to determine how the occurrence of each event would affect the price, dividends, and growth potential of every possible stock. However, something approximating this result is achieved much more easily by classifying stocks into groups that have relatively similar risk characteristics, for example, classifications by industries such as oils, chemicals, steel, paper, air frame, farm equipment, motors, etc. Many future events will produce similar consequences for all of the companies in a given group. For example, a depression will affect most steel companies in a similar manner, and this may differ from the effect of the event on the air frame industry. This suggests that early in the process of investment decision making, management may wish to classify investments into categories in such a way that investment proposals in the same category have similar risk characteristics. That is, a group of investments that would be affected in a similar manner by a wide range of possible events (say, the general level of business activity) would be placed in the same category. It is highly desirable that the categories chosen be defined so that not only new investment proposals but also the existing assets of the firm can be classified in terms of the same categories.

Any such system of classification will be somewhat crude, and the type of classification that will be desirable and feasible will vary from company to company. In many large companies, a classification of investments according to the operating division to which they would be assigned may be appropriate. In other cases the key considerations may be product line, stage of processing, type of technological process used, the type of customer for whom the product is intended, or the geographical location of the investment. Decisions about what bases of classification will be used and about how detailed a classification system should be used are matters of judgment about which no general rules can be given. The aim should be to develop a system that is sufficiently simple so that its use is practical, and so that investments in the same category have a relatively high degree of similarity in terms of the way they would be affected by the most important kinds of uncertain events (for example, the business cycle).

Having classified investment proposals and existing investments into a reasonable set of categories, management may want to consider what proportion of its assets it would like to have in each of the categories. Some categories may be attractive because they promise unusually good immediate earning possibilities and the expected net present values are high. Other categories may not be especially profitable in the near future, but may seem to present opportunities for growth in terms of large and profitable future investment opportunities. Still other categories may be attractive mainly because they offer opportunities for risk diversification and earnings stability (the insurance effect).

It may be reasonable for management to set tentative goals in terms of the proportion of the total assets of the company that it would like to have invested in each of these categories. In terms of these target proportions, investment goals can be derived by comparing the existing proportions with the target proportions. The setting of targets in terms of the proportion of total assets that should be in each category is desirable because the old assets affect the risk characteristics of the new investments.

If there are more investment opportunities than the target proportion, management must weigh the relative advantages of increased expected present values and increased variability against less expected values and less variability. Identifying the effect of an investment, despite the above classification scheme, is not apt to be easy or exact.

Obviously, the preceding approach is not an exact technique for separating acceptable and nonacceptable investments.

ESTIMATING THE PORTFOLIO EFFECTS OF ADDING AN INVESTMENT

Previously we concluded that for many purposes the decision maker would want to know how the outcomes that might occur for his whole portfolio would be affected if a new investment were added to the portfolio. Suppose that for each individual investment ten outcomes are possible. If there are two such investments, the joint probability distribution of the two investments may have one hundred possible outcomes. If there are three such investments, their joint probability distribution may have one thousand possible outcomes. In a practical situation with a large number of separate investments to be considered, it would be very difficult to estimate directly the joint probability distribution of the outcomes of all the investments. We will attempt to give an approximate but somewhat more easily applied method for evaluating how a new investment might affect the risks of existing investments.

We want to distinguish in what respect possible states of nature may differ. We can think of each possible future state of nature as consisting of many separate components. For example, the level of GNP that will prevail might be one component of a state of nature. If we specify a particular level of GNP we will identify not one particular state of nature, but rather all of the possible states that have in common that level of GNP. For a particular investment another relevant aspect of future states of nature might be the average retail price of gasoline. Corresponding to any particular level of GNP we might have separate states of nature corresponding to retail gasoline prices of 30 cents, 35 cents, or 40 cents.

In connection with a particular investment we will wish to describe the future states of nature only insofar as components of those possible future states are materially relevant to our ability to predict the outcome of the investment. For example, if we could predict the outcome of the investment by knowing the future level of GNP and of gasoline prices, but without knowing the future level of copper prices, then future copper prices would be irrelevant for purposes of describing the states of nature of that investment.

Examples

To illustrate the approach we will present a series of examples. In these examples we will assume that at most two components of future possible states of nature are relevant and that these components are statistically independent. We also assume that for each component only two values are possible. Specifically we will assume that the first component can take on the values of A or B and that the second component can take on the values C or D. Thus a future state of nature will be completely specified if we pick one letter from each of these two groups. For example, the letters A,D will specify one future state of nature and the letters B,D another possible state. If for a particular investment all outcomes would be the same regardless of whether the state of nature that occurred was characterized by A or by B, we would say that the first component is irrelevant for that investment, and we might describe a state of nature as being characterized only by C and D.

We can imagine that we have two coins, a nickel and a quarter. The actual state of nature will be determined by flipping each coin and specifying for each whether the outcome was a head or a tail. To generate probabilities of the possible states we will assume that each of the coins is fair and that the flips are independent.

In each of the following examples we will assume that there is an old investment to which we are already committed and a new investment we are considering. We will show how the probability distribution of outcomes of a combined portfolio of the new and old investments could be determined. Finally we shall see that under some conditions the effect of adding new investments to the portfolio can be estimated if we know what aspects of states of nature are relevant to both investments, and if we know how the value of the relevant aspects of states of nature common to both investments affect the outcomes of each of the investments.

The first example is given in Table 1 and in Figure 1. The relevant states of nature for the old investment are A and B. Each of these has an equal probability of occurring. The net present value of the cash flows associated with the old investment are assumed to be 200 if the state of nature A occurs and −100 if the state of nature B occurs. The expected present value for the old investment is 50. The new investment is similar except that its outcomes depend only on the second component of our state of nature. The new investment has a net present value of 200 if C occurs and a −100 if D occurs, and the expected value of the new investment is again 50.

Table 1. Portfolio Effects of Two Investments: Pure Risk Averaging (Independent Investments)

Relevant states of nature (1)	Marginal probabilities (2)	Outcomes (3)	(2) × (3) (4)
Old investment:			
A	.5	200	100
B	.5	−100	−50
Expected outcome			50
New investment:			
C	.5	200	100
D	.5	−100	−50
Expected outcome			50
Combined investment: (.5 of old and .5 of new)			
AC	.25	200	50.00
AD	.25	50	12.50
BC	.25	50	12.50
BD	.25	−100	−25.00
Expected outcome			50.00

The third part of Table 1 shows the probability distribution of the combined outcomes of the two investments, when we buy .5 of each investment. For the combination the outcomes of the flip of both the nickel and the quarter are relevant. In Figure 1 the outcomes for the two individual investments and for their combination are shown in a tree diagram form.

In this example no components of states of nature are common to the two separate investments. The result is that when we combine the two investments into a portfolio there is a tendency for the risks associated with the individual investments to be pooled or averaged. Note that for either of the two investments considered by itself, the average outcome is $50. However, $50 is not a possible outcome for either of the investments. The possible outcomes of $200 and −$100

are either $150 more than the average or $150 less than the average.
Each of the possible outcomes has a probability of one half if we
consider individual investments by themselves.

If we consider the combination of .5 of each of the old and the
new investment, the average outcome is still 50. Now the probability
is .5 that the actual outcome will equal the average outcome. The

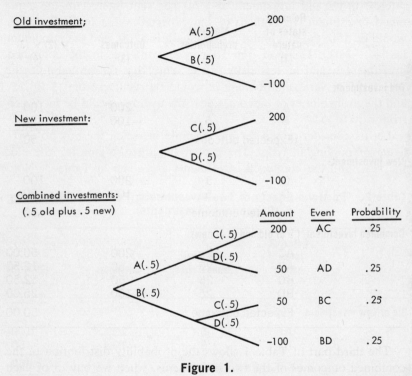

Figure 1.

other two possible outcomes are still 150 more than the average, or
150 less than the average; but the probability of each of these extreme
possibilities is only .25 whereas before it was .5.

Now assume the new portfolio consisted of 100 per cent of the
old and 100 per cent of the new (instead of 50 per cent). The new
portfolio would be bigger than the old investment by itself—that is,
the expected net present value of cash flows is greater, and the maximum possible gain and the maximum possible loss are now twice as
large as they would be if only the old investment had been retained,
or if we retained only .5 of the two investments. If the combined

portfolio were owned by an individual investor, this increase in scale might be highly significant. However, from the point of view of an outside stockholder who owned a share in such an enterprise, changes in absolute scale may be of little importance, because he can offset them by determining what fraction of the shares he owns. Consider an investor whose entire portfolio could be either a 100 per cent interest in the old investment or a 50 per cent interest in the combined investment. In both cases the expected value of his holdings would be $50; the maximum possible gain is $200, and the maximum loss is $-\$100$. However, the 50 per cent interest in the combined investment would be less risky in the sense that the probabilities of very large or very small outcomes would be reduced from .5 to .25, and the probabilities of outcomes near the average would be increased from zero to .5.

Let us consider now a second example in which there is no averaging or pooling of risks. The probability distributions for the old, the new, and the combined investments are given in Table 2. Note

Table 2. Portfolio Effects of Two Investments: Pure Risk Multiplying (Dependent Investments)

Relevant states of nature (1)	Marginal probabilities (2)	Outcomes (3)	(2) × (3) (4)
Old or new investment:			
A	.5	200	100
B	.5	−100	−50
Expected outcome			50
Combined investments:			
A	.5	400	200
B	.5	−200	−100
Expected outcome			100

that the old and the new investments are exactly alike, in respect to both the states of nature on which they depend, and the outcomes that can occur. In Figure 2 a tree diagram corresponding to either of the investments taken separately and to the combination of the two investments is presented.

In this example, the two individual investments depend on common aspects of the state of nature, and the nature of the dependence is exactly the same for the two investments. When we combine two such investments there is no risk averaging. The expected value of the combined investment is twice the expected value of either of the investments taken individually. The maximum and minimum outcomes for the combined investment are exactly twice the maximum outcome for each of the individual investments. Finally, and most importantly, the probabilities for the maximum and minimum for

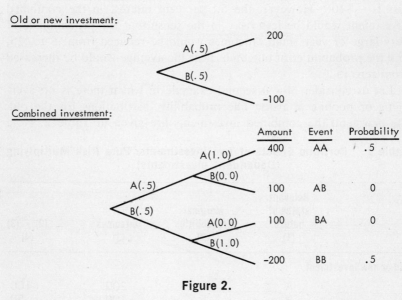

Figure 2.

the combined investments are just as large as for the maximum and minimum of the individual investments. An individual investor would presumably be indifferent as to whether he owned a 100 per cent share in the old investment or a 50 per cent share in the combined investment. This situation might be described as risk multiplying.

A third simple example is described in Table 3. The corresponding tree diagrams are given in Figure 3. This example is similar to the second example in that the same components of the states of nature are relevant to the old and the new investments. The outcomes for both of these investments are solely determined by whether a state of nature is characterized by A or B. However, in this case, the nature of the dependency is different. The old investment is the same as in

Table 3. Portfolio Effects of Two Investments: Defensive Case (Dependent Investments)

	Relevant states of nature (1)	Marginal probabilities (2)	Outcomes (3)	(2) × (3) (4)
Old investment:				
	A	.5	200	100
	B	.5	−100	−50
	Expected outcome			50
New investment:				
	A	.5	−100	−50
	B	.5	200	100
	Expected outcome			50
Combined investment:				
	A	.5	100	50
	B	.5	100	50
	Expected outcome			100

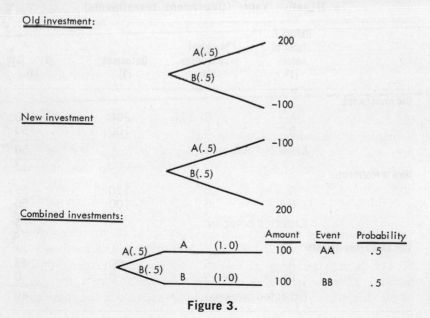

Old investment:

A(.5)

B(.5)

200

−100

New investment

A(.5)

B(.5)

−100

200

Combined investments:

A(.5)

B(.5)

		Amount	Event	Probability
A	(1.0)	100	AA	.5
B	(1.0)	100	BB	.5

Figure 3.

the previous examples. The new investment has unfavorable outcomes associated with states of nature characterized by A, favorable outcomes associated with states of nature characterized by B. In both cases the expected outcomes are equal to $50. When we combine two such investments, we find that not only is the expected outcome $100 but this is the only possible outcome. It occurs regardless of whether the state of nature is A or B. The new investment in this example might be described as a defensive investment with respect to the old. Combining the defensive with the old investment reduces the uncertainty associated with the combination.

It might be difficult to find a new defensive investment that is profitable as an individual investment and also completely eliminates the uncertainty associated with the old. In some circumstances investors might be willing to accept a defensive investment even if its expected value is negative—for example, the investment illustrated in Table 4 and Figure 4. In this case we assume that both the old and new investments depend on states A and B. The old investment has possible outcomes of 200 if A occurs and −100 if B occurs. The expected outcome in this case is 50. The new investment has an

Table 4. Portfolio Effects of Two Investments: Defensive Case with a Negative Value (Dependent Investments)

	Relevant states of nature (1)	Marginal probabilities (2)	Outcomes (3)	(2) × (3) (4)
Old investment:				
	A	.5	200	100
	B	.5	−100	−50
	Expected outcome			50
New investment:				
	A	.5	−110	−55
	B	.5	+100	50
	Expected outcome			−5
Combined investments:				
	A	.5	90	45
	B	.5	0	0
	Expected outcome			45

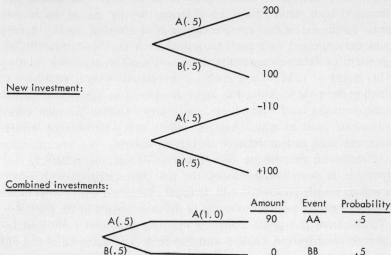

Figure 4.

outcome of −110 if A occurs and of +100 if B occurs. The expected outcome in this case is −5. Note that the new investment is defensive compared to the old (its favorable outcome occurs in those circumstances when the outcome of the old investment would be unfavorable). If we considered the combined investment, we find that the expected value $45 is the sum of the expected values of the two investments taken individually. By combining the new defensive investment with the old we eliminate the possibility of a loss. The risk characteristics of the combined investment are such that many persons might prefer it to the old investment taken by itself, even though the expected value of the combined investment is less than the expected value of the old investment. The investor who prefers the combination is willing to undertake the new investment even though its expected value is negative. The new investment is in many respects analogous to an insurance policy.

A SIMPLIFIED APPROACH

Up to now we have considered cases in which the two investments either depended on exactly the same aspects of future states of nature or had no common components. When we compare two investments, we may find that some components of future states of nature are relevant to both, while others are relevant to only one of the investments. To the extent that some component of a future state of nature is uniquely relevant to a particular invesment and is statistically independent of other components there will tend to be some pooling or averaging of risks. When such an investment with a positive expected present value is not too large compared to other investments in the portfolio, and when there are a large number of such other investments each of which has its unique components (the investments are independent relative to certain events), the uncertainties associated with the unique components will become relatively less important. In such circumstances, the risk characteristics with which we will be mainly concerned will be those associated with components of states of nature relevant to many of the investments in the portfolio.

To illustrate this point, consider the old, new, and combined investments described in Table 5 and Figure 5. The outcome of the old

Table 5. Portfolio Effects of Two Investments

	Relevant states of nature (1)	Marginal probabilities (2)	Outcomes (3)	(2) × (3) (4)
Old investment:				
	A	.5	600	300
	B	.5	−300	−150
				EMV = 150
New investment:				
	AC	.25	400	100
	AD	.25	100	25
	BC	.25	100	25
	BD	.25	−200	−50
				EMV = 100
Combined investment:				
	AC	.25	1,000	250
	AD	.25	700	175
	BC	.25	−200	−50
	BD	.25	−500	−125
				EMV = 250

investment depends on whether A or B has occurred. The new investment is a combination of the two investments described in Table 1. The profitability of the new combination will depend on whether A or B has occurred and also on whether C or D has occurred. Whether A or B has occurred is a common factor for both the old and new investments, but whether C or D has occurred is uniquely relevant to the new investment. If we analyze the combined investment, we find that four possible states of nature are relevant. It would become exceedingly complex to analyze investments in detail in this way if there were many investments and many different states of nature.

Combined investments:

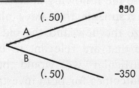

	Amount	Event	Probability
	1,000	AC	.25
	700	AD	.25
	−200	BC	.25
	−500	BD	.25

Simplified tree of combined investments:

(.50)	850
A	
B	
(.50)	−350

Figure 5.

It is interesting to see to what extent we can simplify our analysis without leaving out too much relevant information. If we examine the tree diagram for the combined investment we note that the most important information of the total outcomes is given if we know whether the state of nature obtained is characterized by A or aspect B. The expected value of the outcomes given that state A has occurred is 850, and all the outcomes are desirable. The expected value of the outcomes given that state B has occurred is −350, and all the outcomes given state B are undesirable. The bottom half of Figure 5 presents a simplified version of the analysis for this complex investment, in which are shown only the payoffs of the A and B states of nature. The combined investment has an expected value of 250 and conditional expected outcomes of 850 and −350 for events A and B. Referring to the detailed tree of Figure 5, we find that if A occurs, the actual outcome will be equal to 1,000 or 700 and will differ from the conditional expected value of 850 by 150. If event B occurs we find that the expected outcome given B is −350, and the actual outcomes will be −200, or −500. The difference from the conditional expected value of −350 is again plus or minus 150.

By considering only those states of nature (say, the general level of business activity) that are common to both of the old and new investment we have simplified the analysis, though we do lose some information. If we were considering a large number of investments, the amount of. simplification resulting from this approximation would be very great. However, there is the requirement that the amount of information lost by ignoring the other states be small. If events C and D have great influence on a large investment (for example, if event AD leads to a −800 outcome), these outcomes must also be considered.

SUMMARY

One might propose the following analysis of how a new investment would affect the investments that have already been accepted. We should try to analyze the new and the old investments to determine the states of nature that are relevant to both the new and the old investments. In particular we would be interested in knowing whether favorable outcomes for both investments would tend to occur at the same time (in which case the combination would tend to be risk multiplying), or whether good outcomes for one of the investments tend to be associated with poor outcomes for the other (in which case the new investment would tend to be defensive when combined with the old). The magnitude of these effects could be estimated by considering the conditional expected outcomes of both the new and the old with respect to the common relevant states of nature. We would consider how the distribution of the outcomes of the new investment compared to that of the old investment. We would be less concerned with the outcomes of the new investment that depended on states of nature unique to it (these would tend to average out if there were a large number of such investments) than with the outcomes depending on the same states of nature as a large percentage of the current assets. For example, a firm already vulnerable to a business recession would prefer investments that were less affected by general business activity. A firm currently making electronic tubes (and vulnerable to the inroads of transistors) might not be sympathetic to investing in more facilities for producing tubes. To some extent the type of analysis described in this section can be made in a qualitative manner with the decision maker comparing in an intuitive manner the expected results with and without the investment being considered.

INVESTMENTS AND STOCK VALUES

In principle (though not in practice) there is a very simple test of whether an investment is worthwhile in terms of the taste and preferences of the financial community as a whole. An investment is worthwhile in these terms if the consequence of making the investment is to increase immediately the present value of the firm's securities by more than the cost of the investment.

In practice it is not easy to implement this criteria. The market prices of common stocks change from day to day for a wide variety of reasons. It is difficult to estimate to what extent a change in the price of a common stock derives from changes in the market's estimate of the earning potential and the associated risks of a company's recent investments. In part, the difficulties arise because price changes may be due to a wide range of reasons, many of which have nothing to do with the earning potential of a particular company. In part they arise because the market is not always aware of the earning potential of the investments a firm has undertaken. In some instances, the market price may reflect an anticipation of the earning potential of investments the firm has not yet undertaken. In other cases, the market price may not react until some time after the investments have been made.

To illustrate this criterion suppose for simplicity that a firm is financed wholly from common stock equity and has no appreciable amounts of debt outstanding. The price per share is $100 and the earnings and dividends in a typical year are $10 per share. In a given year this company undertakes a series of investments that together have essentially the same risk characteristics as the investments that have previously been made by the firm. The new investments are expected to raise a typical year's earnings and dividends from $10 per share to $11 per share. If the investments are financed from internally generated funds, we might predict under these circumstances that the price per share would rise from $100 to $110 as the market became aware of the earning potential of the new investments. That is, if the earning potential of the company had increased by 10% as a result of these new investments, and if the risk characteristics remained unchanged, we might expect that the price per share would also increase by an equal percentage. Whether or not this new set of investments was considered desirable by the financial community would depend upon other opportunities available to the investors, and the cost of the investments. If the investments cost less than $10 per share, we would conclude that the investments were considered desirable by the financial community. If they cost more than $10 per share we would say that they had been considered undesirable by the financial community, and that the stockholders would have benefited more by a cash disbursement equal to the cost of the investment.

To understand the logic of this we need only consider what the consequences would have been to a typical shareholder if the investments had been rejected. If the stocks had been selling for $100 per share and no investments were made during the period, then presumably as far as the investment policy is concerned, there would be no reason to expect a change in the price per share. However, the firm would have an amount of earnings that we can imagine it distributes to the stockholders in the form of an extra dividend. Suppose that the investments if undertaken would have cost $10. If the investments are not undertaken then an extra dividend equal to $10 is declared. In the latter case, at the end of the period the stockholder would have a share worth $100, plus $10 in extra dividends, and the investor is just as well off as when the firm invested the funds, driving the price up to $110. In both cases his total assets were equal to $110.

On the other hand, if the investment necessary to increase earnings by $1 had cost only $5.00 per share, the stockholder would have had $100, plus a $5.00 extra dividend, if the investment had been rejected. With the investment he would have had a share of stock worth $110, or $5.00 more than without the investment.

This approach applies only if it is reasonable to assume that the investments undertaken by a firm during a given period generate earnings that have the same risk characteristics as the investments previously undertaken.

The investments may not have the same characteristics as investments previously made but rather may improve the quality of the risk characteristics the market associates with the company's earnings. To take an extreme case, suppose a company whose shares have been selling for $100 per share, based on earnings and dividends of $10 per share, now undertakes some investments at a cost of $10 per share. The investments result in no measurable increase in a typical year's earnings, but they reduce the risk associated with these earnings. If the market judges that the quality of the stock has increased, then it might be willing to price the stock on the basis of a higher multiple of its earning (a lower discount rate or a smaller risk adjustment) than was previously the case. If because of the increase in quality, the price per share goes from $100 to $110, we may still conclude that the investments were worthwhile.

CONCLUSIONS

The corporation should take the nature of the risk associated with the investment and its interaction with the risks of other investments into consideration. The process by which risk is incorporated into the decision can be complex. However, there remains the mechanism of the security markets and this helps simplify the decision process tremendously. Assuming investors who are able and willing to diversify, the only risk components that need be taken into account by the corporation (from the point of view of stockholders) are those that the individual investor cannot eliminate by diversifying his portfolio.[4] This suggests that many investments that have been traditionally considered to be highly risky, such as exploring for new reserves of oil, may turn out to require a relatively small risk premium.

However, corporate management may wish to apply a significant risk premium to large investments that could jeopardize the existence of the firm. If a manager has special skills and experience that make him more valuable to his present employer than to other firms, and if he derives a large fraction of his income from his employment, then he is less able than most stockholders to diversify against events that could threaten the continued existence of the firm.

[4] See William F. Sharpe, "Capital Asset Prices: A Theory of Market Equilibrium Under Conditions of Risk," *Journal of Finance* **XIX** (Sept., 1964), pp. 425–442.

If we rely on the market exchanges and portfolio diversification by the investor to accomplish the incorporation of risk, then for a wide range of investments the firm can make its decisions primarily on expected net present value. Allowances for risk, either in the discount rate or in the measurement of the consequences, would be significant mainly for investments that are very large or where the results have a large variance compared to the net expected value of the investment.

If we drop the assumption of a large publicly owned firm then we can no longer assume that the investor has attained diversification. Now, the investor may be adversely affected by a decision made using expected net present value (an investment may have too much risk, i.e., there is too large a probability of a large loss). The corporation may try to take into consideration the affairs of this investor, but this is very difficult since the investor may be seeking risk in the hope of attaining large gains, or may be a risk avertor.

For practical business decision making, agreement on the exact method of incorporating risk into the analysis is less important than agreement that varying the rate of discount is not a good way of accomplishing the objective of taking risk into consideration. It is true that most persons would require a higher return for risky investments than for less risky investments; however, trying to determine the minimum acceptable rate of discount for different situations is a difficult task.

The use of a discount rate lower than the cost of capital (traditionally computed to be approximately .10) to adjust for the time value of money is an exciting and controversial departure from current capital budgeting practice, but a reasonable evolution. It makes eligible for consideration many investments that would otherwise be excluded. While it does not mean that these investments will be automatically accepted (they still may be screened for risk), it does mean that relatively safe, long-lived investments with low average returns will receive more consideration than they might receive using the cost of capital as the discount rate. It is impossible to predict whether more, less, or the same amount of investment will result from the use of the lower rate of discount and a supplemental risk analysis. We would strongly suspect that more investments would result. Currently investments are screened using the cost of capital, but then risk criteria are applied intuitively to reduce the number of eligible investments. The use of a lower rate of discount would increase the number of eligible investments, thus tending to increase the number that could be ultimately accepted.

QUESTIONS AND PROBLEMS

16–1. The Boeing Airplane Company in 1965 was faced with a major decision: to what extent should it independently develop a supersonic air transport?

The estimates of cost of developing such a plane ranged from one billion to two billion dollars. During the period of decision the English and the French were acting jointly in the development of such a plane, and the United States government considered undertaking a similar project. The reader is referred to the financial reports of Boeing for the year 1965 for financial information.

Required: If you were advising the president of Boeing, what would you suggest? If you were advising the President of the United States what would you suggest?

16–2.

Change in current wealth	Sam's utility	Bill's utility
$		
−40	−100	−100
−20	− 40	− 20
0	0	0
80	40	100
100	60	110
200	300	150

A ticket in a lottery costs $40. If it turns out to be a winning ticket, a prize of $240 will be received. The probability is .3 that the ticket purchased will be a winner. If the ticket purchased is not a winning ticket, no prize is received. The lottery will be conducted a short time after the ticket is purchased.

(a) Suppose Sam is interested in maximizing expected utility. He can buy one ticket, or half a ticket (in which case the cost is half as much, and he receives $120 if the ticket wins), or not play in the lottery. What should he do?

(b) Suppose Bill is interested in maximizing expected utility. He has the same alternatives as Sam. What decision will he make?

Suppose it will be possible to buy a half interest in two different tickets. In this case the probability that both tickets will be winners is .09; the probability that both tickets wil be losers is .49; the probability that one ticket (but not both) will be a winner is .42.

(c) Would Sam prefer a half interest in two different tickets or a whole interest in one ticket?

(d) Would Bill prefer a half interest in each of two different tickets or a whole interest in one ticket?

(e) What would be your preference?

16-3. Assume there are two investments of different risk. A return of .05 is required on one investment; on the other a return of .10 is required. Compare the present values obtained for each investment for expected cash flows of $1,000,000 one period, twenty years, and fifty years from now at the required rates of return.

16-4. The ABC Company issued $1,000 bonds with a coupon interest rate of .05 per year at a price to yield .06 (the price was $885.30 per bond). The life of the bonds is 20 years.

Required: Give three different reasons as to why the bond yield is .06.

16-5. The ABC Company has issued a $1,000 .05 bond with a four-year life. The current interest rate for risk free securities is .05. Assume the following probabilities of payment apply: (The probability of collecting in a given year is statistically independent of whether or not a collection occurred in the previous year. Missed collections are not made up.)

Principal or interest of period	Probability of collection	Probability of no collection
1	1.0	0.0
2	.9	.1
3	.6	.4
4	.5	.5

(a) Assuming that you are willing to pay the expected present value, what amount would you pay for this bond? (b) If the investor pays the amount in (a), what is the approximate cost to the firm issuing the bond? (c) What is the market price of this investment likely to be?

16-6. The ABC Company has been offered a certain investment that yields .05. It can borrow funds at .06, and the interest rate on government securities of a similar maturity is .04. There are no taxes. Should the investment be accepted?

16–7. The capital structure of the ABC Company is .8 stock .2 long term debt. Assume that investors have a time value of money of .05, and there is a corporate tax rate of .4. What is the appropriate rate of discount?

16–8. The ABC Company wants to use its cost of capital in evaluating investments. By a secret process it has succeeded in obtaining the forecasts of future dividends used by investors currently purchasing the stock. By equating the present value of these dividends to the price of the stock it has obtained a number that it considers to be an estimator of the cost of common stock funds.

Required: Comment on the suitability of the measure obtained.

16–9. The Eatwell Company is considering the purchase of a new machine to replace one currently in use. The new machine would cost $100,000 and be depreciated over a four-year period on a straight-line basis. It would have no salvage value. Ignore the investment tax credit in making your analysis.

Let us suppose that the new equipment whose purchase is proposed is to be used to replace an older machine that is fully depreciated and has no salvage value. The older machine could be continued in use for another four years, if this were economically desirable. Both machines could be used to produce a part that is a component of one of the company's products. The company's engineering department estimates that the use of the proposed new machine would most likely result in a reduction of 25 cents per unit in the manufacturing cost of the component. This cost reduction calculation takes into consideration savings in direct labor, material, and variable overhead, on a before-tax basis; the cost attributed to depreciation on the new machine is not included in this calculation.

There is some chance that the savings may not be as great as anticipated. The engineering department considers that there is .1 probability the machine produces savings of 15 cents per unit, and it further believes that there is .9 probability that savings of 25 cents per unit will actually be realized.

Because the total savngs that will be realized will depend on the number of units produced, the sales department of the company was asked to estimate total sales for the next four years for the product.

The product has an established and stable market. The sales department expected that demand would continue at the present rate for the next four years, in which case total sales would amount to 600,000 units, but added an important qualification. It was known that a competitor was about to introduce a product that might be more satisfactory than the company's product to some consumers. If the competitive product is successful, unit sales for the four-year period might be only 400,000. However, the sales department believed the probability is only .3 that the competitor's product would be successful.

Considering both the engineering and the technical uncertainties connected with the proposed new equipment, four possible outcomes (events) need to be considered. These outcomes and their probabilities are given in Table 1. The joint probabilities were calculated on

Table 1.   Joint Probabilities of Possible Outcomes Associated with Use of New Equipment

Unit cost reduction	Unit sales		Marginal probability
	400,000	600,000	
$0.25	.27	.63	.90
0.15	.03	.07	.10
Marginal probability	.30	.70	1.00

the assumption that the unit cost reduction achieved by the machine would be statistically independent of the unit sales of the product. The assumption seems reasonable in this instance.

The financial consequences of these four outcomes are described as follows, assuming a .4 tax rate.

Although the cash inflows that might result from using the new equipment are uncertain, the cash outflows associated with a decision to acquire the new equipment, and the tax savings from depreciation, are not uncertain.

The Eatwell Company produces about 100 different food products, which are distributed through retail foodstores. The machine in question would be used to help manufacture one of these products. The product in question accounts for about 3 per cent of sales and of net profits.

Table 2.   Annual After-Tax Savings Before Depreciation

Event	Unit cost reduction	Unit sales for 4 years	(1) Probability (1)	(2) Total before taxes (2)	(3) Savings after taxes (3) × .6	(4) Annual after-tax savings (4) × ¼	(5) Expectation (1) × (4)
				$	$	$	$
e_1	$0.25	600,000	.63	150,000	90,000	22,500	14,175
e_2	0.25	400,000	.27	100,000	60,000	15,000	4,050
e_3	0.15	600,000	.07	90,000	54,000	13,500	945
e_4	0.15	400,000	.03	60,000	36,000	9,000	270
	Total		1.00				19,440

Eatwell has a capital structure consisting of 80 per cent equity and 20 per cent debt. It is able to borrow money on a long-term basis at 5 per cent (before taxes). The financial committee estimates that the company's average cost of capital is 10 per cent.

The company has no established policy as to the minimum acceptable level of return. It feels that both profitability and risk need to be considered in deciding whether or not an investment is desirable.

Should Eatwell purchase this new machine? What data would you use to defend your judgment?

16–10. The ABC Book Company is considering investing $3,000,000 in an advanced teaching mechanism. If the advanced mechanism is successful, the company expects the investment to have a net present value of $4,000,000. If it is unsuccessful, the investment has a negative net present value of $2,000,000. The probability of success is .7 and failure .3. A loss of $2,000,000 would be very material to this firm.

The company is also considering investing $1,000,000 in a new method of producing books. The method has a .4 probability of being workable. If the method works, the net present value of this investment is computed to be $2,000,000 if the teaching mechanism fails and $0 if the teaching mechanism is successful. If the method of producing books is not successful, there will be a net loss of $1,000,000 resulting from this investment, with a successful teaching mechanism; and the company will break even on this investment if the teaching mechanism is not successful.

Payoffs of $1,000,000 investment in book production

Successful book method	Successful teaching mechanism	
	Yes	No
Yes	0	$2,000,000
No	−$1,000,000	0

Required: Should the company undertake either or both of the investments?

16–11. The Rokal Company is a small regional hardware wholesaler. In recent years the company has been earning approximately $500,000 per year after taxes. Approximately half of the earnings have been paid out as dividends. The stock is closely held by descendants of the founder, many of whom rely on their dividends for a substantial part of their personal income. The board of directors of the company consists of the principal stockholders or their representatives, including the president. Day-to-day management of the company is concentrated in the hands of the president, Mr. John Chalishan, who it is generally agreed is the only family member capable of effectively running the business. The board is consulted on important policy matters. Their main objective is to have the company maintain a stable dividend, with some growth if possible.

Recently several of the board members have become concerned about the possible dangers to dividend stability arising from the fact that management is so heavily concentrated in the hands of the president. In case of a serious sickness or unexpected death, there would be no one else capable of quickly and effectively taking over the management. The board recognized that, in time, an effective professional manager could be found to replace Mr. Chalishan. It also recognized that the company would suffer some financial impairment if it operated without an experienced and energetic head for the 6 to 24 months that would be required to find a new president. The ability of the company to pay its regular dividend during such an interim period was questionable.

The possibility of hiring a potential replacement now was considered but rejected. A person of the necessary experience and ability would be expensive; he would have no real future with the company if Mr. Chalishan, who was only forty-seven years old, remained in good health, and might become a source of friction and factionalism.

The board members finally concluded that the purchase of an insurance policy on Mr. Chalishan's life in the amount of $500,000 would be the best way of handling this risk. Inquiries with an insurance broker indicated that a single payment of $15,000 would provide a five-year term policy on Mr. Chalishan's life, assuming he passed the usual medical examination. The policy provided for renewal if desired with no subsequent medical examination.

When the subject was raised at a board meeting, Mr. Chalishan reacted rather coolly and asked to have the subject tabled until the next meeting. This was done. At the subsequent meeting Mr. Chalishan presented an analysis of the proposed life insurance policy as an investment, which he felt it was. He recommended that the proposal should be rejected on the grounds that it was an obviously unprofitable investment. He presented Exhibit I to justify his opinion.

Exhibit I.   Analysis of Life Insurance Policy as an Investment

A. Present-value analysis

Year	Cash flow	Probability *	Expected cash flow	Present-value factor †	Present value
0	−$15,000	1.000		1.0000	−$15,000
1	$500,000	0.005	$2,500	.9524	$2,381
2	500,000	0.005	2,500	.9070	2,268
3	500,000	0.005	2,500	.8638	2,160
4	500,000	0.005	2,500	.8227	2,057
5	500,000	0.005	2,500	.7835	1,959
				Net Present Value	−$4,177

B. Rate of return analysis

The discounted cash flow rate of return on the expected cash flows associated with this policy is approximately minus 6 per cent.

* Probability based on mortality experience for males of like age and occupation.
† Using a 5 per cent discount rate.

Can the purchase of a life insurance policy be treated as an investment? Why? Is it reasonable for the Rokal Company to purchase this policy?

BIBLIOGRAPHY

ARTICLES ON CAPITAL BUDGETING

Alchian, Armen A. "The Rate of Interest, Fisher's Rate of Return over Costs, and Keynes' Internal Rate of Return," *American Economic Review*, December 1955, pp. 938–943.

———— "The Role of Securities in the Optimal Allocation of Risk-Bearing," *The Review of Economic Studies*, April 1964, pp. 91–96.

Arrow, Kenneth J. "Alternative Approaches to the Theory of Choice in Risk-Taking Situations," *Econometrica*, October 1951, pp. 404–437.

———— "The Portfolio Approach to the Demand for Money and Other Assets, Comment," *The Review of Economics and Statistics: Supplement*, February 1963, pp. 24–27.

Bailey, Martin J. "Formal Criteria for Investment Decisions," *Journal of Political Economy*, October 1959, pp. 476–488.

Baumol, William J. "An Expected Gain-Confidence Limit Criterion for Portfolio Selection," *Management Science*, October 1963, pp. 174–182.

Bernhard, Richard H. "Discount Methods for Expenditure Evaluation— A Clarification of Their Assumptions," *Journal of Industrial Engineering*, January-February 1962, pp. 19–27.

Bernoulli, Daniel. "Exposition of a New Theory on the Measurement of Risk," Translation, Louise Sommer, *Econometrica*, January 1954, pp. 23–36.

Bierman, Harold Jr., and Seymour Smidt. "Capital Budgeting and the Problem of Reinvesting Cash Proceeds," *Journal of Business*, October 1957, pp. 276–279.

Bodenhorn, Diran. "On the Problem of Capital Budgeting," *Journal of Finance*, December 1959, pp. 473–492.

———— "A Cash Flow Concept of Profit," *Journal of Finance*, March 1964, pp. 16–31.

Boness, A. James. "A Pedagogic Note on the Cost of Capital," *Journal of Finance*, March 1964, pp. 99–106.

Borch, Karl. "A Note on Utility and Attitudes to Risk," *Management Science*, July 1963, pp. 697–700.

Boulding, Kenneth. "The Theory of a Single Investment," *Quarterly Journal of Economics*, May 1935, pp. 475–494.

Charnes, Abraham; Cooper, William W.; and Miller, Merton H. "Application of Linear Programming to Financial Budgeting and the Costing of Funds," *Journal of Business*, January 1959, pp. 20–46.

Christenson, Charles. "Construction of Present Value Tables for Use in Evaluating Capital Investment Opportunities," *Accounting Review*, October 1955, pp. 666–672.

Clower, Robert W. "An Investigation into the Dynamics of Investment," *Economic Review*, March 1954, pp. 64–81.

Coleman, John R. Jr.; Smidt, Seymour; and York, Robert. "Optimum

Plant Design for Seasonal Production," *Management Science,* July 1964, pp. 778–785.

Coleman, John R., and York, Robert. "Optimum Plant Design for a Growing Market," *Industrial and Engineering Chemistry,* January 1964, pp. 28–34.

Cord, Joel. "A Method for Allocating Funds to Investment Projects When Returns Are Subject to Uncertainty," *Management Science,* January 1964, pp. 335–341.

Dryden, Myles. "The MAAPI Urgency Rating as an Investment Ranking Criterion," *Journal of Business,* October 1960, pp. 327–341.

———— "Measuring the Productivity of Capital," *Harvard Business Review,* January-February 1954, pp. 120–130.

Durand, David. "Costs of Debt and Equity Funds for Business: Trends and Problems of Measurement," in *Conference on Research in Business Finance,* National Bureau Economic Research, New York, 1952.

———— "Growth Stocks and the St. Petersburg Paradox," *Journal of Finance,* September 1957, pp. 348–363.

———— "The Cost of Capital in an Imperfect Market: A Reply to Modigliani and Miller," *American Economic Review,* September 1959, pp. 639–654.

Dusenberry, James B. "The Portfolio Approach to the Demand for Money and Other Assets," *The Review of Economics and Statistics: Supplement,* February 1963, pp. 9–24.

Dyckman, T. R. "Allocating Funds to Investment Projects When Returns Are Subject to Uncertainty: A Comment," *Management Science,* November 1964, pp. 348–350.

Eckstein, Otto. "Investment Criteria for Economic Development and the Theory of Intertemporal Welfare Economics," *Quarterly Journal of Economics,* February 1957, pp. 56–85.

Fama, Eugene. "Portfolio Selection in a Stable Paretian Market," *Management Science,* January 1965, pp. 404–419.

Fisher, Lawrence. "Determinants of Risk Premiums on Corporate Bonds," *Journal of Political Economy,* June 1959, pp. 217–237.

Freund, Rudolf J. "The Introduction of Risk in a Programming Model," *Econometrica,* July 1956, pp. 253–263.

Friedman, Milton J., and Savage, Leonard J. "The Utility Analysis of Choices Involving Risk," *Journal of Political Economy,* August 1948, pp. 279–304.

Gabor, Andre, and Pearce, I. F. "The Place of Money Capital in the Theory of Production," *Quarterly Journal of Economics,* November 1958, pp. 537–557.

Gordon, Myron J. "The Payoff Period and the Rate of Profit," *Journal of Business,* October 1955, pp. 253–261.

———— "Optimal Investment and Financing Policy," *The Journal of Finance,* May 1963, pp. 264–272.

———— "Security and Investment: Theory and Evidence." *The Journal of Finance,* December 1964, pp. 607–618.

———— and Shapiro, Eli. "Capital Equipment Analysis: The Required Rate of Profit," *Management Science,* October 1956, pp. 102–110.

Hertz, David B. "Risk Analysis in Capital Investment," *Harvard Business Review,* January-February 1964, pp. 95–106.

Hicks, John R. "Liquidity," *The Economic Journal,* December, 1962, pp. 787–802.

Hildreth, Clifford G. "Note on Maximization Criteria," *Quarterly Journal of Econoimcs,* November, 1946, pp. 156–164.

Hillier, Frederick S. "The Derivation of Probabilistic Information for the Evaluation of Risky Investments," *Management Science,* April, 1963, pp. 443–457.

Hirshleifer, Jack. "On the Theory of Optimal Investment Decision," *Journal of Political Economy,* August, 1958, pp. 329–352.

———— "Risk, the Discount Rate and Investment Decisions," *American Economic Review,* May, 1961, pp. 112–120.

———— "Efficient Allocation of Capital in an Uncertain World," *American Economic Review,* Papers and Proceedings, May 1964, pp. 77–85.

Holt, Charles C., and Shelton, John P. "The Implications of the Capital Gains Tax for Investment Decisions," *Journal of Finance,* December 1961, pp. 559–580.

Kalecki, Michal. "The Principle of Increasing Risk," in *Essays in the Theory of Economic Fluctuations.* London: Allen and Unwin, 1939.

Lange, Oscar. "The Place of Interest in the Theory of Production," *Review of Economic Studies,* June 1936, pp. 159–192.

Latane, Henry A. "Criteria for Choice Among Risky Ventures," *Journal of Political Economy,* April 1959, pp. 144–155.

———— "Investment Criteria—A Three Asset Portfolio Balance Model," *Review of Economics and Statistics,* November 1963, pp. 427–430.

Lerner, Eugene M., and Carleton, Willard T. "The Integration of Capital Budgeting and Stock Valuation," *The American Economic Review,* September 1964, pp. 681–702.

Lintner, John. "Distribution of Incomes of Corporations Among Dividends, Retained Earnings, and Taxes," *American Economic Review,* May 1956, pp. 97–113.

———— "Dividends, Earnings, Leverage, Stock Prices and the Supply of Capital to Corporations," *Review of Economics and Statistics,* August 1962, pp. 246–269.

———— "The Cost of Capital and Optimal Financing of Corporate Growth," *Journal of Finance,* May 1963, pp. 292–310.

———— "Optimal Dividends and Corporate Growth Under Uncertainty," *Quarterly Journal of Economics,* February 1964, pp. 49–95.

———— "The Valuation of Risk Assets and the Selection of Risky Investments in Stock Portfolios and Capital Budgets," *Review of Economics and Statistics,* February 1965, pp. 13–37.

Lorie, James H., and Savage, Leonard J. "Three Problems in Capital Rationing," *Journal of Business,* October 1955, pp. 229–239.

Malkiel, Burton G. "Expectations, Bond Prices, and the Term Structure of Interest Rates," *Quarterly Journal of Economics*, May 1962, pp. 197–218.

Manne, Alan S. "Capacity Expansion and Probabilistic Growth," *Econometrica*, October 1961, pp. 632–649.

Markowitz, Harry M. "Portfolio Selection," *Journal of Finance*, March 1952, pp. 77–91.

Marschak, Jacob. "Money and the Theory of Assets," *Econometrica*, October 1938.

Martin, A. D. "Mathematical Programming of Portfolio Selection," *Management Science*, January 1955, pp. 152–166.

Miller, Roger F. "A Note on the Theory of Investment and Production," *Quarterly Journal of Economics*, November 1959, pp. 672–681.

Modigliani, Franco, and Miller, Merton H. "The Cost of Capital, Corporation Finance, and the Theory of Investment," *American Economic Review*, June 1958, pp. 261–297.

———— "The Cost of Capital, Corporation Finance, and the Theory of Investment: Reply," *American Economic Review*, September 1959, pp. 655–669.

———— "Dividend Policy, Growth, and the Valuation of Shares," *The Journal of Business*, October 1961, pp. 411–433.

———— "Corporate Income Taxes and the Cost of Capital: A Correction," *American Economic Review*, June 1963, pp. 433–442.

Naslund, Bertil, and Whinston, Andrew. "A Model Multi-Period Investment Under Uncertainty," *Management Science*, January 1962, pp. 184–200.

Norton, Frank E. "Administrative Organization in Capital Budgeting," *Journal of Business*, October 1955, pp. 291–295.

Ortner, Robert. "The Concept of Yield on Common Stock," *Journal of Finance*, May 1964, pp. 186–198.

Pratt, John W.; Raiffa, Howard; and Schlaifer, Robert. "The Foundations of Decision Under Uncertainty," *Journal of American Statistical Association*, June 1964, pp. 353–375.

Preinreich, Gabriel A. D. "The Economic Life of Industrial Equipment," *Econometrica*, January 1940, pp. 12–44.

Reiter, Stanley. "Choosing an Investment Program Among Interdependent Projects," *The Review of Economic Studies*, February 1963, pp. 32–36.

Roberts, Harry V. "Current Problems in the Economics of Capital Budgeting," *Journal of Business*, January 1957, pp. 12–16.

Roy, Andrew D. "Safety First and the Holding of Assets," *Econometrica*, July 1952, pp. 431–449.

Sharpe, William F. "A Simplified Model for Portfolio Analysis," *Management Science*, January 1963, pp. 277–293.

———— "Capital Asset Prices: A Theory of Market Equilibrium Under Conditions of Risk," *Journal of Finance*, September 1964, pp. 425–442.

Shillinglaw, Gordon. "Residual Values in Investment Analysis," *Journal of Business*, October 1955, pp. 275–284.

——— "Guides to Internal Profit Measurement," *Harvard Business Review*, March-April 1957.

Smith, Vernon L. "Depreciation, Market Valuation and Investment Theory," *Management Science*, July 1963, pp. 690–698.

Solomon, Ezra. "Measuring a Company's Cost of Capital," *Journal of Business*, October 1955, pp. 240–252.

——— "The Arithmetic of Capital Budgeting Decisions," *Journal of Business*, April 1956, pp. 124–129.

——— "Leverage and the Cost of Capital," *The Journal of Finance*, May 1963, pp. 273–279.

Tintner, John. "Optimal Dividends and Corporate Growth Under Uncertainty," *The Quarterly Journal of Economics*, February 1964, pp. 49–95.

Tobin, James. "Liquidity Preference as Behavior Towards Risk," *The Review of Economic Studies*, February 1958, pp. 65–86.

Walter, James F. "Dividend Policies and Common Stock Prices," *Journal of Finance*, March 1956, pp. 29–41.

——— "Liquidity and Corporate Spending," *Journal of Finance*, December 1953, pp. 369–387.

——— "Dividend Policy: Its Influence on the Value of the Enterprise," *The Journal of Finance*, May 1963, pp. 280–291.

Weaver, James B. "False and Multiple Solutions by the Discounted Cash Flow Method for Determining Interest Rate of Return," *Engineering Economics*, Spring 1958, p. 1–31.

Wright, John F. "Notes on the Marginal Efficiency of Capital," *Oxford Economic Papers*, July 1963, pp. 124–129.

BOOKS ON CAPITAL BUDGETING

Alchian, Armen A. *Economic Replacement Policy*. (Santa Monica, California: RAND Corporation, April 1952).

Barges, Alexander. *The Effect of Capital Structure on the Cost of Capital*. (Ford Foundation Doctoral Dissertation Winner.) (Englewood Cliffs: Prentice-Hall, 1963).

Barish, Norman R. *Economic Analysis for Engineering and Managerial Decision Making*. (New York: McGraw-Hill, 1963).

Bowman, Edward H., and Fetter, Robert B. *Analyses of Industrial Operations*. (Homewood, Illinois: Richard D. Irwin, 1959).

Bryce, Murray D. *Industrial Development: A Guide for Accelerating Economic Growth*. (New York: McGraw-Hill, 1960).

Carlson, Sune. *A Study on the Pure Theory of Production*. (New York: Kelley and Millman, 1956).

Carter, Charles F., and others. *Uncertainty and Business Decisions*. (Liverpool University Press, 1957).

Clarkson, Goeffrey P. E. *Portfolio Selection: A Simulation of Trust Investment*. (Ford Foundation Doctoral Dissertation Winner). (Englewood Cliffs: Prentice-Hall, 1962).

Coleman, John R., Jr. *Optimum Plant Design Under Variable Demand.* Cornell University Ph.D. Dissertation, 1963.

Cootner, Paul H. (ed.). *The Random Character of Stock Market Prices.* (Cambridge: The M.I.T. Press, 1964).

Dean, Joel. *Capital Budgeting.* (New York: Columbia University Press, 1951).

Debreau, Gerard. *Theory of Value.* (New York: J. Wiley & Sons, 1959).

Donaldson, Gordon. *Corporate Debt Capacity.* Boston: Division of Research, Harvard Graduate School of Business Administration, 1961.

Eckstein, Otto. *Water Resource Development.* (Cambridge, Mass.: Harvard University Press, 1958).

Farrar, Donald E. *The Investment Decision Under Uncertainty* (Ford Foundation Doctoral Dissertation Winner). (Englewood Cliffs: Prentice-Hall, 1962).

Fisher, Irving. *The Nature of Capital and Income.* (New York: The Macmillan Company, 1906).

————— *The Theory of Interest* (reprint). (New York: Kelley & Millman, Inc., 1954).

Fredrikson, E. Bruce. *Frontiers of Investment Analysis.* (Scranton, Pa.: International Textbook Company, 1965).

Gaffney, M. Mason. *Concepts of Financial Maturity of Timber and Other Assets.* Agricultural Economics Information Series No. 62. (Raleigh: North Carolina State College, 1957).

Good, Irving J. *Probability and Weighting of Evidence.* (London: C. Griffin, 1950).

Gordon, Myron J. *The Investment, Financing and Valuation of the Corporation.* (Homewood, Illinois: Richard D. Irwin, 1962).

Grant, Eugene L., and Ireson, William G. *Principles of Engineering Economy,* 4th ed. (New York: The Ronald Press Co., 1960).

Grayson, C. Jackson, Jr. *Decisions Under Uncertainty: Drilling Decisions by Oil and Gas Operators.* (Boston: Harvard University Graduate School of Business Administration, 1960).

Hart, Albert G. *Anticipations, Uncertainty, and Dynamic Planning, Studies in Business Administration.* (Chicago: University of Chicago Press, 1940.

Hirshleifer, Jack; DeHaven, James; and Milliman, Jerome. *Water Supply, Economics, Technology & Policy.* (Chicago: University of Chicago Press, 1960).

Howard, Ronald A. *Dynamic Programming and Markov Processes.* (New York: M.I.T. Technology Press and J. Wiley & Sons, 1960).

Kaufman, Gordon M. *Statistical Decision and Related Techniques in Oil and Gas Exploration.* (Englewood Cliffs: Prentice-Hall, 1963).

Keirstead, Bruce S. *Capital Interest and Profits.* (New York: J. Wiley & Sons, 1959).

Krutilla, John, and Eckstein, Otto. *Multi Purpose River Development.* (Baltimore: Johns Hopkins Press, 1958).

Lutz, Friedrich and Vera. *The Theory of Investment of the Firm.* (Princeton: Princeton University Press, 1951).

Lutz, F. A. *The Theory of Capital.* (New York: St. Martin's Press, 1961).

Maass, Arthur A. *Design of Water-Resource Systems: New Techniques for Relating Economic Objectives, Engineering Analysis* . . . . Cambridge, Mass.: Harvard University Press, 1962.

Markowitz, Harry M. *Portfolio Selection: Efficient Diversification of Investments,* Cowles Foundation Monograph #16. New York: J. Wiley & Sons, 1959.

Marris, Robin. *The Economics of Capital Utilization.* (Cambridge, Eng.: Cambridge University Press, 1964).

Marglin, Stephen A. *Approaches to Dynamic Investment Planning.* Amsterdam: North Holland Publishing Co., 1963.

Masse, Pierre. *Optimal Investment Decisions: Rules for Action and Criteria for Choice.* Englewood Cliffs: Prentice-Hall, 1962.

———— *Le Choix des Investissements-Criteres et methodes,* 2nd ed. Paris: Dunod, 1964.

McKean, Roland N. *Efficiency in Government Through Systems Analysis.* New York: J. Wiley & Sons, 1958.

Merrett, A. J., and Sykes, Albert. *The Finance and Analysis of Capital Projects.* London: Longmans Green and Co., Ltd., 1963.

Renshaw, Edward F. *Toward Responsible Government: An Economic Appraisal of Federal Investment in Water Resource Programs.* Chicago: Idyia Press, 1957.

Schlaifer, Robert. *Probability and Statistics for Business Decisions.* New York: McGraw-Hill, 1959.

Smith, Don T. *The Effects of Taxation on Corporate Financial Policy.* Boston: Harvard Graduate School of Business Administration, 1952.

Smith, Vernon L. *Investment and Production.* Cambridge, Mass.: Harvard University Press, 1961.

Solomon, Ezra (ed.). *The Management of Corporate Capital.* New York: The Free Press of Glencoe, 1959.

———— *The Theory of Financial Management.* New York: Columbia University Press, 1964.

Terborgh, George. *Business Equipment Policy.* Washington, D. C.: Machinery and Allied Products Institute, 1958.

Tinbergen, Jan. *The Design of Development.* Baltimore: The John Hopkins Press, 1958.

United Nations, Economic Commission for Latin America. *Manual on Economic Development Projects.* New York: 1958.

U. S. Department of the Interior. *Proposed Practices for Economic Analysis of River Basin Projects; Report to the Federal Inter-Agency River Basin Committee.* Washington: Government Printing Office, 1950.

Vancil, Richard F. *Leasing of Industrial Equipment.* New York: McGraw-Hill, 1963.

Vandell, Robert F., and Vancil, Richard F. *Cases in Capital Budgeting.* Homewood: Richard D. Irwin, 1962.

Weingartner, H. Martin. *Mathematical Programming and the Analysis of Capital Budgeting Problems.* (Ford Foundation Doctoral Dissertation Winner). Englewood Cliffs: Prentice-Hall, 1963.

Williams, John B. *The Theory of Investment Value.* Cambridge, Mass.: Harvard University Press, 1938.

Appendix

TABLES

Table A.   Present Value of $1.00

$$(1 + r)^{-n}$$

n/r	1.0%	1.1%	1.2%	1.3%	1.4%
1	.990099	.989120	.988142	.987167	.986193
2	.980296	.978358	.976425	.974498	.972577
3	.970590	.967713	.964847	.961992	.959149
4	.960980	.957184	.953406	.949647	.945906
5	.951466	.946769	.942101	.937460	.932847
6	.942045	.936468	.930930	.925429	.919967
7	.932718	.926279	.919891	.913553	.907265
8	.923483	.916201	.908983	.901829	.894739
9	.914340	.906232	.898205	.890256	.882386
10	.905287	.896372	.887554	.878831	.870203
11	.896324	.886620	.877030	.867553	.858188
12	.887449	.876973	.866630	.856420	.846339
13	.878663	.867431	.856354	.845429	.834654
14	.869963	.857993	.846200	.834580	.823130
15	.861349	.848658	.836166	.823869	.811766
16	.852821	.839424	.826251	.813296	.800558
17	.844377	.830291	.816453	.802859	.789505
18	.836017	.821257	.806772	.792556	.778604
19	.827740	.812322	.797205	.782385	.767854
20	.819544	.803483	.787752	.772345	.757253
21	.811430	.794741	.778411	.762433	.746798
22	.803396	.786094	.769181	.752649	.736487
23	.795442	.777541	.760061	.742990	.726318
24	.787566	.769081	.751048	.733455	.716290
25	.779768	.760713	.742142	.724042	.706401
26	.772048	.752437	.733342	.714750	.696648
27	.764404	.744250	.724646	.705578	.687029
28	.756836	.736152	.716054	.696523	.677544
29	.749342	.728143	.707563	.687585	.668189
30	.741923	.720220	.699173	.678761	.658963
35	.705914	.681883	.658692	.636311	.614712
40	.671653	.645586	.620554	.596516	.573432
45	.639055	.611221	.584624	.559210	.534924
50	.608039	.578685	.550775	.524237	.499002

Table A.   Present Value of $1.00 (cont'd)

n/r	1.5%	1.6%	1.7%	1.8%	1.9%
1	.985222	.984252	.983284	.982318	.981354
2	.970662	.968752	.966848	.964949	.963056
3	.956317	.953496	.950686	.947887	.945099
4	.942184	.938480	.934795	.931127	.927477
5	.928260	.923701	.919169	.914663	.910184
6	.914542	.909155	.903804	.898490	.893213
7	.901027	.894837	.888696	.882603	.876558
8	.887711	.880745	.873841	.866997	.860214
9	.874592	.866875	.859234	.851667	.844175
10	.861667	.853224	.844871	.836608	.828434
11	.848933	.839787	.830748	.821816	.812988
12	.836387	.826562	.816862	.807285	.797829
13	.824027	.813545	.803207	.793010	.782953
14	.811849	.800734	.789781	.778989	.768354
15	.799852	.788124	.776579	.765215	.754028
16	.788031	.775712	.763598	.751684	.739968
17	.776385	.763496	.750834	.738393	.726171
18	.764912	.751473	.738283	.725337	.712631
19	.753607	.739639	.725942	.712512	.699343
20	.742470	.727991	.713807	.699914	.686304
21	.731498	.716526	.701875	.687538	.673507
22	.720688	.705242	.690143	.675381	.660949
23	.710037	.694136	.678607	.663439	.648625
24	.699544	.683205	.667263	.651708	.636531
25	.689206	.672446	.656109	.640185	.624662
26	.679021	.661856	.645142	.628866	.613015
27	.668986	.651433	.634358	.617746	.601585
28	.659099	.641174	.623754	.606823	.590368
29	.649359	.631077	.613327	.596094	.579360
30	.639762	.621139	.603075	.585554	.568558
35	.593866	.573747	.554328	.535584	.517492
40	.551262	.529970	.509521	.489879	.471013
45	.511715	.489534	.468336	.448074	.428708
50	.475005	.452183	.430479	.409837	.390203

Table A.   Present Value of $1.00 (cont'd)

n/r	2.0%	2.1%	2.2%	2.3%	2.4%
1	.980392	.979432	.978474	.977517	.976562
2	.961169	.959287	.957411	.955540	.953674
3	.942322	.939556	.936801	.934056	.931323
4	.923845	.920231	.916635	.913056	.909495
5	.905731	.901304	.896903	.892528	.888178
6	.887971	.882766	.877596	.872461	.867362
7	.870560	.864609	.858704	.852846	.847033
8	.853490	.846826	.840220	.833671	.827181
9	.836755	.829408	.822133	.814928	.807794
10	.820348	.812349	.804435	.796606	.788861
11	.804263	.795640	.787119	.778696	.770372
12	.788493	.779276	.770175	.761189	.752316
13	.773033	.763247	.753596	.744075	.734684
14	.757875	.747549	.737373	.727346	.717465
15	.743015	.732173	.721500	.710993	.700649
16	.728446	.717114	.705969	.695008	.684228
17	.714163	.702364	.690772	.679382	.668191
18	.700159	.687918	.675902	.664108	.652530
19	.686431	.673769	.661352	.649177	.637237
20	.672971	.659911	.647116	.634581	.622302
21	.659776	.646338	.633186	.620314	.607716
22	.646839	.633044	.619556	.606368	.593473
23	.634156	.620023	.606219	.592735	.579563
24	.621721	.607271	.593169	.579408	.565980
25	.609531	.594780	.580400	.566382	.552715
26	.597579	.582547	.567906	.553648	.539761
27	.585862	.570565	.555681	.541200	.527110
28	.574375	.558829	.543720	.529032	.514756
29	.563112	.547335	.532015	.517138	.502691
30	.552071	.536078	.520563	.505511	.490909
35	.500028	.483169	.466894	.451183	.436015
40	.452890	.435482	.418759	.402694	.387259
45	.410197	.392502	.375586	.359415	.343955
50	.371528	.353763	.336864	.320788	.305494

Table A. Present Value of $1.00 (cont'd)

n/r	2.5%	2.6%	2.7%	2.8%	2.9%
1	.975610	.974659	.973710	.972763	.971817
2	.951814	.949960	.948111	.946267	.944429
3	.928599	.925887	.923185	.920493	.917812
4	.905951	.902424	.898914	.895422	.891946
5	.883854	.879555	.875282	.871033	.866808
6	.862297	.857266	.852270	.847308	.842379
7	.841265	.835542	.829864	.824230	.818639
8	.820747	.814369	.808047	.801780	.795567
9	.800728	.793732	.786803	.779941	.773146
10	.781198	.773618	.766118	.758698	.751357
11	.762145	.754013	.745976	.738033	.730182
12	.743556	.734906	.726365	.717931	.709603
13	.725420	.716282	.707268	.698376	.689605
14	.707727	.698131	.688674	.679354	.670170
15	.690466	.680440	.670569	.660851	.651282
16	.673625	.663197	.652939	.642851	.632928
17	.657195	.646390	.635774	.625341	.615090
18	.641166	.630010	.619059	.608309	.597755
19	.625528	.614045	.602784	.591740	.580909
20	.610271	.598484	.586937	.575622	.564537
21	.595386	.583318	.571506	.559944	.548627
22	.580865	.568536	.556481	.544693	.533165
23	.566697	.554129	.541851	.529857	.518139
24	.552875	.540087	.527606	.515425	.503537
25	.539391	.526400	.513735	.501386	.489346
26	.526235	.513061	.500229	.487729	.475554
27	.513400	.500059	.487077	.474445	.462152
28	.500878	.487387	.474272	.461522	.449127
29	.488661	.475036	.461803	.448952	.436470
30	.476743	.462998	.449663	.436723	.424169
35	.421371	.407232	.393581	.380400	.367673
40	.372431	.358183	.344494	.331341	.318702
45	.329174	.315042	.301530	.288609	.276254
50	.290942	.277097	.263923	.251388	.239459

Table A. Present Value of $1.00 (cont'd)

n/r	3.0%	3.1%	3.2%	3.3%	3.4%
1	.970874	.969932	.968992	.968054	.967118
2	.942596	.940768	.938946	.937129	.935317
3	.915142	.912481	.909831	.907192	.904562
4	.888487	.885045	.881620	.878211	.874818
5	.862609	.858434	.854283	.850156	.846052
6	.837484	.832622	.827793	.822997	.818233
7	.813092	.807587	.802125	.796705	.791327
8	.789409	.783305	.777253	.771254	.765307
9	.766417	.759752	.753152	.746616	.740142
10	.744094	.736908	.729799	.722764	.715805
11	.722421	.714751	.707169	.699675	.692268
12	.701380	.693260	.685241	.677323	.669505
13	.680951	.672415	.663994	.655686	.647490
14	.661118	.652197	.643405	.634739	.626199
15	.641862	.632587	.623454	.614462	.605608
16	.623167	.613566	.604122	.594833	.585695
17	.605016	.595117	.585390	.575830	.566436
18	.587395	.577224	.567238	.557435	.547810
19	.570286	.559868	.549649	.539627	.529797
20	.553676	.543034	.532606	.522388	.512377
21	.537549	.526706	.516091	.505700	.495529
22	.521893	.510869	.500088	.489545	.479235
23	.506692	.495508	.484582	.473906	.463476
24	.491934	.480609	.469556	.458767	.448236
25	.477606	.466158	.454996	.444111	.433497
26	.463695	.452142	.440888	.429924	.419243
27	.450189	.438547	.427217	.416190	.405458
28	.437077	.425361	.413970	.402894	.392125
29	.424346	.412571	.401133	.390023	.379231
30	.411987	.400166	.388695	.377564	.366762
35	.355383	.343516	.332055	.320988	.310300
40	.306557	.294885	.283669	.272890	.262530
45	.264439	.253140	.242334	.231999	.222114
50	.228107	.217304	.207021	.197235	.187920

Table A. Present Value of $1.00 (cont'd)

n/r	3.5%	3.6%	3.7%	3.8%	3.9%
1	.966184	.965251	.964320	.963391	.962464
2	.933511	.931709	.929913	.928122	.926337
3	.901943	.899333	.896734	.894145	.891566
4	.871442	.868082	.864739	.861411	.858100
5	.841973	.837917	.833885	.829876	.825890
6	.813501	.808801	.804132	.799495	.794889
7	.785991	.780696	.775441	.770227	.765052
8	.759412	.753567	.747773	.742030	.736335
9	.733731	.727381	.721093	.714865	.708696
10	.708919	.702106	.695364	.688694	.682094
11	.684946	.677708	.670554	.663482	.656491
12	.661783	.654158	.646629	.639193	.631849
13	.639404	.631427	.623557	.615793	.608132
14	.617782	.609486	.601309	.593249	.585305
15	.596891	.588307	.579854	.571531	.563335
16	.576706	.567863	.559165	.550608	.542190
17	.557204	.548131	.539214	.530451	.521838
18	.538361	.529084	.519975	.511031	.502250
19	.520156	.510699	.501422	.492323	.483398
20	.502566	.492952	.483532	.474300	.465253
21	.485571	.475823	.466279	.456936	.447789
22	,469151	.459288	.449643	.440208	.430981
23	.453286	.443328	.433599	.424093	.414803
24	.437957	.427923	.418129	.408567	.399233
25	.423147	.413053	.403210	.393610	.384248
26	.408838	.398700	.388823	.379200	.369825
27	.395012	.384846	.374950	.365318	.355943
28	.381654	.371473	.361572	.351944	.342582
29	.368748	.358564	.348671	.339060	.329723
30	.356278	.346105	.336231	.326648	.317346
35	.299977	.290007	.280378	.271077	.262093
40	.252572	.243002	.233803	.224960	.216460
45	.212659	.203616	.194965	.186689	.178772
50	.179053	.170613	.162578	.154929	.147646

Table A. Present Value of $1.00 (cont'd)

n/r	4.0%	4.1%	4.2%	4.3%	4.4%
1	.961538	.960615	.959693	.958773	.957854
2	.924556	.922781	.921010	.919245	.917485
3	.888996	.886437	.883887	.881347	.878817
4	.854804	.851524	.848260	.845012	.841779
5	.821927	.817987	.814069	.810174	.806302
6	.790315	.785770	.781257	.776773	.772320
7	.759918	.754823	.749766	.744749	.739770
8	.730690	.725094	.719545	.714045	.708592
9	.702587	.696536	.690543	.684607	.678728
10	.675564	.669103	.662709	.656382	.650122
11	.649581	.642750	.635997	.629322	.622722
12	.624597	.617435	.610362	.603376	.596477
13	.600574	.593117	.585760	.578501	.571339
14	.577475	.569757	.562150	.554651	.547259
15	.555265	.547317	.539491	.531784	.524195
16	.533908	.525761	.517746	.509860	.502102
17	.513373	.505054	.496877	.488840	.480941
18	.493628	.485162	.476849	.468687	.460671
19	.474642	.466054	.457629	.449364	.441256
20	.456387	.447698	.439183	.430838	.422659
21	.438834	.430066	.421481	.413076	.404846
22	.421955	.413127	.404492	.396046	.387783
23	.405726	.396856	.388188	.379718	.371440
24	.390121	.381226	.372542	.364063	.355785
25	.375117	.366211	.357526	.349054	.340791
26	.360689	.351788	.343115	.334663	.326428
27	.346817	.337933	.329285	.320866	.312670
28	.333477	.324623	.316012	.307638	.299493
29	.320651	.311838	.303275	.294955	.286870
30	.308319	.299556	.291051	.282794	.274780
35	.253415	.245033	.236935	.229113	.221556
40	.208289	.200434	.192882	.185621	.178641
45	.171198	.163952	.157019	.150386	.144038
50	.140713	.134111	.127824	.121839	.116138

Table A.   Present Value of $1.00 (cont'd)

n/r	4.5%	4.6%	4.7%	4.8%	4.9%
1	.956938	.956023	.955110	.954198	.953289
2	.915730	.913980	.912235	.910495	.908760
3	.876297	.873786	.871284	.868793	.866310
4	.838561	.835359	.832172	.829001	.825844
5	.802451	.798623	.794816	.791031	.787268
6	.767896	.763501	.759137	.754801	.750494
7	.734828	.729925	.725059	.720230	.715437
8	.703185	.697825	.692511	.687242	.682018
9	.672904	.667137	.661424	.655765	.650161
10	.643928	.637798	.631732	.625730	.619791
11	.616199	.609750	.603374	.597071	.590840
12	.589664	.582935	.576288	.569724	.563241
13	.564272	.557299	.550419	.543630	.536931
14	.539973	.532790	.525710	.518731	.511851
15	.516720	.509360	.502111	.494972	.487941
16	.494469	.486960	.479571	.472302	.465149
17	.473176	.465545	.458043	.450670	.443421
18	.452800	.445071	.437482	.430028	.422709
19	.433302	.425498	.417843	.410332	.402964
20	.414643	.406786	.399086	.391538	.384141
21	.396787	.388897	.381171	.373605	.366197
22	.379701	.371794	.364060	.356494	.349091
23	.363350	.355444	.347717	.340166	.332785
24	.347703	.339813	.332108	.324586	.317240
25	.332731	.324869	.317200	.309719	.302422
26	.318402	.310582	.302961	.295533	.288295
27	.304691	.296923	.289361	.281998	.274829
28	.291571	.283866	.276371	.269082	.261991
29	.279015	.271382	.263965	.256757	.249753
30	.267000	.259447	.252116	.244997	.238087
35	.214254	.207201	.200385	.193801	.187438
40	.171929	.165475	.159270	.153302	.147564
45	.137964	.132152	.126590	.121267	.116172
50	.110710	.105540	.100616	.095926	.091459

Table A. Present Value of $1.00 (cont'd)

n/r	5.0%	5.1%	5.2%	5.3%	5.4%
1	.952381	.951475	.950570	.949668	.948767
2	.907029	.905304	.903584	.901869	.900158
3	.863838	.861374	.858920	.856475	.854040
4	.822702	.819576	.816464	.813367	.810285
5	.783526	.779806	.776106	.772428	.768771
6	.746215	.741965	.737744	.733550	.729384
7	.710681	.705961	.701277	.696629	.692015
8	.676839	.671705	.666613	.661566	.656561
9	.644609	.639110	.633663	.628268	.622923
10	.613913	.608097	.602341	.596645	.591009
11	.584679	.578589	.572568	.566615	.560729
12	.556837	.550513	.544266	.538096	.532001
13	.530321	.523799	.517363	.511012	.504745
14	.505068	.498382	.491790	.485292	.478885
15	.481017	.474197	.467481	.460866	.454350
16	.458112	.451187	.444374	.437669	.431072
17	.436297	.429293	.422408	.415640	.408987
18	.415521	.408461	.401529	.394720	.388033
19	.395734	.388641	.381681	.374853	.368153
20	.376889	.369782	.362815	.355986	.349291
21	.358942	.351838	.344881	.338068	.331396
22	.341850	.334765	.327834	.321052	.314417
23	.325571	.318521	.311629	.304893	.298309
24	.310068	.303064	.296225	.289547	.283025
25	.295303	.288358	.281583	.274973	.268525
26	.281241	.274365	.267664	.261133	.254768
27	.267848	.261052	.254434	.247990	.241715
28	.255094	.248384	.241857	.235508	.229331
29	.242946	.236331	.229902	.223654	.217582
30	.231377	.224863	.218538	.212397	.206434
35	.181290	.175350	.169609	.164062	.158701
40	.142046	.136739	.131635	.126726	.122004
45	.111297	.106630	.102163	.097887	.093793
50	.087204	.083150	.079289	.075610	.072106

Table A. Present Value of $1.00 (cont'd)

n/r	5.5%	5.6%	5.7%	5.8%	5.9%
1	.947867	.946970	.946074	.945180	.944287
2	.898452	.896752	.895056	.893364	.891678
3	.851614	.849197	.846789	.844390	.842000
4	.807217	.804163	.801125	.798100	.795090
5	.765134	.761518	.757923	.754348	.750793
6	.725246	.721135	.717051	.712994	.708964
7	.687437	.682893	.678383	.673908	.669466
8	.651599	.646679	.641801	.636964	.632168
9	.617629	.612385	.607191	.602045	.596948
10	.585431	.579910	.574447	.569041	.563690
11	.554911	.549157	.543469	.537846	.532285
12	.525982	.520035	.514162	.508361	.502630
13	.498561	.492458	.486435	.480492	.474627
14	.472569	.466343	.460204	.454151	.448184
15	.447933	.441612	.435387	.429255	.423215
16	.424581	.418194	.411908	.405723	.399636
17	.402447	.396017	.389695	.383481	.377371
18	.381466	.375016	.368681	.362458	.356347
19	.361579	.355129	.348799	.342588	.336494
20	.342729	.336296	.329990	.323807	.317747
21	.324862	.318462	.312195	.306056	.300044
22	.307926	.301574	.295359	.289278	.283328
23	.291873	.285581	.279431	.273420	.267543
24	.276657	.270437	.264363	.258431	.252637
25	.262234	.256096	.250107	.244263	.238562
26	.248563	.242515	.236619	.230873	.225271
27	.235605	.229654	.223859	.218216	.212720
28	.223322	.217475	.211788	.206253	.200869
29	.211679	.205943	.200367	.194947	.189678
30	.200644	.195021	.189562	.184260	.179111
35	.153520	.148512	.143673	.138996	.134475
40	.117463	.113095	.108893	.104851	.100963
45	.089875	.086124	.082533	.079094	.075802
50	.068767	.065585	.062553	.059665	.056912

Table A. Present Value of $1.00 (cont'd)

n/r	6%	7%	8%	9%	10%	11%
1	0.9434	0.9346	0.9259	0.9174	0.9091	0.9009
2	0.8900	0.8734	0.8573	0.8417	0.8264	0.8116
3	0.8396	0.8163	0.7938	0.7722	0.7513	0.7312
4	0.7921	0.7629	0.7350	0.7084	0.6830	0.6587
5	0.7473	0.7130	0.6806	0.6499	0.6209	0.5935
6	0.7050	0.6663	0.6302	0.5963	0.5645	0.5346
7	0.6651	0.6227	0.5835	0.5470	0.5132	0.4817
8	0.6274	0.5820	0.5403	0.5019	0.4665	0.4339
9	0.5919	0.5439	0.5002	0.4604	0.4241	0.3909
10	0.5584	0.5083	0.4632	0.4224	0.3855	0.3522
11	0.5268	0.4751	0.4289	0.3875	0.3505	0.3173
12	0.4970	0.4440	0.3971	0.3555	0.3186	0.2858
13	0.4688	0.4150	0.3677	0.3262	0.2897	0.2575
14	0.4423	0.3878	0.3405	0.2992	0.2633	0.2320
15	0.4173	0.3624	0.3152	0.2745	0.2394	0.2090
16	0.3936	0.3387	0.2919	0.2519	0.2176	0.1883
17	0.3714	0.3166	0.2703	0.2311	0.1978	0.1696
18	0.3503	0.2959	0.2502	0.2120	0.1799	0.1528
19	0.3305	0.2765	0.2317	0.1945	0.1635	0.1377
20	0.3118	0.2584	0.2145	0.1784	0.1486	0.1240
21	0.2942	0.2415	0.1987	0.1637	0.1351	0.1117
22	0.2775	0.2257	0.1839	0.1502	0.1228	0.1007
23	0.2618	0.2109	0.1703	0.1378	0.1117	0.0907
24	0.2470	0.1971	0.1577	0.1264	0.1015	0.0817
25	0.2330	0.1842	0.1460	0.1160	0.0923	0.0736
26	0.2198	0.1722	0.1352	0.1064	0.0839	0.0663
27	0.2074	0.1609	0.1252	0.0976	0.0763	0.0597
28	0.1956	0.1504	0.1159	0.0895	0.0693	0.0538
29	0.1846	0.1406	0.1073	0.0822	0.0630	0.0485
30	0.1741	0.1314	0.0994	0.0754	0.0573	0.0437
35	0.1301	0.0937	0.0676	0.0490	0.0356	0.0259
40	0.0972	0.0668	0.0460	0.0318	0.0221	0.0154
45	0.0727	0.0476	0.0313	0.0207	0.0137	0.0091
50	0.0543	0.0339	0.0213	0.0134	0.0085	0.0054

Table A. Present Value of $1.00 (cont'd)

n/r	12%	13%	14%	15%	16%	17%
1	0.8929	0.8850	0.8772	0.8696	0.8621	0.8547
2	0.7972	0.7831	0.7695	0.7561	0.7432	0.7305
3	0.7118	0.6931	0.6750	0.6575	0.6407	0.6244
4	0.6355	0.6133	0.5921	0.5718	0.5523	0.5337
5	0.5674	0.5428	0.5194	0.4972	0.4761	0.4561
6	0.5066	0.4803	0.4556	0.4323	0.4104	0.3898
7	0.4523	0.4251	0.3996	0.3759	0.3538	0.3332
8	0.4039	0.3762	0.3506	0.3269	0.3050	0.2848
9	0.3606	0.3329	0.3075	0.2843	0.2630	0.2434
10	0.3220	0.2946	0.2697	0.2472	0.2267	0.2080
11	0.2875	0.2607	0.2366	0.2149	0.1954	0.1778
12	0.2567	0.2307	0.2076	0.1869	0.1685	0.1520
13	0.2292	0.2042	0.1821	0.1625	0.1452	0.1299
14	0.2046	0.1807	0.1597	0.1413	0.1252	0.1110
15	0.1827	0.1599	0.1401	0.1229	0.1079	0.0949
16	0.1631	0.1415	0.1229	0.1069	0.0930	0.0811
17	0.1456	0.1252	0.1078	0.0929	0.0802	0.0693
18	0.1300	0.1108	0.0946	0.0808	0.0691	0.0592
19	0.1161	0.0981	0.0829	0.0703	0.0596	0.0506
20	0.1037	0.0868	0.0728	0.0611	0.0514	0.0433
21	0.0926	0.0768	0.0638	0.0531	0.0443	0.0370
22	0.0826	0.0680	0.0560	0.0462	0.0382	0.0316
23	0.0738	0.0601	0.0491	0.0402	0.0329	0.0270
24	0.0659	0.0532	0.0431	0.0349	0.0284	0.0231
25	0.0588	0.0471	0.0378	0.0304	0.0245	0.0197
26	0.0525	0.0417	0.0331	0.0264	0.0211	0.0169
27	0.0469	0.0369	0.0291	0.0230	0.0182	0.0144
28	0.0419	0.0326	0.0255	0.0200	0.0157	0.0123
29	0.0374	0.0289	0.0224	0.0174	0.0135	0.0105
30	0.0334	0.0256	0.0196	0.0151	0.0116	0.0090
35	0.0189	0.0139	0.0102	0.0075	0.0055	0.0041
40	0.0107	0.0075	0.0053	0.0037	0.0026	0.0019
45	0.0061	0.0041	0.0027	0.0019	0.0013	0.0009
50	0.0035	0.0022	0.0014	0.0009	0.0006	0.0004

Table A.   Present Value of $1.00 (cont'd)

n/r	18%	19%	20%	21%	22%	23%
1	0.8475	0.8403	0.8333	0.8264	0.8197	0.8130
2	0.7182	0.7062	0.6944	0.6830	0.6719	0.6610
3	0.6086	0.5934	0.5787	0.5645	0.5507	0.5374
4	0.5158	0.4987	0.4823	0.4665	0.4514	0.4369
5	0.4371	0.4190	0.4019	0.3855	0.3700	0.3552
6	0.3704	0.3521	0.3349	0.3186	0.3033	0.2888
7	0.3139	0.2959	0.2791	0.2633	0.2486	0.2348
8	0.2660	0.2487	0.2326	0.2176	0.2038	0.1909
9	0.2255	0.2090	0.1938	0.1799	0.1670	0.1552
10	0.1911	0.1756	0.1615	0.1486	0.1369	0.1262
11	0.1619	0.1476	0.1346	0.1228	0.1122	0.1026
12	0.1372	0.1240	0.1122	0.1015	0.0920	0.0834
13	0.1163	0.1042	0.0935	0.0839	0.0754	0.0678
14	0.0985	0.0876	0.0779	0.0693	0.0618	0.0551
15	0.0835	0.0736	0.0649	0.0573	0.0507	0.0448
16	0.0708	0.0618	0.0541	0.0474	0.0415	0.0364
17	0.0600	0.0520	0.0451	0.0391	0.0340	0.0296
18	0.0508	0.0437	0.0376	0.0323	0.0279	0.0241
19	0.0431	0.0367	0.0313	0.0267	0.0229	0.0196
20	0.0365	0.0308	0.0261	0.0221	0.0187	0.0159
21	0.0309	0.0259	0.0217	0.0183	0.0154	0.0129
22	0.0262	0.0218	0.0181	0.0151	0.0126	0.0105
23	0.0222	0.0183	0.0151	0.0125	0.0103	0.0086
24	0.0188	0.0154	0.0126	0.0103	0.0085	0.0070
25	0.0160	0.0129	0.0105	0.0085	0.0069	0.0057
26	0.0135	0.0109	0.0087	0.0070	0.0057	0.0046
27	0.0115	0.0091	0.0073	0.0058	0.0047	0.0037
28	0.0097	0.0077	0.0061	0.0048	0.0038	0.0030
29	0.0082	0.0064	0.0051	0.0040	0.0031	0.0025
30	0.0070	0.0054	0.0042	0.0033	0.0026	0.0020
35	0.0030	0.0023	0.0017	0.0013	0.0009	0.0007
40	0.0013	0.0010	0.0007	0.0005	0.0004	0.0002
45	0.0006	0.0004	0.0003	0.0002	0.0001	0.0001
50	0.0003	0.0002	0.0001	0.0001	0.0000	0.0000

n/r	24%	25%	26%	27%	28%	29%
1	0.8065	0.8000	0.7937	0.7874	0.7813	0.7752
2	0.6504	0.6400	0.6299	0.6200	0.6104	0.6009
3	0.5245	0.5120	0.4999	0.4882	0.4768	0.4658
4	0.4230	0.4096	0.3968	0.3844	0.3725	0.3611
5	0.3411	0.3277	0.3149	0.3027	0.2910	0.2799
6	0.2751	0.2621	0.2499	0.2383	0.2274	0.2170
7	0.2218	0.2097	0.1983	0.1877	0.1776	0.1682
8	0.1789	0.1678	0.1574	0.1478	0.1388	0.1304
9	0.1443	0.1342	0.1249	0.1164	0.1084	0.1011
10	0.1164	0.1074	0.0992	0.0916	0.0847	0.0784
11	0.0938	0.0859	0.0787	0.0721	0.0662	0.0607
12	0.0757	0.0687	0.0625	0.0568	0.0517	0.0471
13	0.0610	0.0550	0.0496	0.0447	0.0404	0.0365
14	0.0492	0.0440	0.0393	0.0352	0.0316	0.0283
15	0.0397	0.0352	0.0312	0.0277	0.0247	0.0219
16	0.0320	0.0281	0.0248	0.0218	0.0193	0.0170
17	0.0258	0.0225	0.0197	0.0172	0.0150	0.0132
18	0.0208	0.0180	0.0156	0.0135	0.0118	0.0102
19	0.0168	0.0144	0.0124	0.0107	0.0092	0.0079
20	0.0135	0.0115	0.0098	0.0084	0.0072	0.0061
21	0.0109	0.0092	0.0078	0.0066	0.0056	0.0048
22	0.0088	0.0074	0.0062	0.0052	0.0044	0.0037
23	0.0071	0.0059	0.0049	0.0041	0.0034	0.0029
24	0.0057	0.0047	0.0039	0.0032	0.0027	0.0022
25	0.0046	0.0038	0.0031	0.0025	0.0021	0.0017
26	0.0037	0.0030	0.0025	0.0020	0.0016	0.0013
27	0.0030	0.0024	0.0019	0.0016	0.0013	0.0010
28	0.0024	0.0019	0.0015	0.0012	0.0010	0.0008
29	0.0020	0.0015	0.0012	0.0010	0.0008	0.0006
30	0.0016	0.0012	0.0010	0.0008	0.0006	0.0005
35	0.0005	0.0004	0.0003	0.0002	0.0002	0.0001
40	0.0002	0.0001	0.0001	0.0001	0.0001	0.0000
45	0.0001	0.0000	0.0000	0.0000	0.0000	
50	0.0000					

Table A.   Present Value of $1.00 (cont'd)

n/r	30%	31%	32%	33%	34%	35%
1	0.7692	0.7634	0.7576	0.7519	0.7463	0.7407
2	0.5917	0.5827	0.5739	0.5653	0.5569	0.5487
3	0.4552	0.4448	0.4348	0.4251	0.4156	0.4064
4	0.3501	0.3396	0.3294	0.3196	0.3102	0.3011
5	0.2693	0.2592	0.2495	0.2403	0.2315	0.2230
6	0.2072	0.1979	0.1890	0.1807	0.1727	0.1652
7	0.1594	0.1510	0.1432	0.1358	0.1289	0.1224
8	0.1226	0.1153	0.1085	0.1021	0.0962	0.0906
9	0.0943	0.0880	0.0822	0.0768	0.0718	0.0671
10	0.0725	0.0672	0.0623	0.0577	0.0536	0.0497
11	0.0558	0.0513	0.0472	0.0434	0.0400	0.0368
12	0.0429	0.0392	0.0357	0.0326	0.0298	0.0273
13	0.0330	0.0299	0.0271	0.0245	0.0223	0.0202
14	0.0253	0.0228	0.0205	0.0185	0.0166	0.0150
15	0.0195	0.0174	0.0155	0.0139	0.0124	0.0111
16	0.0150	0.0133	0.0118	0.0104	0.0093	0.0082
17	0.0116	0.0101	0.0089	0.0078	0.0069	0.0061
18	0.0089	0.0077	0.0068	0.0059	0.0052	0.0045
19	0.0068	0.0059	0.0051	0.0044	0.0038	0.0033
20	0.0053	0.0045	0.0039	0.0033	0.0029	0.0025
21	0.0040	0.0034	0.0029	0.0025	0.0021	0.0018
22	0.0031	0.0026	0.0022	0.0019	0.0016	0.0014
23	0.0024	0.0020	0.0017	0.0014	0.0012	0.0010
24	0.0018	0.0015	0.0013	0.0011	0.0009	0.0007
25	0.0014	0.0012	0.0010	0.0008	0.0007	0.0006
26	0.0011	0.0009	0.0007	0.0006	0.0005	0.0004
27	0.0008	0.0007	0.0006	0.0005	0.0004	0.0003
28	0.0006	0.0005	0.0004	0.0003	0.0003	0.0002
29	0.0005	0.0004	0.0003	0.0003	0.0002	0.0002
30	0.0004	0.0003	0.0002	0.0002	0.0002	0.0001
35	0.0001	0.0001	0.0001	0.0000	0.0000	0.0000
40	0.0000	0.0000	0.0000			
45						
50						

n/r	36%	37%	38%	39%	40%	41%
1	0.7353	0.7299	0.7246	0.7194	0.7143	0.7092
2	0.5407	0.5328	0.5251	0.5176	0.5102	0.5030
3	0.3975	0.3889	0.3805	0.3724	0.3644	0.3567
4	0.2923	0.2839	0.2757	0.2679	0.2603	0.2530
5	0.2149	0.2072	0.1998	0.1927	0.1859	0.1794
6	0.1580	0.1512	0.1448	0.1386	0.1328	0.1273
7	0.1162	0.1104	0.1049	0.0997	0.0949	0.0903
8	0.0854	0.0806	0.0760	0.0718	0.0678	0.0640
9	0.0628	0.0588	0.0551	0.0516	0.0484	0.0454
10	0.0462	0.0429	0.0399	0.0371	0.0346	0.0322
11	0.0340	0.0313	0.0289	0.0267	0.0247	0.0228
12	0.0250	0.0229	0.0210	0.0192	0.0176	0.0162
13	0.0184	0.0167	0.0152	0.0138	0.0126	0.0115
14	0.0135	0.0122	0.0110	0.0099	0.0090	0.0081
15	0.0099	0.0089	0.0080	0.0072	0.0064	0.0058
16	0.0073	0.0065	0.0058	0.0051	0.0046	0.0041
17	0.0054	0.0047	0.0042	0.0037	0.0033	0.0029
18	0.0039	0.0035	0.0030	0.0027	0.0023	0.0021
19	0.0029	0.0025	0.0022	0.0019	0.0017	0.0015
20	0.0021	0.0018	0.0016	0.0014	0.0012	0.0010
21	0.0016	0.0013	0.0012	0.0010	0.0009	0.0007
22	0.0012	0.0010	0.0008	0.0007	0.0006	0.0005
23	0.0008	0.0007	0.0006	0.0005	0.0004	0.0004
24	0.0006	0.0005	0.0004	0.0004	0.0003	0.0003
25	0.0005	0.0004	0.0003	0.0003	0.0002	0.0002
26	0.0003	0.0003	0.0002	0.0002	0.0002	0.0001
27	0.0002	0.0002	0.0002	0.0001	0.0001	0.0001
28	0.0002	0.0001	0.0001	0.0001	0.0001	0.0001
29	0.0001	0.0001	0.0001	0.0001	0.0001	0.0000
30	0.0001	0.0001	0.0001	0.0001	0.0000	
35	0.0000	0.0000	0.0000	0.0000		
40						
45						
50						

Table A. Present Value of $1.00 (cont'd)

n/r	42%	43%	44%	45%	46%	47%	48%
1	0.7042	0.6993	0.6944	0.6897	0.6849	0.6803	0.6757
2	0.4959	0.4890	0.4823	0.4756	0.4691	0.4628	0.4565
3	0.3492	0.3420	0.3349	0.3280	0.3213	0.3148	0.3085
4	0.2459	0.2391	0.2326	0.2262	0.2201	0.2142	0.2084
5	0.1732	0.1672	0.1615	0.1560	0.1507	0.1457	0.1408
6	0.1220	0.1169	0.1122	0.1076	0.1032	0.0991	0.0952
7	0.0859	0.0818	0.0779	0.0742	0.0707	0.0674	0.0643
8	0.0605	0.0572	0.0541	0.0512	0.0484	0.0459	0.0434
9	0.0426	0.0400	0.0376	0.0353	0.0332	0.0312	0.0294
10	0.0300	0.0280	0.0261	0.0243	0.0227	0.0212	0.0198
11	0.0211	0.0196	0.0181	0.0168	0.0156	0.0144	0.0134
12	0.0149	0.0137	0.0126	0.0116	0.0107	0.0098	0.0091
13	0.0105	0.0096	0.0087	0.0080	0.0073	0.0067	0.0061
14	0.0074	0.0067	0.0061	0.0055	0.0050	0.0045	0.0041
15	0.0052	0.0047	0.0042	0.0038	0.0034	0.0031	0.0028
16	0.0037	0.0033	0.0029	0.0026	0.0023	0.0021	0.0019
17	0.0026	0.0023	0.0020	0.0018	0.0016	0.0014	0.0013
18	0.0018	0.0016	0.0014	0.0012	0.0011	0.0010	0.0009
19	0.0013	0.0011	0.0010	0.0009	0.0008	0.0007	0.0006
20	0.0009	0.0008	0.0007	0.0006	0.0005	0.0005	0.0004
21	0.0006	0.0005	0.0005	0.0004	0.0004	0.0003	0.0003
22	0.0004	0.0004	0.0003	0.0003	0.0002	0.0002	0.0002
23	0.0003	0.0003	0.0002	0.0002	0.0002	0.0001	0.0001
24	0.0002	0.0002	0.0002	0.0001	0.0001	0.0001	0.0001
25	0.0002	0.0001	0.0001	0.0001	0.0001	0.0001	0.0001
26	0.0001	0.0001	0.0001	0.0001	0.0001	0.0000	0.0000
27	0.0001	0.0001	0.0001	0.0000	0.0000		
28	0.0001	0.0000	0.0000				
29	0.0000						
30							
35							
40							
45							
50							

Table B.   Present Value of $1 Received per Period

$$\frac{1 - (1 + r)^{-n}}{r}$$

n/r	1.0%	1.1%	1.2%	1.3%	1.4%
1	.99010	.98912	.98814	.98717	.98619
2	1.97040	1.96748	1.96457	1.96167	1.95877
3	2.94099	2.93519	2.92941	2.92366	2.91792
4	3.90197	3.89237	3.88282	3.87330	3.86383
5	4.85343	4.83914	4.82492	4.81076	4.79667
6	5.79548	5.77561	5.75585	5.73619	5.71664
7	6.72819	6.70189	6.67574	6.64975	6.62391
8	7.65168	7.61809	7.58473	7.55158	7.51864
9	8.56602	8.52432	8.48293	8.44183	8.40103
10	9.47130	9.42070	9.37048	9.32066	9.27123
11	10.36763	10.30732	10.24751	10.18822	10.12942
12	11.25508	11.18429	11.11414	11.04464	10.97576
13	12.13374	12.05172	11.97050	11.89007	11.81041
14	13.00370	12.90971	12.81670	12.72465	12.63354
15	13.86505	13.75837	13.65286	13.54852	13.44531
16	14.71787	14.59780	14.47911	14.36181	14.24587
17	15.56225	15.42809	15.29557	15.16467	15.03537
18	16.39827	16.24934	16.10234	15.95723	15.81398
19	17.22601	17.06167	16.89955	16.73961	16.58183
20	18.04555	17.86515	17.68730	17.51196	17.33908
21	18.85698	18.65989	18.46571	18.27439	18.08588
22	19.66038	19.44598	19.23489	19.02704	18.82237
23	20.45582	20.22353	19.99495	19.77003	19.54869
24	21.24339	20.99261	20.74600	20.50348	20.26498
25	22.02316	21.75332	21.48814	21.22752	20.97138
26	22.79520	22.50576	22.22148	21.94228	21.66803
27	23.55961	23.25001	22.94613	22.64785	22.35505
28	24.31644	23.98616	23.66218	23.34438	23.03260
29	25.06579	24.71430	24.36975	24.03196	23.70079
30	25.80771	25.43452	25.06892	24.71072	24.35975
31	26.54229	26.14691	25.75980	25.38077	25.00962
32	27.26959	26.85154	26.44249	26.04222	25.65051
33	27.98969	27.54851	27.11709	26.69519	26.28255
34	28.70267	28.23789	27.78368	27.33977	26.90587
35	29.40858	28.91977	28.44237	27.97608	27.52058
40	32.83469	32.21950	31.62051	31.03722	30.46915
45	36.09451	35.34358	34.61463	33.90692	33.21972
50	39.19612	38.30136	37.43540	36.59715	35.78557

Table B. Present Value of $1 Received per Period (cont'd)

n/r	1.5%	1.6%	1.7%	1.8%	1.9%
1	.98522	.98425	.98328	.98232	.98135
2	1.95588	1.95300	1.95013	1.94727	1.94441
3	2.91220	2.90650	2.90082	2.89515	2.88951
4	3.85438	3.84498	3.83561	3.82628	3.81699
5	4.78264	4.76868	4.75478	4.74094	4.72717
6	5.69719	5.67784	5.65859	5.63943	5.62038
7	6.59821	6.57267	6.54728	6.52204	6.49694
8	7.48593	7.45342	7.42112	7.38904	7.35716
9	8.36052	8.32029	8.28036	8.24070	8.20133
10	9.22218	9.17352	9.12523	9.07731	9.02976
11	10.07112	10.01330	9.95598	9.89913	9.84275
12	10.90751	10.83987	10.77284	10.70641	10.64058
13	11.73153	11.65341	11.57604	11.49942	11.42353
14	12.54338	12.45415	12.36583	12.27841	12.19189
15	13.34323	13.24227	13.14241	13.04363	12.94592
16	14.13126	14.01798	13.90600	13.79531	13.68588
17	14.90765	14.78148	14.65684	14.53370	14.41206
18	15.67256	15.53295	15.39512	15.25904	15.12469
19	16.42617	16.27259	16.12106	15.97155	15.82403
20	17.16864	17.00058	16.83487	16.67147	16.51033
21	17.90014	17.71711	17.53674	17.35900	17.18384
22	18.62082	18.42235	18.22689	18.03439	17.84479
23	19.33086	19.11649	18.90549	18.69782	18.49341
24	20.03041	19.79969	19.57276	19.34953	19.12995
25	20.71961	20.47214	20.22887	19.98972	19.75461
26	21.39863	21.13399	20.87401	20.61858	20.36762
27	22.06762	21.78543	21.50837	21.23633	20.96921
28	22.72672	22.42660	22.13212	21.84315	21.55958
29	23.37608	23.05768	22.74545	22.43925	22.13894
30	24.01584	23.67882	23.34852	23.02480	22.70749
31	24.64615	24.29017	23.94152	23.60000	23.26545
32	25.26714	24.89190	24.52460	24.16503	23.81300
33	25.87895	25.48416	25.09793	24.72007	24.35035
34	26.48173	26.06708	25.66168	25.26529	24.87767
35	27.07559	26.64083	26.21601	25.80088	25.39516
40	29.91585	29.37684	28.85172	28.34005	27.84144
45	32.55234	31.90411	31.27438	30.66254	30.06799
50	34.99969	34.23854	33.50121	32.78684	32.09457

Table B. Present Value of $1 Received per Period (cont'd)

n/r	2.0%	2.1%	2.2%	2.3%	2.4%
1	.98039	.97943	.97847	.97752	.97656
2	1.94156	1.93872	1.93588	1.93306	1.93024
3	2.88388	2.87828	2.87269	2.86711	2.86156
4	3.80773	3.79851	3.78932	3.78017	3.77105
5	4.71346	4.69981	4.68622	4.67270	4.65923
6	5.60143	5.58258	5.56382	5.54516	5.52659
7	6.47199	6.44719	6.42252	6.39800	6.37363
8	7.32548	7.29401	7.26274	7.23168	7.20081
9	8.16224	8.12342	8.08488	8.04660	8.00860
10	8.98259	8.93577	8.88931	8.84321	8.79746
11	9.78685	9.73141	9.67643	9.62191	9.56783
12	10.57534	10.51068	10.44660	10.38310	10.32015
13	11.34837	11.27393	11.20020	11.12717	11.05483
14	12.10625	12.02148	11.93757	11.85452	11.77230
15	12.84926	12.75365	12.65907	12.56551	12.47295
16	13.57771	13.47077	13.36504	13.26052	13.15718
17	14.29187	14.17313	14.05581	13.93990	13.82537
18	14.99203	14.86105	14.73172	14.60401	14.47790
19	15.67846	15.53482	15.39307	15.25318	15.11513
20	16.35143	16.19473	16.04019	15.88777	15.73744
21	17.01121	16.84107	16.67337	16.50808	16.34515
22	17.65805	17.47411	17.29293	17.11445	16.93863
23	18.29220	18.09413	17.89915	17.70718	17.51819
24	18.91393	18.70140	18.49231	18.28659	18.08417
25	19.52346	19.29618	19.07272	18.85297	18.63688
26	20.12104	19.87873	19.64062	19.40662	19.17664
27	20.70690	20.44930	20.19630	19.94782	19.70375
28	21.28127	21.00813	20.74002	20.47685	20.21851
29	21.84438	21.55546	21.27204	20.99399	20.72120
30	22.39646	22.09154	21.79260	21.49950	21.21211
31	22.93770	22.61659	22.30196	21.99365	21.69151
32	23.46833	23.13084	22.80035	22.47668	22.15968
33	23.98856	23.63452	23.28801	22.94886	22.61688
34	24.49859	24.12783	23.76518	23.41042	23.06336
35	24.99862	24.61100	24.23207	23.86160	23.49937
40	27.35548	26.88180	26.42004	25.96985	25.53087
45	29.49016	28.92849	28.38244	27.85151	27.33520
50	31.42361	30.77317	30.14252	29.53095	28.93777

Table B. Present Value of $1 Received per Period (cont'd)

n/r	2.5%	2.6%	2.7%	2.8%	2.9%
1	.97561	.97466	.97371	.97276	.97182
2	1.92742	1.92462	1.92182	1.91903	1.91625
3	2.85602	2.85051	2.84501	2.83952	2.83406
4	3.76197	3.75293	3.74392	3.73494	3.72600
5	4.64583	4.63248	4.61920	4.60598	4.59281
6	5.50813	5.48975	5.47147	5.45329	5.43519
7	6.34939	6.32529	6.30134	6.27751	6.25383
8	7.17014	7.13966	7.10938	7.07929	7.04940
9	7.97087	7.93339	7.89619	7.85924	7.82254
10	8.75206	8.70701	8.66230	8.61793	8.57390
11	9.51421	9.46103	9.40828	9.35597	9.30408
12	10.25776	10.19593	10.13464	10.07390	10.01369
13	10.98318	10.91221	10.84191	10.77227	10.70329
14	11.69091	11.61034	11.53059	11.45163	11.37346
15	12.38138	12.29078	12.20116	12.11248	12.02474
16	13.05500	12.95398	12.85409	12.75533	12.65767
17	13.71220	13.60037	13.48987	13.38067	13.27276
18	14.35336	14.23038	14.10893	13.98898	13.87052
19	14.97889	14.84443	14.71171	14.58072	14.45142
20	15.58916	15.44291	15.29865	15.15634	15.01596
21	16.18455	16.02623	15.87015	15.71629	15.56459
22	16.76541	16.59476	16.42663	16.26098	16.09775
23	17.33211	17.14889	16.96849	16.79084	16.61589
24	17.88499	17.68898	17.49609	17.30626	17.11943
25	18.42438	18.21538	18.00983	17.80765	17.60877
26	18.95061	18.72844	18.51005	18.29538	18.08433
27	19.46401	19.22850	18.99713	18.76982	18.54648
28	19.96489	19.71589	19.47140	19.23134	18.99561
29	20.45355	20.19092	19.93321	19.68029	19.43208
30	20.93029	20.65392	20.38287	20.11702	19.85625
31	21.39541	21.10519	20.82071	20.54185	20.26846
32	21.84918	21.54502	21.24704	20.95510	20.66906
33	22.29188	21.97370	21.66216	21.35710	21.05837
34	22.72379	22.39152	22.06637	21.74816	21.43670
35	23.14516	22.79875	22.45995	22.12856	21.80438
40	25.10278	24.68525	24.27798	23.88067	23.49303
45	26.83302	26.34453	25.86927	25.40682	24.95677
50	28.36231	27.80396	27.26210	26.73615	26.22555

Table B. Present Value of $1 Received per Period (cont'd)

n/r	3.0%	3.1%	3.2%	3.3%	3.4%
1	.97087	.96993	.96899	.96805	.96712
2	1.91347	1.91070	1.90794	1.90518	1.90244
3	2.82861	2.82318	2.81777	2.81237	2.80700
4	3.71710	3.70823	3.69939	3.69059	3.68182
5	4.57971	4.56666	4.55367	4.54074	4.52787
6	5.41719	5.39928	5.38146	5.36374	5.34610
7	6.23028	6.20687	6.18359	6.16044	6.13743
8	7.01969	6.99017	6.96084	6.93170	6.90274
9	7.78611	7.74993	7.71400	7.67831	7.64288
10	8.53020	8.48683	8.44379	8.40108	8.35868
11	9.25262	9.20159	9.15096	9.10075	9.05095
12	9.95400	9.89485	9.83620	9.77808	9.72045
13	10.63496	10.56726	10.50020	10.43376	10.36794
14	11.29607	11.21946	11.14360	11.06850	10.99414
15	11.93794	11.85204	11.76706	11.68296	11.59975
16	12.56110	12.46561	12.37118	12.27780	12.18545
17	13.16612	13.06073	12.95657	12.85363	12.75188
18	13.75351	13.63795	13.52381	13.41106	13.29969
19	14.32380	14.19782	14.07346	13.95069	13.82949
20	14.87747	14.74085	14.60606	14.47308	14.34187
21	15.41502	15.26756	15.12215	14.97878	14.83740
22	15.93692	15.77843	15.62224	15.46832	15.31663
23	16.44361	16.27393	16.10682	15.94223	15.78011
24	16.93554	16.75454	16.57638	16.40100	16.22834
25	17.41315	17.22070	17.03138	16.84511	16.66184
26	17.87684	17.67284	17.47226	17.27503	17.08108
27	18.32703	18.11139	17.89948	17.69122	17.48654
28	18.76411	18.53675	18.31345	18.09412	17.87867
29	19.18845	18.94932	18.71458	18.48414	18.25790
30	19.60044	19.34949	19.10328	18.86170	18.62466
31	20.00043	19.73762	19.47992	19.22721	18.97936
32	20.38877	20.11409	19.84488	19.58103	19.32240
33	20.76579	20.47923	20.19853	19.92355	19.65416
34	21.13184	20.83339	20.54121	20.25513	19.97501
35	21.48722	21.17691	20.87327	20.57612	20.28531
40	23.11477	22.74563	22.38534	22.03365	21.69030
45	24.51871	24.09227	23.67708	23.27277	22.87900
50	25.72976	25.24827	24.78058	24.32621	23.88471

Table B. Present Value of $1 Received per Period (cont'd)

n/r	3.5%	3.6%	3.7%	3.8%	3.9%
1	.96618	.96525	.96432	.96339	.96246
2	1.89969	1.89696	1.89423	1.89151	1.88880
3	2.80164	2.79629	2.79097	2.78566	2.78037
4	3.67308	3.66438	3.65571	3.64707	3.63847
5	4.51505	4.50229	4.48959	4.47695	4.46436
6	5.32855	5.31109	5.29372	5.27644	5.25925
7	6.11454	6.09179	6.06916	6.04667	6.02430
8	6.87396	6.84536	6.81694	6.78870	6.76063
9	7.60769	7.57274	7.53803	7.50356	7.46933
10	8.31661	8.27484	8.23340	8.19226	8.15142
11	9.00155	8.95255	8.90395	8.85574	8.80792
12	9.66333	9.60671	9.55058	9.49493	9.43976
13	10.30274	10.23814	10.17413	10.11072	10.04790
14	10.92052	10.84762	10.77544	10.70397	10.63320
15	11.51741	11.43593	11.35530	11.27550	11.19654
16	12.09412	12.00379	11.91446	11.82611	11.73873
17	12.65132	12.55192	12.45368	12.35656	12.26056
18	13.18968	13.08101	12.97365	12.86759	12.76281
19	13.70984	13.59171	13.47507	13.35992	13.24621
20	14.21240	14.08466	13.95861	13.83422	13.71147
21	14.69797	14.56048	14.42488	14.29115	14.15925
22	15.16712	15.01977	14.87453	14.73136	14.59024
23	15.62041	15.46310	15.30813	15.15545	15.00504
24	16.05837	15.89102	15.72625	15.56402	15.40427
25	16.48151	16.30407	16.12946	15.95763	15.78852
26	16.89035	16.70277	16.51829	16.33683	16.15834
27	17.28536	17.08762	16.89324	16.70215	16.51429
28	17.66702	17.45909	17.25481	17.05409	16.85687
29	18.03577	17.81766	17.60348	17.39315	17.18659
30	18.39205	18.16376	17.93971	17.71980	17.50394
31	18.73628	18.49784	18.26395	18.03449	17.80937
32	19.06887	18.82031	18.57661	18.33766	18.10334
33	19.39021	19.13157	18.87812	18.62973	18.38628
34	19.70068	19.43202	19.16887	18.91111	18.65859
35	20.00066	19.72203	19.44925	19.18218	18.92069
40	21.35507	21.02772	20.70803	20.39578	20.09076
45	22.49545	22.12179	21.75771	21.40292	21.05712
50	23.45562	23.03853	22.63302	22.23871	21.85522

Table B. Present Value of $1 Received per Period (cont'd)

n/r	4.0%	4.1%	4.2%	4.3%	4.4%
1	.96154	.96061	.95969	.95877	.95785
2	1.88609	1.88340	1.88070	1.87802	1.87534
3	2.77509	2.76983	2.76459	2.75937	2.75416
4	3.62990	3.62136	3.61285	3.60438	3.59594
5	4.45182	4.43934	4.42692	4.41455	4.40224
6	5.24214	5.22511	5.20818	5.19132	5.17456
7	6.00205	5.97994	5.95794	5.93607	5.91433
8	6.73274	6.70503	6.67749	6.65012	6.62292
9	7.43533	7.40157	7.36803	7.33473	7.30165
10	8.11090	8.07067	8.03074	7.99111	7.95177
11	8.76048	8.71342	8.66674	8.62043	8.57449
12	9.38507	9.33085	9.27710	9.22381	9.17097
13	9.98565	9.92397	9.86286	9.80231	9.74231
14	10.56312	10.49373	10.42501	10.35696	10.28957
15	11.11839	11.04105	10.96450	10.88874	10.81376
16	11.65230	11.56681	11.48225	11.39860	11.31586
17	12.16567	12.07186	11.97912	11.88744	11.79680
18	12.65930	12.55702	12.45597	12.35613	12.25747
19	13.13394	13.02308	12.91360	12.80549	12.69873
20	13.59033	13.47077	13.35278	13.23633	13.12139
21	14.02916	13.90084	13.77426	13.64941	13.52623
22	14.45112	14.31397	14.17876	14.04545	13.91402
23	14.85684	14.71082	14.56694	14.42517	14.28546
24	15.24696	15.09205	14.93949	14.78923	14.64124
25	15.62208	15.45826	15.29701	15.13829	14.98203
26	15.98277	15.81005	15.64013	15.47295	15.30846
27	16.32959	16.14798	15.96941	15.79381	15.62113
28	16.66306	16.47260	16.28542	16.10145	15.92062
29	16.98371	16.78444	16.58870	16.39641	16.20749
30	17.29203	17.08400	16.87975	16.67920	16.48227
31	17.58849	17.37176	17.15907	16.95034	16.74547
32	17.87355	17.64818	17.42713	17.21029	16.99758
33	18.14765	17.91372	17.68438	17.45953	17.23906
34	18.41120	18.16880	17.93127	17.69850	17.47036
35	18.66461	18.41383	18.16821	17.92761	17.69192
40	19.79277	19.50162	19.21710	18.93904	18.66726
45	20.72004	20.39141	20.07097	19.75848	19.45368
50	21.48218	21.11925	20.76608	20.42236	20.08777

Table B. Present Value of $1 Received per Period (cont'd)

n/r	4.5%	4.6%	4.7%	4.8%	4.9%
1	.95694	.95602	.95511	.95420	.95329
2	1.87267	1.87000	1.86734	1.86469	1.86205
3	2.74896	2.74379	2.73863	2.73349	2.72836
4	3.58753	3.57915	3.57080	3.56249	3.55420
5	4.38998	4.37777	4.36562	4.35352	4.34147
6	5.15787	5.14127	5.12475	5.10832	5.09196
7	5.89270	5.87120	5.84981	5.82855	5.80740
8	6.59589	6.56902	6.54232	6.51579	6.48942
9	7.26879	7.23616	7.20375	7.17156	7.13958
10	7.91272	7.87396	7.83548	7.79729	7.75937
11	8.52892	8.48371	8.43885	8.39436	8.35021
12	9.11858	9.06664	9.01514	8.96408	8.91345
13	9.68285	9.62394	9.56556	9.50771	9.45038
14	10.22283	10.15673	10.09127	10.02644	9.96223
15	10.73955	10.66609	10.59338	10.52141	10.45018
16	11.23402	11.15305	11.07295	10.99372	10.91532
17	11.70719	11.61859	11.53100	11.44438	11.35875
18	12.15999	12.06367	11.96848	11.87441	11.78145
19	12.59329	12.48916	12.38632	12.28475	12.18442
20	13.00794	12.89595	12.78541	12.67628	12.56856
21	13.40472	13.28485	13.16658	13.04989	12.93476
22	13.78442	13.65664	13.53064	13.40638	13.28385
23	14.14777	14.01209	13.87835	13.74655	13.61663
24	14.49548	14.35190	14.21046	14.07113	13.93387
25	14.82821	14.67677	14.52766	14.38085	14.23629
26	15.14661	14.98735	14.83062	14.67639	14.52459
27	15.45130	15.28427	15.11998	14.95838	14.79942
28	15.74287	15.56814	15.39636	15.22747	15.06141
29	16.02189	15.83952	15.66032	15.48422	15.31116
30	16.28889	16.09897	15.91244	15.72922	15.54925
31	16.54439	16.34701	16.15323	15.96300	15.77621
32	16.78889	16.58414	16.38322	16.18607	15.99258
33	17.02286	16.81084	16.60289	16.39892	16.19883
34	17.24676	17.02757	16.81269	16.60202	16.39546
35	17.46101	17.23477	17.01308	16.79582	16.58290
40	18.40158	18.14185	17.88788	17.63954	17.39665
45	19.15635	18.86626	18.58319	18.30694	18.03730
50	19.76201	19.44479	19.13584	18.83488	18.54166

n/r	5.0%	5.1%	5.2%	5.3%	5.4%
1	.95238	.95147	.95057	.94967	.94877
2	1.85941	1.85678	1.85415	1.85154	1.84892
3	2.72325	2.71815	2.71307	2.70801	2.70296
4	3.54595	3.53773	3.52954	3.52138	3.51325
5	4.32948	4.31753	4.30564	4.29381	4.28202
6	5.07569	5.05950	5.04339	5.02736	5.01140
7	5.78637	5.76546	5.74467	5.72399	5.70342
8	6.46321	6.43717	6.41128	6.38555	6.35998
9	7.10782	7.07628	7.04494	7.01382	6.98290
10	7.72173	7.68437	7.64728	7.61046	7.57391
11	8.30641	8.26296	8.21985	8.17708	8.13464
12	8.86325	8.81347	8.76412	8.71517	8.66664
13	9.39357	9.33727	9.28148	9.22619	9.17139
14	9.89864	9.83566	9.77327	9.71148	9.65027
15	10.37966	10.30985	10.24075	10.17234	10.10462
16	10.83777	10.76104	10.68512	10.61001	10.53570
17	11.27407	11.19033	11.10753	11.02565	10.94468
18	11.68959	11.59879	11.50906	11.42037	11.33272
19	12.08532	11.98744	11.89074	11.79523	11.70087
20	12.46221	12.35722	12.25356	12.15121	12.05016
21	12.82115	12.70906	12.59844	12.48928	12.38156
22	13.16300	13.04382	12.92627	12.81033	12.69597
23	13.48857	13.36234	13.23790	13.11523	12.99428
24	13.79864	13.66541	13.53413	13.40477	13.27731
25	14.09394	13.95376	13.81571	13.67975	13.54583
26	14.37519	14.22813	14.08338	13.94088	13.80060
27	14.64303	14.48918	14.33781	14.18887	14.04232
28	14.89813	14.73756	14.57967	14.42438	14.27165
29	15.14107	14.97390	14.80957	14.64803	14.48923
30	15.37245	15.19876	15.02811	14.86043	14.69566
31	15.59281	15.41271	15.23584	15.06214	14.89152
32	15.80268	15.61628	15.43331	15.25369	15.07734
33	16.00255	15.80997	15.62102	15.43560	15.25365
34	16.19290	15.99426	15.79945	15.60836	15.42092
35	16.37419	16.16961	15.96906	15.77242	15.57962
40	17.15909	16.92669	16.69933	16.47687	16.25918
45	17.77407	17.51707	17.26610	17.02101	16.78160
50	18.25593	17.97744	17.70598	17.44131	17.18323

n/r	5.5%	5.6%	5.7%	5.8%	5.9%
1	.94787	.94697	.94607	.94518	.94429
2	1.84632	1.84372	1.84113	1.83854	1.83597
3	2.69793	2.69292	2.68792	2.68293	2.67797
4	3.50515	3.49708	3.48904	3.48103	3.47305
5	4.27028	4.25860	4.24697	4.23538	4.22385
6	4.99553	4.97973	4.96402	4.94838	4.93281
7	5.68297	5.66263	5.64240	5.62228	5.60228
8	6.33457	6.30931	6.28420	6.25925	6.23445
9	6.95220	6.92169	6.89139	6.86129	6.83139
10	7.53763	7.50160	7.46584	7.43033	7.39508
11	8.09254	8.05076	8.00931	7.96818	7.92737
12	8.61852	8.57079	8.52347	8.47654	8.43000
13	9.11708	9.06325	9.00991	8.95703	8.90463
14	9.58965	9.52960	9.47011	9.41118	9.35281
15	10.03758	9.97121	9.90550	9.84044	9.77602
16	10.46216	10.38940	10.31740	10.24616	10.17566
17	10.86461	10.78542	10.70710	10.62964	10.55303
18	11.24607	11.16043	11.07578	10.99210	10.90938
19	11.60765	11.51556	11.42458	11.33469	11.24587
20	11.95038	11.85186	11.75457	11.65849	11.56362
21	12.27524	12.17032	12.06676	11.96455	11.86366
22	12.58317	12.47189	12.36212	12.25383	12.14699
23	12.87504	12.75748	12.64155	12.52725	12.41453
24	13.15170	13.02791	12.90592	12.78568	12.66717
25	13.41393	13.28401	13.15602	13.02994	12.90573
26	13.66250	13.52652	13.39264	13.26081	13.13100
27	13.89810	13.75618	13.61650	13.47903	13.34372
28	14.12142	13.97365	13.82829	13.68528	13.54459
29	14.33310	14.17959	14.02866	13.88023	13.73427
30	14.53375	14.37462	14.21822	14.06449	13.91338
31	14.72393	14.55930	14.39756	14.23865	14.08251
32	14.90420	14.73418	14.56722	14.40326	14.24222
33	15.07507	14.89979	14.72774	14.55885	14.39303
34	15.23703	15.05662	14.87961	14.70590	14.53544
35	15.39055	15.20513	15.02328	14.84490	14.66992
40	16.04612	15.83759	15.63345	15.43360	15.23792
45	16.54773	16.31922	16.09592	15.87769	15.66437
50	16.93152	16.68598	16.44643	16.21268	15.98455

Table B. Present Value of $1 Received per Period (cont'd)

n/r	6%	7%	8%	9%	10%
1	0.9434	0.9346	0.9259	0.9174	0.9091
2	1.8334	1.8080	1.7833	1.7591	1.7355
3	2.6730	2.6243	2.5771	2.5313	2.4869
4	3.4651	3.3872	3.3121	3.2397	3.1699
5	4.2124	4.1002	3.9927	3.8897	3.7908
6	4.9173	4.7665	4.6229	4.4859	4.3553
7	5.5824	5.3893	5.2064	5.0330	4.8684
8	6.2098	5.9713	5.7466	5.5348	5.3349
9	6.8017	6.5152	6.2469	5.9952	5.7590
10	7.3601	7.0236	6.7101	6.4177	6.1446
11	7.8869	7.4987	7.1390	6.8051	6.4951
12	8.3838	7.9427	7.5361	7.1607	6.8137
13	8.8527	8.3577	7.9038	7.4869	7.1034
14	9.2950	8.7455	8.2442	7.7862	7.3667
15	9.7122	9.1079	8.5595	8.0607	7.6061
16	10.1059	9.4466	8.8514	8.3126	7.8237
17	10.4773	9.7632	9.1216	8.5436	8.0216
18	10.8276	10.0591	9.3719	8.7556	8.2014
19	11.1581	10.3356	9.6036	8.9501	8.3649
20	11.4699	10.5940	9.8181	9.1285	8.5136
21	11.7641	10.8355	10.0168	9.2922	8.6487
22	12.0416	11.0612	10.2007	9.4424	8.7715
23	12.3034	11.2722	10.3711	9.5802	8.8832
24	12.5504	11.4693	10.5288	9.7066	8.9847
25	12.7834	11.6536	10.6748	9.8226	9.0770
26	13.0032	11.8258	10.8100	9.9290	9.1609
27	13.2105	11.9867	10.9352	10.0266	9.2372
28	13.4062	12.1371	11.0511	10.1161	9.3066
29	13.5907	12.2777	11.1584	10.1983	9.3696
30	13.7648	12.4090	11.2578	10.2737	9.4269
31	13.9291	12.5318	11.3498	10.3428	9.4790
32	14.0840	12.6466	11.4350	10.4062	9.5264
33	14.2302	12.7538	11.5139	10.4644	9.5694
34	14.3681	12.8540	11.5869	10.5178	9.6086
35	14.4982	12.9477	11.6546	10.5668	9.6442
40	15.0463	13.3317	11.9246	10.7574	9.7791
45	15.4558	13.6055	12.1084	10.8812	9.8628
50	15.7619	13.8007	12.2335	10.9617	9.9148

n/r	11%	12%	13%	14%	15%
1	0.9009	0.8929	0.8850	0.8772	0.8696
2	1.7125	1.6901	1.6681	1.6467	1.6257
3	2.4437	2.4018	2.3612	2.3216	2.2832
4	3.1024	3.0373	2.9745	2.9137	2.8550
5	3.6959	3.6048	3.5172	3.4331	3.3522
6	4.2305	4.1114	3.9975	3.8887	3.7845
7	4.7122	4.5638	4.4226	4.2883	4.1604
8	5.1461	4.9676	4.7988	4.6389	4.4873
9	5.5370	5.3282	5.1317	4.9464	4.7716
10	5.8892	5.6502	5.4262	5.2161	5.0188
11	6.2065	5.9377	5.6869	5.4527	5.2337
12	6.4924	6.1944	5.9176	5.6603	5.4206
13	6.7499	6.4235	6.1218	5.8424	5.5831
14	6.9819	6.6282	6.3025	6.0021	5.7245
15	7.1909	6.8109	6.4624	6.1422	5.8474
16	7.3792	6.9740	6.6039	6.2651	5.9542
17	7.5488	7.1196	6.7291	6.3729	6.0472
18	7.7016	7.2497	6.8399	6.4674	6.1280
19	7.8393	7.3658	6.9380	6.5504	6.1982
20	7.9633	7.4694	7.0248	6.6231	6.2593
21	8.0751	7.5620	7.1015	6.6870	6.3125
22	8.1757	7.6446	7.1695	6.7429	6.3587
23	8.2664	7.7184	7.2297	6.7921	6.3988
24	8.3481	7.7843	7.2829	6.8351	6.4338
25	8.4217	7.8431	7.3300	6.8729	6.4641
26	8.4881	7.8957	7.3717	6.9061	6.4906
27	8.5478	7.9426	7.4086	6.9352	6.5135
28	8.6016	7.9844	7.4412	6.9607	6.5335
29	8.6501	8.0218	7.4701	6.9830	6.5509
30	8.6938	8.0552	7.4957	7.0027	6.5660
31	8.7331	8.0850	7.5183	7.0199	6.5791
32	8.7686	8.1116	7.5383	7.0350	6.5905
33	8.8005	8.1354	7.5560	7.0482	6.6005
34	8.8293	8.1566	7.5717	7.0599	6.6091
35	8.8552	8.1755	7.5856	7.0700	6.6166
40	8.9511	8.2438	7.6344	7.1050	6.6418
45	9.0079	8.2825	7.6609	7.1232	6.6543
50	9.0417	8.3045	7.6752	7.1327	6.6605

Table B.   Present Value of $1 Received per Period (cont'd)

n/r	16%	17%	18%	19%	20%
1	0.8621	0.8547	0.8475	0.8403	0.8333
2	1.6052	1.5852	1.5656	1.5465	1.5278
3	2.2459	2.2096	2.1743	2.1399	2.1065
4	2.7982	2.7432	2.6901	2.6386	2.5887
5	3.2743	3.1993	3.1272	3.0576	2.9906
6	3.6847	3.5892	3.4976	3.4098	3.3255
7	4.0386	3.9224	3.8115	3.7057	3.6046
8	4.3436	4.2072	4.0776	3.9544	3.8372
9	4.6065	4.4506	4.3030	4.1633	4.0310
10	4.8332	4.6586	4.4941	4.3389	4.1925
11	5.0286	4.8364	4.6560	4.4865	4.3271
12	5.1971	4.9884	4.7932	4.6105	4.4392
13	5.3423	5.1183	4.9095	4.7147	4.5327
14	5.4675	5.2293	5.0081	4.8023	4.6106
15	5.5755	5.3242	5.0916	4.8759	4.6755
16	5.6685	5.4053	5.1624	4.9377	4.7296
17	5.7487	5.4746	5.2223	4.9879	4.7746
18	5.8178	5.5339	5.2732	5.0333	4.8122
19	5.8775	5.5845	5.3162	5.0700	4.8435
20	5.9288	5.6278	5.3527	5.1009	4.8696
21	5.9731	5.6648	5.3837	5.1268	4.8913
22	6.0113	5.6964	5.4099	5.1486	4.9094
23	6.0442	5.7234	5.4321	5.1668	4.9245
24	6.0726	5.7465	5.4509	5.1822	4.9371
25	6.0971	5.7662	5.4669	5.1951	4.9476
26	6.1182	5.7831	5.4804	5.2060	4.9563
27	6.1364	5.7975	5.4919	5.2151	4.9636
28	6.1520	5.8099	5.5016	5.2228	4.9697
29	6.1656	5.8204	5.5098	5.2292	4.9747
30	6.1772	5.8294	5.5168	5.2347	4.9789
31	6.1872	5.8371	5.5227	5.2392	4.9824
32	6.1959	5.8437	5.5277	5.2430	4.9854
33	6.2034	5.8493	5.5320	5.2462	4.9878
34	6.2098	5.8541	5.5356	5.2489	4.9898
35	6.2153	5.8582	5.5386	5.2512	4.9915
40	6.2335	5.8713	5.5482	5.2582	4.9966
45	6.2421	5.8773	5.5523	5.2611	4.9986
50	6.2463	5.8801	5.5541	5.2623	4.9995

n/r	21%	22%	23%	24%	25%
1	0.8264	0.8197	0.8130	0.8065	0.8000
2	1.5095	1.4915	1.4740	1.4568	1.4400
3	2.0739	2.0422	2.0114	1.9813	1.9520
4	2.5404	2.4936	2.4483	2.4043	2.3616
5	2.9260	2.8636	2.8035	2.7454	2.6893
6	3.2446	3.1669	3.0923	3.0205	2.9514
7	3.5079	3.4155	3.3270	3.2423	3.1611
8	3.7256	3.6193	3.5179	3.4212	3.3289
9	3.9054	3.7863	3.6731	3.5655	3.4631
10	4.0541	3.9232	3.7993	3.6819	3.5705
11	4.1769	4.0354	3.9018	3.7757	3.6564
12	4.2784	4.1274	3.9852	3.8514	3.7251
13	4.3624	4.2028	4.0530	3.9124	3.7801
14	4.4317	4.2646	4.1082	3.9616	3.8241
15	4.4890	4.3152	4.1530	4.0013	3.8593
16	4.5364	4.3567	4.1894	4.0333	3.8874
17	4.5755	4.3908	4.2190	4.0591	3.9099
18	4.6079	4.4187	4.2431	4.0799	3.9279
19	4.6346	4.4415	4.2627	4.0967	3.9424
20	4.6567	4.4603	4.2786	4.1103	3.9539
21	4.6750	4.4756	4.2916	4.1212	3.9631
22	4.6900	4.4882	4.3021	4.1300	3.9705
23	4.7025	4.4985	4.3106	4.1371	3.9764
24	4.7128	4.5070	4.3176	4.1428	3.9811
25	4.7213	4.5139	4.3232	4.1474	3.9849
26	4.7284	4.5196	4.3278	4.1511	3.9879
27	4.7342	4.5243	4.3316	4.1542	3.9903
28	4.7390	4.5281	4.3346	4.1566	3.9923
29	4.7430	4.5312	4.3371	4.1585	3.9938
30	4.7463	4.5338	4.3391	4.1601	3.9950
31	4.7490	4.5359	4.3407	4.1614	3.9960
32	4.7512	4.5376	4.3421	4.1624	3.9968
33	4.7531	4.5390	4.3431	4.1632	3.9975
34	4.7546	4.5402	4.3440	4.1639	3.9980
35	4.7559	4.5411	4.3447	4.1644	3.9984
40	4.7596	4.5439	4.3467	4.1659	3.9995
45	4.7610	4.5449	4.3474	4.1664	3.9998
50	4.7616	4.5452	4.3477	4.1666	3.9999

Table B. Present Value of $1 Received per Period (cont'd)

n/r	26%	27%	28%	29%	30%	31%
1	0.7937	0.7874	0.7813	0.7752	0.7692	0.7634
2	1.4235	1.4074	1.3916	1.3761	1.3609	1.3461
3	1.9234	1.8956	1.8684	1.8420	1.8161	1.7909
4	2.3202	2.2800	2.2410	2.2031	2.1662	2.1305
5	2.6351	2.5827	2.5320	2.4830	2.4356	2.3897
6	2.8850	2.8210	2.7594	2.7000	2.6427	2.5875
7	3.0833	3.0087	2.9370	2.8682	2.8021	2.7386
8	3.2407	3.1564	3.0758	2.9986	2.9247	2.8539
9	3.3657	3.2728	3.1842	3.0997	3.0190	2.9419
10	3.4648	3.3644	3.2689	3.1781	3.0915	3.0091
11	3.5435	3.4365	3.3351	3.2388	3.1473	3.0604
12	3.6059	3.4933	3.3868	3.2859	3.1903	3.0995
13	3.6555	3.5381	3.4272	3.3224	3.2233	3.1294
14	3.6949	3.5733	3.4587	3.3507	3.2487	3.1522
15	3.7261	3.6010	3.4834	3.3726	3.2682	3.1696
16	3.7509	3.6228	3.5026	3.3896	3.2832	3.1829
17	3.7705	3.6400	3.5177	3.4028	3.2948	3.1931
18	3.7861	3.6536	3.5294	3.4130	3.3037	3.2008
19	3.7985	3.6642	3.5386	3.4210	3.3105	3.2067
20	3.8083	3.6726	3.5458	3.4271	3.3158	3.2112
21	3.8161	3.6792	3.5514	3.4319	3.3198	3.2147
22	3.8223	3.6844	3.5558	3.4356	3.3230	3.2173
23	3.8273	3.6885	3.5592	3.4384	3.3253	3.2193
24	3.8312	3.6918	3.5619	3.4406	3.3272	3.2209
25	3.8342	3.6943	3.5640	3.4423	3.3286	3.2220
26	3.8367	3.6963	3.5656	3.4437	3.3297	3.2229
27	3.8387	3.6979	3.5669	3.4447	3.3305	3.2236
28	3.8402	3.6991	3.5679	3.4455	3.3312	3.2241
29	3.8414	3.7001	3.5687	3.4461	3.3316	3.2245
30	3.8424	3.7009	3.5693	3.4466	3.3321	3.2248
31	3.8432	3.7015	3.5697	3.4470	3.3324	3.2251
32	3.8438	3.7019	3.5701	3.4473	3.3326	3.2252
33	3.8443	3.7023	3.5704	3.4475	3.3328	3.2254
34	3.8447	3.7026	3.5706	3.4477	3.3329	3.2255
35	3.8450	3.7028	3.5708	3.4478	3.3330	3.2256
40	3.8458	3.7034	3.5712	3.4481	3.3332	3.2257
45	3.8460	3.7036	3.5714	3.4482	3.3333	3.2258
50	3.8461	3.7037	3.5714	3.4483	3.3333	3.2258

n/r	32%	33%	34%	35%	36%	37%
1	0.7576	0.7519	0.7463	0.7407	0.7353	0.7299
2	1.3315	1.3172	1.3032	1.2894	1.2760	1.2627
3	1.7663	1.7423	1.7188	1.6959	1.6735	1.6516
4	2.0957	2.0618	2.0290	1.9969	1.9658	1.9355
5	2.3452	2.3021	2.2604	2.2200	2.1807	2.1427
6	2.5342	2.4828	2.4331	2.3852	2.3388	2.2939
7	2.6775	2.6187	2.5620	2.5075	2.4550	2.4043
8	2.7860	2.7208	2.6582	2.5982	2.5404	2.4849
9	2.8681	2.7976	2.7300	2.6653	2.6033	2.5437
10	2.9304	2.8553	2.7836	2.7150	2.6495	2.5867
11	2.9776	2.8987	2.8236	2.7519	2.6834	2.6180
12	3.0133	2.9314	2.8534	2.7792	2.7084	2.6409
13	3.0404	2.9559	2.8757	2.7994	2.7268	2.6576
14	3.0609	2.9744	2.8923	2.8144	2.7403	2.6698
15	3.0764	2.9883	2.9047	2.8255	2.7502	2.6787
16	3.0882	2.9987	2.9140	2.8337	2.7575	2.6852
17	3.0971	3.0065	2.9209	2.8398	2.7629	2.6899
18	3.1039	3.0124	2.9260	2.8443	2.7668	2.6934
19	3.1090	3.0169	2.9299	2.8476	2.7697	2.6959
20	3.1129	3.0202	2.9327	2.8501	2.7718	2.6977
21	3.1158	3.0227	2.9349	2.8520	2.7734	2.6991
22	3.1180	3.0246	2.9365	2.8533	2.7746	2.7000
23	3.1197	3.0260	2.9377	2.8543	2.7754	2.7008
24	3.1210	3.0271	2.9386	2.8550	2.7760	2.7013
25	3.1220	3.0279	2.9392	2.8556	2.7765	2.7017
26	3.1227	3.0285	2.9397	2.8560	2.7768	2.7019
27	3.1233	3.0289	2.9401	2.8563	2.7771	2.7022
28	3.1237	3.0293	2.9404	2.8565	2.7773	2.7023
29	3.1240	3.0295	2.9406	2.8567	2.7774	2.7024
30	3.1242	3.0297	2.9407	2.8568	2.7775	2.7025
31	3.1244	3.0299	2.9408	2.8569	2.7776	2.7025
32	3.1246	3.0300	2.9409	2.8569	2.7776	2.7026
33	3.1247	3.0301	2.9410	2.8570	2.7777	2.7026
34	3.1248	3.0301	2.9410	2.8570	2.7777	2.7026
35	3.1248	3.0302	2.9411	2.8571	2.7777	2.7027
40	3.1250	3.0303	2.9412	2.8571	2.7778	2.7027
45	3.1250	3.0303	2.9412	2.8571	2.7778	2.7027
50	3.1250	3.0303	2.9412	2.8571	2.7778	2.7027

Table B. Present Value of $1 Received per Period (cont'd)

n/r	38%	39%	40%	41%	42%	43%
1	0.7246	0.7194	0.7143	0.7092	0.7042	0.6993
2	1.2497	1.2370	1.2245	1.2122	1.2002	1.1883
3	1.6302	1.6093	1.5889	1.5689	1.5494	1.5303
4	1.9060	1.8772	1.8492	1.8219	1.7954	1.7694
5	2.1058	2.0699	2.0352	2.0014	1.9686	1.9367
6	2.2506	2.2086	2.1680	2.1286	2.0905	2.0536
7	2.3555	2.3083	2.2628	2.2189	2.1764	2.1354
8	2.4315	2.3801	2.3306	2.2829	2.2369	2.1926
9	2.4866	2.4317	2.3790	2.3283	2.2795	2.2326
10	2.5265	2.4689	2.4136	2.3605	2.3095	2.2605
11	2.5555	2.4956	2.4383	2.3833	2.3307	2.2801
12	2.5764	2.5148	2.4559	2.3995	2.3455	2.2938
13	2.5916	2.5286	2.4685	2.4110	2.3560	2.3033
14	2.6026	2.5386	2.4775	2.4192	2.3634	2.3100
15	2.6106	2.5457	2.4839	2.4249	2.3686	2.3147
16	2.6164	2.5509	2.4885	2.4290	2.3722	2.3180
17	2.6206	2.5546	2.4918	2.4319	2.3748	2.3203
18	2.6236	2.5573	2.4941	2.4340	2.3766	2.3219
19	2.6258	2.5592	2.4958	2.4355	2.3779	2.3230
20	2.6274	2.5606	2.4970	2.4365	2.3788	2.3238
21	2.6285	2.5616	2.4979	2.4372	2.3794	2.3243
22	2.6294	2.5623	2.4985	2.4378	2.3799	2.3247
23	2.6300	2.5628	2.4989	2.4381	2.3802	2.3250
24	2.6304	2.5632	2.4992	2.4384	2.3804	2.3251
25	2.6307	2.5634	2.4994	2.4386	2.3806	2.3253
26	2.6310	2.5636	2.4996	2.4387	2.3807	2.3254
27	2.6311	2.5637	2.4997	2.4388	2.3808	2.3254
28	2.6313	2.5638	2.4998	2.4389	2.3808	2.3255
29	2.6313	2.5639	2.4999	2.4389	2.3809	2.3255
30	2.6314	2.5640	2.4999	2.4389	2.3809	2.3255
31	2.6315	2.5640	2.4999	2.4390	2.3809	2.3255
32	2.6315	2.5640	2.4999	2.4390	2.3809	2.3256
33	2.6315	2.5641	2.5000	2.4390	2.3809	2.3256
34	2.6315	2.5641	2.5000	2.4390	2.3809	2.3256
35	2.6215	2.5641	2.5000	2.4390	2.3809	2.3256
40	2.6316	2.5641	2.5000	2.4390	2.3810	2.3256
45	2.6316	2.5641	2.5000	2.4390	2.3810	2.3256
50	2.6316	2.5641	2.5000	2.4390	2.3810	2.3256

Table B. Present Value of $1 Received per Period (cont'd)

n/r	44%	45%	46%	47%	48%	49%
1	0.6944	0.6897	0.6849	0.6803	0.6757	0.6711
2	1.1767	1.1653	1.1541	1.1430	1.1322	1.1216
3	1.5116	1.4933	1.4754	1.4579	1.4407	1.4239
4	1.7442	1.7195	1.6955	1.6720	1.6491	1.6268
5	1.9057	1.8755	1.8462	1.8177	1.7899	1.7629
6	2.0178	1.9831	1.9495	1.9168	1.8851	1.8543
7	2.0957	2.0573	2.0202	1.9842	1.9494	1.9156
8	2.1498	2.1085	2.0686	2.0301	1.9928	1.9568
9	2.1874	2.1438	2.1018	2.0613	2.0222	1.9844
10	2.2134	2.1681	2.1245	2.0825	2.0420	2.0030
11	2.2316	2.1849	2.1401	2.0969	2.0554	2.0154
12	2.2441	2.1965	2.1507	2.1068	2.0645	2.0238
13	2.2529	2.2045	2.1580	2.1134	2.0706	2.0294
14	2.2589	2.2100	2.1630	2.1180	2.0747	2.0331
15	2.2632	2.2138	2.1665	2.1211	2.0775	2.0357
16	2.2661	2.2164	2.1688	2.1232	2.0794	2.0374
17	2.2681	2.2182	2.1704	2.1246	2.0807	2.0385
18	2.2695	2.2195	2.1715	2.1256	2.0815	2.0393
19	2.2705	2.2203	2.1723	2.1263	2.0821	2.0398
20	2.2712	2.2209	2.1728	2.1267	2.0825	2.0401
21	2.2717	2.2213	2.1731	2.1270	2.0828	2.0403
22	2.2720	2.2216	2.1734	2.1272	2.0830	2.0405
23	2.2722	2.2218	2.1736	2.1274	2.0831	2.0406
24	2.2724	2.2219	2.1737	2.1275	2.0832	2.0407
25	2.2725	2.2220	2.1737	2.1275	2.0832	2.0407
26	2.2726	2.2221	2.1738	2.1276	2.0833	2.0408
27	2.2726	2.2221	2.1738	2.1276	2.0833	2.0408
28	2.2726	2.2222	2.1739	2.1276	2.0833	2.0408
29	2.2727	2.2222	2.1739	2.1276	2.0833	2.0408
30	2.2727	2.2222	2.1739	2.1276	2.0833	2.0408
31	2.2727	2.2222	2.1739	2.1276	2.0833	2.0408
32	2.2727	2.2222	2.1739	2.1277	2.0833	2.0408
33	2.2727	2.2222	2.1739	2.1277	2.0833	2.0408
34	2.2727	2.2222	2.1739	2.1277	2.0833	2.0408
35	2.2727	2.2222	2.1739	2.1277	2.0833	2.0408
40	2.2727	2.2222	2.1739	2.1277	2.0833	2.0408
45	2.2727	2.2222	2.1739	2.1277	2.0833	2.0408
50	2.2727	2.2222	2.1739	2.1277	2.0833	2.0408

Table C. Present Value of Depreciation Charges from $1.00 of Assets Depreciated over _n_ Years, Using the Sum-of-the-Years'-Digits Depreciation Method, Discounting at _r_ Per Cent per Year, Assuming No Salvage Value *

n	1%	2%	3%	4%	5%
3	0.983580	0.967639	0.952159	0.937121	0.922507
4	0.980344	0.961356	0.943005	0.925262	0.908099
5	0.977125	0.955135	0.933984	0.913629	0.894031
6	0.973922	0.948974	0.925093	0.902218	0.880293
7	0.970734	0.942873	0.916330	0.891023	0.866876
8	0.967562	0.936831	0.907692	0.880038	0.853771
9	0.964405	0.930848	0.899179	0.869260	0.840968
10	0.961264	0.924923	0.890786	0.858684	0.828460
11	0.958139	0.919054	0.882513	0.848304	0.816238
12	0.955029	0.913243	0.874357	0.838117	0.804294
13	0.951934	0.907487	0.866317	0.828119	0.792621
14	0.948854	0.901786	0.858390	0.818304	0.781211
15	0.945790	0.896140	0.850574	0.808669	0.770057
16	0.942740	0.890548	0.842867	0.799210	0.759152
17	0.939705	0.885009	0.835268	0.789923	0.748488
18	0.936685	0.879523	0.827775	0.780805	0.738060
19	0.933680	0.874089	0.820386	0.771850	0.727861
20	0.930689	0.868706	0.813099	0.763056	0.717885
21	0.927713	0.863375	0.805913	0.754420	0.708125
22	0.924751	0.858093	0.798825	0.745937	0.698577
23	0.921804	0.852862	0.791835	0.737605	0.689234
24	0.918871	0.847679	0.784940	0.729420	0.680091
25	0.915952	0.842545	0.778139	0.721379	0.671142
26	0.913047	0.837459	0.771430	0.713478	0.662383
27	0.910157	0.832421	0.764812	0.705715	0.653808
28	0.907280	0.827430	0.758283	0.698087	0.645412
29	0.904417	0.822485	0.751843	0.690591	0.637192
30	0.901568	0.817586	0.745488	0.683224	0.629142
31	0.898733	0.812732	0.739219	0.675983	0.621258
32	0.895911	0.807923	0.733033	0.668866	0.613535
33	0.893102	0.803158	0.726929	0.661870	0.605970
34	0.890308	0.798438	0.720906	0.654992	0.598558
35	0.887527	0.793760	0.714962	0.648230	0.591295
36	0.884759	0.789126	0.709097	0.641581	0.584179
37	0.882004	0.784534	0.703308	0.635043	0.577204
38	0.879263	0.779984	0.697595	0.628615	0.570367
39	0.876534	0.775475	0.691957	0.622292	0.563666
40	0.873819	0.771007	0.686391	0.616074	0.557095
41	0.871116	0.766580	0.680898	0.609958	0.550653
42	0.868427	0.762193	0.675476	0.603942	0.544336
43	0.865750	0.757846	0.670123	0.598023	0.538141
44	0.863086	0.753537	0.664839	0.592201	0.532065
45	0.860434	0.749268	0.659623	0.586472	0.526105
46	0.857795	0.745036	0.654473	0.580836	0.520258
47	0.855169	0.740843	0.649388	0.575290	0.514521
48	0.852555	0.736687	0.644368	0.569831	0.508892
49	0.849953	0.732568	0.639411	0.564460	0.503368
50	0.847364	0.728486	0.634516	0.559173	0.497946

* Values tabled are

$$C(n,r) = \sum_{i=1}^{n} \frac{2(n-i+1)}{n(n+1)(1+r)^i}$$

Table C.   Sum-of-the-Years'-Digits (cont'd)

n	6%	7%	8%	9%	10%
3	0.908300	0.894486	0.881048	0.867973	0.855247
4	0.891491	0.875412	0.859841	0.844756	0.830135
5	0.875151	0.856955	0.839408	0.822481	0.806142
6	0.859266	0.839089	0.819715	0.801101	0.783209
7	0.843821	0.821791	0.800728	0.780574	0.761279
8	0.828799	0.805040	0.782417	0.760858	0.740298
9	0.814188	0.788815	0.764753	0.741914	0.720217
10	0.799974	0.773096	0.747709	0.723706	0.700988
11	0.786143	0.757863	0.731257	0.706197	0.682566
12	0.772683	0.743098	0.715372	0.689355	0.664911
13	0.759582	0.728783	0.700031	0.673150	0.647983
14	0.746828	0.714902	0.685210	0.657550	0.631744
15	0.734410	0.701439	0.670888	0.642529	0.616160
16	0.722317	0.688377	0.657043	0.628059	0.601198
17	0.710538	0.675703	0.643657	0.614115	0.586827
18	0.699064	0.663401	0.630710	0.600674	0.573017
19	0.687885	0.651459	0.618184	0.587713	0.559741
20	0.676799	0.639863	0.606063	0.575209	0.546973
21	0.666373	0.628601	0.594329	0.563144	0.534688
22	0.656022	0.617660	0.582967	0.551496	0.522864
23	0.645931	0.607030	0.571963	0.540249	0.511478
24	0.636091	0.596698	0.561302	0.529385	0.500508
25	0.626495	0.586656	0.550970	0.518886	0.489937
26	0.617134	0.576891	0.540955	0.508738	0.479745
27	0.608001	0.567396	0.531244	0.498925	0.469915
28	0.599090	0.558159	0.521826	0.489433	0.460429
29	0.590394	0.549173	0.512689	0.480248	0.451273
30	0.581906	0.540429	0.503823	0.471358	0.442432
31	0.573619	0.531918	0.495217	0.462751	0.433891
32	0.565529	0.523632	0.486861	0.454414	0.425637
33	0.557628	0.515564	0.478746	0.446337	0.417657
34	0.549912	0.507707	0.470863	0.438509	0.409940
35	0.542374	0.500053	0.463203	0.430920	0.402474
36	0.535010	0.492595	0.455758	0.423561	0.395247
37	0.527815	0.485328	0.448521	0.416422	0.388251
38	0.520782	0.478244	0.441483	0.409494	0.381476
39	0.513909	0.471338	0.434638	0.402770	0.374911
40	0.507189	0.464604	0.427978	0.396242	0.368548
41	0.500619	0.458037	0.421498	0.389901	0.362379
42	0.494194	0.451630	0.415189	0.383741	0.356396
43	0.487911	0.445379	0.409048	0.377755	0.350592
44	0.481764	0.439280	0.403067	0.371936	0.344958
45	0.475751	0.433326	0.397241	0.366278	0.339490
46	0.469868	0.427514	0.391565	0.360775	0.334179
47	0.464110	0.421839	0.386034	0.355421	0.329019
48	0.458475	0.416296	0.380643	0.350212	0.324006
49	0.452958	0.410883	0.375386	0.345141	0.319132
50	0.447557	0.405594	0.370260	0.340203	0.314393

Table C.   Sum-of-the-Years'-Digits (cont'd)

n	11%	12%	13%	14%	15%
3	0.842856	0.830790	0.819035	0.807581	0.796417
4	0.815958	0.802209	0.788868	0.775920	0.763348
5	0.790365	0.775124	0.760394	0.746152	0.732375
6	0.766001	0.749442	0.733498	0.718140	0.703339
7	0.742793	0.725072	0.708074	0.691759	0.676091
8	0.720676	0.701935	0.684023	0.666892	0.650496
9	0.699586	0.679954	0.661256	0.643433	0.626432
10	0.679466	0.659057	0.639686	0.621284	0.603786
11	0.660260	0.639179	0.619238	0.600354	0.582453
12	0.641917	0.620259	0.599837	0.580559	0.562340
13	0.624389	0.602239	0.581419	0.561824	0.543359
14	0.607631	0.585066	0.563920	0.544077	0.525430
15	0.591601	0.568690	0.547283	0.527252	0.508479
16	0.576259	0.553065	0.531455	0.511289	0.492439
17	0.561569	0.538146	0.516385	0.496132	0.477248
18	0.547495	0.523895	0.502028	0.481728	0.462847
19	0.534005	0.510273	0.488341	0.468031	0.449185
20	0.521068	0.497244	0.475284	0.454995	0.436212
21	0.508655	0.484776	0.462819	0.442580	0.423883
22	0.496739	0.472838	0.450912	0.430747	0.412156
23	0.485295	0.461400	0.439530	0.419460	0.400994
24	0.474299	0.450436	0.428644	0.408687	0.390361
25	0.463727	0.439919	0.418225	0.398397	0.380222
26	0.453560	0.429828	0.408247	0.388562	0.370549
27	0.443776	0.420138	0.398686	0.379154	0.361313
28	0.434357	0.410829	0.389519	0.370150	0.352487
29	0.425285	0.401881	0.380723	0.361526	0.344043
30	0.416544	0.393276	0.372280	0.353262	0.335971
31	0.408117	0.384997	0.364171	0.345336	0.328238
32	0.399990	0.377026	0.356377	0.337730	0.320826
33	0.392148	0.369350	0.348882	0.330427	0.313720
34	0.384579	0.361953	0.341672	0.323411	0.306901
35	0.377269	0.354821	0.334730	0.316666	0.300353
36	0.370207	0.347943	0.328045	0.310178	0.294063
37	0.363382	0.341305	0.321603	0.303934	0.288015
38	0.356783	0.334897	0.315391	0.297921	0.282197
39	0.350400	0.328707	0.309400	0.292127	0.276598
40	0.344223	0.322726	0.303617	0.286541	0.271205
41	0.338244	0.316944	0.298034	0.281154	0.266008
42	0.332453	0.311351	0.292640	0.275955	0.260998
43	0.326844	0.305941	0.287427	0.270935	0.256164
44	0.321407	0.300703	0.282387	0.266086	0.251499
45	0.316136	0.295632	0.277511	0.261399	0.246993
46	0.311024	0.290719	0.272792	0.256868	0.242640
47	0.306064	0.285957	0.268223	0.252484	0.238432
48	0.301250	0.281341	0.263798	0.248241	0.234362
49	0.296577	0.276863	0.259510	0.244133	0.230424
50	0.292038	0.272519	0.255353	0.240153	0.226611

Table C.   Sum-of-the-Years'-Digits (cont'd)

n	16%	17%	18%	19%	20%
3	0.785532	0.774917	0.764562	0.754459	0.744599
4	0.751137	0.739274	0.727743	0.716534	0.705633
5	0.719044	0.706139	0.693640	0.681532	0.669796
6	0.689067	0.675298	0.662010	0.649179	0.636783
7	0.661035	0.646559	0.632633	0.619230	0.606323
8	0.634793	0.619745	0.605314	0.591467	0.578172
9	0.610202	0.594697	0.579874	0.565692	0.552115
10	0.587133	0.571272	0.556153	0.541729	0.527957
11	0.565469	0.549339	0.534006	0.519418	0.505526
12	0.545104	0.528779	0.513303	0.498616	0.484666
13	0.525939	0.509484	0.493925	0.479195	0.465237
14	0.507885	0.491356	0.475764	0.461039	0.447116
15	0.490862	0.474305	0.458723	0.444041	0.430189
16	0.474793	0.458249	0.442714	0.428108	0.414354
17	0.459612	0.443114	0.427657	0.413152	0.399522
18	0.445254	0.428832	0.413477	0.399097	0.385608
19	0.431663	0.415341	0.400110	0.385872	0.372540
20	0.418784	0.402583	0.387493	0.373412	0.360248
21	0.406571	0.390508	0.375573	0.361659	0.348673
22	0.394977	0.379066	0.364297	0.350561	0.337758
23	0.383962	0.368214	0.353621	0.340068	0.327454
24	0.373487	0.357912	0.343501	0.330136	0.317715
25	0.363517	0.348122	0.333899	0.320726	0.308499
26	0.354021	0.338812	0.324779	0.311801	0.299767
27	0.344967	0.329948	0.316110	0.303326	0.291487
28	0.336329	0.321503	0.307860	0.295271	0.283625
29	0.328081	0.313450	0.300002	0.287607	0.276152
30	0.320199	0.305763	0.292511	0.280309	0.269044
31	0.312661	0.298422	0.285364	0.273353	0.262274
32	0.305446	0.291403	0.278538	0.266716	0.255820
33	0.298536	0.284688	0.272014	0.260378	0.249663
34	0.291914	0.278259	0.265774	0.254321	0.243783
35	0.285562	0.272099	0.259800	0.248528	0.238162
36	0.279466	0.266192	0.254077	0.242981	0.232786
37	0.273611	0.260524	0.248590	0.237668	0.227638
38	0.267984	0.255082	0.243325	0.232573	0.222705
39	0.262573	0.249853	0.238270	0.227684	0.217975
40	0.257366	0.244825	0.233413	0.222990	0.213435
41	0.252353	0.239988	0.228744	0.218479	0.209076
42	0.247524	0.235331	0.224251	0.214142	0.204886
43	0.242868	0.230845	0.219926	0.209969	0.200856
44	0.238378	0.226521	0.215759	0.205951	0.196978
45	0.234045	0.222351	0.211743	0.202079	0.193243
46	0.229861	0.218327	0.207869	0.198347	0.189644
47	0.225819	0.214441	0.204131	0.194747	0.186174
48	0.221912	0.210688	0.200521	0.191273	0.182826
49	0.218134	0.207060	0.197034	0.187918	0.179594
50	0.214479	0.203552	0.193664	0.184676	0.176473

Table D. Present Value of Depreciation Charges from $1.00 of Assets Depreciated over n Years, Using the Twice Straight-Line Declining Balance Depreciation Method, Discounting at r Per cent per Year, Assuming No Salvage Value *

n	1%	2%	3%	4%	5%
3	.985753	.971890	.958397	.945260	.932465
4	.981570	.963759	.946539	.929883	.913765
5	.977620	.956126	.935471	.915611	.896505
6	.973593	.948394	.924329	.901332	.879339
7	.969722	.941004	.913741	.887838	.863203
8	.965781	.933528	.903095	.874349	.847170
9	.961962	.926325	.892896	.861498	.831973
10	.958088	.919063	.882674	.848693	.816918
11	.954316	.912033	.872833	.836432	.802576
12	.950500	.904965	.862998	.824248	.788403
13	.946772	.898100	.853497	.812540	.774853
14	.943010	.891213	.844023	.800930	.761488
15	.939326	.884508	.834848	.789745	.748676
16	.935615	.877793	.825713	.778670	.736058
17	.931974	.871243	.816850	.767980	.723936
18	.928312	.864693	.808038	.757408	.712010
19	.924714	.858295	.799475	.747187	.700533
20	.921098	.851904	.790970	.737088	.689251
21	.917543	.845654	.782695	.727311	.678378
22	.913973	.839416	.774483	.717659	.667697
23	.910459	.833309	.766484	.708302	.657388
24	.906935	.827220	.758552	.699071	.647267
25	.903462	.821253	.750819	.690114	.637488
26	.899982	.815306	.743155	.681281	.627890
27	.896550	.809476	.735677	.672703	.618607
28	.893112	.803668	.728269	.664247	.609498
29	.889721	.797971	.721036	.656027	.600680
30	.886326	.792298	.713874	.647927	.592029
31	.882974	.786729	.706876	.640049	.583647
32	.879620	.781187	.699949	.632287	.575425
33	.876309	.775744	.693178	.624731	.567452
34	.872995	.770330	.686477	.617289	.559631
35	.869722	.765009	.679923	.610041	.552042
36	.866449	.759718	.673438	.602902	.544599
37	.863214	.754516	.667093	.595945	.537370
38	.859981	.749344	.660816	.589094	.530281
39	.856784	.744259	.654672	.582414	.523391
40	.853589	.739204	.648595	.575837	.516633
41	.850430	.734231	.642643	.569420	.510063
42	.847273	.729289	.636757	.563101	.503617
43	.844150	.724426	.630991	.556934	.497346
44	.841031	.719594	.625289	.550862	.491193
45	.837945	.714838	.619701	.544933	.485204
46	.834863	.710113	.614176	.539095	.479328
47	.831813	.705461	.608760	.533391	.473604
48	.828767	.700840	.603405	.527776	.467988
49	.825752	.696289	.598153	.522287	.462514
50	.822742	.691769	.592961	.516883	.457143

* Values tabled are

$$D(n,r) = \sum_{i=1}^{n} \frac{d_i}{(1+r)^i}$$

where $d_i = \begin{cases} (2/n)(1 - 2/n)^{i-1} & \text{for } i < k \\ \dfrac{(1 - 2/n)^{k-1}}{n+1-k} & \text{for } i > k \end{cases}$ and k is the smallest integer greater than or equal to $(n/2 + 1)$.

Table D.   Twice Straight-Line Declining Balance (cont'd)

n	6%	7%	8%	9%	10%
3	.919999	.907850	.896007	.884459	.873195
4	.898161	.883049	.868405	.854212	.840448
5	.878113	.860399	.843330	.826873	.810998
6	.858291	.838135	.818819	.800297	.782525
7	.839757	.817424	.796132	.775819	.756424
8	.821445	.797073	.773962	.752024	.731181
9	.804178	.777979	.753259	.729907	.707825
10	.787165	.759267	.733076	.708455	.685282
11	.771038	.741615	.714123	.688399	.664295
12	.755187	.724354	.695683	.668981	.644070
13	.740105	.708006	.678296	.650747	.625155
14	.725308	.692046	.661403	.633114	.606944
15	.711188	.676885	.645423	.616490	.589849
16	.697352	.662101	.629912	.600443	.573398
17	.684121	.648022	.615200	.585272	.557908
18	.671167	.634304	.600928	.570615	.543003
19	.658756	.621213	.587360	.556731	.528930
20	.646613	.608464	.574202	.543320	.515386
21	.634960	.596275	.561668	.530587	.502568
22	.623565	.584409	.549515	.518288	.490228
23	.612613	.573046	.537917	.506587	.478522
24	.601907	.561985	.526671	.495281	.467249
25	.591605	.551378	.515921	.484505	.456532
26	.581536	.541054	.505496	.474090	.446205
27	.571835	.531140	.495515	.464146	.436369
28	.562355	.521489	.485834	.454531	.426886
29	.553212	.512211	.476552	.445336	.417837
30	.544278	.503178	.467546	.436441	.409106
31	.535651	.494483	.458901	.427921	.400760
32	.527222	.486017	.450509	.419674	.392703
33	.519076	.477859	.442442	.411764	.384988
34	.511116	.469914	.434610	.404104	.377534
35	.503416	.462249	.427071	.396746	.370386
36	.495891	.454783	.419749	.389616	.363474
37	.488606	.447573	.412693	.382758	.356836
38	.481485	.440547	.405836	.376109	.350413
39	.474586	.433757	.399221	.369706	.344236
40	.467841	.427138	.392791	.363494	.338254
41	.461301	.420735	.386580	.357504	.332493
42	.454907	.414491	.380540	.351689	.326910
43	.448702	.408445	.374701	.346076	.321527
44	.442633	.402549	.369018	.340624	.316306
45	.436740	.396834	.363520	.335354	.311265
46	.430976	.391258	.358166	.330233	.306373
47	.425374	.385850	.352981	.325279	.301644
48	.419894	.380571	.347930	.320460	.297051
49	.414565	.375446	.343034	.315794	.292607
50	.409349	.370443	.338262	.311254	.288288

Table D. Twice Straight-Line Declining Balance (cont'd)

n	11%	12%	13%	14%	15%
3	.862205	.851479	.841009	.830785	.820799
4	.827096	.814139	.801561	.789345	.777477
5	.795677	.780884	.766593	.752782	.739427
6	.765462	.749069	.733311	.718155	.703569
7	.737891	.720170	.703213	.686975	.671415
8	.711362	.692499	.674530	.657399	.641054
9	.686922	.667114	.648326	.630487	.613533
10	.663444	.642841	.623381	.604978	.587558
11	.641678	.620426	.600432	.581597	.563831
12	.620795	.599014	.578601	.559443	.541436
13	.601339	.579138	.558408	.539018	.520855
14	.582687	.560159	.539199	.519662	.501419
15	.565240	.542468	.521351	.501731	.483465
16	.548517	.525574	.504369	.484727	.466494
17	.532823	.509768	.488526	.468906	.450743
18	.517778	.494669	.473441	.453890	.435837
19	.503615	.480496	.459318	.439865	.421946
20	.490034	.466948	.445860	.426537	.408781
21	.477215	.454194	.433219	.414046	.396465
22	.464915	.441993	.421160	.402160	.384774
23	.453276	.430474	.409799	.390984	.373799
24	.442102	.419446	.398950	.380335	.363365
25	.431503	.409008	.388700	.370291	.353538
26	.421320	.399004	.378899	.360707	.344178
27	.411640	.389513	.369616	.351643	.335337
28	.402333	.380407	.360728	.342981	.326903
29	.393467	.371749	.352289	.334766	.318913
30	.384935	.363433	.344200	.326906	.311278
31	.376792	.355509	.336501	.319432	.304026
32	.368948	.347891	.329112	.312271	.297087
33	.361449	.340617	.322065	.305446	.290478
34	.354219	.333617	.315293	.298897	.284144
35	.347294	.326919	.308820	.292643	.278100
36	.340612	.320467	.302593	.286633	.272297
37	.334201	.314283	.296630	.280882	.266747
38	.328010	.308319	.290887	.275348	.261413
39	.322061	.302594	.285377	.270043	.256300
40	.316309	.297067	.280063	.264932	.251379
41	.310775	.291752	.274957	.260023	.246655
42	.305420	.286616	.270028	.255288	.242101
43	.300261	.281670	.265284	.250732	.237722
44	.295264	.276886	260699	.246333	.233496
45	.290443	.272273	.256280	.242095	.229425
46	.285770	.267806	.252005	.237998	.225492
47	.281255	.263492	.247879	.234044	.221698
48	.276876	.259312	.243882	.230218	.218029
49	.272641	.255271	.240021	.226521	.214484
50	.268529	.251351	.236277	.222940	.211052

Table D.   Twice Straight-Line Declining Balance (cont'd)

n	16%	17%	18%	19%	20%
3	.811044	.801511	.792194	.783085	.774177
4	.765944	.754731	.743827	.733220	.722897
5	.726509	.714007	.701903	.690179	.678819
6	.689524	.675993	.662949	.650369	.638231
7	.656495	.642180	.628435	.615231	.602537
8	.625447	.610531	.596266	.582613	.569537
9	.597406	.582052	.567419	.553463	.540141
10	.571048	.555386	.540513	.526374	.512921
11	.547053	.531189	.516172	.501941	.488440
12	.524488	.508516	.493443	.479202	.465728
13	.503814	.487801	.472734	.458535	.445137
14	.484356	.468368	.453365	.439263	.425989
15	.466428	.450508	.435606	.421633	.408508
16	.449534	.433726	.418965	.405154	.392209
17	.433891	.418222	.403621	.389989	.377236
18	.419128	.403626	.389212	.375779	.363236
19	.405398	.390077	.375859	.362632	.350301
20	.392417	.377297	.363290	.350281	.338171
21	.380295	.365382	.351588	.338798	.326907
22	.368814	.354118	.340548	.327981	.316315
23	.358052	.343575	.330225	.317880	.306431
24	.347840	.333588	.320464	.308341	.297111
25	.338234	.324205	.311301	.299395	.288377
26	.329101	.315298	.302616	.290926	.280118
27	.320483	.306900	.294434	.282955	.272349
28	.312275	.298913	.286662	.275390	.264984
29	.304506	.291359	.279316	.268244	.258031
30	.297092	.284160	.272323	.261448	.251423
31	.290056	.277331	.265693	.255008	.245164
32	.283330	.270810	.259368	.248870	.239203
33	.276930	.264609	.253355	.243037	.233540
34	.270802	.258676	.247608	.237465	.228135
35	.264956	.253020	.242131	.232157	.222986
36	.259350	.247600	.236887	.227078	.218062
37	.253991	.242420	.231876	.222226	.213360
38	.248844	.237449	.227070	.217576	.208855
39	.243913	.232689	.222469	.213124	.204544
40	.239170	.228112	.218049	.208850	.200407
41	.234618	.223722	.213809	.204750	.196439
42	.230234	.219495	.209729	.200808	.192625
43	.226018	.215432	.205808	.197019	.188960
44	.221953	.211515	.202030	.193371	.185432
45	.218038	.207745	.198394	.189859	.182037
46	.214257	.204105	.194885	.186473	.178764
47	.210611	.200596	.191503	.183208	.175610
48	.207086	.197205	.188235	.180056	.172565
49	.203682	.193930	.185081	.177013	.169625
50	.200387	.190762	.182030	.174071	.166785

Table E. e^{-x}

	0	.01	.02	.03	.04
0	1.000000	.990050	.980199	.970446	.960789
.10	.904837	.895834	.886920	.878095	.869358
.20	.818731	.810584	.802519	.794534	.786628
.30	.740818	.733447	.726149	.718924	.711770
.40	.670320	.663650	.657047	.650509	.644036
.50	.606531	.600496	.594521	.588605	.582748
.60	.548812	.543351	.537944	.532592	.527292
.70	.496585	.491644	.486752	.481909	.477114
.80	.449329	.444858	.440432	.436049	.431711
.90	.406570	.402524	.398519	.394554	.390628
1.00	.367879	.364219	.360595	.357007	.353455
1.10	.332871	.329559	.326280	.323033	.319819
1.20	.301194	.298197	.295230	.292293	.289384
1.30	.272532	.269820	.267135	.264477	.261846
1.40	.246597	.244143	.241714	.239309	.236928
1.50	.223130	.220910	.218712	.216536	.214381
1.60	.201897	.199888	.197899	.195930	.193980
1.70	.182684	.180866	.179066	.177284	.175520
1.80	.165299	.163654	.162026	.160414	.158817
1.90	.149569	.148080	.146607	.145148	.143704
2.00	.135335	.133989	.132655	.131336	.130029
2.10	.122456	.121238	.120032	.118837	.117655
2.20	.110803	.109701	.108609	.107528	.106459
2.30	.100259	.099261	.098274	.097296	.096328
2.40	.090718	.089815	.088922	.088037	.087161
2.50	.082085	.081268	.080460	.079659	.078866
2.60	.074274	.073535	.072803	.072078	.071361
2.70	.067206	.066537	.065875	.065219	.064570
2.80	.060810	.060205	.059606	.059013	.058426
2.90	.055023	.054476	.053934	.053397	.052866
3.00	.049787	.049292	.048801	.048316	.047835
3.10	.045049	.044601	.044157	.043718	.043283
3.20	.040762	.040357	.039955	.039557	.039164
3.30	.036883	.036516	.036153	.035793	.035437
3.40	.033373	.033041	.032712	.032387	.032065
3.50	.030197	.029897	.029599	.029305	.029013
3.60	.027324	.027052	.026783	.026516	.026252
3.70	.024724	.024478	.024234	.023993	.023754
3.80	.022371	.022148	.021928	.021710	.021494
3.90	.020242	.020041	.019841	.019644	.019448
4.00	.018316	.018133	.017953	.017774	.017597
4.10	.016573	.016408	.016245	.016083	.015923
4.20	.014996	.014846	.014699	.014552	.014408
4.30	.013569	.013434	.013300	.013168	.013037
4.40	.012277	.012155	.012034	.011914	.011796
4.50	.011109	.010998	.010889	.010781	.010673
4.60	.010052	.009952	.009853	.009755	.009658
4.70	.009095	.009005	.008915	.008826	.008739
4.80	.008230	.008148	.008067	.007987	.007907
4.90	.007447	.007372	.007299	.007227	.007155

Table E. e^{-x} (cont'd)

	.05	.06	.07	.08	.09
0	.951229	.941765	.932394	.923116	.913931
.10	.860708	.852144	.843665	.835270	.826959
.20	.778801	.771052	.763379	.755784	.748264
.30	.704688	.697676	.690734	.683861	.677057
.40	.637628	.631284	.625002	.618783	.612626
.50	.576950	.571209	.565525	.559898	.554327
.60	.522046	.516851	.511709	.506617	.501576
.70	.472367	.467666	.463013	.458406	.453845
.80	.427415	.423162	.418952	.414783	.410656
.90	.386741	.382893	.379083	.375311	.371577
1.00	.349938	.346456	.343009	.339596	.336216
1.10	.316637	.313486	.310367	.307279	.304221
1.20	.286505	.283654	.280832	.278037	.275271
1.30	.259240	.256661	.254107	.251579	.249075
1.40	.234570	.232236	.229925	.227638	.225373
1.50	.212248	.210136	.208045	.205975	.203926
1.60	.192050	.190139	.188247	.186374	.184520
1.70	.173774	.172045	.170333	.168638	.166960
1.80	.157237	.155673	.154124	.152590	.151072
1.90	.142274	.140858	.139457	.138069	.136695
2.00	.128735	.127454	.126186	.124930	.123687
2.10	.116484	.115325	.114178	.113042	.111917
2.20	.105399	.104350	.103312	.102284	.101266
2.30	.095369	.094420	.093481	.092551	.091630
2.40	.086294	.085435	.084585	.083743	.082910
2.50	.078082	.077305	.076536	.075774	.075020
2.60	.070651	.069948	.069252	.068563	.067881
2.70	.063928	.063292	.062662	.062039	.061421
2.80	.057844	.057269	.056699	.056135	.055576
2.90	.052340	.051819	.051303	.050793	.050287
3.00	.047359	.046888	.046421	.045959	.045502
3.10	.042852	.042426	.042004	.041586	.041172
3.20	.038774	.038388	.038006	.037628	.037254
3.30	.035084	.034735	.034390	.034047	.033709
3.40	.031746	.031430	.031117	.030807	.030501
3.50	.028725	.028439	.028156	.027876	.027598
3.60	.025991	.025733	.025476	.025223	.024972
3.70	.023518	.023284	.023052	.022823	.022596
3.80	.021280	.021068	.020858	.020651	.020445
3.90	.019255	.019063	.018873	.018686	.018500
4.00	.017422	.017249	.017077	.016907	.016739
4.10	.015764	.015608	.015452	.015299	.015146
4.20	.014264	.014122	.013982	.013843	.013705
4.30	.012907	.012778	.012651	.012525	.012401
4.40	.011679	.011562	.011447	.011333	.011221
4.50	.010567	.010462	.010358	.010255	.010153
4.60	.009562	.009466	.009372	.009279	.009187
4.70	.008652	.008566	.008480	.008396	.008312
4.80	.007828	.007750	.007673	.007597	.007521
4.90	.007083	.007013	.006943	.006874	.006806

INDEX